THEOROI AND INITIATES IN SAMOTHRACE

Hesperia Supplements

The *Hesperia* Supplement series (ISSN 1064-1173) presents book-length studies in the fields of Greek archaeology, art, language, and history. Founded in 1937, the series was originally designed to accommodate extended essays too long for inclusion in the journal *Hesperia*. Since that date the Supplements have established a strong identity of their own, featuring single author monographs, excavation reports, and edited collections on topics of interest to researchers in classics, archaeology, art history, and Hellenic studies.

Hesperia Supplements are electronically archived in JSTOR (www.jstor.org), where all but the most recent titles may be found. For order information and a complete list of titles, see the ASCSA website (www.ascsa.edu.gr).

Hesperia Supplement 37

THEOROI AND INITIATES IN SAMOTHRACE

The Epigraphical Evidence

NORA M. DIMITROVA

The American School of Classical Studies at Athens
2008

Cover illustration: Record of initiates from Thasos and Philippi on marble plaque found in the Sacristy in Samothrace. Archaeological Museum of Samothrace, inv. no. 39.547

Library of Congress Cataloging-in-Publication Data

Dimitrova, Nora M., 1971–
    Theoroi and initiates in Samothrace : the epigraphical evidence / Nora M. Dimitrova.
        p.   cm. — (Hesperia supplement ; 37)
    Includes bibliographical references and index.
    ISBN 978-0-87661-537-9 (alk. paper)
    1. Samothrace Island (Greece)—Religion. 2. Gods, Samothracian. 3. Inscriptions, Greek—Greece—Samothrace Island. 4. Samothrace Island (Greece)—Antiquities. I. Title.
BL793.S3D56 2008
292.080939′11—dc22   2008029512

092608/L8

PREFACE

I have received much encouragement and welcome help in completing this manuscript, which originated as a Ph.D. dissertation five years ago and has undergone many revisions and additions since. I am very grateful to the Classics Department at Cornell University, where I had a valuable educational and personal experience as a Ph.D. candidate, and especially to Alan Nussbaum and Hayden Pelliccia for their help with my academic work at Cornell and for their humanity in difficult times.

My work on Samothracian inscriptions has been generously supported by James R. McCredie, director of the New York Institute of Fine Arts and of the excavations at Samothrace. I am very grateful for his permission to publish new material. All photographs were taken by me unless otherwise indicated.

I have profited greatly from my discussions with Bonna Wescoat of Emory University, author of the forthcoming publication of the Eastern Hill of the Samothracian Sanctuary.

I am also deeply indebted to Dimitris Matsas and Chryssa Karadima-Matsa of the 19th Ephoreia of Prehistoric and Classical Antiquities, for their help and wonderful hospitality.

John Mansfield of the Epigraphy Project at Cornell University kindly supervised my completion of a full bibliography of Samothracian inscriptions, which was of great use in creating the bibliographical lemmata for this work.

I am very grateful to Klaus Hallof for his kind permission to examine squeezes at the Berlin-Brandenburgische Akademie der Wissenschaften, and to the Department of Greek, Roman, and Etruscan Antiquites, Musée du Louvre, for allowing me to study their Samothracian inscriptions and publish their photographs.

The travel grants I have received from the Hirsch Fund for Archaeology and the Mario Einaudi Center for International Studies at Cornell University have significantly facilitated my trips to Samothrace and the completion of this work.

I am much obliged to the editors and the anonymous *Hesperia* Supplement reviewers, who suggested valuable corrections and revisions to this manuscript. I am especially grateful to Michael Fitzgerald for the meticulous care, precision, and helpfulness of his editorial work.

Last, but not least, it would be impossible to overestimate the help and inspiration I have received from Kevin Clinton, a dearest friend and a loving husband.

CONTENTS

ILLUSTRATIONS

TABLES

EDITORIAL SYMBOLS

The editorial symbols follow those in Sterling Dow's *Conventions in Editing: A Suggested Reformulation of the Leiden System* (Durham 1969).

[ ]	restoration
< >	editorial correction
( )	resolution of abbreviation
{ }	editorial deletion
Γ̣	ambiguous Greek letter
ḅ	ambiguous Latin letter
α̠	letter read in earlier edition but no longer visible
.	trace(s) of a letter consistent with more than one interpretation
[. . . .]	lacuna of approximately four letters
[- - - -]	lacuna of unknown number of letters
- - - - - - - -	lacuna of unknown number of lines
[*IMT* 1031]	edition not based on autopsy

The following designations are also used:

5.A	document 5, side A
5.*b*	document 5, fragment *b*
5.i	document 5, first inscription
5.II	document 5, second column

Per standard scholarly practice, Thracian names are accented if they are attested only in Greek literary sources but unattested epigraphically; they are unaccented otherwise.

INTRODUCTION

The core of this work is an edition of all documents pertaining to sacred ambassadors *(theoroi)* and initiates *(mystai* and *epoptai)* in Samothrace. These documents, which constitute the majority of all Samothracian inscriptions, form a crucial body of evidence for the Samothracian Mysteries of the Great Gods, the most famous mystery cult in antiquity after the Eleusinian Mysteries. Despite the fame of the Samothracian Mysteries and their great popularity in the Hellenistic and Roman periods, there is still much uncertainty with regard to the identity of the Great Gods, the form of the Mysteries, and the function of several buildings in the sanctuary. The inscriptions edited here shed some light on these questions—more so than the monumental royal dedications and other Samothracian documents not included here. As direct sources of information they are especially valuable, as the literary evidence pertaining to the Samothracian Mysteries is often inconsistent and difficult to interpret. The entire body of evidence, literary and epigraphical, will be discussed by Kevin Clinton in *Samothrace* 12: *The Religion of the Sanctuary of the Great Gods.* The present volume presents the most significant epigraphical documents and the conclusions that can be drawn from them concerning the religious functions of the sanctuary and the people who came to experience the religion of Samothrace. The conclusions do not pretend to be exhaustive; it is hoped that this collection of epigraphical evidence will serve as a stimulus to further questions, and that the picture that emerges from the epigraphical evidence will provide a perspective helpful in assessing other evidence concerning the sanctuary, the city, and the cults of Samothrace.

The inscriptions from Samothrace have never been collected in a single edition. About three-fourths of them (including unpublished material) concern theoroi and initiates. Of the 113 documents published by Carl Fredrich (in *IG* XII.8) and Friedrich Hiller von Gaertringen (in *IG* XII Supplement), 68 concern theoroi and initiates. P. M. Fraser's edition of Samothracian inscriptions on stone (*Samothrace* 2.1) includes 91 documents found or acquired during the American excavations from 1939 through 1957, 47 of which concern theoroi and initiates (including nos. 6, 13, 17, 19; appendixes I, IIIA, IV; and nos. 62 and 63, the two prohibition inscriptions). Many new inscriptions have come to light since then; some have appeared in periodicals whereas others are published here for the first time.

2

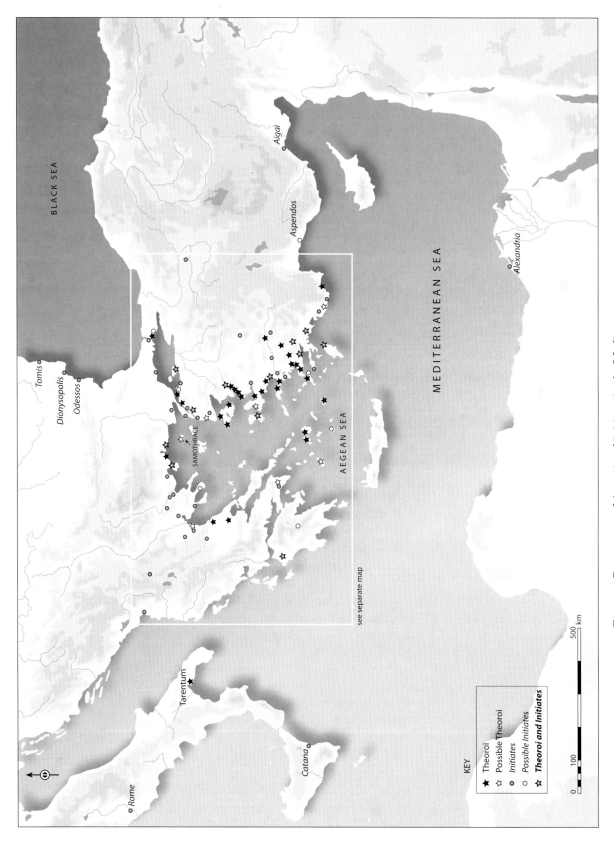

Figure 1. Provenance of theoroi and initiates in the Mediterranean. R. J. Robertson

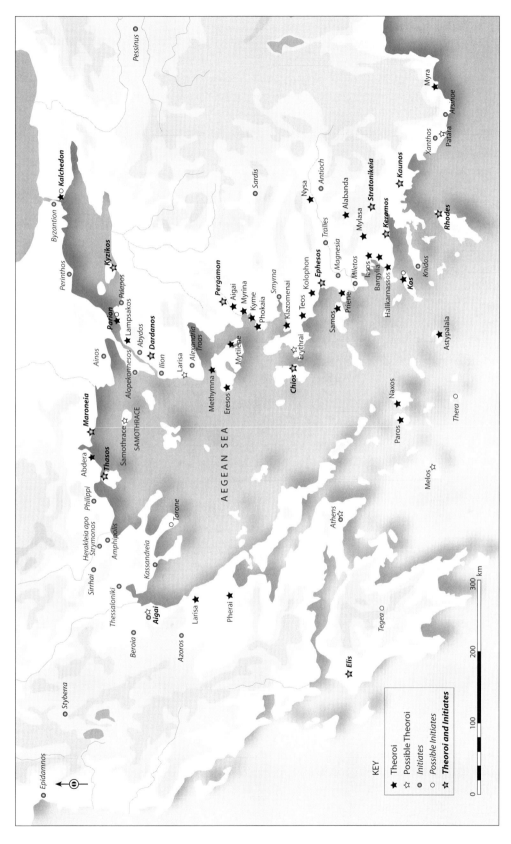

Figure 2. Provenance of theoroi and initiates in the Aegean. R. J. Robertson

The present collection contains all relevant published documents, with corrections and additions, and all relevant unpublished inscriptions that I was able to identify in the Archaeological Museum of Samothrace in the course of my examination of the fragments deposited there. My criterion for inclusion was that a fragment contain at least one name or meaningful word pertaining to the topic of theoroi or initiates. In addition to the documents from Samothrace, I have included two pertinent inscriptions of uncertain provenance (**25, 29**), and several from other sites associated with the Samothracian Mysteries, namely, Kos, Iasos, Priene, Rhodes, Tomis, and Dionysopolis (Appendixes I, II). The total number of inscriptions is 179, including 171 main documents, edited in Parts I and II, and the 8 inscriptions presented in Appendixes I and II, which are indirectly related to the topic.

My presentation of each document includes the following elements, in accordance with standard epigraphical publications: a physical description of the stone, bibliography, text, epigraphical commentary, and general commentary. Part I comprises documents concerning theoroi in Samothrace, and Part II, those concerning initiates. Each part is prefaced by a discussion of various problems associated with theoroi and initiates, respectively.

The most immediate and straightforward results were prosopographical. The study contains the most up-to-date lists of theoroi and initiates in Samothrace, including about 500 names corrected from previous publications and about 100 new names.[1] Even though a list of initiates was published by Susan Cole in 1984,[2] the list of theoroi presented here is the first of its kind. The total number of known theoroi is now estimated to be approximately 250, and that of initiates some 700, not including heavily damaged partial names. Fourteen new names of eponymous kings, the major Samothracian magistrates, have been added as well.

This new information naturally allows us also to change the map of cities that sent visitors to Samothrace (Figs. 1, 2). A couple of cities that sent theoroi have been added to those previously known, and two previously known have become doubtful. Seven new cities that sent certain or presumable initiates have been added, but two previously known must now be considered as only possible.

Another welcome by-product of this new look at the epigraphical evidence is that we have been able to define the functions of the theoroi in Samothrace with greater clarity. Counter to the traditional assumption that theoroi went to Samothrace to attend a special festival, perhaps the Mysteria, we now know that the city of Samothrace made them proxenoi, at least during the 2nd century B.C. and possibly the 1st; that they received various honors and were probably initiated; and that some of them set up dedications to the Great Gods. Only two documents (Appendix I.**2** and I.**3**) mention festival attendance; they provide no evidence for a special festival of the Mysteries, but for the strong possibility that the Dionysia constituted the major Samothracian festival at which theoroi were present. In any case, theoroi must have visited the island for other reasons as well, as suggested in particular by Appendix I.**4** and I.**5**.

With regard to the broader aims of this study, some results may be mentioned here. Document **26**, for instance, gives valuable insight into

1. A new record of initiates found in 2005 provides several new names: Parmenios Zoilou Andrios, and the Alexandrians Philakes Pleistonymou and Pleistonymos Philakou; the publication of this document is forthcoming.

2. Cole 1984, appendix III.

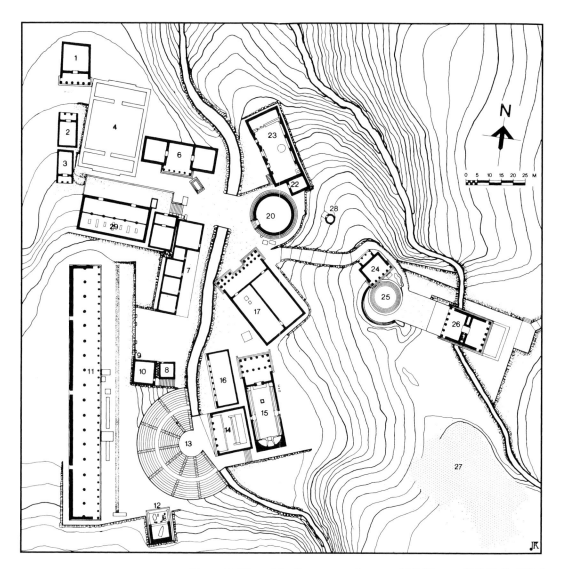

Figure 3. Plan of the Sanctuary of the Great Gods at Samothrace: (1–3) unidentified Late Hellenistic buildings; (4) unfinished Early Hellenistic building; (6) Milesian dedication; (7) dining rooms; (8, 10) unidentified niche; (9) Archaistic niche; (11) stoa; (12) Nike monument; (13) theater; (14) altar court; (15) Hieron; (16) Hall of Votive Gifts; (17) Hall of Choral Dancers; (20) Rotunda of Arsinoe; (22) Sacristy; (23) Anaktoron; (24) Dedication of Philip III and Alexander IV; (25) theatral area; (26) Propylon of Ptolemy II; (27) Southern Necropolis; (28) Doric Rotunda; (29) Neorion. Lehmann 1998, plan IV

the political history of both the Thessalian League and Samothrace in the middle of the 2nd century B.C., including Rome's war with Perseus and related events. It also challenges the traditional view that mainland Greece was extremely poorly represented by theoroi in Samothrace.

As far as initiation itself is concerned, we learn much from **29**, including the use of the term *Kabiros* in documents regarding the Samothracian cult. The same monument offers a valuable detail about a little-known benefit of Samothracian initiation—a happier lot in the afterlife. This text, the only one known to associate initiation at Samothrace with a happy afterlife, helps explain why the formula *mystai eusebeis* typically appears in Samothracian records of initiation. Furthermore, the documents concerning initiates supplement our understanding of their social status (among them we find slaves, freedmen, ordinary citizens, high officials, and kings); the dates of the initiation records (at least from ca. 180 B.C. until A.D. 186); the stages of initiation (preliminary purification, *myesis,* and *epopteia*); the existence of a special festival; and the display of initiation records in certain areas of the sanctuary (Fig. 3).

The documents presented here provide new and emend old information about the people who visited Samothrace as theoroi and those who were initiated into the Mysteries of the Great Gods. The monograph is intended for anyone interested in Greek religion and mystery cults, Greek and Latin epigraphy, prosopography, and Samothracian history and cult in particular.

PART I: DOCUMENTS CONCERNING THEOROI
IN SAMOTHRACE

CHAPTER I

THEOROS AND THEOROI

In attempting to understand the purpose and functions of the theoroi who appear in Samothracian documents, we should briefly consider what is known about their functions elsewhere, both from literary descriptions and from inscriptions. A full treatment of theoroi, desirable as it may be, would require a separate monograph; here a summary of the facts must suffice.[1]

ETYMOLOGY OF THEOROS AND FUNCTIONS OF THEOROI

It is customary to begin a discussion of the functions of theoroi with an analysis of the etymology of *theoros*, but this is more problematic than it might seem.[2] The basic meaning of the word *theoros* is "observer," and the act of observation is called *theoria*.[3] The second component of the word is cognate with the verb ὁράω, "to see,"[4] but the first element is a matter of dispute. The traditionally proposed etymology is that it represents the word θέα (sight), as the etymological dictionaries of Frisk and Chantraine attest.[5] Chantraine draws attention, however, to the following difficulties:

1. The principal study remains that of Boesch (1908), though it is focused on the festival-announcing class of theoroi. Perlman 2000 is the principal study of *theorodokoi*, focused primarily on the Peloponnese.

2. I am very grateful to Alan Nussbaum for his help in clarifying the etymology of *theoros*.

3. James Ker (2000) points out that the notion of observation present in the semantics of "theoros" is not a passive one, but presupposes guarding and preservation. He compares other words with the suffix -oros, all of which denote "watching over" something, and not merely "seeing." I am grateful to Leslie Kurke for this reference.

4. Although the connection with ὁράω seems certain, the traditional reconstruction of a digamma in the second element of the word (i.e., *-ϝορός) is problematic. There is no evidence that a digamma was ever present in the Greek derivatives of ὁράω. Therefore the more likely explanation for the rough breathing is that it represents *h*, which in turn comes from Indo-European *s*, the root of the word being reconstructed as *ser-/suer-. The form *suer- must be reflected in the Germanic group *warian*, cognate with English "beware." The Greek word may simply reflect the form *ser-. Thus the reconstructed early Greek form of *theoros* should be *θεαΗορός (cf. φρουρός

from προΗορός) and not *θεαϝορός; see Buck 1953, p. 443.

5. Frisk 1960–1972; Chantraine 1968–1980. This is also the view expressed in the illuminating article by Ian Rutherford (2000), who outlines the various meanings of *theoros* and related words and concludes that the application of these terms to pilgrimage and sacred envoys "is best explained by the hypothesis that the prestige activity of watching the Panhellenic games was the dominant paradigm for other forms of sacred visitation" (p. 146). I am grateful to Hayden Pelliccia for bringing this article to my attention.

θέα is a strictly Attic form, which cannot satisfactorily explain the dialectal variations; and the meaning of *theoros* is frequently loaded with religious significance, which is hard to reconcile with the notion of mere observation.

Let us consider Chantraine's first objection. The Attic form θέα comes from *thæuæ (cf. Ionic θέη < θήη), which in turn comes from Proto-Greek *thau-a < Indo-European *dheuh₂u-.[6] This means that the dialectal variations of the word *theoros* cannot be explained if its first element was the word for sight. The Doric form of the word *theoros* is θεαρός, which cannot come regularly from θέα (sight), since the Doric version of the word is θάα (cf. θαέομαι, θατήρ), which is regularly derived from *thau-a. It would be difficult to explain the Doric form of the word *theoros* and its derivatives as a result of Attic influence, since it is abundantly attested, even in early inscriptions.[7] The Boiotian form θιαωρία[8] is also difficult to explain as deriving from the word for sight, since one would expect an alpha instead of the iota, which reflects a raising of the *e*-sound present in the Doric form θεαρός. In fact, some Doric variants also have the form θιαρός,[9] so the Boiotian form must be influenced by the Doric. Other notable dialectal variants are the Thessalian θεουρός and the Ionic θευρός.[10]

Let us turn now to the second objection raised by Chantraine, namely, the pervasive religious connotations of the term *theoros,* which, together with the obvious phonological difficulties of reconciling the word for sight with the dialectal variations, have prompted scholars to look for an alternative explanation for the first element of the word. Koller interprets the meaning of θεωρός as "the one observing the will of the god."[11] Buck argues that "if not actually derived from the stem of θεός, a very early popular association with it is the most probable explanation of the title."[12] The word for god, derived from Indo-European *dheh₁s- (cf. Latin < *fasno < *fesno), would give in Proto-Greek *theh-, which does not contradict any of the dialectal variants, pointing to *theh-a-horo-.

While the phonology of the term *theoros* definitely favors the word for god as its first component, the semantics of the word presents certain problems, since there are early instances in which it is used to denote simple observation, apparently without religious significance. For example, the term *theoros* was applied to local officials in Thasos, Tegea, Mantinea, Naupaktos, Megara, Pergamon, and elsewhere.[13] The officials on Thasos are

6. The reason for the restoration of the glide is the cognate word θαῦμα (wonder), which derives from the root *thau- < *dheuh₂u-.

7. See, e.g., *IvO* 7 (before 500–450 B.C.), 13 (before 500–450 B.C.), 36 (before 365–363 B.C.); *SEG* XXII 315 (4th century B.C.), XXVI 445 (ca. 350 B.C.), XXXIII 2767 (318–316 B.C.), XXXVII 340 (early 4th century B.C.).

8. Attested in Bechtel 1887, 1.227; cf. Buck 1953, p. 443.

9. E.g., *I.Magnesia* 25, 34, 38, 43.

10. θεουρός is attested in a Magnes- ian copy of a decree in honor of a citizen of Kassandreia in Thessaly (*I.Magnesia* 62); Buck explains the ου as influenced by Attic, with Thessalian coloring. θευρός is attested in some Thasian lists of theoroi: *IG* XII.8 267 (3rd century B.C.), 351 (4th century B.C.), 352 (4th century B.C.), 358 (3rd century B.C.).

11. Koller 1958, p. 285.

12. Buck 1953, p. 444.

13. Also in Arkadian Orchomenos, Pellana, Paros, and Aigina; see Müller 1817, pp. 134–135; Boesch 1908, pp. 5–6; Haussoullier 1917, pp. 143–147. For adding Pergamon to the list, see Robert, *OMS* 6, pp. 210–213. Boesch lists Phaselis, Oropos, and Troezen as well, but Haussoullier excludes them from his list on account of insufficient evidence. For instance, in the case of Oropos, the one inscription mentioning a *theoros* (*IG* VII 424) contains the form θεωροῦ followed by a name in the genitive, but it is too fragmentary to allow any definite conclusions about the usage of the term.

known from inscriptions in which they appear as eponymous magistrates (with the formula ἐπὶ θεωρῶν) whose duty was to record ψηφίσματα.[14] Xenophon mentions the Tegean magistrates in recounting the unsuccessful efforts of Kallibios and Proxenos to unite all the people of Arkadia: their followers were "defeated . . . in the council of officials" (ἡττώμενοι . . . ἐν τοῖς θεαροῖς).[15] The theoroi in Mantinea are noted in connection with a treaty between Athens, Argos, Mantinea, and Elis:[16] together with the *polemarchs* they were to administer the oath that had to be sworn by every party to the treaty. The inscriptions mentioning the officials in Naupaktos include a decree about the friendship between Naupaktos and Keos, dated ἐπὶ θεωροῦ (*SGDI* 1424), and three manumission documents, dated with the formula γραμματεύοντος θεαροῖς (*SGDI* 1425, 1426, 1428). Megara presents an interesting case: in *IG* VII 39 and 40, officials who dedicate offerings to Apollo Prostaterios are called θεαροί.[17] Similarly, the evidence from Pergamon consists of a dedication to Apollo (*I.Pergamon* I 4) that lists names of θεαροί.

It seems likely that in the case of these local authorities the metaphorical meaning of the word "observer" was originally implied, that is, a supervisor of some kind. The observation was understood as a form of control, as is the case, for example, with the English words "inspector" and "supervisor." The Spartan officers in control of the ephebes were called βιδιαῖοι, the literal meaning of which is "overseers."[18] The Ionic variants of the word, attested in the examples from Thasos and in one of the aforementioned documents from Naupaktos (*SGDI* 1424), support the hypothesis that *theoros* meant "overseer," since these forms can easily have the word for sight as their first element. The Doric forms, however, attested in the documents from Tegea, Megara, and Pergamon, as well as in the other three inscriptions from Naupaktos, present the phonological problems discussed above. In the cases of Megara and Pergamon, one can argue that the θεαροί there may have had religious functions, since they dedicated offerings to Apollo. For Naupaktos and Tegea, however, there is no evidence that the officials had any sacred duties. Therefore we must assume either that the officials did have religious duties but we do not have any information about them, or that the title was applied by analogy with other places where they were sacred officials of some kind.

It is noteworthy that most of the places having theoroi as local officials are in Arkadia. Was the *theoria* as a local magistracy an Arkadian institution? A more-or-less distant connection with Arkadia can be found for some of the non-Arkadian places listed above, as Louis Robert shows.[19] On the other hand, it is also conceivable, and in my view even more likely, that the institution was widespread throughout Greece but remained better preserved in Arkadia. Support for this possibility can be found in Aristotle's *Politics:* τὸ γὰρ ἀρχαῖον οἱ δῆμοι καθίστασαν πολυχρονίους τὰς δημιουργίας καὶ τὰς θεωρίας.[20]

Tourists, that is, sightseers, were also called theoroi. This is another instance in which the word denotes observation, with no religious connotation. In discussing what laws should be enforced regarding travel to foreign places, Plato states that only public officials over the age of 40 should be permitted to go abroad. Among these he lists κήρυκες, πρεσβεῖαι, and

14. E.g., *IG* XII.8 263, 267, 268, 353, 355. These inscriptions mention the word *theoros,* while over 80 other documents belonging to the same group list only names without the heading. This is the most significant record of theoroi as local officials: their names were inscribed on the walls of the so-called Passage of the Theoroi.

15. Xen. *Hell.* 6.5.7.

16. Thuc. 5.47.

17. In *IG* VII 190 there may be another instance of theoroi as Megarian local officials, but the inscriptoin is too damaged to provide certain evidence.

18. I owe this reference to Jeremy Rau.

19. *OMS* 6, pp. 212–213.

20. Arist. *Pol.* 1310b20; cf. also Robert, *OMS* 6, p. 213.

some θεωροί.[21] By *theoroi* he means those who wish "*to see* the affairs of the rest of mankind" (τὰ τῶν ἄλλων ἀνθρώπων πράγματα θεωρῆσαι).[22] The meaning of θεωρία as travel for the purposes of sight-seeing or inspection is also attested in Herodotus (1.29–30), Isocrates (*Trapez.* 359a), and Plato (*Rep.* 7.556c).

Theoroi were also the official representatives of a Greek city at festivals. The act of observing is clearly one of their functions, since official delegations were sent in order to view the festival.[23] This meaning is attested in Thucydides 3.104 (σύν τε γὰρ γυναιξὶ καὶ παισὶν ἐθεώρουν, ὥσπερ νῦν ἐς τὰ Ἐφέσια Ἴωνες) and in Aristophanes' *Wasps* 1188–1189 (ἐγὼ δὲ τεθεώρηκα πώποτ' οὐδαμοῦ, / πλὴν ἐς Πάρον). The precise translation of θεωρέω in these examples is "to go in order to watch."[24] Watching, however, was not the only function of the festival-attending theoroi; they also participated in the sacrifices for the god in whose honor a festival was held. This is nicely illustrated by Plutarch in his *Demetrius,* where he portrays the extreme obsequiousness of Stratokles, who suggests that instead of ordinary messengers, theoroi should be sent to Demetrios and Antigonos.[25] Plutarch's description of theoroi as those who sacrifice on behalf of their cities at festivals illustrates the importance of their religious functions. Representation of one's city was not only a matter of political prestige, both for the city and for the individual ambassadors,[26] but it also involved some diplomatic activity.[27] The head of the group was usually called *architheoros,* and his office (the *architheoria*) was one that entailed considerable expense, which we find recorded in inscriptions and literary sources.[28] The number of theoroi per city, according to inscriptions, was typically two or three. The host cities were responsible for their entertainment, and had special officials known as *theorodokoi* to provide them with food and shelter.[29] Both the theoroi and the *theorodokoi* were honored by their cities in various ways.

Two definitions of the term *theoroi* give a useful perspective on their duties: (1) in *Suda,* s.v. οἱ εἰς θυσίαν πεμπόμενοι καὶ τὰς ἑορτάς, καὶ θεωρὶς ναῦς, δι᾽ ἧς πεμπόμενοι ἐπὶ τὰς θυσίας τὰς ἀποδήμους ὑπὲρ τῆς πατρίδος, ἢ καὶ ἐπὶ τοὺς ἱεροὺς ἀγῶνας καὶ ἄλλας πανηγύρεις οἱ θεωροὶ ἐστέλλοντο καὶ εἰς χρηστήρια; and (2) in a scholion to Aristophanes' *Peace* 342, θεωροὺς δὲ ἐκάλουν τοὺς ἀπὸ τῶν πόλεων δημοσίᾳ ἐκπεμπομένους συνθύσοντας καὶ συμπανηγυρίσοντας.[30] It is noteworthy that in both definitions the offering of sacrifices is considered a function separate from that of attending festivals. This adds a different nuance to the meaning of *theoroi*—that of envoys sent to distant sanctuaries on behalf of their cities, but not necessarily during festivals.[31] In many cases, of course, the sacrifice would have been offered in conjunction with festival attendance.

21. *Leg.* 950d–e.

22. *Leg.* 951a.

23. Cf., e.g., Dillon 1997, p. 21.

24. See *TLG,* s.v. θεωρέω: "ludos spectatum venio."

25. Plut. *Demetr.* 11a: τὸ δὲ ὑπερφυέστατον ἐνθύμημα τοῦ Στρατοκλέους . . . ἔγραψε ὅπως οἱ πεμπόμενοι κατὰ ψήφισμα δημοσίᾳ πρὸς Ἀντίγονον ἢ Δημήτριον ἀντὶ

πρεσβευτῶν θεωροὶ λέγοιντο,[21] καθάπερ οἱ Πυθοῖ καὶ Ὀλυμπίαζε τὰς πατρίους θυσίας ὑπὲρ τῶν πόλεων ἀνάγοντες ἐν ταῖς Ἑλληνικαῖς ἑορταῖς. On the distinction between *presbeutai* and theoroi, see p. 15.

26. Plato, e.g., is particularly strict when describing the moral qualities that the envoys sent to the Panhellenic festivals should possess in order to give

a good name to their city (*Leg.* 950e).

27. Dillon 1997, pp. 22–24.

28. Arist. *Eth. Nic.* 1122a; Plut. *Nic.* 3.5–6; *IG* II² 1635, etc.

29. Perlman 2000; Boesch 1908, pp. 105–106.

30. Holwerda 1982, p. 55, 342b–c.

31. This is supported by inscriptions; see the discussions of Delos and Delphi, pp. 14–15.

The last word in the *Suda* definition adds another interesting detail about the functions of theoroi: they could be envoys sent to consult an oracle. This meaning is paralleled in Sophokles' *Oedipus Tyrannus* and *Oedipus at Colonus*.[32] According to Harpokration, the usage of *theoros* to mean an oracle consultant reflects an association with the word θεός: θεωροὶ λέγονται οὐ μόνον οἱ θεαταί, ἀλλὰ καὶ οἱ εἰς θεοὺς πεμπόμενοι.[33] Plutarch ([*De mus*] 27) claims that in days of old the Greeks were not familiar with music from the theater, but music dwelled in temples; hence he derives the etymology of both θέατρον and θεωρεῖν from θεός. The sentence quoted above from Harpokration is continued by an eloquent attempt to explain the meaning of *theoros* as someone who takes care of divine matters: καὶ ὅλως τοὺς τὰ θεῖα φυλάττοντας τῶν θεῶν φροντίζοντας οὕτως ὠνόμαζον, ὤρην γὰρ ἔλεγον τὴν φροντίδα.

Thus the other major usage of the word θεωρός, in addition to "observer," is "envoy sent to the gods." The meaning of θεωρία as "sacred mission" is nicely illustrated in Plato's *Phaedo* (58b), where Phaedo explains that Socrates' execution was delayed until the return of the ship that the Athenians sent annually to Delos, in fulfillment of their vow to Apollo after Theseus saved the 14 youths and maidens from the Minotaur: τῷ οὖν Ἀπόλλωνι εὔξαντο, ὡς λέγεται, τότε, εἰ σωθεῖεν, ἑκάστου ἔτους θεωρίαν ἀπάξειν εἰς Δῆλον.

The meaning of *theoros* as an official sacred delegate is consistent with yet another usage of the word: those whom a city sent to announce the beginning of a festival were also called *theoroi* in most cities. Notable exceptions were Athens and Olympia, where festival announcers were referred to as *spondophoroi*.[34] It has been suggested that this was the older term, kept for special celebrations such as the Mysteries or the Olympic games.[35] This would be hard to prove, however, since the term is not attested before the second quarter of the 4th century B.C. for Athens,[36] and the preserved Olympian inscriptions mentioning *spondophoroi* are from the 1st century B.C. and later.[37]

Perhaps the different terminology is to be explained by the fact that the duty of the *spondophoroi* was to herald the sacred truce[38] (or at least this was the political intention behind the terminology), while the announcing theoroi were simply sacred delegates, whose mission needed to be more fully specified. Thus in some inscriptions they are called οἱ ἐπαγγέλλοντες θεωροί,[39] to be distinguished, presumably, from non-announcing theoroi. Other inscriptions provide detail about the specific duties of the announcing theoroi, namely, to announce the festival, the sacrifices, and the sacred truce. The festival-announcing theoroi were also entertained by *theorodokoi* and given public honors.

---

32. Soph. *OT* 112–115: Οι. πότερα δ᾽ ἐν οἴκοις, ἢ ᾽ν ἀγροῖς ὁ Λάιος, / ἢ γῆς ἐπ᾽ ἄλλης τῷ δε συμπίπτει φόνῳ; / Κρ. θεωρός, ὥς ἔφασκεν, ἐκδημῶν πάλιν / πρὸς οἶκον οὐκεθ᾽ ἵκεθ᾽, ὡς ἀπεστάλη; *OC* 412–413: Οι. ἃ δ᾽ ἐννέπεις, κλύουσα τοῦ λέγεις, τέκνον; / Ισ. ἀνδρῶν θεωρῶν Δελφικῆς ἀφ᾽ ἑστίας.

33. Harp., s.v. θεωρικά.

34. I.e., "people bringing the sacred truce," a title originally given to "assistants who bring a libation to a priest"; see Clinton's introduction to *I.Eleusis* 2.

35. Dillon 1997, p. 5.

36. *Agora* XVI 56, lines 1–24 (= Clinton, *I.Eleusis* 138).

37. *IvO* 59, 62, 64, 65, 69, 74, 75, 77, 79, 80, etc.

38. *I.Eleusis* 2.

39. E.g., *IG* XII Suppl. (1939) 138 (Miletos). It is interesting that in some inscriptions (e.g., *I.Magnesia* 40) the festival announcers are simply called οἱ ἐπαγγέλλοντες, "the men," or "those chosen to announce the festival" (cf. Dillon 1997, p. 12; Boesch 1908, pp. 9–10).

The term *theoros*, then, did not mean solely "sacred envoy," but was applied to various offices. Nor was it the only term the Greeks had for "sacred envoy"; inscriptions show that they were known by various other titles in various places. The sacred delegates of Kyzikos and Rhodes, for example, were called *hieropoioi*, as **50**, **58**, and **59** attest.[40] Another Samothracian document, **47**, uses the terms *katangeleus* and *hieragogos*, presumably with the same meaning. These were all titles given by cities to their sacred envoys, or simply titles of local officials whose duties included those of a sacred envoy. The titles changed over time; *synthytes* was used for sacred envoys during the Principate.[41]

The religious functions of theoroi, as opposed to the simple notion of observing, can be explained, according to the *TLG*, by their having two different components as their sources, θέα versus θεός, which resulted in two homonymous formations. This is a logical scenario and may explain the phonological problems with the term. Its only flaw is that in some instances of theoroi being local officials we have the Doric form *thearos*, which must come from the word for god. On the other hand, we know very little about the actual functions of these local officials, so it is possible that they had sacred duties as well.

To summarize, the basic meanings of the term θεωρός ranged from observer (local or traveling) to sacred envoy of some kind. Perhaps these two basic meanings were the result of homonymous formations from θέα and θεός, respectively.

THEOROI IN INSCRIPTIONS

Over 500 inscriptions recording theoroi have been preserved.[42] Some of these concern local officials, as noted above, but in most documents the term is used to denote sacred envoys sent to present (sacrificial) offerings at a distant shrine, to attend religious celebrations, or to invite people to join the celebrations of their home city.

The term *theoros* occurs most frequently in the records of Thasian officials; the temple inventories on Delos;[43] the catalogues of Pythaists in Delphi;[44] the decrees regarding the Koan sanctuary of Asklepios and its immunity;[45] the Magnesian inscriptions concerning the Leukophryena festival;[46] and honorary decrees in praise of prominent Romans in Ephesos.[47]

40. See Robert 1963, p. 67: "Ces gens ont été nommés 'hiéropes' pour être envoyés aux fêtes de Samothrace; le terme équivaut exactement à 'théores' ou à 'synthytai.'" Cf. Smith (1972, esp. pp. 538–539), who points out that the title of *hieropoioi* apparently did not exist in Rhodes for regular officials but was given to those "on special missions to Samothrace."

41. Robert, *OMS* 5, 1989, p. 647.

42. The number includes the inscriptions containing the word *theoros*, but it must be noted that in some cases, names of theoroi (e.g., in Thasos, Delphi, and Samothrace) are preserved without their title.

43. E.g., *IG* XI 161, 199, 287; *I.Délos* 291, 298, 313, 1421, 1425, 1430, 1432, 1441, 1450. For a complete list of the inscriptions with references to theoroi, arranged geographically, see

Bruneau 1970, pp. 94–100.

44. E.g., *FdD* III.2 2, 4, 7, 8, 9, 10, 14, 16, 27, 57, 58.

45. Herzog and Klaffenbach 1952, nos. 2, 3, 4, 5, 6, 7, 8, 9, 11, 12, 13, 14, 15, 16, 17, 18.

46. E.g., *I.Magnesia* 37, 41, 42, 44, 45, 47, 48, 80, 81.

47. E.g., *I.Ephesos* 1264, 1266, 1352, 1360, 1480, 1513, 1751.

The Thasian inscriptions list names of local theoroi, who served each year, usually in groups of three. Their names were inscribed on the walls of the so-called Passage of the Theoroi over the course of several centuries (starting in the 4th century B.C.).[48]

The Delian catalogues (mostly 3rd century B.C.) enumerate gifts from various cities, which were represented by certain officials among whom *architheoroi* and theoroi are frequently listed.[49] These gifts were sacred offerings, sent during different times of the year. The function of the theoroi mentioned in these inscriptions was simply to bring the offerings, most commonly called ἀπαρχαί, as a token of respect for the cult of Apollo Delios.[50] They were neither attending nor announcing a festival. The presentation of sacred offerings from distant places has a long tradition as a cultic activity at Delos; it brings to mind, for example, the offerings of the Hyperboreans, which were sent to Apollo along a specific route and passed from one city to another. Thus, as Bruneau notes, Kallimachos's verses in the *Hymn to Delos*, ἀλλά τοι ἀμφιετεῖς δεκατηφόροι αἰὲν ἀπαρχαί / πέμπονται, πᾶσαι δὲ χοροὺς ἀνάγουσι πόληες, have been supplemented by rich epigraphical documentation.[51]

The Pythaist lists (2nd–1st century B.C.), inscribed on the walls of the Athenian Treasury at Delphi, record the sending to Delphi of the sacred embassy known as the *Pythais*. They include names of both theoroi and Pythaists, but their exact duties are unclear.[52] It is interesting to note that the head of the Pythaists is frequently called *architheoros*. This points to a similarity between the functions of theoroi and Pythaists, and more precisely, indicates that the *Pythais* can be viewed as a kind of *theoria*. In the Pythaist lists the theoroi are sacred envoys who participate in the presentation of sacrifices and first fruits to Apollo. They were not sent as festival attendees: the *Pythais* was a specific Athenian institution not connected with any Delphic festival.[53]

The inscriptions on Kos (242 B.C.) are copies of decrees, issued by various cities, concerning the Koan theoroi whose mission was to announce the festival in honor of Asklepios. The Koan representatives visited cities spread over a vast territory that included Sparta, Messene, Thelphoussa, Elis, Aigeira, Phthiotic Thebes, Megara, Amphipolis, Philippi, Pella, Ainos, Maroneia, Corcyra, Neapolis, Elea, and Iasos. The decrees mention that the Koan theoroi announced not only the festival, but also the sacrifices and truce accompanying it, and list the honors bestowed on them, such as the grant of the requested immunity (ἀσυλία) for their sanctuary, an invitation to the Prytaneion, and the donation of funds for the sacrifices.

The inscriptions concerning Magnesian theoroi (3rd–2nd century B.C.) are other cities' decrees accepting the festival in honor of Artemis Leukophryena. It is interesting that in these documents the people who announced the festivals served as both *presbeutai* and theoroi. This specification is consistent with the above-quoted passage in Plutarch's *Demetrius*, where the implied difference between *presbeutai* and theoroi lies in the sacred character of the latter. One can compare *IG* VII 4140–4142, where delegates from Akraiphiai, inviting the Orchomenians to attend the festival of Apollo Ptoios, are referred to as πρεσβευταὶ καὶ θεωροί. Their duties consist of delivering to the Orchomenian officials a letter acknowledging

48. For a recent discussion and bibliography, see Graham 2001.

49. A very useful recent summary of the Delian inventories is provided in Rutherford 1998, pp. 81–82. I owe this reference to Hayden Pelliccia.

50. Bruneau 1970, pp. 111–112.

51. Callim. *Hymn* 4.278–279; see Bruneau 1970, p. 93.

52. *FdD* III.2 17.

53. Boethius 1918, p. 137.

the friendly relations between the two cities and inviting them to accept the sacrifice, sacred truce, safety, and contest associated with the Ptoia.

The inscriptions in Ephesos (2nd–3rd century A.D.) are decrees in honor of various Roman officials who had become Ephesian theoroi at the Olympic games. These documents are noteworthy because most include names of women, who were generously given other honorary titles (priestess, etc.) in addition to having served as theoroi, which was "evidently a very high honor," as van Bremen notes.[54]

The examples above were chosen to illustrate the variety of functions that the office of the theoroi involved. An explanation for this variety can be found in the general meaning of *theoros* as a sacred envoy, whose specific duties differed from place to place and changed over time.

THEOROI IN SAMOTHRACIAN INSCRIPTIONS

In the case of Samothrace, the majority of records concerning theoroi represent lists of names, preceded by an ethnic. They can be further divided into (1) wall blocks of Thasian marble inscribed with theoroi records (Chap. 2), and (2) other stones bearing inscriptions concerning Samothracian theoroi (Chap. 3).

The most striking feature of the wall blocks is that their height is ca. 0.35 m (Table 1). This led Benndorf to conclude that they belonged to a single building, which he thought was the Doric "Old Temple" (presently known as the Hall of Choral Dancers).[55] The main reason for this conclusion was that the other buildings have wall blocks of large dimensions, and that the frieze of the building, whose height can be estimated at ca. 0.33 m (see below), would be roughly in harmony with the size of **16**, a 0.42 m high Doric architrave block bearing a record of theoroi-initiates. Alternatively, Susan Cole has suggested that the building might have been the Ionic Milesian dedication.

Recording the names of officials on walls of buildings was not an isolated practice. Two approximate parallels for lists of theoroi come to mind: as mentioned above, the Athenian Treasury in Delphi held names of Pythaists (who were essentially theoroi), and the walls of the Thasian Passage of the Theoroi contained numerous inscriptions with names of theoroi, recorded over a few centuries. Of course, in the Thasian context the theoroi were local officials, not religious ambassadors, but the idea of setting up theoroi records on a wall of a Samothracian building may well have been a mechanical imitation of the example of Thasos, which prominently displayed its own theoroi records. Moreover, the practice of setting up inscriptions on walls was not unknown in Samothrace, but is also attested for Samothracian decrees: *IG* XII.8 151–155 and *Samothrace* 2.1 1 are on wall blocks made of local limestone that must have belonged to a building intended to display important decrees of the city.

It is still impossible to determine which building displayed the theoroi records. Apparently none of the excavated buildings in the sanctuary has wall blocks that match the dimensions of the theoroi blocks. It is possible, therefore, that the building that displayed them was not in the sanctuary

54. Bremen 1996, p. 88; cf. also Robert, *OMS* 5, pp. 669–674.

55. Conze 1880, pp. 97–101. For this building, also called *Temenos* for a time, see Lehmann 1998, pp. 73–78.

TABLE 1. DIMENSIONS OF WALL BLOCKS WITH THEOROI RECORDS

Block Number	Height (m)	Width (m)	Thickness (m)	Letter Height (m)
FULLY PRESERVED				
5	0.35	1.56	0.22	0.01–0.015 (i), 0.015–0.02 (ii)
8	0.35	1.09	0.21	0.012
9	0.35	1.10	0.20	0.012–0.015
13	0.355	1.37	0.22	0.02
14	0.355	1.104	0.19	0.04 (line 1), 0.02 (I), 0.012–0.015 (II)
PARTIALLY PRESERVED				
1	0.35	0.44	0.24	0.018 (lines 1–2), 0.015 (lines 3–10)
2	0.36	0.84	?	0.018–0.021, 0.022–0.029 (line 2)
6	0.355	0.61	0.08	0.015 (i), 0.02 (ii), omicron and delta 0.01
7	0.35	0.45	0.19	0.01–0.012 (II), 0.015 (I)
10	0.355	1.02	0.08	0.015 (I), 0.015–0.02 (II), 0.015 (III), omicron 0.01
11	0.35	0.62	0.20	0.01–0.015 (left), 0.015–0.02 (right)
12	0.35	0.42	0.17	0.02
15	0.355	0.52	0.08	0.02
16	0.42	1.38	0.075	0.04
17	0.355	1.08	0.18	0.015 (i), 0.02 (ii.1–3), 0.017–0.02 (ii.4–7), 0.015–0.018 (iii)
62	0.35	0.795	0.19	0.03 (i.1–5), 0.025 (i.6, ii)

proper, but elsewhere within the city walls of Samothrace. Since many of the blocks mention the granting of *proxenia* to the theoroi by the city of Samothrace, it would be logical to seek the building with theoroi records in the city, or in a location closely associated with it. Unfortunately this cannot be verified until the city area is thoroughly excavated. Some of the blocks with theoroi records were later reused in the church of the Monastery of Christ; other uninscribed blocks from the same original building lie in the church ruins.

If the Doric architrave block came from the building with the records of theoroi, and if its preserved height is indeed close to the original height (see the physical description of **16**), it would allow for a partial reconstruction of the building's dimensions. The architrave's preserved height is ca. 0.42 m, and the regula was 0.215 m wide. Therefore the corresponding height of the triglyph would be ca. 0.323 m (the width of the regula multiplied by 3/2), and that of the entablature 0.743 m (0.420 + 0.323 m). These dimensions are too small for a standard temple or for any of the excavated buildings in the sanctuary. A stoa is a possible candidate, but of course this is merely a hypothesis that cannot be checked for the time being. I mention it here only to provide some idea of what we might be looking for, if indeed the architrave block belonged to the same building as the other theoroi blocks.

As for the arrangement of text on the wall blocks, it is clear that the inscriptions were carved while the building was standing, since some continue from one block to another: **7–13**, inscription i are continuations of inscriptions carved on the block above; **5**, inscription i evidently continues from the blocks above and on the left; and **10** and **13**, inscription ii must continue to the block on the right. It is possible that **1** was above **10**, and **6** above **11**. Inscription **5.ii**, however, is clearly confined to a single block, since in two places names are divided between two lines instead of carrying over to the block on the right. It is possible that the right edge of this block was at a corner.

The order of the documents in Part I is thematic: first are the records of theoroi-proxenoi that preserve the opening formula (**1–6**), followed by the records of theoroi-proxenoi that lack the opening formula (**7–13.i**); then the records of theoroi-initiates (**13.ii–17**) are presented; and lastly, miscellaneous documents concerning theoroi in Samothrace (**18–28**).

In terms of the shapes of the stones, the 28 documents in Part I concerning theoroi in Samothrace are on wall blocks (**1, 2, 5–17**, and probably **23**), monument bases (**4, 26, 27**, and probably **21**), stelai (**18, 22**, and probably **24**), a round altar (**28**), an architrave block (**16**), and blocks (**19, 25**) and fragments (**20**) of unclear purpose. Inscription **3** was probably on a wall block, given its layout, but the stone's shape and dimensions are unknown.

The wall blocks with theoroi records are ca. 0.35 m high and ca. 0.20 m thick, and they probably belonged to the same building, as discussed above. They contain records of either (1) theoroi-proxenoi (i.e., theoroi who were also proxenoi, **1, 2**, and probably **3, 5–13.i**), or (2) theoroi-initiates (i.e., theoroi who are expressly called initiates, **13.ii–17**). The main difference between the lists of theoroi-proxenoi and theoroi-initiates is that the first contain many ethnics and were set up by Samothrace, while the latter record only one city and were presumably set up by the theoroi themselves.[56] It should be added that there is one other block of similar appearance, **62**, containing records of initiates only. It must come from the same building, and the records on it were probably inscribed at roughly the same time as the other lists of theoroi-initiates.

The records of theoroi-proxenoi date from the 2nd and 1st centuries B.C. (except **4**); the securely dated ones, however, all belong to the 2nd century. These records tell us that sacred ambassadors from certain cities have become proxenoi, that is, honorary representatives of Samothrace in their own cities. Some (**1–3, 5.ii, 6**) contain an opening formula of the type ἐπὶ βασιλέως - - οἵδε πρόξενοι ἐγένοντο τῆς πόλεως θεωροὶ παραγενόμενοι.[57] The formula usually takes up the first two lines and is carved in larger letters than the rest of the inscription. The lines below are occupied by ethnics in either the nominative plural or the genitive plural,[58] followed by several names, usually with patronymics. The lists are inscribed in vertical columns, not restricted to one block. Some blocks whose width happens to be better preserved (**5, 6**) display more than one inscription. Inscription **5.ii** is a record of theoroi-proxenoi, while **5**, inscription i, inscribed to the left of **5**, inscription ii, is a similar list of names preceded by an ethnic, but without the opening formula.

I have provisionally assigned the other blocks containing lists of names preceded by ethnics (**7–13.i**) to the category of theoroi-proxenoi records (note the question mark in each document's title); it seems logical to assume that these documents lack the usual opening formula because it was inscribed on the block above.

56. Cole 1984, p. 54.

57. Inscription **4** has a different formula, which is probably related to its different shape; the block must have been part of an enormous monument, but the inscription on it may not be original.

58. According to Benndorf (Conze 1880, pp. 97–98; cf. *Samothrace* 2.1, p. 62), the lists with ethnics in the nominative plural are older than the ones with genitive plurals. There is no reason, however, that the nominative should predate the genitive in the expression of the ethnic.

The exact number of records of theoroi-proxenoi is unknown because some of the blocks contain columns of different letter sizes (e.g., **10**), and it cannot be determined whether they belong to different inscriptions. On the other hand, **6** and **11** may have belonged together, given their similar layout and lettering.

Four (**13.ii–15, 17**) of the five lists of theoroi-initiates (**13.ii–17**) are inscribed on the same type of ca. 0.35 m high blocks that the records of theoroi-proxenoi are. In fact, **13**, inscription ii occupies the vacant space after the end of **13**, inscription i, an older list probably of theoroi-proxenoi. The records of theoroi-initiates, dating to the 1st century B.C. and the 1st century A.D. (except perhaps **16**), are later than the lists of theoroi-proxenoi. Therefore we can speculate that the initial purpose of the building with records of theoroi was to display the names of the theoroi-proxenoi, and that names of theoroi-initiates were inscribed later in the vacant spaces, after the practice of granting *proxenia* to the theoroi had lost its vitality. This could also explain why **16**, the architrave block discussed above, contains a list of theoroi-initiates: perhaps it was originally uninscribed, and later, when the wall blocks of the building were already occupied, the list was added above the wall.

Two records of theoroi-initiates (**14, 15**) contain names of initiates who were not themselves theoroi, but were simply accompanying the theoroi. This provides another argument in support of the idea that the records of theoroi-initiates were set up by individuals and not by the city of Samothrace. Perhaps the theoroi-initiates, having asked the relevant Samothracian officials for permission, paid a fee in order to have their names inscribed on the building with records of theoroi. Further support for this suggestion is provided by **17**, which comprises three inscriptions: **17**, inscription i is illegible; **17**, inscription ii is a record of two theoroi-initiates and one initiate from Stratonikeia; and **17**, inscription iii is a record of a single initiate from Sardis, added in the vacant space below **17**, inscription ii.

The other inscriptions concerning Samothracian theoroi are on stones of various kinds. Inscriptions **18** and **20** are fragments with ethnics and names, possibly belonging to theoroi records; **19** is a block of unclear purpose, perhaps reused for inscribing names of theoroi and initiates; and **21** is probably a base that held a dedication, but it is unclear whether the ethnic inscribed on it concerns theoroi.

Inscription **22**, on a large stele, with names preceded by ethnics, was included by Fraser in the lists of theoroi. Although there is no certain indication that it contained a record of theoroi, this seems probable, since its layout resembles that of the other theoroi inscriptions. Its suggested 3rd-century B.C. date corresponds to the date of Appendix I.3, which calls for publication of the names of the theoroi "on the stele" (lines 11–12), apparently referring to a stele on which the names of theoroi must have been annually recorded. This implies that before the records of theoroi were inscribed on a building, they were published on stelai, at least in the 3rd century B.C. Inscription **23** is on what is probably a wall block larger than the standard 0.35 m high blocks, with lists of names and ethnics, presumably of theoroi. Inscription **24** is known only from a copy made by the Italian traveler Cyriacus of Ancona; like **22**, it must have been on a stele, listing names preceded by an ethnic, the first of which is that of Samothrace. It has traditionally been thought of as a list of theoroi because of its layout, but this is not certain. The presence of Samothracians, if the reading is correct, would point to a different group of officials, since it seems unlikely that Samothrace sent theoroi to itself.

Inscription **25**, on a block in the Archaeological Museum in Istanbul and published by Fraser as a Samothracian list of theoroi, contains ethnics and names, but its provenance and nature remain unknown. Inscription **26** is a dedication by the Thessalian League to the Samothracian gods. The official representatives of the league, two Pheraian and two Larisaean citizens, are called theoroi. Inscription **27** is on a statue base, and **28** is on a round altar; both were dedicated by theoroi from Paros. Appendix I.**1** and I.**2** represent inscriptions from Kos, I.**3** and I.**4** are copies of Samothracian decrees from Iasos, and I.**5** is a Prienian copy of a Samothracian decree; all concern theoroi in Samothrace.

CHAPTER 2

RECORDS OF THEOROI INSCRIBED ON WALL BLOCKS

Inscriptions **1–13.i** concern theoroi-proxenoi, and **13.ii–17** pertain to theoroi-initiates.

1   Record of theoroi-proxenoi from Larisa, Ephesos, and Kyme   Fig. 4

Wall block of Thasian marble, broken on the right, damaged in the upper left corner. A rectangular dowel hole and a pry hole are visible on top at the right. The back is secondarily smoothed, presumably for use in the Genoese Towers, in whose vicinity the block was found. Archaeological Museum of Samothrace, courtyard, inv. 52.779.

H. 0.35 m, W. 0.44 m, Th. 0.24 m; L.H. 0.018 m (lines 1–2), 0.015 m (lines 3–10).

Ed. Fraser, *Samothrace* 2.1 (1960) 23.

Cf. Robert 1963, p. 67; Robert and Robert, *BullÉp* 1964 372 (*ad* line 3); Cook 1968, p. 38, n. 8; 1973, p. 221; [*IMT* 543].

2nd century B.C.?

[ἐπὶ β]ασιλέως Θεοδώρου [τοῦ - - *nomen patris* - - οἵδε πρόξενοι ἐγένοντο - -],
[. . . ?] τῶν πόλεων θεωροὶ πα[ραγενόμενοι]

      Λαρισαῖοι   Ἐφέσιοι
      [. .]ΡΑΣ Ἀριστομένους   Ἡράκλειτος [- - - - - - -]
5   [Εὔ]δημος Εὐδήμου   Ἰσόδικος ΣΑ[- - - - - - -]
      [Ἀ]ντίγονος Θερσίππου 15 Ἑρμαγόρας [- - - - - - -]
      Δημήτριος Νικολάου.   - - - - - - - - - - - - - - - - - -
        Κυμαῖοι·
      Φαέννης Ἰκεσίου
10   [Φ]αέννης Φαέννου τοῦ Ἰκεσίου
      . Ε . . ⁵ . . Ν[- - - - - -]

Fraser. **1**, *fin.* τῆς πόλεως Fraser, τοῦ δήμου *vel* τῆς πόλεως Dimitrova. **2** [τῶνδε] τῶν πόλεων Fraser.

Epigraphical Commentary
Fraser suggests a date in the late 3rd–early 2nd century B.C. on the basis of the lettering. A 2nd-century date seems more likely to me, in view of

the broken-bar alpha (uncommon before the middle of the 2nd century B.C.) and since the hand resembles that of **26**, which is securely dated to 170–140 B.C. There may have been a third column; see Fraser, p. 66. The readings are largely those of Fraser. The inscription closely resembles **10** in hand and matches **10**, column I in letter height, so it is possible that the present inscription was located above **10**, if the columns of the latter (or at least column III) belonged to different records. If column III belonged to the same record, then **1** and **10** are from different records, since Kyme is mentioned in both of them; see **10**, Epigraphical Commentary.

Line 2: The space before τῶν πόλεων seems too small to restore [τῶνδε]. If any word is to be restored, it should occupy two or three letters at most. A vacant space is also possible; cf. **5**, inscription ii.

Line 3: First letter: lower part of a right oblique stroke. The second, third, and fourth letters are clear.

Line 4: First preserved letter: clear rho.

Line 11: Unclear traces of letters except for the E and the N.

Lines 16–end: The stone is badly damaged and it is unclear whether the inscription was continued.

Commentary

Line 1: The name Theodoros is attested for an eponymous king; see *ad* **34**. [οἵδε πρόξενοι ἐγένοντο τῆς πόλεως] is a well-documented and certainly possible restoration. I have suggested the variant [οἵδε πρόξενοι ἐγένοντο τοῦ δήμου] on the assumption that πόλις might have been avoided, since it occurs in the following line. For the phrase πρόξενοι τοῦ δήμου, see *ad* **4**.

Line 2: The formula restored by Fraser, [τῶνδε] τῶν πόλεων θεωροὶ πα[ραγενόμενοι], is also restored by Salviat in a record of theoroi found in 1961 (**4**, inscription ii): [τῶνδε τῶν πό]λεων θεωροὶ | [παραγενόμενοι]. If the restoration is correct, then [τῶνδε] should occur at the end of line 1 (or be split between the two lines, which is unlikely); see Epigraphical Commentary. The phrase is logical but unparalleled. The repetition of the demonstrative (οἵδε πρόξενοι . . . [τῶνδε] τῶν πόλεων) seems stylistically awkward. An alternative suggestion would be simply [οἵδε πρόξενοι ἐγένοντο τῆς πόλεως / τοῦ δήμου] | τῶν πόλεων θεωροὶ πα[ραγενόμενοι], with a vacant space before τῶν πόλεων. Another possibility is [ἐκ / ἀπὸ] τῶν πόλεων θεωροὶ πα[ραγενόμενοι]. Parallels for the phrase [ἐκ / ἀπὸ] τῶν πόλεων θεωροί occur in *I.Priene* 111.XVIII, lines 175, 189, and in 118.A, line 15—the difference being that the participle in those examples is παρεπιδημοῦντες.

Line 3: Following Bean, Fraser assumes that Larisa-on-Hermos is meant, apparently because of its geographic proximity to Ephesos and Kyme; in his introduction (p. 14), however, he discusses this Larisa as certainly identified with the Larisa-on-Hermos. Robert and Robert suggest Larisa in Thessaly. The names that follow are too common to allow for any definite conclusions, except that Ἀντίγονος was extremely popular in Thessaly, because of Macedonian influence. Thessalian theoroi from Larisa are also listed in a new document (**26**). A Larisaean inscription containing two decrees in accordance with Philip V's letters to the Thessalians mentions a Samothracian, who is given citizenship.[1] On the other hand,

1. *IG* XI.2 517; cf. *Samothrace* 2.1, p. 9.

Figure 4. Record of theoroi-proxenoi from Larisa, Ephesos, and Kyme (1)

no connection between Samothrace and Larisa-on-Hermos is known. The matter is further complicated by the existence of two other Larisas in Asia Minor: the Troadic and Ephesian ones. Cook (1973, p. 221) suggests that Larisa in the Troad is more likely to have sent theoroi than Larisa-on-Hermos, which was not a very significant city in the Hellenistic and Roman periods, while the Ephesian Larisa was even less important than the one on the Hermos and perhaps lacked even the status of a city. There is no evidence, however, for any connections between Larisa in the Troad and Samothrace. Thus the suggestion that Larisa in Thessaly is meant is slightly preferable.[2]

Line 4: A name like Δωρᾶς is possible.

Lines 9–10: Apparently father and son. Φαέννης is a very rare name, as Robert points out (p. 67; cf. Bechtel [1917] 1964, p. 441). The form of the name is Aeolic, as Bechtel and Robert remark, corresponding to the Attic Φάνης. It is interesting to note that the Aeolic form Φάεννος is more common; it is attested four times in Attica.

2   Record of theoroi-proxenoi from Halikarnassos, Kolophon, and Ephesos

Wall block of Thasian marble, damaged at top and bottom. Found in Chora, built into the church of Ayios Nikolaos, now lost. I saw a squeeze in the Berlin Academy in May 2004.

H. 0.36 m, W. 0.84 m, Th.?; L.H. 0.018–0.021 m, 0.022–0.029 m (line 2).

Edd. Blau and Schlottmann 1855, p. 621, no. 13; Conze 1860, p. 68; [Michel 1900, no. 868]; Fredrich, *IG* XII.8 164.

Cf. Conze 1880, p. 97; Kern 1893, pp. 377–378, n. 1; Habicht 1972.

2. Cf. Pounder and Dimitrova 2003, p. 36, n. 23.

2nd–1st century B.C.?

    ἐπὶ βασιλ[έως- - *nomen* - - τοῦ- - *nomen patris* - -οἵδε πρόξενοι ἐγένοντο]
    τῆς πόλεως θ[εωροὶ παραγεν|όμενοι]
       Ἁλικαρνασεῖς·
    Μενεκράτης Μενεκράτου τοῦ Μητροδ|[ώρου]
5   Φύλης Ἑρμίου
    Μηνόδοτος Ἀπολλωνίου
       Κολοφώνιοι·
    Νικάνωρ Μηνοφίλου
    Βίσθα<ρ>ος Ἀπολλᾶ
10   Ἐφέσιοι·
    Θέοφις Νικοστράτου
    Θεμισταγόρας Εὐέλθοντος.

Fredrich. **1** . . . ΣΙ . . . . ΙΑΣ Blau and Schlottmann, ΕΙ . . . . A _ . . . .
Conze. **2** ΣΘ Blau and Schlottmann. **9** Βίσθα<ρ>ος Habicht. **12** ΝΤΟΣ Blau and
Schlottmann, Conze *legerunt*.

Epigraphical Commentary

Fredrich dates the inscription to the 1st century B.C. on the basis of its
lettering, but the 2nd century B.C. cannot be excluded.

    Lines 2, 4, end: The text probably continues on an adjacent block.

    Line 9: Βισθαῖος, squeeze. The iota is clear, and there is not enough
space to suppose a rho.

Commentary

Line 4: A Μενεκράτης Μενεκράτου occurs in *I.Halikarnassos* 51.2 (undated),
but the name Μενεκράτης is too common to allow an identification.

    Line 5: Fredrich notes that another Φύλης from Halikarnassos,
Φύλης Πολυγνώτου, is attested in an inscription found in Astypalaia (*IG*
XII.3 213.8). The same person also occurs in a series of Rhodian inscriptions (*IG* XII.1 69.1, 85.5, and many others) dated to the middle and
second half of the 3rd century B.C. The name Φύλης is otherwise poorly
attested.

    Line 9: Βισθαῖος is a hapax. However, Βίσθαρος occurs as a Kolopho-
nian name in *I.Kolophon* 6.IV.451 and 6.VI.627, as Habicht points out
(p. 112). It is possible that the stone carver made a mistake.

    Line 11: Θέοφις seems to be a hapax.

    Line 12: Θεμισταγόρας is attested as an Ephesian name in *I.Ephesos*
563.28.

3   Record of theoroi-proxenoi from Priene and Samos

    The inscription is known from the copy made by Cyriacus of Ancona,
Cod. Vat. Lat. 5250, folio 20, verso. Its dimensions are unknown. It was
probably on a wall block.

    Edd. [Ziebarth 1906, p. 411, no. 2]; [Fredrich, *IG* XII.8 165].

    Cf. Mommsen, *CIL* III (1873) 713; Conze 1880, p. 98, IX; Hiller von
Gaertringen, *I.Priene* (1906) 540; Robert and Robert, *BullÉp* 1958 270;
Robert 1963, pp. 67–69.

Middle of 2nd century B.C.

[ἐπὶ βασιλέως - - *nomen* - - τοῦ - - *nomen patris* - -]
[οἵδε πρόξενοι ἐγένοντο τῆς πόλεως]
θε<ω>ροὶ παραγενόμενοι·
          Πριηνεῖς·
5   Φίλιος Θρασ<υ>βούλου
     Βασιλείδης Ἀπολλοδώρου
     τοῦ Ποσ<ε>ιδωνίου
          Σάμιοι·
     Ἀπολλ<ώ>νιος Μελαινέως
10   Ἀρχέπολις Καλλιστράτου
     Ἀρίστιππος <Ἀρ?>μένου *vel* Φαμενοῦ
     Ἑρμέας Δαμοκράτε<ο>ς.
     ἀ<γ>ορανομοῦντος Ἀπολλοδώρου
     τοῦ Πυθαράτου.

Fredrich. **3** ΘΕΟΡΟΙ Cyriacus. **5** ΘΡΑΣΕΙΒΟΥΛΟΥ Cyriacus. **7** ΠΟΣΙΔΩΝΙΟΥ Cyriacus. **9** ΑΠΟΛΛΟΝΙΟΣ Cyriacus. **11** ΡΑΜΕΝΟΥ Cyriacus, <Φ>αμενοῦ *vel* Ἀρμένου Fredrich. **12** ΔΑΜΟΚΡΑΤΕΩΣ Cyriacus. **13** ΑΤΟΡΑΝΟΜΟΥΝΤΟΣ Cyriacus.

Commentary

Lines 1–2: It is possible that the text, restored by Fredrich in these two lines, was inscribed on the block above, if we assume that this monument consisted of wall blocks. We do not know, however, what shape it had.

Line 5: The spelling Θρασειβούλου, recorded by Cyriacus, may be an example of etacism, and not necessarily his mistake. The Φίλιος Θρασυβούλου honored in *I.Priene* 234 as a victor in the boys' pankration may be the same person. The Θρασύβουλος Φιλίου mentioned in *I.Priene* 255.3–6 may be the son of the *theoros* in the present inscription, as Hiller von Gaertringen remarks (p. 151).

Line 6: Fredrich notes that Ἀπολλόδωρος Ποσειδωνίου, the father of Basileides, is known from *I.Priene* 37, a decree set up in the early 2nd century B.C., so he dates the inscription to the middle of the 2nd century. An Ἀπολλόδωρος Ποσειδωνίου is also honored in other documents from Priene: *I.Priene* 65, 186, 236, and 237. One of them is especially interesting (186):

Βασιλείδης καὶ Καλλινίκη
τὸν αὐτῶν πατέρα
Ἀπολλόδωρον Ποσειδωνίου
ἱερητεύοντα Βασιλεῖ
καὶ Κούρησιν.

This 2nd-century B.C. round statue base must have supported a statue of Ἀπολλόδωρος Ποσειδωνίου, who served as a priest of Basileus (Zeus Kretagenes) and the Kouretes, as Hiller von Gaertringen comments, though he is not sure whether the honorand is the same person as the Ἀπολλόδωρος Ποσειδωνίου in *I.Priene* 65, 236, or 237. *I.Priene* 37 tells us that the real father of Apollodoros was Artemidoros, and that he was son of Poseidonios by adoption. One wonders whether this Poseidonios could be related to Poseidonios son of Herodes, the father of the poet Herodes, who was honored as a judge in *I.Priene* 63 and praised in an honorary decree by Samothrace, *I.Priene* 68–70 (see Appendix I.5). Poseidonios, however, is a relatively frequent name in Priene, so such a connection seems unlikely. Ἀπολλόδωρος Ποσειδωνίου is probably to be identified with the one mentioned in the other Prienian documents. His son Basileides must be the same as the *theoros* here, since Basileides is a relatively rare name.

Line 9: The patronymic Μελαινέως may occur in another Samian document, *IG* XII 6, 130, which has Μελαι[ν (2nd century B.C.).

Line 10: A descendant of Ἀρχέπολις Καλλιστράτου is attested in *IG* XII 6.1 322.1–2 (1st century A.D.).

Line 11: The rare name Φαμενός is attested in *SEG* XXVIII 1431, while Ἅρμενος is more common.

Line 13: The use of the formula ἀγορανομοῦντος + name to date a document is attested in 11 other Samothracian documents with eight preserved names; see Index. The function of the official is unclear. In most of these documents an eponymous king is mentioned at the beginning, before the *agoranomos*, who occurs sometimes in the beginning, sometimes at the end of a document. Robert (pp. 67–68) calls officials like the Samothracian *agoranomoi* "pseudo-eponyms," to be distinguished from the actual eponymous magistrates. He suggests that in the case of Samothrace the ἀγορανόμος was probably concerned with the organization of a large-scale πανήγυρις. Robert cites instances of πανηγύρεως ἀγορανόμος, a title he considers equivalent to πανηγυριάρχης, and concludes that the ἀγορανόμος was of considerable importance for the practical aspects of the Samothracian festivals (p. 69). This is an attractive suggestion. We know from Livy (45.5.6) that the *basileus* was the chief magistrate of Samothrace and that he addressed the assembly in 168 B.C. regarding Perseus's capture. Therefore, if the *basileus* was concerned with the city affairs in general, it is likely that another official had to deal with the increasing needs of the Sanctuary of the Great Gods, and that official may well have been the *agoranomos*.

4 Record of theoroi-proxenoi from Ephesos, Alabanda, Fig. 5
Klazomenai, Astypalaia, and Kos

Three joining fragments of Thasian marble, forming a block of a large monument base preserved on all sides. The top, back, and bottom are rough-picked, and the sides have anathyrosis. A rectangular dowel hole and a pry hole are visible on top, and an end dowel hole appears at the right edge. Archaeological Museum of Samothrace, courtyard, inv. 61.502 *(a)*. Fragments *b* and *c*, joined by Wolters (*apud* Fredrich), have no inventory numbers. Fragment *c* was found in the house of Anagnostes Bourgares; fragment *b* was considered lost by Fredrich, and must have reappeared in the museum later; fragment *a* was found on July 5, 1961, by P. Bernard in the area of the Genoese Towers. I associated *a* with *b* + *c* in July 2001.

H. 0.18 m, W. (combined) 1.04 m, Th. 0.57 m; L.H. 0.02 m (lines 1–2), 0.012 m (lines 3–end).

Figure 5. Record of theoroi-proxenoi from Ephesos, Alabanda, Klazomenai, Astypalaia, and Kos (4)

Edd. *a*, Salviat 1962, pp. 274–275; *c*, Blau and Schlottmann 1855, p. 622, no. 16; Conze 1860, p. 67; *b* + *c*, Kern 1893, pp. 368–369, no. 11; Fredrich, *IG* XII.8 168.

1st to 2nd century A.D.?

	Col. I	Col. II	Col. III
a, i	*a*, ii	*b*, ii	*c*, ii
[- - - - - - - - - -]*traces*	επὶ βας[ιλέως - - - -]ΚΛΕΙΟΥΣ τ[οῦ - - - *nomen patris* - - - οἵδε ἐγένοντο]
[ἀπὸ τῶν πό]λεων θεωροὶ	πρόξεν[οι τοῦ] δήμου παραγενηθέντες ἀ[πὸ τῶν πόλεων θεωροί]

...

Fredrich, Salviat. **1–3** Dimitrova. **1** επὶ βας[ιλέως - - -οἵδε] Salviat, [ἐπὶ βασιλέως . . . .]α [οἵ]δ[ε πρόξενοι ἐγένοντο τῆς πόλεως] *supplevit* Wolters (*apud* Fredrich). **2** πρόξεν[οι ἐγένοντο τῆς πόλεως- - -] Salviat, [θεωροὶ τοῦ δή]μου παραγενηθέντες Α[- - -] Fredrich. **3** [- - -τῶνδε τῶν πό]λεων θεωροὶ [παραγενόμενοι] Salviat. **II.7** [Κ]ρατῖνος Fredrich. **III.5** Πολυκλε[ίους] Fredrich. **III.6** Dimitrova, Βά[ττ]αλος Νο- - - Fredrich, ΑΥΤΑ Fredrich.

Epigraphical Commentary

The letters are uneven and inelegant, dated by Fredrich to ca. A.D. 100. The first two lines, containing the opening formula, are inscribed in larger letters.

Line 1: Dotted letters: unclear traces.

Line 2: The delta and eta of δήμου are visible.

Line II.7: ΠΥΘΙΩΝΑ, *lapis*.

Line II.9: A piece was broken off the stone on the left, and only the sigma is now visible.

Line III.3: Perhaps the sigma was omitted from the line below. It may have been the final letter of the ethnic, inscribed above by the carver in order to avoid transferring a single letter to a different block.

Lines III.4–5: The name Ξενοκράτης was presumably omitted and added later.

Line III.5: The iota of ΠΟΛΥΚΛΕΙ is visible.

Line III.6: Nothing is visible now after the omicron. The name is crowded between lines above and below it.

Commentary

The block contains two records of theoroi-proxenoi, i and ii. Only a small part of the opening formula of i is preserved, since the beginning of this part of the text was inscribed on the block to the left. Most of ii is preserved: only the end of the opening formula in lines 1 and 2 is missing, having been placed on the block to the right. This shows that the records were inscribed while the blocks were still together. It is unclear from which structure they came. The dowel holes on the top and right, as well as the joint surfaces on the two sides, show that there was at least one block to the left, one to the right, and three blocks on top; this suggests a monument of considerable size. The theoroi records on it may not be original.

Line 2: Fredrich observes that the aorist participle παραγενηθέντες is attested only here, and Fraser (p. 67) notes that the formula, as restored by Fredrich (οἵδε πρόξενοι ἐγένοντο τῆς πόλεως θεωροὶ τοῦ δήμου παραγενηθέντες), is otherwise unrecorded. The expression πρόξενοι τοῦ δήμου, on the other hand, is attested in hundreds of inscriptions.

Line 6: Βά<ττ>αλος, suggested by Fredrich, is not attested. Βακχύλ(λ)ος is a common name and is confirmed by the stone.

5   Record of theoroi-proxenoi from Alabanda, Kyme, Mytilene,   Fig. 6
    Bargylia, Naxos, Maroneia, Priene, Kaunos, Abdera, Samos,
    Kos, Rhodes, Iasos, Stratonikeia, Pergamon, Parion, and
    Ephesos

Wall block of Thasian marble, apparently preserved on all sides, reused as the front lintel block of the inner door of the Church of Christ (placed upside down).

H. 0.35 m, W. 1.56 m, Th. 0.22 m; L.H. 0.01–0.015 m (inscription i), 0.015–0.02 m (inscription ii).

Edd. Conze 1880, pp. 96–97; [Michel 1900, no. 867]; Fredrich, *IG* XII.8 170.

Cf. Salač 1925, p. 159; Hiller von Gaertringen, *IG* XII Suppl. (1939), p. 148; Ohlemutz 1940, p. 435, n. 5; Fraser, *Samothrace* 2.1 (1960), pp. 72–73, appendix III B, no. 4; Robert 1963, pp. 63–64; Hansen 1971, pp. 435–436; [*IMT* 1031].

About 150 B.C. or shortly thereafter

See text opposite.

Fredrich. **22** Παιώνιος Fredrich, Π<α>ιώνιος Fraser, Πριώνιος *lapis.* **41** Δόρκος Μητροδώρου Fredrich (*in minusculis*), Δόρκος Μητροδότου Fredrich (*in maiusculis*), Salač, Fraser. **50** Σωσ[ικ]λείδο[υ Fredrich, Σωσ[αν]δρίδου Salač, Σωσα[ν]δρίδου Fraser. **65** Ῥ[οδί]ων Fraser. **73** Ματροκλεί<ου>-|ους Fredrich, Ἰατροκλεί<ου>-|ους Salač, Fraser. **75** [Πολ]- / [Ε]ὐ- Fredrich.

Figure 6. Record of theoroi-proxenoi from Alabanda, Kyme, Mytilene, Bargylia, Naxos, Maroneia, Priene, Kaunos, Abdera, Samos, Kos, Rhodes, Iasos, Stratonikeia, Pergamon, Parion, and Ephesos (5)

i, Col. I

[- - -]
[- - -]
[- - -]
[- - -]
5 [- -]ΟΠΙΜΟΥ
[- - -]
[- -]ΙΜΟΥ
[- -]
[- -]ΝΙΟΥ
10 [- -]ΟΥ
[- -ο]ι·
[- -]ΣΟΥ
[- -Ἀν]τίγνορος
[- -]
15 [- -]ΙΝΟΥ
[- -]
[- -]
[- -]ΧΑΡΙΟΣ

i, Col. II

ΞΕΝΟΥ
20 Ἀλαβανδεῖς·
Λυσίας Λυσίου τοῦ Λυσίου
Πρίανος Μιννίωνος
40 Διόδοτος Ζήνωνος
τοῦ Θύρσου
Κυμαῖοι·
25 Ἀπολλοφάνης Ἀπολλοδόρου
Θεόδωρος Φιλοδόξου
τοῦ Φιλοξένου
45 Μυτιληναῖοι·
30 Κάλλιππος Εὐκλείδου
Διοφάνης Ζωίλου
Βαργυλιῆται·
Ἱεροκλῆς Σαμιάδου
Βρύων Ἱεροκλείους
35 Νάξιοι·
Θεοκλῆς Νυμφο[δ]ώρ[ο]υ
ΣΩΣΙΚ[- - - - - - - -]

ii, Col. I

[ἐπὶ βα]σιλέως
τῆς πόλεως
Μαρωνιτῶν·
Διόδοτος Ζήνωνος
Δόρκος Μητροδότου
Πριηνέων·
Μοσχίων Ἀναξίλου
Φιλέας Κράτητος
Καυνίων·
Ἀντίπατρος Ἰατροκλείους
τοῦ Ἡρακιστίωνος
Ἑρμοκράτης Ζήνωνος·
Ἕρμων ᵒᵒᵒ Κυδίου.

ii, Col. II

Λη[τογ]ένου
Θεωροὶ
Ἀβδηριτῶν·
Νικομήδης Διοδόρου
Ἑρμογένης Ἀγαθοκλέους
55 Σαμίων·
Ζωΐλος Ζωΐλου
Φιλόξενος Δράκοντος
Θεοδέκτης Προτσίδου
Κοῖον·
60 Εὐκλείδης Ἀντιγόνου
Ἀγησικράτης Εὔφρονος
Ἀπατούριος Ἀπατουρίου. 75

ii, Col. III

τοῦ Σοσα[ν]δρίδου
παραγεν[όμενο]ι
65 Ῥ[οδί]ον·
Εὐάρατος Εὐάρατου
Τιμάπολις Εὐφραγόρου
καθ' ὑοθεσίαν δὲ Τιμαπόλιος
Φίλιννος Ζωΐλου
70 Ἰασέον· Βίλλαρος Ἑρμίου
Ἀντιλέων Μενεκράτου
Στρατονικέον· Χρυσάωρ
Ἀρτεμιδώρου τοῦ Ἰατροκλεί{ου}-
ους τοῦ Γλαυκίου
Π[ρέ]πων {ωΝ}υδόρου 75

ii, Col. IV

[οἵδε πρόξενοι ἐγ[έ]νο[ντο]
Ζωΐλος Ζωΐλου τοῦ Ἀρισ[το]-
μένου
παρὰ βασιλέως Ἀττάλου·
80 Μάνδρον, Ἀπολλότιμος
Παριανῶν· Βασιλείδης
Ἀριστομένου, Ἠγεκρά-
της Διονυσίου
Δημήτριος Εὐμένους
85 Ἐφεσίον·
Θεόδοτος Βαδρομίου
Ἀρτεμίδωρος Ἀρτεμιδώρου
[Ἀ]πολλόδωρος Νικησάνδρου.

Epigraphical Commentary

The block contains two inscriptions, i and ii. Inscription i is now very hard to read and to check against its published editions. Fraser notes that it is written in "a very strange angular slanting hand." It must also be a record of theoroi-proxenoi, apparently a continuation from the blocks above and to the left. Inscription ii, however, is obviously confined to the block: in lines 77–78 and 82–83 names were divided between lines when the carver reached the edge of the stone. This arrangement may have been used for stylistic purposes or because the right end of the block fell at a corner.

The most legible part of the stone is inscription ii, column I. Fredrich observes that the hand of inscription ii, columns II and III–IV is different from that of inscription ii, column I, though the inscription is the same.

Lines ii.1–2: The letters of the heading are slightly larger and more spaced out.

Line 22: The second letter is a rho.

Line 75: ὠνυδώρου, *lapis*. The omega nu of the preceding name have apparently been repeated by mistake.

Commentary

This is the largest preserved block with theoroi records. It shows that it was typical to fit more than one inscription on one block. Presumably the beginning of inscription i was on an adjacent block.

Line 22: Πριώνιος is not attested in inscriptions, while Παιώνιος is a common name, as Fraser notes; hence his correction. I prefer to leave Πριώνιος, as it is on the stone, in view of the name Πριών, attested in a Delian epitaph (*SEG* XXVII 456). On the name Μιννίων see **13**, inscription i, *ad* line 11. It is interesting that in both cases the theoroi are from Alabanda, but it is unclear whether they are related.

Lines 37, 50: The name Λητογένης, though regularly formed, is not attested epigraphically. One wonders whether a delta should be read instead of the lambda, in which case Δη[μο]γένης, a well-attested name, could be restored.

Line 56: Ζώϊλος Ζωΐλου occurs in *IG* XII 6.1 182 (2nd century B.C.) as a victor in various games; he may be the same person (Hallof).

Line 58: Θεοδέκτης is a relatively rare name, but it occurs in another Samian inscription, *IG* XII 6.1 29 (306–301 B.C.), and possibly in *IG* XII 6.1 176. Πρωταΐδου is a hapax.

Line 66: Εὐάρατος is very common on Rhodes. Fredrich quotes *IG* XII.1 792, but the name occurs in many other Rhodian inscriptions.

Line 67: Τιμάπολις Εὐφραγόρου also appears in *IG* XII.1 836, as Fredrich remarks. He is also attested in *Lindos* 223 and 228, while his son and grandson are attested in *Lindos* 252 (ca. 115 B.C.). *Lindos* 223 is dated ca. 149 B.C. and 228 is dated to 138 B.C.; record ii therefore is probably to be dated to the middle of the 2nd century B.C. or shortly thereafter.

Line 69: Φίλιννος with double nu is very rare.

Line 70: Βίλλαρος is a very rare name, but it occurs also in *I.Iasos* 194.

Line 72: Robert (pp. 63–64) proves that Stratonikeia in Karia is meant: the name Χρυσάωρ is typically Karian, and Ἰατροκλῆς is attested only in Karia and Ionia. Moreover, Χρυσάωρ is to be connected with Ζεύς Χρυσαώριος, who was a major Karian deity and had a sanctuary near Stratonikeia (Robert, p. 63).

Line 79: Fredrich observes that Attalos II or more likely III is meant. Attalos II seems to be the preferable candidate, since the inscription is to be dated around the 140s B.C. (see *ad* line 67). Of course, a slightly later date cannot be excluded.

Line 80: It is strange that the king's ambassadors do not have patronymics (cf. **26**). Ἀπολλότιμος is a hapax.

Line 88: Νικησάνδρου is a hapax.

6 Record of theoroi-proxenoi from Myrina, Samos, Kos, and Teos   Fig. 7

Fragment of a wall block of Thasian marble, broken on the left, with traces of claw-chisel at bottom. The back was cut off for shipping purposes in the 19th century. Found built into a house. Paris, Musée du Louvre, inv. Ma. 4183. I saw the stone in July 2001.

H. 0.355 m, W. 0.61 m, Th. 0.08 m; L.H. 0.015 m (inscription i), 0.02 m (inscription ii), omicron, delta 0.01 m.

Edd. Blau and Schlottmann 1855, p. 623, no. 17; Conze 1860, pp. 67–68; Fredrich, *IG* XII.8 171.

Cf. Robert 1935a, pp. 487–488; Hiller von Gaertringen, *IG* XII Suppl. (1939), p. 148; Robert 1963, p. 62.

2nd century B.C.?

i
```
   [ἐπὶ βασιλέως - nomen - τοῦ Με]νεσθέως
   [οἵδε πρόξενοι τῆς πόλεω]ς ἐγένοντο
   [θεωροὶ παραγενόμεν]οι Μυριναίων·
        [Διο]νύσιος Μυός
5        Πυθαγόρας Ἡρακλεί-
   [- - - - - - - -]ΔΟΧΟΥ        του
   [- - - - - - - -]
   [- - - - - - - - -Ο]Υ
   [- - - - - - - - -]ΤΟΥ
10 [- - - - - - - - -]
   [- - - - - - - - - -]ΤΟΣ
   [- - - - - - - - - -]ΩΣ
   [- - - - - - - - - -]Ν·
   [- - - - - - - - -]ΞΕΝΟΥ
15 [- - - - - - - - - -]ΧΟΥ
   [- - - - - - - - - -]
   - - - - - - - - - - -
```

ii
```
   ἐπὶ βασιλέ[ως Μητρώνα?]-
   κτος τοῦ ΑΘΗΝΑ[- - -]
   οἵδε πρόξενοι τη[ς πόλε]-
20 ως ἐγένοντο θεω[ροὶ πα]-
   ραγενόμενοι Σαμ[ίων]·
   Ἀδήριτος Θερσάνδ[ρου]
   Δημήτριος Ἀρτέμων[ος]
   Θαλῆς Ἡρακλείδου
25   Κωΐων·
   Φαίνιππος Δημοκράτ[ου]
   Καλλικράτης Φιλιππί[δου]
   Τηΐων·
   Ἀγαθοκλῆς ΑΠΟΛΔ[- - -]
   - - - - - - - - - - - - - - - - - - -
```

Fredrich. **13** [- - - - - ο]ι Fredrich. **21** Σαυ[αίων] *vel* Σαυ[ίων] Fredrich, Σαμ[ίων] Hiller, Robert 1935a.

Epigraphical Commentary

The lettering is very similar to that of **11** and **26**. Fredrich dates the inscription to ca. 100 B.C. on the basis of its lettering, but I prefer a 2nd-century date in view of its close resemblance to **26**.

Line 1: First preserved letter: two bottom parts of verticals; the second, bottom horizontal.

Line 6: First preserved letter: right bottom part of a triangle.

Line 13: A faint nu is discernible.

Line 18: The last five letters are very faint now.

Lines 20, 22, 26, 27, 29: The underlined letters reflect damage on the stone that must have occurred after its publication in *IG* XII Supplement.

Figure 7. Record of theoroi-proxenoi from Myrina, Samos, Kos, and Teos (6). Photo © C. Larrieu, courtesy Musée du Louvre, Department of Greek, Roman, and Etruscan Antiquities

Commentary

It is possible that this inscription was the beginning of the record in **11**, given the similar letters and layout. If so, then it must have been placed on the block above **11**.

Line 1: For eponymous kings attested on Samothracian coins as MENE and ἈΘΗΝΑ see Fredrich, *IG* XII.8, p. 41. Metronax is a name commonly associated with eponymous kings; see **46**, **89**, and Fredrich, *IG* XII.8, p. 41.

Line 3: It is unclear which Myrina is meant; see *ad* **9**.

Lines 5–6: The cutter omitted the name of Pythagoras Herakleitou, then tried to fit it below [Διο]νύσιος Μυός, but ran out of space for the last three letters.

Lines 8, 11, 14, 17: Presumably ethnics, as Fredrich notes.

Line 14: Fredrich restores [- - -ο]ι, but there are other possibilities for the ending of an ethnic (e.g., -αι) and, more importantly, the genitive plural is more likely than the nominative; cf. Μυριναίων in line 3.

Line 23: On the restoration, see also Robert (1963, p. 62), who notes that the name Ἀδήριτος is typical of Samians.

Line 29: An Ἀγαθοκλῆς Ἀπολλοδώρου is attested in *I. Teos* 87, but it is unclear whether he is the same person, since names with Ἀπολλο- as their first component are rather frequently attested.

Figure 8. Record of theoroi-prox-
enoi(?) from Alabanda and Stratonikeia (7)

7   Record of theoroi-proxenoi(?) from Alabanda and Stratonikeia   Fig. 8

Wall block of Thasian marble, broken on the left and right, badly worn.
The back is rough-picked. Found in Chora. Archaeological Museum of
Samothrace, courtyard, inv. 39.1131.

H. 0.35 m, W. 0.45 m, Th. 0.19 m; L.H. 0.01–0.012 m (col. II), 0.015 m
(col. I).

Ed. Fraser, *Samothrace* 2.1 (1960) 24.

Cf. Robert 1963, pp. 63–64.

2nd century B.C.?

	Col. I	Col. II
	[- - - - - - - -]ON	[- - - - - - - - - -]ΙΟΣ ΚΑ[- - -]
	[- - - - -]ΑΝ[- -]	Μενεκράτης ΘΕ[- - - - - -]
	[. . .]	[- - - -]ασίων
	[. . .]	Ἀρισταγόρας ΜΗΝ[- - - - - -]
5	[. . .]	ΜΗ[. ᶜᵃ·⁵ .]Σ [Δ]ημη[τρίου]
	[. . .]	Θεο[φῶ?]ν [. . .]ΙΟΥ
	[. . .]	Διοκλῆς Ἡγήμονος
	[. . .]	Δημήτριος ΜΕΝΕ[- - - - - -]
	- - - - -	Ἀλαβ[ανδέων]
10		Διονύσιος Ε[. .]Υ[- - - - - -]
		Διονύσιος [- - - - - -]
		Στρατο[νικέων]
		ΕΝ[. . . .]Σ [- - - - - - -]
		[. .]ω[. .]ΗΣ [- - - - - - -]
		- - - - - - - - - - - - - - - - - -

Fraser. **II.2** Μ[. . 5 . .]ΘΕ[- - - -] Fraser, Μενεκράτης ΘΕ[- - - - -] Dimitrova.
II.3 [- - - -]ασίων Dimitrova, . . . τ̣α̣ι(ω)ν Fraser. **II.4** ΜΗΤ Fraser, ΜΗΝ Dimitrova.
II.5 ΜΕ̣Ν[. . 5 . .]Σ Fraser.

Epigraphical Commentary

The date is roughly based on the letter forms. According to Fraser, "how far the stone extended to the left and right, and how many columns there originally were, cannot be determined. The photograph reveals more than the stone itself or the squeeze."

Line I.3–end: Mostly illegible traces.

Line II.3: What Fraser read as nu is omega, with scratches resembling nu. It is followed by a left vertical.

Commentary

Lines 1–2: Fraser notes that larger letters suggest a heading; but only the letters in the first column are larger, and they must belong to another record. Column II, which must have begun on the block above, contains names.

Line II.3: Fraser points out that this must have been an ethnic because of the indentation, and that the final nu should allow for restoring the ethnic in the genitive plural.

Line II.12: Presumably Karian Stratonikeia is meant; see *ad* **5**.

8   Record of theoroi-proxenoi(?) from Priene, Halikarnassos, Klazomenai, Thasos, Maroneia, Abdera

Wall block of Thasian marble, heavily damaged. It is lying outside the Church of Christ, to the left of the entrance. An end dowel hole is visible on the right, and a dowel hole on top.

H. 0.35 m, W. 1.09 m, Th. 0.21 m; L.H. 0.012 m.

Edd. Conze 1860, pp. 70–71; Fredrich, *IG* XII.8 161.

Cf. Lehmann-Hartleben 1939, p. 144; Fraser, *Samothrace* 2.1 (1960), p. 72, appendix III B, no. 2.

2nd century B.C.

```
      [- - - - - - - - - - - - - - - - - - - - - - - - - - - - - - -]
      Ἀτ[- - - - - - -]ΟΜΑΧΟΥ, Ἀπολλῶ Ἀρχεπόλι[δος]
      [- - - - - - - - - - - - - -]Λ[- - - - - - - - - - - - - - - -]
      Σ . . [. .]ΑΣ Ἀριστέου, Διονυσόδωρος ΑΡΤΕΜΙ[- - -]
  5      [Πρι]ηνεῖς·
      Θεόμνηστος Ἀκρισίου, Νύμφων Καλλικράτο[υ]
         Ἁλικαρνασσεῖς· Ἀντίπατρος Φανίππου
      Ἱεροκ[λ]ῆς Μενοίτου, Ἀντίπατρος Ἀντιπάτρου
         Κλαζομέν<ι>οι·
 10   Σίμων Κλεοβούλου, Ἀσκληπιάδης Ἀπολλο[- - -]
         Θάσιοι·
      Δημέας Ἀ[. . .]ν[.]μάχου, Φανόλεως Σωσιπόλ[ιδος]
         Μαρωνῖται·
      Ἐπικράτης Ἁλιάρχου, Ἀριστόβου[λ]ος Ἀριστ[- -]
 15      Ἀβδηρῖται·
      Διονύσιος Διο[ν]υσίου, Ἀρχαγόρας Ἀριστόνο[υ].
```

Fredrich. **4** Σωδ[άμ]ας Fredrich, Ἀρτεμι[δώρου?] Fredrich. **8** Ἀντιπάτρου Fredrich. **12** Ἀ[μυ]ν[ο]μάχου Fredrich, Ἀ[μει]ν[ο]μάχου Hiller (*apud* Fredrich).

Epigraphical Commentary

The stone was practically illegible when Fraser saw it: "It was badly defaced across the inscribed surface in 1938 (the new inscription is conveniently dated, as is an earlier one of 1758). The inscription (particularly the first pair of names in each line) is now worn almost beyond legibility, and it is barely possible to follow the text as printed in *IG*, let alone correct it." Now the legibility is even worse.

Line 8: The left oblique stroke printed in Fredrich's majuscule copy as the last letter of Ἀντιπάτρου can belong only to an upsilon, so I have removed the dot under it.

Commentary

Line 4: Σωδάμας is not attested, but Σώδαμος and Σωδαμίδας, however, are.

Line 6: A Νύμφων Καλλικράτου was sent as a δικαστής to Troadic Alexandia (*I.Priene* 44), as Fredrich notes. Most probably he is the same person, since the name is relatively rare. Θεόμνηστος Ἀκρισίου is not attested, but Ἀκρίσιος occurs in Priene several times (*I.Priene* 42, 111, 313). As Fredrich notes, it cannot be proven that the *stephanephoros* Ἀκρίσιος mentioned in *I.Priene* 111 was the grandson of the father of Θεόμνηστος in the present inscription.

Line 7: Φάνιππος does not occur in Halikarnassos, as far as I know, but the name is very frequent on Thasos.

Line 12: The name Δημέας is attested elsewhere on Thasos (*IG* XII Suppl. (1939) 429, line 9). Ἀμυνόμαχος seems to occur only in Attic inscriptions, while Ἀμεινόμαχος, though regularly formed (cf. Ἀμεινόνικος, for example), is not attested epigraphically. Φανόλεως is a very common Thasian name.

Line 14: The rare name Ἁλίαρχος is attested on a lead tablet from Sicily (*SEG* XXXIX 1013; cf. also *SEG* XXXVII 1806).

9   Record of theoroi-proxenoi(?) from Phokaia, Dardanos,   Fig. 9
        Aigai, Myrina, Kyzikos, Chios, Eresos, and Nysa

Wall block of Thasian marble, preserved on all sides. There is anathyrosis on the left and right, an end dowel hole at the bottom right edge, and a dowel hole on top, roughly centered, with a pry hole to its left. The back is rough-picked, the top and bottom smooth-picked. The block was outside the Church of Christ when Fraser saw it in 1954; it was recently moved to the Old School Lab of the Ephoreia of Prehistoric and Classical Antiquities in Palaiopolis.

H. 0.35 m, W. 1.10 m, Th. 0.20 m; L.H. 0.012–0.015 m.

Edd. Kern 1894; Fredrich, *IG* XII.8 162.

Cf. Bechtel 1898, p. 82; Fraser, *Samothrace* 2.1 (1960), p. 72, appendix III B, no. 3; Habicht 1972; [*IMT* 107].

2nd century B.C.?

Col. I	Col. II	Col. III

Col. I

Φωκαιεῖς·
Διονύσιος Θεοδώρου
[..] . ΔΙ . ΟΣ Ματρίου
Δαρδανεῖς·
5 [Ζ]ώπυρος Μητροδώρου
Αἴσιμος Ἑρμογένου
Αἰγαιεῖς·
Νικογένης Ἑρμογένου
νεώτερος
10 [Ἐ]πίγονος [. .]ΟΝΑΤΟΥ
Μ[υρ]ιναῖοι·
[Ἀ]γαθ[ό]στρατος Πραξιφάνου
[Φ]ί[λι]ππος Νικηράτου

Col. II

Κυζικηνοί·
15 Νικογένης Ἀττάλου
Μαιάνδριος Ἀγήνορος
Ἁλικαρνασσεῖς·
Ἱεροκλῆς Δημητρίου
Ἱεροκλῆς Μενεστράτου
20 Ἱεροκλῆς Μενεστράτου
τοῦ Περικλείους
Ἱεροκλῆς Ἱεροκλείους
τοῦ Μενεστράτου
Χῖοι·
25 Φιλοκράτης Τιμοκρίτου
Διόφαντος Δημητρίου
Νικία[ς] Μήτρ[ω]νος

Col. III

Μ[. . . .] Ἀντιπάτρου
Σ[ύμ]μαχος Στύρακος
30 Μέντωρ Ἀσκληπιάδου
Διονύσιος Διονυσίου τοῦ Διονυσίου
Θεμίσων Θεμίσωνος
Ἀρίστων Γοργίου
Θεόδωρος Ἀμύντου
35 Διόφαντος Μαγεδάτου
Γοργίας Ἀρίστωνος
Ἐρέσιοι·
Ἀγησιμένης Βάκχου
Πρωτίων Ναίωνος
40 Νυσαιεῖς·
Θεόδωρος Ἀπολλωνί[ο]υ.

Fredrich. **4** Ἐπ]ίδι̣κος Fredrich. **10** [Λε *vel* Θε]ονάτου Fredrich.

Epigraphical Commentary

The inscription is now almost illegible, so I have largely reprinted Fredrich's text. Fredrich dates the inscription to the 2nd century B.C. on the basis of its lettering.

Line 4: First preserved letter is a vertical; fourth letter a left vertical.

Commentary

Line 3: Ἐπίδικος is a very rare name, and not the only possible restoration; Εὐθύδικος, for instance, is much more common.

Lines 6, 8: It is interesting that the patronymics are the same; the second one might have been repeated by mistake.

Lines 7, 11: Fredrich assumes that Aigai and Myrina are the Asiatic cities situated near Pergamon, since the catalogue lists theoroi from Asia Minor. This seems a likely conjecture. Lemnian Myrina cannot be excluded, however, since it is close enough to Asia Minor to be associated with such a list; Eresos and Samos, for example, are listed in the inscription but are not on the mainland. Moreover, the typical appellation of the citizens of

Figure 9 *(opposite).* Record of theoroi-proxenoi(?) from Phokaia, Dardanos, Aigai, Myrina, Kyzikos, Chios, Eresos, and Nysa (9)

Asiatic Myrina is Μυριναῖοι παρὰ Κύμην, as the Athenian tribute lists testify. As for Aigai, the question is more complicated. There are numerous cities with this name: in Achaia, Euboia, Cilicia, near Pergamon, and the Macedonian capital. Among these, the Asiatic Aigai near Pergamon seems the most likely candidate.

Line 15: The patronymic Ἀττάλου gives a valuable insight into the relations between Kyzikos and Samothrace, and consequently, into the functions of theoroi on Samothrace.

First, it occurs in the name of a Cyzicene initiate in **56** and **58**, Ἀσκληπιάδης Ἀττάλου; it is probably the same person in both documents, as Fraser assumes. In **56** he is sent as an envoy in his capacity as ἀρχιτέκτων, called both initiate and *epoptes,* while in **58** he is only an initiate. He has an adopted name in **56**, [.]ικις Μνησιστράτου, while in **58** he is merely Ἀσκληπιάδης Ἀττάλου, which prompts Fraser to conclude that the second inscription is earlier.

Second, in **59** a certain [Δι]ογένης Ἀττάλου is recorded as a *hieropoios* sent by the Cyzicene demos. It is tempting to restore the name in the present inscription, [Νικ]ογένης, instead of [Δι]ογένης, and certainly possible: Conze's drawing shows that there is room for nu, iota, and kappa before the omicron.

Line 16: The name Μαιάνδριος is attested in other Cyzicene inscriptions (*I.Kyz.* 1447.B; 1462, line 17; 1543).

Lines 22–23: Ἱεροκλῆς Ἱεροκλείους τοῦ Μενεστράτου may have been a son of either Ἱεροκλῆς Μενεστράτου τοῦ Περικλείους or Ἱεροκλῆς Μενεστράτου, mentioned in lines 19–21.

Lines 28–36: Fredrich notes that it is uncertain whether these are theoroi from Chios. There is a large number of names without an ethnic, and even if we suppose an ethnic preceding line 28 the list is still too long. We find a similar situation in **22**, lines 27–37. There are several possible explanations for the long list. First, a city might send a large number of sacred envoys to reflect its own stature. Another possibility is that theoroi from the same city were sent more than once during a year. A third possibility would be to suppose that all members of the sacred delegation were listed as theoroi. Inscriptions **14** and **15** show the opposite phenomenon, namely, that cities sometimes sent a group of ambassadors, all of whom were referred to as initiates (μύσται εὐσεβεῖς), while only the first few among them were theoroi.

Lines 33, 36: Ἀρίστων Γοργίου and Γοργίας Ἀρίστωνος are probably father and son, with the father listed first, although there is no confirming evidence.

Line 35: Μαγεδάτου is a hapax, to my knowledge.

Lines 38: Ἁγησιμένης is a rare name, but attested elsewhere on Lesbos (*IG* XII.2 526), as Habicht notes (p. 110). The theonym Βάκχος is not a typical name for a person. We could suppose that the iota of Βακχίου was omitted by the stone carver or the editors of the inscription, but the condition of the stone makes this impossible to determine.

10   Record of theoroi-proxenoi(?) from Kyzikos, Eresos,   Fig. 10
         Kolophon, Kyme, Teos, Priene, and the *koinon* of
         Dionysiac *technitai* from Ionia and the Hellespont

Wall block of Thasian marble, preserved on the right. A rectangular dowel hole and a pry hole are visible on top, ca. 0.43 m from the right edge. The back is cut and secondarily smoothed. Found in "the lower part of the castle" (Conze). Paris, Musée du Louvre, inv. Ma. 4181. I saw the stone in July 2001.

H. 0.355 m, W. 1.02 m, Th. 0.08 m; L.H. 0.015 m (col. I), 0.015–0.02 m (col. II), 0.015 m (col. III), omicron 0.01 m.

Edd. Conze 1860, p. 65; Fredrich, *IG* XII.8 163; [*IMT* 1575].

Cf. Ziebarth 1896, p. 85; Salviat, Chapouthier, and Salač 1956, p. 144, with n. 3; Aneziri 2003, p. 154, with n. 74, and p. 287, with n. 86.

Figure 10. Record of theoroi-prox-enoi(?) from Kyzikos, Eresos, Kolophon, Kyme, Teos, Priene, and the koinon of Dionysiac *technitai* from Ionia and the Hellespont (10).
Photo © M. and P. Chuzeville, courtesy Musée du Louvre, Department of Greek, Roman, and Etruscan Antiquities

2nd–1st century B.C.?

Col. I	Col. II	Col. III
[- -]ΕΙΟΥ	Ἀλεξίμαχος Πυθί[ωνος]	[Κ]τήσιππος [- - - - - -]
[- -]ΟΙ ·	15 Πυθίας Ἀμάρδιδος	Σωσιγένης Σ . [.³⁻⁴.]ΙΟ[Υ]
[- -]ΡΟΣ Μενεκράτου	Κυζικηνοί ·	Κολοφώνιοι ·
[- -]ΥΡΟΣ Βακχίου	Παρμενίσκος Ἀριστέως	25 Μητρόδωρος Δωροθέου
5 [- -Μ]ενάνδρου	Φιλόξενος Φιλοξένου	Δημήτριος Μηνοφάντου
[Θάσιο?]ι ·	Ἐρέσιοι ·	Κυμαῖοι ·
[- -Φα?]νόλεω	20 Ἀρχέλαος Ἀριστώνακτος	Ἀρτεμίδωρος καὶ Ἀπ|[ολλωνίδης?]
[- -]ΚΡΑΤΟΥ	Ἀγέλαος Εὐμέδοντος.	οἱ Ἀπολλωνίδου
[- - - - -]		30 Τήϊοι
10 [- - - -]ΩΝΟΣ		Ἡρόφιλος Ἀθηναίου
[- - - -]ΙΝΟΥ		Νέανδρος Νεάνδρου
[- - - -]		Πριηνεύς
[- - - - - -]		Παρμενίων Παρμενίω[νος]
		35 τοῦ κοινοῦ τῶν πε|[ρὶ τὸν Διόνυσον]
		τεχνειτῶν τῶν|[ἀπὸ Ἰωνίας]
		καὶ Ἑλλησπόντου
		Διομήδης Μητροδώρου
		Ἀθηνικῶν Σατύρ[ου].

Fredrich. **3** [- - -π]υρος Fredrich. **5** [τοῦ Με]νάνδρου *vel* [φύσει δὲ Με] νάνδρου Fredrich. **7** [Φα *vel* Κρι?]νόλεω Fredrich. **14** Πυθίω[νος] Fredrich. **22** Κτήσιππος Fredrich. **23** Σω[σιβ]ίου Fredrich, *fortasse* Σω[σιγέ]νου Dimitrova. **37** Ἑλλησπόντο|[υ] Fredrich.

Epigraphical Commentary

The three columns have different letter heights, but it is unclear whether they belonged to one, two, or three inscriptions. It seems likely that at least column III was part of a different inscription, since it is separated from column II by a much greater distance than that between columns I and II, and the spacing between the lines of III is narrower than that of either I or II. Moreover, the larger letters of II and the vacant space after it strongly suggest that it was the end of a record. The hand is similar to those of **6, 11, 26**, and especially **1**. For the possibility that **1** and **10** could belong together, see *ad* **1**. Fredrich dates the inscription to the 1st century B.C. on the basis of its lettering, but in view of its resemblance to **26**, I prefer a 2nd-century date, though the 1st century is possible.

Line 5: Traces of the epsilon can be made out.

Line 7: First preserved letter: right vertical.

Line 11: First preserved letter: right vertical.

Line 14: Last preserved letter: nothing visible now.

Line 22: First preserved letter: nothing visible now; second and fifth letters: middle vertical; third, sixth, and seventh letters: two vertical lines; eighth and ninth letters: clear omicron and sigma.

Line 23: Last letter before the first brackets: unclear traces; the first letter after the brackets, a vertical line; the last letter, nothing visible.

Line 37: Last letter: left diagonal with the right position for upsilon.

Commentary

Line 7: Κρινόλεως is a very rare name, while Φανόλεως occurs more often, and is extremely common on Thasos.

Line 15: Ἀμάρδιδος seems to be a hapax. Ἀμαρδίακος occurs in an inscription from Tanais, *CIRB* 1279.

Lines 17–18: Παρμενίσκος Ἀριστέως and Φιλόξενος Φιλοξένου occur as initiates and *hieropoioi* in **58**, as Fredrich, and later Fraser, point out.

Line 31: The name Ἡρόφιλος is attested elsewhere in Teos: *I.Teos* 83.14, 87.1.23, 104.5.

Line 34: Παρμενίων, a very common Greek name, is attested elsewhere in Priene: *I.Priene* 238.3, 313.344, 313.579.

Lines 35–end: The Dionysiac artists, guilds of actors and musicians, functioned as independent states, with their own assemblies, officials, and religious life.[3] They are attested from the 3rd century B.C. until at least the 3rd century A.D. The *technitai* enjoyed royal patronage in the Hellenistic kingdoms and Imperial Rome. They also had various privileges (personal immunity during travels, tax exemption, etc.) deriving from their club membership. The most famous guilds were those of the Isthmus and Nemea (later based in Argos and Thebes); of Athens; of Egypt; and of Ionia and the Hellespont (mentioned in the present document). The *technitai* of Ionia and the Hellespont were granted immunity, as two Delphic documents show (*IG* IX.1 175, ca. 237/6 B.C.; *FdD* III.3 218.B, ca. 235 B.C.); they also issued decrees (*IG* XI.4 1061 [172–167 B.C.], 1136; *I.Iasos* 65); and sent ambassadors (*I.Cos* 7, 81 B.C.). Inscription **10** shows that their theoroi visited Samothrace. The names mentioned here are otherwise unattested. It is possible, as Salviat suggests (p. 144), that the presence of Dionysiac artists reflects the importance of dramatic performances at the Samothracian festival.

3. See *L'Association dionysiaque;* Stephanis 1988; Aneziri 2003.

11 Record of theoroi-proxenoi(?) from Kos, Bargylia,   Fig. 11
Klazomenai, and a *koinon* of Dionysiac artists

Figure 11. Record of theoroi-prox-
enoi(?) from Kos, Bargylia, Klazomenai, and a *koinon* of Dionysiac
artists (**11**)

Wall block of Thasian marble, broken above and on the left. An end
dowel hole is visible at the left bottom edge. The inscription was found in
the Genoese Towers, in the course of archaeological work undertaken by the
Ephoreia of Prehistoric and Classical Antiquities in 1995. Archaeological
Museum of Samothrace, courtyard. No inv. no.

H. 0.35 m, W. 0.62 m, Th. 0.20 m; L.H. 0.01–0.015 m (left), 0.015–
0.02 m (right).

Unpublished. Mentioned in Karadima 1995, p. 492.

2nd century B.C.?

```
     [- - - - - - - - - - - -] .          . . [- - - - - - - - - - - - - - - - - - - - - - - - -]
     Β . [. .ᶜᵃ·⁶. .] . ΙΟΣ                vacat ΝΥΜ[. .ᶜᵃ·⁶. .]ΕΥ . [- - -]
     Ζώϊλος Διοδώρου          15  τοῦ κοινοῦ τῶν π[ερὶ τὸν Διόνυσον]
     Πύθων Με[.]ωνος               τεχνιτῶν [- - - - - - - - - - - - - -]
  5      Κωίων                    Ἄρατος ΣΤΡΑΤ[- - - - - - - - - -]
     Φρασίδης Λυκούργου          Νουμήνιος ΔΑ[- - - - - - - - - - - -]
     Ἄνθιππος Τιμοξένου          Ταραντῖνος
         Βαργυλιητῶν                         vacat
     Σόλων Ἄβρωνος
 10      Κλαζομενίων
     Μητρόδωρος Ἀθηναγόρου
     Πύθερμος Φανοπόλιος
     vacat
```

Epigraphical Commentary
The letters are carefully carved and clear, except in the first two lines,
where the surface of the stone is damaged. The hand is consistent with
2nd-century B.C. documents, and resembles those of **6** and **26**; see **6**, Epigraphical Commentary.

Commentary

This block has the format of a record of theoroi-proxenoi. The vacant spaces at the bottom suggest that this was the end of a list, whose beginning was presumably inscribed on a block above. Further, the letters preserved in the second line do not seem to be larger or to indicate an opening formula in any other way. For the possibility that **11** belonged with **6**, see **6**, Commentary.

Lines 15–16: For the listing of Dionysiac *technitai*, see *ad* **10**.

Lines 17–18: The names Ἄρατος and Νουμήνιος are attested without patronymics for other Dionysiac *technitai* (see Stephanis 1988, s.vv.), but no identification is possible.

Line 19: Presumably the ethnic Ταραντῖνος refers to Νουμήνιος. Fifteen other *technitai* from Tarentum are known, according to Stephanis 1988, p. 554. This is the first Tarentine attested as visiting Samothrace. This need not mean, however, that Tarentum sent theoroi to Samothrace, but rather that the guild of Dionysiac artists sent theoroi, and one of them happened to be from Tarentum.

12 Record of theoroi-proxenoi(?) from Kyzikos and Mylasa   Fig. 12

Wall block of Thasian marble, broken only on the right, found in Chora. Archaeological Museum of Samothrace, courtyard. No inv. no. I saw a squeeze in the Berlin Academy in May 2004.

H. 0.35 m, W. 0.42 m, Th. 0.17 m; L.H. 0.02 m.

Edd. Kern 1893, p. 354, no. 3; Fredrich, *IG* XII.8 169.

Beginning of 2nd century B.C.?

```
        [ . . . ] . ΤΗΣ . Μ . . . . Π . . [- -]
        [- - - - - - - - - - -]Ο[- - -]
        [. . ? .] . ΛΚ[. . . .]Ι ·
        [. . .]ΛΙΣ . Λ . . . ΙΟΥ
    5   [. . .]ΜΗ[- - - - -]ΟΠΟΣ
                Μυλασεῖς ·
        [. . 5 . .]ΜΟΣ Φιλοδήμο[υ]
        [. . .] ΑΜΦ . ΗΣ Ἑρμίου ·
                Κυζικηνῶν
    10  [- - -]ΝΟΣ Ποσειδέου
        - - - - - - traces - - - - - - -
```

Fredrich. 3 . λκ[. . . ο]ι ·, [Ζ]ακ[ύνθιο]ι? Fredrich. 5 [Ἑρ]μῆ[ς Μέρ]οπος Fredrich. 10 [μη]νὸς Ποσειδεῶν[ος] Fredrich.

Epigraphical Commentary

The inscription is almost illegible. Fredrich dates it to the beginning of the 2nd century B.C. on the basis of its letter style.

Commentary

Line 3: Possibly an ethnic, as Fredrich suggests.

Line 9: The genitive of the ethnic is surprising, given the nominative in line 6.

Line 10: One would expect a name of a Cyzicene ambassador rather than a month, and the squeeze clearly shows an omicron instead of the omega of the word Poseideon; hence my reading. Poseideos is a rarer form of the common name Posideos.

13 Records of theoroi-proxenoi(?) from Kyzikos, Halikarnassos, Kaunos, Alabanda, and Dardanos (inscription i), and of theoroi-initiates from Keramos (inscription ii)

Figure 12. Record of theoroi-proxenoi(?) from Kyzikos and Mylasa (12)

Wall block of Thasian marble, apparently preserved on all sides, reused as the inner door lintel of the Church of Christ; the inscription appears on the underside of the lintel. The top and right sides are smooth, the bottom apparently so; clamp cuttings are visible above and on the left and right.

H. 0.355 m, W. 1.37 m, Th. 0.22 m; L.H. 0.02 m.

Edd. Blau and Schlottmann 1855, p. 616; Conze 1860, pp. 69–70; Fredrich, *IG* XII.8 160.

Cf. Conze 1880, p. 85, no. 2; Fraser, *Samothrace* 2.1 (1960), p. 72, appendix III B, no. 1; [*IMT* 1576].

2nd century B.C.? (inscription i), 1st century B.C.? (inscription ii)

i   [. . . .]οι·

     [- -]ος Ἀριδείκου, Κράτης Κράτητος

         Κυζικηνοί·

     [- -]δωρος Μιδίου, Ἄρχιππος Ἀριστίωνος

5   Ἁλικαρνασσεῖς

     [- -]νίας Μελάντου, Μόσχος Μόσχου

         [Κ]αύνιοι·

     [- -]Πυρρίχου, Βελλεροφόντης Ἅγιος,

     [- -]ας Τίμωνος

10   Ἀλαβανδεῖς·

     [- -]ν Ἰάσονος, ὁ φύσει Μιννίωνος, Πάμφιλος Ἀπολλωνίου

         Δαρδανεῖς·

     [Με]νέλαος Ἀντήνορος, Δείφιλος Μηνίου.

                                       Ἀρτεμίδωρος

15   Σιληνοῦ

                                 vacat

ii   ἐπὶ βασιλέως Πυθίωνος τοῦ[- -]

               Κεραμιητῶν θεωροὶ

               μύσται εὐσεβεῖς·

               Ἱεροκλῆς Δημητρίου τοῦ Μοσχ[- -]

20   Ἀριστομένης Ἀριστομένους

               καθ᾽ υοθεσίαν δὲ Δωροθέου

               ἐουσεβὴς μύσ(της) *(sic)*

                     εὐ<σ>ε(βής)

Fredrich. **1** [Ῥόδι]οι? Hiller [*apud* Fredrich]. **4** [-δ]ωρος Fredrich, δωρος Dimitrova. **6** [- -]Μελάντου Fredrich, [- -]νίας Μελάντου Dimitrova. **8** [- - Πυ]ρρίχου Fredrich, Πυρρίχου Dimitrova. **13** [- -]λαος Fredrich, [Με]νέλαος Dimitrova. **16**, *fin.* [Ἀριδήλου?] Fredrich. **19** Μοσ||[χ- -] Fredrich. **22** μίσ(της) Fredrich.

Epigraphical Commentary
The right part of the stone is better preserved. The hand of inscription ii resembles closely those of **15** and **17.ii**. The dating is based on letter style (Fredrich, commentary). In 2004 a piece was broken off below the block, which allowed additional letters to be read on the left in lines 4, 6, 8, 13.

Lines 16–21: The hand is different and presumably later.

Line 19: Parts of the chi can be detected.

Lines 22–23: Fredrich: "nihili sunt." The letters are different (lunate sigma and epsilon) and carelessly executed.

Commentary
Only the second inscription, ii, is a list of theoroi-initiates. The earlier inscription, i, was probably a list of theoroi-proxenoi, lacking the initial formula. Its layout resembles that of **8**: the ethnics are indented, and often two names are placed on a single line. It is possible, therefore, that **8** and **13** were next, or at least close, to each other.

Line 1: Hiller von Gaertringen suggests [Ῥόδι]οι?, since Ἀριδείκης is a Rhodian name. Another possibility would be [Κῶι]οι? since both Ἀριδείκης and Ἀριδεικεύς occur on Rhodes and Kos.

Line 4: The patronymic Μιδίου is probably from Μ(ε)ιδίας, and not from Μίδιος, which is a very rare name. Curiously enough, a Cyzicene document (*IMT* 1456) frequently mentions the name Μ(ε)ιδίας both in the nominative and the genitive, and offers two possible candidates to match the name in the present document ([Μη]τρόδωρος Μειδίου, line I.56, and Ἀρτεμίδωρος Μειδί[ου], line I.87); the identification is far from certain, however, since the name is so common.

Line 6: The name Μελάντης is attested in documents of Halikarnassos (e.g., *I.Halikarnassos* 73.2, 228.1.8) in the form Μελάντας. Α Μόσχος Μόσχου τοῦ Μοσχίωνος occurs in a Halikarnassian inscription (*I.Halikarnassos* 97.6), but the name is too common to allow for a certain identification.

Lines 8–9: None of the names listed occurs elsewhere in Kaunos. Βελλεροφόντης is a very rare name.

Lines 10–11: The name Μιννίων is typical of Rhodes, Kos, Karia, and Ionia. The patronymic occurs also in **5**, line 22, but it is unclear whether the two theoroi from Alabanda are related. A certain Ἰάσων Μιννίωνος is honored in an inscription from Halikarnassos (*I.Halikarnassos* 9).

Line 13: Only the patronymic Μηνίου among the names listed occurs elsewhere in Dardanos (*IMT* 174).

Lines 14–15: It is unclear whether the name is part of the Dardanian group. It may belong to a list inscribed on the block above.

Line 16: Fredrich notes that the eponymous official is perhaps the same as the one in **57** (*IG* XII.8 186), Πυθίων τοῦ Ἀριδήλου. ΠΥΘ is numismatically attested for a Samothracian eponym; see *IG* XII.8, p. 41. There are two eponymous kings with the name Aridelos attested on Samothrace: Ἀρίδηλος τοῦ Φιλοξένου (57) and Ἀρίδηλος [- - - -]ίχου (58). The abbreviations ἈΝΔΗ, read as Ἀ<ρι>δή(λου), and ἈΡΙ are also seen on Samothracian coins; see *IG* XII.8, p. 41. It is unclear who the father of Πυθίων is.

Line 17: This is the only inscription that mentions Keramos in connection with Samothrace. It is interesting to note that a cult of the Great Gods in Keramos (θεοὶ μεγάλοι Κεραμιῆται) is attested in inscriptions. The ethnic indicates of course that they were not identical with the Samothracian Great Gods; according to Laumonier, they were a Zeus and a local figure associated with either Zeus or Apollo.[4]

14 Record of theoroi-initiates from Dardanos and of Roman   Fig. 13
    initiates of uncertain provenance

Wall block of Thasian marble, broken recently in the upper right corner. The broken-off piece is preserved. Smooth-picked on the left, top, and bottom, rough-picked on back. There may be anathyrosis on the right. The stone was lying outside the Church of Christ in 1954, when Fraser saw it. It was recently moved to the Old School Lab of the Ephoreia of Prehistoric and Classical Antiquities in Palaiopolis.

H. 0.355 m, W. 1.104 m, Th. 0.19 m; L.H. 0.04 m (line 1), 0.02 m (col. I), 0.012–0.015 m (col. II).

Edd. Blau and Schlottmann 1855, p. 615, 4; Conze 1860, p. 70; [Mommsen, *CIL* I (1863) 581]; [Lommatzsch, *CIL* I² (1918) 667]; [Mommsen, *CIL* III (1873) 716]; Conze 1875, p. 43; Fredrich, *IG* XII.8 173; [Degrassi, *ILLRP* I (1957) and I² (1965) 211].

Cf. Conze 1880, p. 98, C; Fraser, *Samothrace* 2.1 (1960), p. 73, appendix III B, no. 5; [*IMT* 104]; Clinton 2001, p. 35.

June 3, 66 B.C.

M(anio) · Lepid(o) L(ucio) Vo[lc]ac(io) co(n)s(ulibus) A. D. III Non(as)
    Iunias   mystae   piei

Col. I	Col. II

Col. I

N(umerius) · [. . . .]ni[. . .] l. · E . [. . .]us
L. · Ne[.]ius *vacat*
5 Q. · Clod<i>us Q. · l. · Agacles
Diodo[t]us · A[th]enogenis
Artemo Nearchi.
    vacat

Col. II

ἐπὶ βασιλέως Ἀρίστωνος τοῦ
    Ἰφικράτους μύσται εὐσεβεῖς
10 θεωροὶ Δαρδανεῖς·
    Λυσιμένης Ἀπολλωνίδου
    Ἀπολλόδωρος Δεινοκλέους
    συμμύσται· *v* Σωκλῆς
    Ὀλυμπιοδώρου
15 ΠΑΤ . . . ΟΣ καὶ Ἀπολλωνίδης
    οἱ Ἀλεξιμάχου
    Διονύσιος Διοδώρου
    Μηνόφαντος Φιλοκράτους
    ἀκόλουθοι·
20 Ἀρτεμίδωρος Εὐημέρου.

Fredrich. **1** M(anio) Lepid(o) L(ucio) Vo[lc]ac(io) Fredrich. **2** mistae Fredrich, mystae Dessau [*apud* Fredrich]. **3** N(umerius) . . . . ni[us N.] l(ibertus) Ep[hor]us(?) Fredrich, N · [. . . .]ni[. . .] l. Ef[. . .]us Degrassi. **13** Σωκλῆς Fraser, Ἰσοκλῆς Fredrich. **15** Πατί[σ]κος *vel* Πάτ[αι]κος Fredrich, *fortasse* Πάτριχος Fraser. **20** Εὔδωρος Fraser.

4. Laumonier 1958, pp. 646–652.

Figure 13. Record of theoroi-initiates from Dardanos and of Roman initiates of uncertain provenance (14)

Epigraphical Commentary

The inscription is now almost obliterated. Its Latin portion was almost illegible even at the time of its first publication in *CIL*. The consular dating is spread over both columns of the inscription and is cut in very large letters.

Line 5: Fredrich's majuscule copy has ΑΓΛCLES, so in order to print Agacles, one has to assume that the stone carver confused the Greek and Roman alphabets.

Commentary

This document is unusual because it has a Latin part in addition to the Greek list of theoroi-initiates. It is curious that Roman *mystae* are listed on the same block as Greek theoroi. In fact, only the first two Greek initiates are also theoroi. The dimensions of the block are compatible with those of the other blocks, but there seems to be no justification for inscribing names of initiates on the same building that held lists of theoroi-proxenoi. One would expect a list of initiates to be placed on an individual stele as a purely private initiative. At least two of the Romans mentioned in this inscription were freed slaves (lines 3, 5), so it is unlikely that they were important to the city of Samothrace. Unfortunately, none of the people listed is attested elsewhere, so we cannot determine whether the Romans came from Dardanos as well. It seems logical that they all came to Samothrace together. The following document, **15**, provides a good parallel for Dardanian initiates listed together with Roman initiates. It would seem that after the recording of theoroi-proxenoi ceased to be a popular practice, names of initiates were inscribed on the same building. The difference is that the records of initiates list a single city; they were perhaps not set up by Samothrace, but privately by the initiates.

Another noteworthy feature of this document is that it reveals a hierarchy in the initiates' status: only the first two are theoroi, the next three are *symmystai*, while the last person mentioned is a servant, *akolouthos*. The use of the plural title *akolouthoi* must be a mistake, unless the list continued on the block below.

Line 8: The abbreviation ΑΡΙ is numismatically attested for a Samothracian eponym; see *ad* **13**. The father of Ariston here may be related to the king in **15**.

Figure 14. Record of theoroi-initiates from Dardanos and of Roman initiates of uncertain provenance (15). Photo © M. and P. Chuzeville, courtesy Musée du Louvre, Department of Greek, Roman, and Etruscan Antiquities

15   Record of theoroi-initiates from Dardanos and of Roman   Fig. 14
     initiates of uncertain provenance

Wall block of Thasian marble, broken on the right; the back was cut off and smoothed for shipping purposes in the 19th century; there may have been an end dowel hole in the lower left edge. Found built into "the bigger tower" (Conze). Paris, Musée du Louvre, inv. Ma. 4184. I saw the stone in July 2001.

H. 0.355 m, W. 0.52 m, Th. 0.08 m; L.H. 0.02 m.

Edd. Blau and Schlottmann 1855, p. 622, no. 15; Conze 1860, pp. 63–64; [Mommsen, *CIL* I (1863) 580]; [Lommatzsch, *CIL* I² (1918) 671]; [Mommsen, *CIL* III (1873) 715]; [Cagnat, *IGR* I.4 (1905) 852]; Fredrich, *IG* XII.8 174; [Degrassi, *ILLRP* I (1957) and I² (1965) 214]; [*IMT* 105].

1st century B.C.?

      ἐπὶ βασιλέως Ἰφικράτους <u>τοῦ</u> [- -]
      θεωροὶ Δαρδανέων
      μύσται εὐσεβεῖς·
      Παυσανίας Διφίλου
  5 Διονύσιος Σκοπίου
      Ἀντίοχος Σκοπίου
      ἀκόλουθος Παυσανίου· Ὅμιλ<u>ος</u>
         mystae · piei
      L. · Veneilius L. · f. · Pollion · Dionysius <u>L.</u> · <u>se</u>[r](vus)
 10 Q<u>.</u> · Acorenus · Q<u>.</u> · l. · Alexsander ·

Fredrich. **1** ΣΤΟΥ Blau and Schlottmann, ΣΤΟ Conze, ΤΟΥ Fredrich. **7** ΛΟΣ *edd.* **9** VS · I · SEB Conze.

Epigraphical Commentary

The letters are carefully done and clear. Their style is very similar to that of **13**, inscription ii, and **17**, inscription ii. The Greek and Roman letters seem to have been executed by the same hand.

The last few letters in lines 1, 7, and 9 are underlined since they can no longer be seen.

Commentary

For the recording of Greek and Roman initiates in addition to the theoroi-initiates, see **14**. The inscription conforms to the dimensions of the other theoroi blocks.

Line 1: The eponymous king may be the father or another relative of the one in **14**, hence the tentative date.

Lines 5–6: Σκόπιος is a very rare name.

Line 7: For the ἀκόλουθος, cf. **14**, Commentary.

Line 10: The name Acorenus, as far as I know, is unattested.

16   Record of theoroi-initiates from Elis   Fig. 15

Doric architrave block of Thasian marble, preserved on both the left and right sides, the top and bottom being close to the original surface. The regulae measure 0.215 m in width, and the space between them ca. 0.25 m. The front surface is light gray, with a secondary reddish coloring. The back was cut and secondarily smoothed in the 19th century for shipping purposes. The stone has damage holes on the right; the broken surfaces are white. Found built into "the lowest tower" (Conze). Paris, Musée du Louvre, inv. Ma. 4186. I saw the stone in July 2001.

H. 0.42 m, W. 1.38 m, Th. 0.075 m; L.H. 0.04 m.

Edd. Blau and Schlottmann 1855, p. 621, no. 12; Conze 1860, p. 64; Bechtel 1887, no. 236; Conze 1880, pp. 98–99; Fredrich, *IG* XII.8 176.

2nd–1st century B.C.?

    ἐπὶ βασιλέως Τεισία τοῦ Κρίτωνος
       Ἠλείων θεωροί
       μύσται εὐσεβεῖς·
      Ἄντανδρος Θεοδώρου
  5 Ἀριστοκράτης Ἀντιφάνεως
    - - - - - - - - *traces* - - - - - - - - - - -

Fredrich. **5** Ἀντιφάνεως Dimitrova, Ἀντιφάνεος Fredrich. **6** Dimitrova.

Figure 15. Record of theoroi-initiates from Elis (**16**). Photo © M. and P. Chuzeville, courtesy Musée du Louvre, Department of Greek, Roman, and Etruscan Antiquities

Epigraphical Commentary

The letters are clear and carefully done.

Line 5: I see an omega.

Line 6: Unclear traces of letters.

Commentary

This architrave block is of crucial importance in trying to reconstruct the
building from which the theoroi blocks came (see discussion above, pp. 16–
17). This is the only inscription that mentions ambassadors from the
Peloponnese. Fredrich suggests a date in the 1st century B.C. or 1st century A.D. on the basis of the letter shapes, which is possible, but I prefer
an earlier date because the eponymous official might be the same as the
one recorded on a pseudo-Rhodian coin that is dated by Richard Ashton
to the first half of the 2nd century B.C.[5] The name Τ(ε)ισίας occurs as a
patronymic of the eponymous king in **62**, a list of initiates inscribed on a
block from the building that held theoroi records.

17   Records of theoroi-initiates from Stratonikeia and Sardis   Fig. 16

Wall block of Thasian marble, broken on the right; the left side has
anathyrosis; the top and bottom are smooth-picked. A rectangular dowel
hole is visible on top, 0.695 m from the left edge. Found 1 km northeast of
Kamariotissa, near the intersection of the main coastal road and the country
road leading to Potamia. Palaiopolis, Old School Lab of the Ephoreia of
Prehistoric and Classical Antiquities, Ephoreia inv. C 80.106.

H. 0.355 m, W. 1.08 m, Th. 0.18 m; L.H. 0.015 m (inscription i),
0.02 m (inscription ii, lines 1–3), 0.017–0.02 m (inscription ii, lines 4–7),
0.015–0.018 m (inscription iii).

Ed. Triantaphyllos 1985, pp. 312–313.

Cf. *SEG* XXXV 964.

1st century B.C.?

i		ii	Στρατονικέων
	[- - - - - - - - - - - - -]		ἐπὶ βασιλέως Δη[- - - -]
	[- - - - - - - - - - - - -]		μύσται [εὐσεβεῖς - - - -]
	[- - - - - - - - - - - - -]		ἀρχιθεωρὸς ΜΕΝ[- - - -]
5	[- - - - - - - - - - - - -]		θεωροὶ ⱽ Ἀριστόλα[ος- -]
	[- - - - - - - - - - - - -]		καθ᾽ ὑοθεσίαν δὲ ΑΝ[- - - -]
	[- - - - - - - - - - - - -]		Ἀρεὺς Φιλοκράτο[υ- -]
	[- - - - - - - - - - - - -]	iii	*vacat*
	[- - - - - - - - - - - - -]		ἐπὶ βασιλέως Ἀπ<ο>λλωνίδ[ου]
10	[- - - - - - - - - -]ΟΣ		τοῦ Θεοδώρου
	[- - - - - - - - - - - - -]		μύστης εὐσεβὴς
	[- - - - - - - - - - - - -]		[Ἀ]ντισθένης Μηνοδότου [τοῦ]
	[- - - - - - - - - -]ΜΥ . . .		Ἀν[τι]σθένου Σαρδιανὸς
	[- - - - - - - - - - - - -]		δικαστὴς
			vacat

Triantaphyllos. **4** θ . τος Triantaphyllos, ἀρχιθεωρὸς Dimitrova. **5** θεωροὶ
Καρ . . τονα Triantaphyllos, θεωροὶ Ἀριστόλα[ος- -] Dimitrova. **12** *fortasse* [τοῦ
Ἀντι]σθένου Pleket (*apud SEG*).

Epigraphical Commentary

The letters of inscription ii, larger and more elongated than those of iii,
resemble the hand(s) of **13**, inscription ii, and **15**. The inscription (at least
ii) can be tentatively dated by its letter forms to the 1st century B.C. The

5. Ashton 1988; see also **26** and **62**.

Figure 16. Records of theoroi-initiates from Stratonikeia and Sardis (17)

letters of inscription iii, added in the vacant space after ii, are consistent with a date in the 1st century B.C., but a later date is also possible. The block contained another inscription on the left, where unclear traces of letters are visible.

Line 4: There is a stray horizontal mark above the rho of ἀρχιθεωρὸς, which gives the appearance of tau.

Line 9: The omicron of Ἀπ<ο>λλωνίδ[is omitted.

Commentary

Inscription i may have been a record of theoroi-proxenoi, ii is a list of theoroi-initiates, and iii is a record of a single initiate from Sardis. Apparently at a certain point only initiates were recorded on the building inscribed with theoroi blocks.

Line 9: An eponymous king with the name Δείνων Ἀπολλωνίδου is attested in **56**, as Triantaphyllos observes.[6] It is unclear whether the two kings are related.

Lines 12, 13: The ethnic Sardianos is otherwise unattested in Samothracian context, as Triantaphyllos notes. Presumably Ἀντισθένης was sent to Samothrace as a judge, and then became initiated. There are numerous inscriptions honoring judges who were sent from one city to another. Poseidonios, son of Herodes, for example, the father of the Prienian poet praised by Samothrace, served as a judge (see *ad* **3**, line 6).

6. In his text there is a slight misprint of the name as Δείνων Ἀπολλωνίδης, but Ἀπολλωνίδου must be a patronymic in the genitive singular.

CHAPTER 3

Records of Theoroi Inscribed on Other Stones

The following documents concerning theoroi[1] (18–28) are inscribed on stelai, unidentified blocks, a statue base, and a round altar.

18 Record of theoroi(?) from Parion   Fig. 17

Fragment of a stele of Thasian marble, preserved on the right, rough-picked on back. Paris, Musée du Louvre, inv. Ma. 4185. I saw the stone in July 2001.

H. 0.165 m, W. 0.20 m, Th. 0.04 m; L.H. 0.02–0.025 m.
Ed. Fredrich, *IG* XII.8 175.
Cf. Fraser, *Samothrace* 2.1 (1960), p. 65; [*IMT* 103].

1st century B.C.?

```
      [- - - - - - -]ὶ Παριανῶ[ν]·
      [- - -]ρος Ἀνδρέ-
      [ου, Ἀπατ?]ούριος Πο-
      [- -ο]υς, Ἀντι-
  5   [- -] . λε-
```

Fredrich. **1** [μύσται εὐσεβεῖς] Fredrich. **2** [θεωρο]ὶ Fredrich. **6** [κ *vel* υ]λε- Fredrich.

Epigraphical Commentary
The lettering, different from that of most other Samothracian inscriptions, is indicative of a 1st-century B.C. date, according to Fredrich.

Line 2: Dotted letters: bottom verticals.
Line 6: Upper diagonals, followed by the apex of a triangle.

Commentary
The restoration proposed by Fredrich in line 1, [μύσται εὐσεβεῖς], is far from certain, so I have not included this inscription among the other records of theoroi-initiates.

Figure 17. Record of theoroi(?) from Parion (18). Photo © C. Larrieu, courtesy Musée du Louvre, Department of Greek, Roman, and Etruscan Antiquities

1. See **132** for possible theoroi from Perinthos.

19   Records of theoroi and initiates   Fig. 18

Fragment of a block of Thasian marble, found in Chora, once built into a wall outside the καφενεῖον τοῦ Γεωργίου, preserved on the right and left. It is unclear whether the top and bottom are preserved. The block is inscribed both on the front (side A) and on the left (side B). Paris, Musée du Louvre, inv. Ma. 4187. I saw the stone in July 2001.

H. 0.45 m, W. 0.31 m, Th. 0.15 m; L.H. 0.02–0.025 m (lines 1–3), 0.015–0.02 m (lines 4–6), 0.05 m (line 8), 0.03 m (line 9), 0.02 m (lines 11–end).

Edd. Blau and Schlottmann 1855, p. 620, nos. 10, 11; Conze 1860, pp. 66–67; Fredrich, *IG* XII.8 177.

Cf. Conze 1860, p. 62; Collini 1990, p. 261.

Date?

Side A

μύσται

εὐσ[ε]βεῖς·

Νικήφορος,

Φιλόστρατος, Δωσί-

5   θεος, Δᾶος, Εὐήμερος,

Ἐπαμινώνδας, Ταλο[υ]-

ρας, Βιθυς.[2]

Side B

[- - - -]F *vacat*

vacat

[- - -θε]ωροί·

10   [- - - -]ΣΠΑΡ

[- - - -π]όλιδος,

[- - -ο]δώρου,

[- - -]ύης Ἀρισ-

[- - -]άτου, Ἡρα-

15   [- - -]όδοτος

[- -], Δημήτρ[ι]-

[ος - -]ς, Νεκ . [. .]

Fredrich. **6–7** ΤΑ . . . ΡΑΣ Blau and Schlottmann, Ταλο[ύ]|ρας Fredrich. **8–9** [ἐπὶ βασιλέως]||[τοῦ δεῖνος τοῦ δεῖνος] Fredrich. **13** *fortasse* Εὐσύης Fredrich.

Epigraphical Commentary

The letters are clear, though a bit uneven.

Line 2: The inscription is now damaged where the second epsilon of εὐσ[ε]βεῖς should have been.

Line 6: The left oblique stroke of what seems to be a lambda looks "broken." The space after the omicron seems to be vacant.

Commentary

This block, 0.45 m high, is much larger than the standard 0.35 m blocks. The names in the inscription on side A are most probably those of slaves, as Fredrich notes, so it must postdate that on side B, which mentions theoroi.

Line 6: The name Ταλορας is unattested, so Ταλο[υ]ρας is a preferable reading. The genitive Ταλουρου occurs in several inscriptions from

2. As noted in the List of Editorial Symbols, I follow the standard scholarly practice of accenting Thracian names if they are attested only in Greek literary sources but unattested epigraphically, and leave them unaccented otherwise.

Figure 18. Records of theoroi and initiates (19): side A *(left)*, side B *(right)*. Photos © M. and P. Chuzeville (left), C. Larrieu (right), courtesy Musée du Louvre, Department of Greek, Roman, and Etruscan Antiquities

Attica and Thessaly. The name itself is considered to be Thracian,[3] and is attested also in the form Tarula(s); see **89**. Initiates with Thracian names are commonly attested in Samothrace (see Chap. 9). This is not surprising, given the geographic proximity and the traditional interest of the Thracians in Samothracian cult. A late-4th-century B.C. inscription from the major Thracian city of Seuthopolis is our earliest epigraphical record of the worship of the Samothracian gods outside Samothrace.[4] Inscription **171** and inscription Appendix II.**3** are from two Thracian cities, Odessos and Dionysopolis, respectively, that mention local worship of the Samothracian Mysteries. It is likely that the pre-Greek settlers of Samothrace came from Thrace, and a Thracian origin of the term *Kabeiros* would certainly make better sense from a geographic and cultic point of view than a Semitic one would.[5] Even Thracian royalty became Samothracian initiates, as is evident from **46**.

Line 8: It is unclear what F means, but it must belong to a different inscription. Fredrich suggests [ἐπὶ βασιλέως]|[τοῦ δεῖνος τοῦ δεῖνος], but the vacant space on the stone does not allow this restoration.

Line 13: A certain Εὐσύης occurs in **50**, as Fredrich points out.

20   Record of theoroi(?) from Kolophon   Fig. 19

Fragment of Thasian marble, broken on all sides. Paris, Musée du Louvre, inv. Ma. 4182. I saw the stone in July 2001.

H. 0.16 m, W. 0.20 m, Th. 0.04 m; L.H. 0.02 m.

Edd. Reinach 1892, p. 204, no. 3; Kern 1893, p. 375, no. 25; Fredrich, *IG* XII.8 166.

3. Detschew 1957, pp. 491–492. I owe this observation to Dimitar Boyadzhiev.

4. *IGBulg* V 5614; Velkov 1991, pp. 7–11, no. 1; Elvers 1994, 266 (*SEG* XLII 661); Tacheva 2000, pp. 28–35; cf. Cole 1984, pp. 59–60, 147–148, no. 14.

5. Collini (1990) argues against the Semitic origin of the term.

Figure 19. Record of theoroi(?) from Kolophon (20). Photo © C. Larrieu, courtesy Musée du Louvre, Department of Greek, Roman, and Etruscan Antiquities

2nd century B.C.?

- - - - - - - - - - - - - - -
Κολοφώ[νιοι] *vel* Κολοφω[νίων]
[Μ]ενε . [- - -] .
- - - - - - - - - - - - - - -

Fredrich. **1** Κολοφώ[νιοι] Fredrich.

Epigraphical Commentary

The lettering resembles that of **1, 6, 10, 11**, and **26**, except that the present inscription has more pronounced serifs. Fredrich thinks the hand suggests a date in the 1st century B.C., but I prefer a 2nd-century B.C. date on account of its similarity to **26**.

Line 2: Of the last letter there are only unclear traces.

Commentary

It is unclear whether this fragment belonged to a list of theoroi.

Line 1: Either the nominative or the genitive plural is possible.

21   Dedication by theoroi(?) from Patara   Fig. 20

Base of Thasian marble, preserved on all sides. The top and the sides are smooth in front and rough-picked on back. The back is rough. A dowel hole and a pour channel are visible above on the left. The block was removed from a wall in Chora, before Fredrich copied it in the local schoolhouse. Archaeological Museum of Samothrace, courtyard. No inv. no.

H. 0.14 m, W. 0.56 m, Th. 0.26 m; L.H. 0.017–0.02 m.

Edd. Kern 1893, p. 370, no. 12; Fredrich, *IG* XII.8 167.

2nd century B.C.?

Παταρεῖς
Ζώπυρο<ς> Σπόνδου
Εὐδαίμων Θράσωνος

Fredrich.

Epigraphical Commentary

The lettering is consistent with 2nd-century B.C. documents, hence Fredrich's dating.

Figure 20. Dedication by theoroi(?)
from Patara (21)

Commentary

The pour channel and the dowel hole suggest that a dedication stood on
top of the block. It is possible that there were other blocks to the right and
the left. It is uncertain whether the inscription is original and whether the
Παταρεῖς mentioned in it were theoroi. If they were theoroi who set up
a dedication to the Great Gods, then this would be another example of
names of theoroi on bases of monuments; cf. **4** and **26**.

22   Record of theoroi(?) from Teos, Methymna, Samos, Kolophon,
Klazomenai, Kaunos, Abdera, Parion, and Kalchedon

Two joining fragments of a stele of Thasian marble, badly worn. Preserved on all sides. Found in Roman aqueduct. Archeological Museum of
Samothrace, courtyard, inv. 38.376.

   H. 1.74 m, W. 0.40–0.45 m, Th. 0.085–0.10 m; L.H. 0.015 m.
   Ed. Fraser, *Samothrace* 2.1 (1960) 22.
   Cf. Lehmann-Hartleben 1939, p. 144; Robert 1963, pp. 51–53, 55,
62; [*IMT* 1032 (*ad* lines 51–64)].

After middle of 3rd century b.c.?

       ἐπὶ βασιλέως [- - - -]νοδώρου τοῦ ΑΙΓ[- - - - - -]
           Τηΐων·
       [. . .⁵. . - - -   - - - - - -]
       Ἀπολλώνιος [. . .]ιπίδου
    5   [. . .] . ίων
       Ἀγαθοφῶν Ἀγαθονίκου
       Ἁμετερός Παντακλέος
       Δαμόπολις Ἁγησιδάμου
           [. .]λίων
   10 Διόδοτος Πρωτοφίλου
       Πύθων Πυθοκρίτου
       Νικόστρατος Ἀριστοβούλου
           Μηθυμναίων
       Θυμητᾶς Δεινα[. . .?]ου
   15 [- - - - - -]ν Μίνδρου

[Πρ]ύτανι[ς] [- - - - - - -]
Πι[. . .⁶. . .]ων [- - - - - -]
Α[- - - - - -   - - - - - - -]
[- - - - - - -   - - - - - - -]
20   Σα[μί]ων·
[- - - - - -   - - - - - - -]
[- - -]άτιος   [- - - -]φου
[- - - - - -   - - - - - - -]
          [Κολο]φων[ίων]
25   [- - - - - -]   Ἡροδ[- - - - - -]
[- - - -]ώνιος   [. . .]π[. .]ίου
          [- - -]ίων
Παυσανίας Πλειστίου
Πλειστοκράτης Ἀρίστωνος
30   Ἀγησίας Στρα[- - - - - -]
[- - - - - -   - - - - -]ηνου
[- - - - - - - - - -] Θεοφίλου
Ἑρμοπείθης Ἀριστόλα
Εὔμηλος Στρατωνύμου
35   [- - - - - -] Ἀθηναγόρα
[- - - - - -] Διονυσίου
Πα[. . . . .]ης Σκαμανδρ[ίου]
          Κλαζομενίων
Ἡραγίτων Δημητρίου
40   Τηλεφάνης Μητροδώρου
Ἀρτέμω[ν] [- - - -]φάνους
          Καυνίων
[- - - - - -]ίων Βοΐσκου
Λυ[. . . .] Πανταλέοντος
45   Ἀβδηριτῶν
Εὐκράτης Ἡρακλείδου
Ἀπολλόδωρο[ς] Πυθοδ[- - - -]
[- - - - - -   - - - - - -]
[- - - - - -   - - - - - -]
50   [- - - - - -   - - - - - -]
          Παριανῶν
[- - - - - -] Ἀπολλωνίου
[- - - - - -   - - - - -]ου
Πολυδ[. . . . .] Ἐπιγόνου
55   [- - -]λλ[.]π[- - - - - - - - -]νος
[- - - - - -   - - - - - -]ν[- - - -]
[- - -]π[- - -   .]υ[. .]μένου
[- -]υ[- - - -   - - - - -]μο[υ]
[- - - -]υ[- -   - - - - - -]
60   [- - - - -   - - - - -]
[- - - - - -   - - -]λ[- - -]
[- - - - - -   -]ν[- - - - -]
Πολύδωρος Διονυσοδότου
Στράτηγος [. . . . .]οθέου

65   Καλχηδονίων
         [- - - - - -   - - - - - -]
         Αμ[- - - -   - - - - - -]ωνος
         Φιλοφάνης [Πυ?]ρρίνου
         [- - - - - -   - - - - -]ς
70   Διογένης Μενύλλου Ῥόδιος
         Πισικράτης Εὐτίμου [. .]ίδιος

Fraser. **1** Ἀ[θ]ανοδώρου Fraser. **3** Πο̣λυμ̣[- - -] Fraser. **5** Μη̣λ̣ί̣ων Bean (*apud* Fraser), Κν̣ιδίων Fraser. **9** Μη̣λ̣ί̣ων Fraser. **14** Δεινα[γόρ]ου Fraser. **37** Παλλάν-τ̣η̣ς Fraser, Πα̣ν̣τ̣α̣κλῆς Robert, *haesitanter*. **68** [Πυ]ρ̣ρίνου Robert, [Μυ]ρρίνου Fraser.

Epigraphical Commentary

The stone is practically illegible now, to such an extent that it seems pointless to underline what can no longer be seen. In 1939 the two fragments made a complete join, as Fraser points out; then a piece was broken off from the lower right corner of the top fragment. The readings are those of Fraser.

Line 1: I see nothing before nu in the name of the eponymous official. Last letter: Fraser has obviously seen a left vertical and a top horizontal, since he reads either gamma or pi.

Line 5: First letter after the brackets: apparently a triangle, since Fraser reads a delta, while Bean reads a lambda.

Line 9: First letter after the brackets: apparently a triangle, since Fraser reads a lambda.

Commentary

Fraser notes that the present inscription is unusual in its form: it is a stele, not a block from a wall. Another curiosity is that there is no record of bestowing *proxenia* on the theoroi. Fraser concludes that although it is tempting to assign the format of stelai listing theoroi who were not made *proxenoi* to an earlier date, the considerably later date of another stele of theoroi, **24** (*IG* XII.8 172), would point to the parallel existence of simple lists of theoroi and lists of theoroi-proxenoi. The date of **24**, however, is uncertain. The present stele must have been set up by Samothrace since it is unlikely that people from all the cities listed would have erected such a monument together. It is uncertain whether the officials listed were theoroi, although this seems probable. It is conceivable that there was a series of stelai and that the title was inscribed on the first.

The hypothesis that the names of theoroi were inscribed on stelai in the 3rd century B.C., a practice replaced by publication on building walls, may be supported by Appendix I.3 (mid-3rd century B.C.?), which calls for publication of the names of the theoroi "on the stele" (lines 11–12). "The stele" is not further explained, presumably because it was generally understood in Samothrace what it meant, namely, the stele on which names of theoroi were annually inscribed.

Line 4: [Εὐρ]ιπίδου seems the most likely among the few possible restorations.

Lines 5–8: Robert (p. 52) points out that in Fraser's text the delta of Κν̣ιδίων is not dotted, while in his commentary it is: "Κν̣ιδίων is not certain.

Knidian theoroi do not occur elsewhere in the lists, and Bean prefers to read the word as Μηλίων, though this seems to me more probable in line 9."

It is interesting to note that the names Ἀγαθοφῶν, Πανταϰλῆς, Δαμόπολις, and Ἁγησίδαμος occur in Rhodian inscriptions: Ἀγαθοφῶν is a very rare name, yet it is attested, to my knowledge, only in the present document and on Rhodes (*Lindos* II 51.c.II, line 55). The rest are especially well documented on Rhodes.[6] Restoring ['Ρο]δίων in line 5 should be considered.

Line 7: The name Ἀμετερός (the accent is on the last syllable) is very rare (e.g., *IG* V.1 1441a.2). Ἡμέτερος does not occur as a name, except for the feminine Ἡμετέρα (*IG* V.2 536; cf. Robert, p. 53).

Line 9: Fraser's reading Μηλίων has been used as evidence for theoroi from Melos, but the reading is uncertain.

Line 10: Πρωτοφίλου is a hapax, to my knowledge.

Line 14: Θυμητᾶς is very rare. The only comparable instance known to me is *IG* II² 6270, Θυμητάδος. As for the patronymic, Δεινά[ρχ]ου is also possible and better attested.

Line 27: Robert suggests that ['Ροδ]ίων can be restored since the following three names are likely to be Rhodian. This would be hard to prove, however, because names such as Παυσανίας and Ἀρίστων are common all over Greece, while Πλειστίας and Πλειστοϰράτης are unattested in Rhodian inscriptions (see below, *ad* lines 28, 29; for a more probable Rhodian list, see above, *ad* lines 5–8).

Lines 27–37: Fraser notes that a group of 10 names preceded by a single ethnic is very unusual. He suggests that an ethnic may be read in line 31, -ηνου—for example, -ηνων.[7] Even if this assumption is correct, the following group of six names still calls for an explanation (cf. *ad* **10**, lines 28–36).

Line 28: Πλείστιος is a rare name, attested only in Delphi, *CID* II 139.40. Fraser has as the nominative in the index Πλειστίας, which is a more common name.

Line 29: Πλειστοϰράτης is not attested epigraphically, to my knowledge.

Line 33: Ἑρμοπείθης seems to be a hapax, while Ἀριστόλας is very common.

Line 34: Στρατώνυμος seems to be a hapax.

Line 37: Παλλάντης, restored by Fraser, is unattested. Robert (p. 53) tentatively suggests Πανταϰλῆς.

Line 39: Ἡραγ(ε)ίτων is a very rare spelling, attested only in *IG* XII.5 881, to my knowledge. Ἡρογ(ε)ίτων, on the other hand, is very common.

Line 43: The patronymic Βοΐσϰου occurs elsewhere in a Kaunian context: *I.Iasos* 18, a decree honoring Ἑστιαῖος Βοΐσϰου Καύνιος.

Line 68: Πύρρινος is a much more commonly attested name than Μύρριν[ος],[8] and the ending is restored, so one cannot be sure about the exact form of the name.

Line 70: The patronymic Μενύλλου occurs elsewhere in Rhodian inscriptions: *Lindos* II 363; *SEG* XXXIII 642.

Line 71: According to Fraser, [Κν]ίδιος is possible, "in which case he was presumably omitted from the Κνίδιοι in lines 5ff." This observation, however, contradicts his former conclusion that the restoration Κνιδίων is only hypothetical. Even though the reading of lines 5 and 9 is uncertain,

6. Πανταϰλῆς / -εύς is listed in *IG* XII.1 258, 765, 1034.II; *Lindos* II 1.A, 51.a, 347.a.III, 347.b.II, 419.III, etc. Δαμόπολις occurs in *IG* XII.1 730; *Lindos* II 270.II, 286, 294.II, 349.II. Ἁγησίδαμος is attested as a Rhodian name in a large number of inscriptions.

7. Robert (1963, p. 52) notes that the upsilon of -ηνου should have been dotted to allow for a variant reading.

8. Myrrinos occurs in *IG* II² 1951, fr. f, col. III, line 161. Fraser lists the nominative in the index as Μυρρίνης, but such a form does not occur for the masculine.

one could still restore [Κν]ίδιος, without necessarily presupposing that the name was omitted earlier. Π(ε)ισικράτης does not occur in Knidian inscriptions, but is quite common on Rhodes. For example, a Πεισικράτης is listed in **50**, a record of Rhodian initiates and *hieropoioi*. One wonders whether [Ῥ]όδιος can be an alternative restoration.

23 Record of theoroi(?) from Ephesos, Rhodes(?), Kyzikos,   Fig. 21
Alabanda, Lampsakos, and Athens(?)

Block of Thasian marble, with anathyrosis on the right, built into the southeast face of a wall of the Gattilusi fortress, ca. 13.50 m to the northwest of the southeast corner of the smaller Gattilusi Tower and ca. 0.33 m above present surface. Eugene Dwyer noticed it in the 1970s, and James Sickinger took a photograph of it in 2002.[9] I located it and copied it briefly in 2003, and examined the text in greater detail in 2004.

H. 0.77 m, W. 1.04 m, Th. inaccessible; L.H. 0.01 m.

Ed. Matsas and Dimitrova 2006, pp. 129–130.

2nd–1st century B.C.?

- -

Col. I   Col. II

[. .^{ca. 6}. .]Ἀπολλοδώρο[υ]
. . νίας Ἀλεξάνδρο[υ]   Θεόξενος ΥΡ . [. .⁵⁻¹⁰. .] *vacat*?
Ἀθήναιος Δημοκράτους   Τιμοκλείδας Α . . [. .⁵⁻¹⁰. .]
   Ἐφέσιοι   Λαμψακηνοί
5 Ἐρασιννίδης Ἐρασιννίδου   Μεμνονίδης . . [. .⁵⁻¹⁰. .]
Ἀπολλωνίδης Κνώσσου   Δωσίθε[ος] . . [. .⁵⁻¹⁰. .]
Ἡρακλείδης Ἐπικράτου   Ἀθην[αῖοι ?]
   Ῥόδιοι

- - - - - - - - - - - - - - - -   - - - - - - - - - - - - - - - -

ΑΛ[. . . . . .¹⁰⁻¹⁵. . . . . .]   *vacat*
10 ΗΡΟ . [. . . . .¹⁰⁻¹⁵. . . . . .]
   Κυζ[ικηνοί]
Μενίσκος Μεν[. .^{ca. 6}. .]
Ἡρακλείδης ΝΑ[. .^{ca. 6}. .]
   Ἀλαβανδεῖ[ς]
15 [Ἡ]ρακλεώτης [. . . .^{ca. 10}. . . .]
[Ἀ]ναξίδημ[ος . . . .^{ca. 10}. . . .]
vacat

Epigraphical Commentary
The inscription is now very worn.

Commentary
This was probably a list of theoroi, as suggested by the format of the inscription, which consists of names preceded by ethnics. It appears to be a wall block, but it is unclear from which building it came; it does not match the dimensions of the other blocks with theoroi records, which have a height of ca. 0.35 m and a thickness of ca. 0.20 m. The date is based on the fact that the known theoroi lists are dated to the 2nd and 1st centuries B.C.; the letter shapes are consistent with this date.

9. I wish to thank both for kindly informing me about the monument and sharing their notes and photograph.

Line I.6: The rare name Knosos is typical of Ephesos, and is usually spelled with a single sigma.

Line II.7: The presence of Athenians, if the reading is correct, probably refers to colonists on Imbros or Lemnos, since Attica was not a common place of origin for visitors to Samothrace; cf. **30**, a record of the initiation of Athenians on Imbros. An Athenian initiate is also mentioned in **29**.

Figure 21. Record of theoroi(?) from Ephesos, Rhodes(?), Kyzikos, Alabanda, Lampsakos, and Athens(?) (23)

24   Record of theoroi(?) from Samothrace(?), Lampsakos, Myra, Ephesos or Eresos, and Thasos

The inscription is known from the copy made by Cyriacus of Ancona, Cod. Vat. Lat. 5250, folio 20, verso. Its dimensions are unknown.

Edd. Ziebarth 1906, p. 412, no. 4; Fredrich, *IG* XII.8 172, with add., p. vii; [*IMT* 22].

Cf. Mommsen, *CIL* III (1873) 713; Fraser, *Samothrace* 2.1 (1960), pp. 62–65.

Ca. 100 B.C.?

> [ἐπὶ] βασιλέως Προκλέους τοῦ Ἀδριανοῦ *(sic)*
>   Σαμοθρᾳκων· *(sic)*
> Ἀπολλώνιος Ἀπολλομένου *(sic)*
> Ἀνδρόνικος Πολυνίκου
> 5   Λα<μ>ψακηνῶν·
> Ἀρτεμίδωρος [Κρ]άντορος
> Αἰσχύλος Αἰσχρίωνος
>   Μυρέων·
> Εὐαγόρας Ἡ[γ]ήτορος

10 Εὔαλ<κ>ος Ὀσέ<ο>του
    Ἀντίγονος Δρόμωνος
        Ἐιεσίων ·
    Σωσίθεος Ἡρακλείδου
    Ἀρτεμίδωρος Ξενίου
15 Δημόδοτος Διονυσίου
        Θασίων ·
    Ἀντιφῶν Σοφοκλείους
    Ἱέ<ρ>ων Ἀριστοφῶντος
    Διοκλῆς Ἡγ[η]σίου
20 Ἀμαντινὸς *(sic)* Φιλοξένου.

Fredrich. **2** *fortasse* Σαμίων. **5** ΛΑΨΑΚΗΝⲰΝ Cyriacus. **9** [Εὐ]μήτορος Wil. [*apud* Fredrich], [Εὐφ]ήτορος Iacobs [*apud* Fredrich], ΗΜΗΤΟΡΟΣ Cyriacus. **10** ΕΥΑΛΟΣ ΟΣΕΟΤΟΥ Cyriacus. **12** Ἐ[ρ *vel* φ]εσίων Fredrich, ΕΙΕΣΙⲰΝ Cyriacus. **18** Ἱέ[ρ]ων Fredrich, ΙΕΓⲰΝ Cyriacus. **19** Ἡγ[η]σίου Fredrich, ΗΓΙΣΙΟΥ Cyriacus.

Commentary

The inscription is unusual in its form: the layout of Cyriacus's copy suggests a stele rather than a block. It is not certain that this is a list of theoroi, but its pattern—ethnics followed by groups of several names—resembles that of the other theoroi documents.

Line 1: The last name must be a mistake, as Fredrich notes. Ἀριδήλου is possible, but cannot be verified. As for Prokles, we should note that the abbreviation ΠΡΟ is numismatically attested for a Samothracian magistrate; see *IG* XII.8, p. 41.

Line 2: The presence of Samothracians is curious, as Fredrich points out. It is unparalleled in lists of either sacred ambassadors or initiates in Samothrace. Perhaps it is a mistake for Σαμίων; cf. Cyriacus's reading of μυστηρίων for μύσται in **58**, line 18 (see Fig. 46).

Line 9: A certain Εὐαγόρας Ἀ[γ]ήτορος occurs in *Lindos* 224 as a priest of Dionysos, but most probably he was a Rhodian.

Line 17: Ἀντιφῶν, son of Σοφοκλῆς, is attested from Thasos, *IG* XII.8 430 (undated) and 441 (ca. 100 B.C.). If ours is the same person, he must have gone to Samothrace as a relatively young ambassador; the second inscription is an epitaph in verse that mentions his untimely death before the age of 30:

ἄρτι με νυμφιδίων ἀπὸ δύσμορον ἅρπασε παστῶν
δαίμων ἐς τριτάταν νισόμενον δεκάδα,
ἄρτι βίου περόωντα κατ᾽ εὐκλέα θέσμια δόξας
στυγνὸς ἄπαιδα δόμοις ἀμφεκάλυψ᾽ Ἀίδας
Ἀντιφόωντα, γοναῖσι Σοφοκλέος ὃν τέκε μάτηρ
Ἡρώ, τᾶι λιπόμαν οὐ τέκος ἀλλὰ τάφον . . .

Yet the epitaph refers to the glory he brought to his fatherland, so it is not impossible that he went to Samothrace as a theoros. Thus I tentatively date the present inscription to ca. 100 B.C., but it could be earlier in light of the hypothesis that it was common practice in the 3rd century to record theoroi on stelai (see *ad* **22**). The other inscription, 430, mentions just his name. A Sophokles, son of Antiphon, attested in *IG* XII.8 312, served as a theoros on Thasos.

Figure 22. Record of theoroi(?) from Myrina and Erythrai (25). *Samothrace* 2.1, pl. XI: appendix III A

25   Record of theoroi(?) from Myrina and Erythrai   Fig. 22

Block of Thasian marble, part of top edge preserved. Archaeological Museum of Istanbul. *Non vidi.*

H. 0.17 m, W. 0.240 m, Th. 0.10 m; L.H. 0.008–0.01 m.

Ed. Fraser, *Samothrace* 2.1 (1960), p. 69, appendix III A.

Date?

Col. I		Col. II	Col. III
- - - - - - - - - -		*vacat*	- - - - - - - - -
- - - - - - - - - -		Λάκων	- - - - - - - - -
- - - - - - - - - -	5	Ἡράκλειτος	*paragr.?* - - - -
- - - - - - - - - -		Πολέμων	Ἡρα[- - - - - -]
[- - - - - - - - -]ν .		*paragr.* Μυριναῖοι	Διοι[- - - - - -]
[- - - - - - - -]ιοι·		Ἀπολλόθεμις 15	*paragr.* Ἐρυ[θραῖοι]
[- - - - - - - -]ος		Ἱερώνυμος.	Διαγό[ρας]
- - - - - - - - - -	10	[*paragr.*] [. . . ?]νιοι·	Ἀριστα[γόρας *vel* -ῖος?]
		[- - - - - -]ος	Εὐθυδά[μας]
		- - - - - - - - -	[*paragr.*]Κλαζομ[ένιοι(?)]

Fraser, *e Roberti ectypo.* **II.7** [Καύ]νιοι Fraser. **III.9** Dimitrova, Κλαζο[μένιος(?)] Fraser.

Epigraphical Commentary

The overly elegant letters are suggestive of a later date. The hand is unlike those of the other theoroi records, as Fraser points out. The *paragraphoi* are noteworthy:[10] they introduce new ethnics. The readings are largely those of Fraser, based on L. Robert's squeeze.

Line I.2: Fraser prints a clear iota for the first preserved letter, but the drawing of the squeeze is unclear at that point.

Line III.12: Left part of a bottom horizontal, whose decorative finials have the right angle for a *paragraphos.*

Line III.19: The kappa and omicron are clear. Two triangles are visible after the kappa. The left upper part of the mu can be discerned.

10. Fraser (*Samothrace* 2.1, p. 70, n. 4) mentions that the same sign occurs in *I.Delos* 313.I, line 14, and 316, lines 62, 111, 113, sqq.

Commentary

Fraser notes that this document must have been Samothracian because of the Thasian marble used. He assumes that it was a list of theoroi. Its most striking feature is the format of the names: they have no patronymic. This is unparalleled among the theoroi documents, except for the two ambassadors of King Attalos in **5**. It is unclear when the document was inscribed. Fraser favors a later date, on the basis of the contrast with the lettering of the other inscriptions. It must be emphasized, however, that both the provenance and the nature of the inscription are far from certain.

Line III.19: Fraser, following Bean, prefers to restore Κλαζο[μένιος] as a personal name since the letters "are not indented and preceded by a *paragraphus*," and points out that "this is not an improbable name for a citizen of Erythrai." In my view the ethnic Κλαζομ[ένιοι] is a more probable reading. It is impossible to see whether it was preceded by a *paragraphos*, and the lack of indentation may be in order to save space, since Κλαζομένιοι is a longer word than most other ethnics. Moreover, Κλαζομένιος is not attested as a personal name.

26   Dedication by the Thessalian League to the Great Gods   Fig. 23

Block of coarse-grained Thasian marble, broken below, smooth on the left, rough-picked on back, moderately rough-picked above. Found in 1986, built into a wall of a Byzantine structure in the northwestern corner of the Ship Building, during American excavations. Two dowel holes with pour channels are visible on top, positioned diagonally. That in the left corner is 0.055 m from the left edge and 0.04 m from the front edge. The dowel hole on the right occurs in a similar position in the upper rear corner, with some lead preserved in it. The positions of the dowel holes suggests that a rectangular object covered the top of the block, possibly a relief. There is a small, shallow, rectangular cutting approximately midway down the left side, 0.045 m from the front edge. In wall of Byzantine structure. Inv. 01.2.

H. 0.804 m, W. 0.47 m, Th. 0.20 m; L.H. 0.01–0.025 m.
Ed. Pounder and Dimitrova 2003.
Cf. McCredie 1990 (mentioned).

170–140 B.C.

   τὸ κοινὸν Θεσσαλῶν
    θεοῖς μεγάλοις
    ἐπὶ θεωρῶν
  vacat ca. 0.02 m
  Δαμοθοίνου τοῦ Λεοντομένους
5 Φιλονίκου τοῦ Φιλίππου
    Φεραίων
  Παμφίλου τοῦ Βαθυκλείους
  Λυκίσκου τοῦ Βαθυκλείους
    Λαρισαίων
  vacat ca. 0.02 m
10   ἐπὶ βασιλέως
  Νυμφοδώρου τοῦ Θεώνδου

Figure 23. Dedication by the Thessalian League to the Great Gods (26)

Epigraphical Commentary

The letters are clear, carefully executed in comparison with most other Samothracian inscriptions, and they are adorned with finials. Omicron and theta are usually smaller (0.01–0.012 m) than the other letters. The hand resembles those of **1, 6, 10,** and **11**. It is consistent with 2nd-century inscriptions (on the reasons for the date, see Commentary), notably with **5**, inscription ii, and a municipal document of Scotussa, dated by the eponyms of the Thessalian League (161/0 B.C.).[11] This is the earliest securely dated Samothracian document with a broken-bar alpha.

Commentary

The commentary is largely reprinted from the *editio princeps*.

This document is a dedication by the Thessalian League to the Great Gods in Samothrace. The Thessalian delegation consists of two

11. Pouilloux 1955, pp. 443–459 (= *SEG* XV 370).

citizens from Pherai and two from Larisa. It is headed by the Pheraian Damothoinos, son of Leontomenes, undoubtedly none other than the *strategos* of the Thessalian League in 161/0.[12] The other three theoroi are unknown, although their names, except that of Bathykles, are attested in Thessaly.[13]

The expression ἐπὶ θεωρῶν in line 3 should be understood as "represented by the theoroi" or something similar. A parallel for this usage can be found in Delian inventory lists (e.g., *IG* XI.2 184, 186, 188, 190, and many others), where a gift by a certain delegation, whose leader is mentioned by name, is referred to as "ἀνάθημα ἐπὶ ἀρχιθεώρου [name]."

Damothoinos, son of Leontomenes (line 4), is known from other inscriptions, where he is mentioned as *strategos* of the league.[14] He belonged to a famous Pheraian family, whose members, attested from the 3rd century B.C. until the 1st century A.D., performed important public duties. Both his great-grandfather Epikratidas and his grandfather Damothoinos II were gymnasiarchs at Pherai, ca. 241 B.C. and ca. 216 B.C., respectively.[15] His father, Leontomenes, son of Damothoinos, was *strategos* of the Thessalian League in 186/5 B.C., as *IG* IX.2 64, 67, and 274 testify. In the next year, 185/4, his brother and Damothoinos's uncle Pausanias held the same office. Damothoinos's grandson, Leontomenes, son of Megalokles, was also *strategos*, ca. 100–90 B.C.[16]

A date before 170 B.C. for the present inscription is unlikely: Damothoinos, son of Leontomenes, would probably have been too young to head the embassy. His father, Leontomenes, son of Damothoinos, was *strategos* in 186/5 B.C., and so was probably between 40 and 55 years old at the time. His son, then, was probably born between ca. 205 and 190 B.C., and in 170 B.C. would have been between 20 and 35 years old—not a very plausible (though theoretically possible) age to hold such an important public office as the head of an embassy.

The eponymous king Nymphodoros, son of Theondas (lines 10–11), is otherwise unattested. The rare name Theondas, however, occurs elsewhere in connection with Samothrace: a Hadra vase from Egypt mentions a Samothracian ambassador to Alexandria, named Theondas, who died in 219 B.C.[17] According to Livy (45.5.6–12), a Theondas was an eponymous king of Samothrace in 168 B.C. The name is also attested on coins, dating perhaps from the same year, 168 B.C.[18] The eponymous king recorded in the

12. Although Damothoinos is not called *architheoros*, the listing of his name before those of the other *theoroi* suggests that he was the most important member of the delegation.

13. For instance, Pamphilos is attested in *IG* IX.2 474.A, line 42, 517, line 54, 557, line 25, 562, line 17; Lykiskos in *IG* IX.2 109.a, line 38, 121, 275, 288, 290.a, 527, 851; Philonikos in *IG* IX.2 65, line 11, 234.I, line 32, 257. Philippos is very common in Thessaly, and is found elsewhere in Pherai (*IG* IX.2 415).

14. Pouilloux 1955, pp. 443–459 (*SEG* XV 370); *Syll.*³ 668 (*SEG* XXVIII 505.19); and possibly Axenidis 1939 (*SEG* XXVIII 505.21). For the two possible restorations in *SEG* XXVIII 505, see Kramolisch 1978, p. 58.

15. See Kramolisch 1978, pp. 28, 31.

16. Kramolisch 1978, p. 31, provides a useful stemma of Damothoinos's family.

17. *SB* 1 1639.

18. Ashton (1988) demonstrates that the name Theondes/Theondas

appears on a posthumous Alexander tetradrachm of the early or mid-2nd century B.C. and on pseudo-Rhodian coins, which he is inclined to date to 168 B.C. and thereby acknowledge their Samothracian origin (I am grateful to Alain Bresson for this reference). For Samothracian coins, see also Münsterberg [1911, 1912, 1914, 1927] 1973, p. 28; *IG* XII.8, p. 41. The name Theondes is also attested (twice) on a lead curse tablet, considered Samothracian by Dusenbery (*Samothrace* 11.2, pp. 1165–1168).

present dedication would have been too old between 170 and 140 B.C. (the suggested date of the document; see below) to be the son of the ambassador Theondas. He would have been at least between 55 and 85 at that time, if we assume that his father had died as early as about age 40, which is possible but unlikely. He might have been the son of the other Theondas, who was king in 168 B.C. This would mean that if the inscription is to be dated ca. 160 B.C., the time of Damothoinos's service as *strategos*, Nymphodoros must have served as eponymous king at a relatively early age (ca. 40), and his father at a relatively late age (ca. 60), which is theoretically possible. A date around 150–140 B.C. would suit this scheme a bit better, but of course one cannot be sure whether the two kings were indeed father and son. It is also unclear whether the ambassador Theondas was related to the eponymous king of 168 B.C., but the time interval suits the possibility that he was the latter's grandfather, thereby conforming to the Greek custom of naming the grandson after his grandfather. In view of the name's rarity, the hypothesis that the eponymous king of 168 B.C. was the grandson of the ambassador Theondas and the father of Nymphodoros in the present inscription is attractive.

Thus a date between 170 and 140 B.C. can be safely suggested, in view of Damothoinos's generalship, which is dated to 161/0 B.C., and of Nymphodoros's possible relation to the eponymous king of 168 B.C.

It is impossible to determine whether there was a specific occasion for the dedication, such as the capture of Perseus by the Romans in August of 168 B.C., followed by the liberation of Samothrace from Macedonian rule. As mentioned above, Theondas was the eponymous king of Samothrace when Perseus was captured, whereas the eponymous magistrate of the present inscription is Nymphodoros, son of Theondas. The inscription, therefore, cannot be dated to a civil year that included August of 168 B.C. If the Samothracian calendar was similar to the Athenian, that is, if the year began with the first new moon after the summer solstice, the first half of 167 B.C. is also precluded. The Thasian year, on the other hand, may have begun with the winter solstice (as did the Parian one), as Jean Pouilloux observed.[19] If Samothrace followed the example of Thasos (and if the Thasian year indeed began in the winter), then the inscription could be dated to 167 B.C., shortly after Perseus's defeat. Too little is known about the Samothracian calendar, however, to make a strong argument. Our only evidence is that Maimakterion and Mounychion were Samothracian months.[20]

19. Pouilloux 1954, p. 149; see also pp. 456–458. A recent discussion of the Thasian and Parian calendars has been provided by Trümpy (1997, pp. 65–72).

20. See Samuel 1972, p. 130. He lists two Samothracian months, Maimakterion (*Samothrace* 2.1 5) and Poseideon (*IG* XII.8 169). It must be noted that Poseideon is most probably a mistake for the name Posideos (see **12**, *ad* line 10). Cole (1984, pp. 40, 119,

n. 333) observes that "neither *Mounychion*, nor *Artemisios* is listed by Samuel as a Samothracian month." Mounychion, which corresponds to Roman May, appears in an initiate list published by McCredie (1965, p. 115). Artemisios is mentioned in another list of initiates (Robert 1936, pp. 52–53, a corrected version of *IG* XII.8 195), but as a Macedonian month, not a Samothracian one. Trümpy 1997, p. 118, lists only Maimakterion for Samothrace.

The document is not unique in mentioning theoroi setting up a dedication in Samothrace. Two inscriptions (**27** and **28**) mention theoroi from Paros offering dedications to the Great Gods. The present inscription adds to the geographic range of cities and institutions connected with Samothrace: now Pherai and Larisa in Thessaly can be included in the list of places that sent sacred ambassadors. Previously the only other place in mainland Greece that was certainly attested as sending theoroi (excluding Macedonia and Thrace, which were traditionally connected with Samothrace) was Elis, as a record of theoroi-initiates (*IG* XII.8 176) testifies.

The new information that Thessaly also sent theoroi prompts us to reexamine the identity of the city of Larisa that is attested in **1** as sending theoroi; see *ad* **1**, line 3. Although it is not certain that Thessalian Larisa is meant, this possibility is now well worth considering.

The document introduced here is also interesting from a historical perspective. After the Second Macedonian War (200–197 B.C.), the Thessalian League was liberated by the Romans. In 194 B.C. T. Quinctius Flamininus reorganized its structure by establishing *strategoi*, who presided over the federal government as annual officers.[21] A typical feature of the new constitution was the council, *synedrion*, which functioned as a representative government.[22] The Greek face of the new organization reflected the Romans' desire to demonstrate that the league was indeed free from Macedonian supremacy. The territory of the refounded state did not include some of the northern areas formerly inhabited by *perioeci*, but in the south it gained Phthiotic Achaia, Aitolian Lamia, and other regions.[23]

The period to follow—the first half of the 2nd century B.C.—directly pertains to our inscription. The Thessalian League experienced a full-fledged revival, marked by considerable political activity with an expanded geographic scope. We learn from a decree of Phokaia, honoring a certain Apollodoros from Priene and dated ca. 190 B.C., that Priene was visited by Thessalian ambassadors.[24] A decree found at Delphi, dated to 186 or 184 B.C.,[25] honors Nikostratos, son of Anaxippos, a prominent citizen of Larisa who fulfilled various diplomatic duties with distinction, including service as a *hieromnemon* of the Thessalians in the reorganized Amphictionic Council, which now consisted of autonomous members (lines 3–4) and was not dependent, as before, on the Aitolians.[26] A decree of the Thessalian League, found in Philia, near the federal sanctuary of Athena Itonia, and dated to 179–165 B.C.,[27] discusses financial aid given to Ambracia by the league and can serve as evidence for their good relations: Ambracian citizens were granted *proxenia* and invited to the sacrifice in honor of Athena Itonia. As Habicht observes,[28] the Thessalian *koinon* also sent theoroi to

21. Livy 34.51.4–6. The reorganization of the Thessalian League by Flamininus and the 10 *legati* (the *strategoi*) are also referred to in *Syll.*³ 674, lines 50–54.

22. Presumably Flamininus drew inspiration from the Achaean League, which had had a *synedrion* for 200 years; cf. Larsen 1968, p. 284.

23. Larsen 1968, p. 282.

24. *I.Priene* 65.8–10.

25. *Syll.*³ 613.

26. See especially Habicht's discussion of the decree (1987, pp. 60–62). For the new Amphictionic Council, see also Lefèbre 1998, p. 205; Sanchez 2001, pp. 496–509.

27. *SEG* XXVI 688.

28. Pers. comm.; see Pounder and Dimitrova 2003, p. 31, n. 1.

Figure 24. Dedication by theoroi
from Paros (27)

the Asklepieia in Mytilene[29] and participated in the Klaria of Kolophon,[30] and Larisa, the capital of the league, honored officials of Eumenes II.[31]

The league fought on the Roman side against Perseus during the Third Macedonian War (171–168 B.C.), and subsequently regained the cities it had indirectly lost to Philip V during the Roman war with Antiochus III and the Aitolians in 192–188 B.C., when Philip had been allowed to conquer some Thessalian territory as a reward for the help he gave the Romans. The Thessalian cavalry performed feats of bravery by helping the Romans at Callicinus[32] in 171 B.C.,[33] and in general played an active part in the war. This was celebrated by the founding of the contest of the Eleutheria in Larisa, commemorating the Thessalians' valor.[34] Thessaly, on the winning side at last, was in a position to exert the influence that must have accompanied victory. In 168 B.C., immediately after Perseus reached Samothrace, embassies from Thessaly were dispatched: L. Aemilius Paullus gave audience to numerous delegations at Pella, *maxime ex Thessalia*.[35] Against this background, the present monument informs us that the Thessalian League sent theoroi to Samothrace—a fact hitherto unknown, and one that enriches our knowledge of Thessalian and Samothracian history in the 2nd century B.C.

27   Dedication by theoroi from Paros   Fig. 24

Fragment of a marble statue base, preserved on top, bottom, and the left. On top at the front left corner there are two small holes and a pour channel leading to the front; in the center there is a cavity for the insertion of a plinth, presumably of a marble statue. Archaeological Museum of Samothrace, inv. 70.456.

H. 0.04 m, W. 0.133 m, Th. 0.18 m; L.H. 0.007 m.
Ed. McCredie 1979, p. 26.
Cf. Bingen *apud SEG* XXIX 797.

2nd century B.C.?

> *vv* Παρίων θεωροὶ Ε[- - - - - - - - - - - - -]
> Δεξίθεος Δημοστρά[του- - - - - - - - - -]
> ἐπὶ βασιλέως Ἀντιφάν[ου *vel* -ους]

McCredie.

29. *IG* XII Suppl. (1939) 3, after 196 B.C.

30. Picard 1922, pp. 345–347.

31. Polyb. 22.6; and *IG* IX.2 512 (= *SEG* XXXI 574) and Gallis 1980 [1981–1982], pp. 246–249, no. 1 (= *SEG* XXXI 575), both inscriptions of 171 or 170 B.C.

32. On the correct version of this name, see Helly 1995, p. 264, n. 150.

33. Livy 42.55–60.

34. *BullÉp* 1964 227; Walbank 1979, p. 305; *IG* IX.2 553.

35. Livy 44.46.9.

Epigraphical Commentary
The letters are clear and carefully done.

Commentary
Bingen dates the document to the 3rd or 2nd century B.C., apparently on the basis of its letter style. I prefer the 2nd century B.C. in view of the broken-bar alpha.

Line 2: Neither Δεξίθεος nor Δημόστρατος is hitherto attested in Paros.

Line 3: The eponymous king is otherwise unknown.

28   Dedication by theoroi from Paros   Fig. 25

Round altar of Thasian marble. Found in 1939 outside the entrance of the Anaktoron. Archaeological Museum of Samothrace, on exhibition in Hall B, inv. 39.914.

H. 0.18 m, Diam. 0.135 m; L.H. 0.005–0.01 m.

Edd. Lehmann-Hartleben 1940, pp. 355–356, fig. 37; Fraser, *Samothrace* 2.1 (1960) 13.

Cf. Lehmann 1955, pp. 82–83 = Lehmann 1998, p. 126; Robert and Robert, *BullÉp* 1964 366.

Figure 25. Dedication by theoroi from Paros (28). *Samothrace* 2.1, pl. VIII:13

2nd century B.C.?

   Παρίων θεωροὶ
   Χαιρίτης
   Τιμοδώρου,
   Χαῖρις
 5 Κρίτωνος
   Θεοῖς
   Μεγάλοις.

  Fraser.

Epigraphical Commentary

The lettering is consistent with 2nd-century B.C. documents, hence Fraser's dating. The second half of the 2nd century is more likely, in view of the broken-bar alpha.

Commentary

Fraser draws attention to a Cretan *thymiaterion* dedicated by a Parian (*IC* I 35 3). He believes that the two monuments are very similar in shape and letter style, and may have been produced on Paros. The lettering, however, is not much different from that of other Samothracian monuments, namely **1, 6, 11,** and **26.** Another counterargument is that the present altar is made of Thasian marble (see Lehmann).

  Lines 2–3: Neither Χαιρίτης nor Τιμόδωρος is attested otherwise on Paros, to my knowledge.

  Line 4: The hypocoristic name Χαῖρις is attested in another Parian document (*IG* XII.5 461), as Fraser remarks.

  Line 5: The name Κρίτων itself is not attested otherwise on Paros, but *IG* XII.5 216 has the form Κριτωνίδεω.

CHAPTER 4

CONCLUSIONS, PART I

PROSOPOGRAPHY

The preceding documents contain approximately 250 names of Samothracian theoroi (see the Index of Names), with nine new names. The previously published names have been collated with the stone where possible, and a large number of them have undergone major or minor corrections.

PROVENANCE OF THE THEOROI

The places of origin of certain or presumable theoroi are Abdera (attested in **5, 8, 22**), Aigai (**9**), Alabanda (**4, 5, 7, 13, 23**), Astypalaia (**4**), Bargylia (**5, 11**), Chios (**9**), Dardanos (**9, 13.i, 14, 15**), Elis (**16**), Ephesos (**1, 2, 4, 5, 23, 24**[?]), Eresos (**9, 10, 24**[?]), Halikarnassos (**2, 8, 13**), Iasos (**5**, Appendix I.3, I.4), Kalchedon (**22**), Kaunos (**5, 13, 22**), Keramos (**13.ii**), Klazomenai (**4, 8, 11, 22**), Kolophon (**2, 10, 20, 22**), Kos (**4–6, 11**, Appendix I.1, I.2), Kyme (**1, 5, 10**), Kyzikos (**9, 10, 12, 13, 23**), Lampsakos (**23, 24**), Larisa in Thessaly (**1**?, **26**), Maroneia (**5, 8**), Methymna (**22**), Mylasa (**12**), Myra (**24**), Myrina (**6, 9, 25**[?]), Mytilene (**5**), Naxos (**5**), Nysa (**9**), Parion (**5, 18, 22**), Paros (**27, 28**), Pergamon (**5**), Pherai (**26**), Phokaia (**9**), Priene (**3, 5, 8, 10**, Appendix I.5), Rhodes (**5, 23**), Samos (**3, 5, 6, 22**), Stratonikeia (**5, 7, 17.ii**), Tarentum (**11**?), Teos (**6, 10, 22**), Thasos (**8, 24**), and possibly Athens (**23**), Erythrai (**25**[?]) and Patara (**21**). There is no positive evidence that Larisa in the Troad (see **1**, *ad* line 3) or Melos (see **22**, *ad* line 9) sent theoroi. Samothrace (**24**) might have been a mistake for Samos.

The geography of these places is consistent with Cole's main conclusions that the best-represented areas in the records of both theoroi and initiates are Macedonia, Thrace, Asia Minor, and the Aegean islands, with "almost total lack of reference to the cities of central Greece," and that the Samothracian clientele seems to have been "limited to a certain defined area."[1] Although more visitors from mainland Greece are now known—**26** mentions theoroi from Larisa and Pherai in Thessaly; **29, 30**, and perhaps **23** record visitors from Athens (or its colonies), while **31** records presumable

1. Cole 1984, p. 43.

initiates from Tegea and Torone—this does not change significantly the ratio of visitors coming from mainland Greece versus those from the best-represented places. This ratio can be explained by the fact that Samothrace certainly was a favorite sanctuary of Macedonian rulers, while cities of central and southern Greece felt a stronger traditional attachment to the Eleusinian Mysteries (this is especially true, of course, for Athens);[2] and that the best-represented cities were either geographically close to Samothrace, or shared religious affinities with it, expressed in the worship of the Samothracian or similar divinities.[3]

INSCRIBING OF THEOROI RECORDS

The records of theoroi were inscribed on wall blocks ca. 0.35 m high that may have come from a building in the city of Samothrace, since no excavated building in the sanctuary matches the hypothetical dimensions reconstructed from the architrave block (**16**), nor does any excavated building in the sanctuary display wall blocks of the same size. The building displayed records of theoroi-proxenoi and of theoroi-initiates dating from the 2nd–1st centuries B.C. (the securely dated inscriptions are from the 2nd century). This implies that the practice of granting *proxenia* to the theoroi was most vital during the 2nd to 1st centuries B.C., but it need not be limited to this period. Earlier theoroi records may have been inscribed on stelai. Records of theoroi were also carved on monument bases, set up usually by the theoroi themselves (except **4**, whose inscription may not be original). At any rate, the fact that the building that displayed the records of theoroi was more likely associated with the city than the sanctuary is consistent with the fact that the visits of the theoroi, through their demonstration of piety, had a primarily political purpose, directed toward the polis of Samothrace; and so they were honored by the city, in decrees (some of which honored their home cities as well) and with grants of *proxenia*. Their status was very different from that of ordinary *mystai*.

FUNCTIONS OF THE THEOROI IN SAMOTHRACE

In modern scholarship the theoroi in Samothrace have traditionally been associated with attendance at a special festival.[4] Two inscriptions provide evidence about festival attendance. The first is an Iasian copy of a Samothracian decree (Appendix I.3, lines 6–9), which recommends that the demos of Iasos and the recently arrived Iasian theoroi receive praise at the Dionysia. The second is a Samothracian decree set up in Kos (Appendix I.2), which states, "and now he [Praximenes] has arrived at the [- - - - -]ia, having been sent as theoros by the Koans" (line 12). It is impossible to restore the festival name in this inscription with certainty. The editor, K. Hallof, suggests the Dionysia or the Mysteria. The Dionysia seem to make better sense, since they fit the space slightly better and are mentioned

2. Ar. *Pax* 277–279 seems to imply that some Athenians were initiates at Samothrace, but very few Athenians appear in the records of initiation; see Chap. 9.

3. See Hemberg 1950, and Cole 1984, chap. 5 and appendix 1, for the geographic distribution of the Samothracian and related cults.

4. E.g., Cole 1984, p. 48.

in line 19 as the event at which Praximenes is to be honored.[5] It is of considerable significance that Praximenes is honored also with a grant of *prohedria* in the ἀγῶνες, but the principal ἀγῶνες in Samothrace will have been the Dionysia. Such a grant would make practically no sense if the theoroi were not expected to attend the Dionysia. The importance of the Dionysia for the theoroi is also signaled by the fact that Dionysiac *technitai* came as theoroi (**10, 11**), most likely because of the special character of the Samothracian Dionysia.

The fact that theoroi were honored and most likely present at the Dionysia can be reconciled with Salviat's views about the Samothracian festival. He emphasizes the importance of theatrical performances, which evidently included dramatization of Samothracian myth.[6] The fact that the poet Dymas was praised for writing a drama about Samothracian myths further points out not only the importance of the Dionysia at Samothrace (Samothracian praise suggests production in Samothrace) but also an interesting connection between dramatic performance and the Samothracian Dionysia and Mysteria. Dramatizations related to Samothracian myth were apparently performed both secretly, during the initiation ceremonies, and publicly, during the Dionysia.[7] This would parallel the situation at Eleusis, where performances enacting Eleusinian myth took place during the Mysteria and sometimes in the theater during the Dionysia.[8] If Praximenes arrived for the Dionysia, as the evidence tends to suggest, it is quite conceivable that the Dionysia constituted the major Samothracian festival that attracted theoroi and other visitors. There is no clear indication that there was a special annual celebration of the Mysteria separate from the various celebrations that, at least in the Roman period, took place repeatedly throughout the sailing season (see Chap. 9).

Moreover, it is on general grounds questionable whether a festival such as the Mysteria, with its promise of personal σωτηρία, had a significant enough public dimension at Samothrace to induce theoroi to come specifically to attend this festival. At Athens there is little evidence that the Mysteria regularly attracted theoroi, in contrast to the Panathenaia and Dionysia.[9] Honors for foreigners at Athens were regularly announced at the latter festivals (not at the Mysteria), just as they were at the Dionysia in Samothrace. Of course theoroi did become initiates in the Samothracian Mysteria, which could have been held close enough to the time of the Dionysia to accommodate the wishes of visitors.

5. Although line 19 is heavily damaged, there is no reason to doubt the restoration Διον]υσ[ίων τῶι ἀγῶνι, since it has numerous contextual parallels all over the Greek world, including other Samothracian documents (Appendix I.**3**, I.**4**, and I.**5**).

6. Salviat, Chapouthier, and Salač 1956, pp. 142–145; cf. Cole 1984, p. 122, n. 410.

7. Chapouthier (1935, pp. 174–175) maintains similar views; cf. Cole 1984,

p. 122, n. 410.

8. See *I.Eleusis* 70 (= *IG* II² 1186), which implies a choral performance in honor of Demeter and Kore at the local Dionysia. Clinton points out that the Dionysia were the main festival of the deme of Eleusis, which had little control over the Athenian festival of the Mysteria and the sanctuary.

9. Apparently *IG* II² 992 (early 2nd century B.C.) is the only document that refers to theoroi who performed

a sacrifice at (presumably) the Greater Mysteria; for the prosopography see Habicht 1994a, pp. 256–260 (*SEG* XL 58), and Günther 1992 (*SEG* XLII 1072). No dedications by theoroi are attested at Eleusis. On foreigners, including ambassadors, attending the Dionysia, see especially Pickard-Cambridge 1988, pp. 58–59; on attendance by theoroi at the Panathenaia, *I.Priene* 45 and Habicht 1994a, p. 260.

The typical activity of the theoroi during their visit is given to us in the Samothracian decree published in Iasos (Appendix I.3, lines 3–4): they performed τὴν θυσίαν καὶ τὴν ἀπαρχὴν καὶ τὴν θεωρίαν τὴν παραγεγενημένην εἰς τὸ ἱερὸν. This was typical of theoroi at festivals in general; cf., for example, the theoroi sent by the cities of Euboia to Chalkis (*IG* XII.9 207, lines 18–20): [ὑπὲρ θεωρῶν· πέμπειν δὲ τ]ὰς πόλεις εἰς τοὺς ἀγῶνας τῶν Διονυσίων καὶ Δημητριείων ἑλομένους θε[ωροὺς κομίζοντας τὸ κατὰ τ]ὸ ψήφισμα καλλιστεῖον, λαμβάνοντας ἀργύριον παρὰ τῆς ἰδίας πόλε[ως δραχμὰς - - - - - - κον]τα καὶ συνπονπεύειν καὶ τᾶλλα πάντα πράττειν κατὰ τὸν Εὐβοϊκὸν νόμο[ν]. The theoroi in Samothrace followed a similar pattern, performing sacrifice (which of course would involve marching in the procession), offering a gift (ἀπαρχὴν), and performing *theoria* at the sanctuary, which, as the evidence tends to suggest, included viewing the Dionysia in the theater at the sanctuary.

On the other hand, the phrases "the first theoroi who arrive from Iasos" (Appendix I.4, line 31) and "the first theoroi who arrive from Priene" (Appendix I.5, lines 9–10) suggest multiple visits, not connected with a particular event; if the theoroi were expected solely or primarily for a particular event, there would be no reason not to mention the event in these references. They imply that it was not clear when the next theoroi from a particular city would arrive, whether to attend a festival or to announce a festival held in their home city or for some other purpose. This means that festival attendance was not the the only function of the theoroi in Samothrace. The evidence does seem to suggest, however, that the Dionysia were a major festival that many theoroi did attend. Of course, many theoroi participated in the Mysteria, though such participation may have been only a secondary purpose of their visit. It should also be noted that an oracle is attested for Samothrace;[10] this too may have been a focus of their piety, paralleled at Delphi, which received many theoroi from Athens.

The majority of the inscriptions suggest that the theoroi were (1) distinguished representatives of their home cities, as the few identified names reveal; (2) participated in sacrifices; (3) made dedications to, and in general, honored, the Great Gods, usually by participating in a great festival such as the Dionysia; and (4), in turn received *proxenia* and other privileges. Many were initiated, as the records of theoroi-initiates show.

10. [Plut.] *Mor.* 229D (= *Apothegmata Laconica,* Lysander 10; *Samothrace* 1 240).

PART II: DOCUMENTS CONCERNING INITIATES IN SAMOTHRACE

CHAPTER 5

RECORDS OF INITIATES

CONTEXT OF THE RECORDS

MYSTERY CULT

The religious context of these Samothracian documents is Greek mystery cult. A brief synopsis of its relevant aspects is given here.[1]

To many modern readers, the term "mystery cult" immediately evokes secrecy. However, in the Classical festival of the Μυστήρια, the notion of secrecy, though significant, was secondary. The central ritual of the Μυστήρια was initiation. The word "initiation," however, is of course derived from the Latin translation of μυστήρια, namely, *initia* (beginnings), but this has had the unfortunate consequence that the word "initiates" is a somewhat imprecise translation of the Greek μύσται, the word for participants in the Μυστήρια who underwent the extraordinary experience (πάθος) of the ritual.[2] The term μύσται is obviously related to μυστήρια, but the ancient word μυστήρια should not be understood in its more modern sense of "secrets" (a sense that is primarily attested in the post-classical period), but rather, as in the case of many ancient Greek festival names, as reflecting a significant element of the ritual performed in the cult. In the case of μυστήρια, the word simply refers to the participants, the μύσται: it is the festival of the μύσται.

The word μύσται is a nominal form from the verb μύω, "to close." The μύσται are "the closed ones."[3] The question then turns on the manner of the "closing": are they closed with respect to their mouths (prohibited from revealing what they experienced), or closed with respect to their eyes (μύω frequently refers to closing the eyes)? Clinton has argued for the latter, pointing out that prohibition against divulging the content of rituals applied to a broad range of cults and was not restricted to *mysteria*; the distinguishing feature of μύσται, therefore, should be more specific. In fact, in some *mysteria* we know that the μύσται were blindfolded, and the custom of providing the initiates with μυσταγωγοί (guides of the μύσται) would be consistent with blindfolding. The practice would have had the effect of increasing the initiates' *pathos*—undergoing a death-like experience—before they could see the extraordinary vision in which the *mysteria* culminated.[4]

1. The best introduction to Greek mystery cults is Burkert 1987. See also Burkert 1993 (on Samothrace), Clinton 1992 and 1993 (on Eleusis), and Clinton 2003 (on Eleusis and Samothrace).

2. Aristotle, fr. 15: τοὺς τελουμένους οὐ μαθεῖν τι δεῖν ἀλλὰ παθεῖν καὶ διατεθῆναι, δηλονότι γενομένους ἐπιτηδείους. On the terminology regarding initiates and initiation, see Dowden 1980, p. 414; Clinton 2003, 2004.

3. Clinton 2003.

4. See Clinton 1992, pp. 86–87; on blindfolds in Mithraic *mysteria*, Merkelbach 1984, pp. 136–137, figs. 29 and 30.

The term *mystai* was given to participants in the Eleusinian, Samothracian, and Andanian Mysteries, as well as Dionysiac mystery rites, but it was apparently not used in all rites that involved some sort of initiation, but only in those specifically called *mysteria* (i.e., those that included the practice of blinding and whose participants were called *mystai*).[5]

In Samothrace, as at Eleusis, the first-time initiates are called *mystai*, "blinded ones," as opposed to the *epoptai*, "viewers," initiates participating in the second stage of the rite. The semantics of *epoptai* thus offers further support for the suggestion that the *mystai* were blindfolded initiates. This gradation, attested first at Eleusis and elsewhere only at Samothrace, apparently originated at Eleusis, where *mystai*, the first-stage initiates, could become *epoptai* at a second participation in the Mysteries after a year's interval.[6] The process of participating as a *mystes* was called μύησις.

The term μύησις, however, also meant a purificatory procedure that was performed prior to initiation, at least in Eleusis and probably also in Samothrace.[7] Presumably the reason for this had to do with the fact that blinding occurred during both the preliminary ceremony and the first stage of the *mysteria;* μύησις was both the process of becoming a μύστης and acting in the *mysteria* as μύστης.[8] For the Eleusinian Mysteria the preliminary *myesis* took place either in the city Eleusinion or at the sanctuary at Eleusis, and was performed by a member of either of the two main priestly clans (Eumolpidai and Kerykes). At Samothrace *myesis* evidently took the form of *thronosis*, whereby a blindfolded person was put in a chair and was the focal point of an ecstatic, terrifying dance by ministers of the cult.[9]

Little is known about the central ritual of the ancient Greek *mysteria*, shrouded as it was in secrecy. Literary, epigraphical, and archaeological evidence tells us that the *mysteria* usually took place at night, and involved a frightening, deathlike experience. The blindfolded initiates at Eleusis, for example, were led in the darkness by a *mystagogos* amidst a cacophony of frightening sounds, until finally the blindfold was removed. They passed from terrifying darkness to immense bright light to experience a vision of the divine, revealed by the hierophant in the Telesterion.[10]

THE SAMOTHRACIAN MYSTERIES

The Samothracian Mysteries also took place at night. Document **29** informs us that at a climax in the rite the initiates saw a sacred light (see **29**, Commentary, and Chap. 9, p. 244). There is good reason to believe that the ceremony celebrated the union of man and woman, expressed in myth by the wedding of Kadmos and Harmonia. It has been traditionally assumed that at Samothrace the first stage of initiation took place in the structure called the Anaktoron, the second in the Hieron. However, James McCredie's discovery in the 1990s of the other half of the building now called the Hall of Choral Dancers revealed that this building, the largest and most central building in the sanctuary, was most likely the Telesterion.[11] Its frieze consisted of the depiction of around 800 dancing women, probably representing a wedding dance.

5. Clinton 2003, p. 50.
6. Clinton 2003, p. 50.
7. Clinton 2003.
8. Clinton 2003, pp. 50–65.
9. Clinton 2003, pp. 61–65.
10. Plut. fr. 178 (= Stobaeus 4.52.49); Clinton 1992, pp. 84–90 with bibliography; Burkert 1987, pp. 91–93, 113–114.
11. Lehmann 1998, pp. 35, 73–78; Clinton 2003, p. 61.

RECORDS OF INITIATES

With regard to the recording of the names of *mystai* on stone, Samothrace is extraordinary. Although *mystai* are mentioned in inscriptions throughout the Greek world, including decrees, sacred laws, dedications, and epitaphs,[12] only in Samothrace do records of initiation appear in such abundance, the vast majority of them set up by the initiates themselves. This practice must have been encouraged by the polis of Samothrace.

Several lists of *mystai eusebeis* are found in Imbros (*IG* XII.8 87, 88, 89, undated; and possibly 85, 4th–3rd century B.C.). It is conceivable that there were many more records, since the Kabirion at Imbros has not been excavated. We do not know whether the Samothracians adopted the practice of recording *mystai eusebeis* from Imbros or vice versa, but the cult of the Kabiri on Imbros never achieved the international reputation of the Samothracian cult.

RECORDS OF INITIATION

Initiation into the mysteries of the Great Gods in Samothrace was sought throughout antiquity, especially during the Hellenistic and Roman periods, when the sanctuary was at the height of its popularity. Yet our attempts to reconstruct the Samothracian Mysteries are impeded by numerous unanswered questions, many of which are quite fundamental. We do not know for certain who the Great Gods were or what function several of the sanctuary buildings served. The origin of the cult is obscure, and the pre-Greek history of Samothrace is only gradually being clarified by excavations.[13] Literary sources are abundant, but often frustratingly confusing. How helpful, then, is the documentary evidence in elucidating the Samothracian cult?

The 143 documents included here in Part II are inscriptions on stone pertaining to initiation. Most of them are records of initiation, and so have considerable prosopographical value in providing information about the people who visited the island to be initiated. The 32 unpublished documents included here add about 100 new names of certain or presumable initiates, while emendations of the republished records modify many previously known names. In addition, the documents in Part II furnish important information about the initiates' places of origin, cultic experience, social status, the dates of initiation records, the stages of initiation, and the existence of an annual festival (see Chap. 9).

Whereas most records of initiation were inscribed on stelai, some appear on bases (**35, 41, 45, 55, 131**), and several on blocks of unclear origin (**33, 53, 60, 68, 95, 97, 128, 138, 148, 157**). What is clear, however, is that "stones were used and re-used often many times," with names "added at the top, in the middle, or at the end of other lists."[14] Some "parasitic" lists were even inscribed on monuments that were originally not meant to record initiates (**39, 41, 45, 55, 76, 131**).

Recording of the initiates' names must have contributed to the prestige of the sanctuary by displaying the diversity and multitude of its worshippers, and this in turn fostered its prosperity. We have 138 certain or probable

12. Decrees: e.g., *IG* X.2 259. Sacred laws: e.g., *LSAM* 84; *LSS* 15, 65. Dedications: e.g., *ISM* II 143; *IG* XII Suppl. 397, 1125; *IG* XII.8 643; *I.Prusa* 48. Epitaphs: e.g., *IG* II² 3639, 3811; *IG* XI.1 313; *IGUR* III 1169.

13. See the account by D. Matsas of the excavations of the 19th Ephoreia of Prehistoric and Classical Antiquities (Komotini) in Lehmann 1998, pp. 165–179, with bibliography, pp. 183–184. On Greek colonization, see Graham 2001.

14. Cole 1984, p. 41.

records of initiation, not including the records of theoroi-initiates presented in Part I, and we must bear in mind that this is but a tiny fraction of their original number. The several limekilns found within the sanctuary are undoubtedly responsible for the destruction of an enormous amount of material, and may explain why we know next to nothing about, for example, sacred personnel. The preserved records of initiation form more than half of the known Samothracian inscriptions (ca. 250, including insignificant fragments), but we should probably imagine that the records of initiation numbered several thousand in antiquity.

Locations of the Records of Initiation

The presumably large number of records naturally raises the question of where they were displayed. If the initiates intended them to advertise their piety, and the Samothracians encouraged this publicity for the benefit of the sanctuary, it is logical to suppose that the records stood in the vicinity of the sanctuary, so that they would make a lasting impression upon all visitors, especially those who were not yet initiated (i.e., those who were not yet allowed to enter the sanctuary, but whom the Samothracians wished to encourage to become initiated). Unfortunately, the vast majority of our inscriptions are scattered throughout the island, far from their original locations, the process of dispersal having begun at least as early as late antiquity and continuing at least through the 19th century.

The excavations revealed many fragments in and near the sanctuary, though, unfortunately, none were found in situ. The findspots suggest several possible areas as original locations. The area around the Stoa on the Western Hill, where many certain and presumable records on initiation were found (**46, 61, 69, 74, 86, 88, 96, 104, 109, 115, 116, 125, 126, 136, 140, 146, 147, 151, 158, 166**), must have been a very suitable place for setting up stelai with names of initiates. Within the Stoa, fragments of stucco covering an early phase of the interior wall show a very interesting feature: "a system of wall decoration which imitated masonry with drafted margins, and other fragments preserve portions of mouldings. The most unusual feature of this wall stucco is the fact that many of the fragments are inscribed."[15] The many inscriptions on this wall clearly were created at different times. One fragment preserves the letters ΒΑΣΙΛΕ at the top of a raised panel, which suggests the beginning of a document with a date according to the eponymous *basileus*, ΒΑΣΙΛΕ[ΥΟΝΤΟΣ or ΕΠΙ] ΒΑΣΙΛΕ[ΩΣ. Another small fragment contains the letters ΟΠΤ at the top of a raised panel that most likely are part of the word ΕΠ]ΟΠΤ[ΑΙ.[16] This surely is to be interpreted as the heading of a list of *epoptai* (mere mention of *epoptai* in a decree is possible but less likely). The interior wall of the Stoa, built in the first half of the 3rd century, may well have served early on as a surface for inscribing lists of *mystai* and *epoptai*. The area surrounding the Stoa also served to display stone documents containing these lists, most probably from at least the beginning of the 2nd century B.C., starting perhaps only after the wall of the Stoa was no longer used for this purpose (the beginning of the 2nd century is the probable date of **64**, the earliest dated list, not found in situ). All this bears upon the issue of whether the Western Hill

15. McCredie 1965, pp. 108–110.
16. McCredie 1965, p. 109, with pl. 31:c. The photograph shows the upper left part of the horizontal stroke of tau and the lower tip of its vertical stroke.

formed part of the sanctuary proper. Given its natural separation from the central buildings by a stream, as well as its somewhat public nature (stoa, monuments, dining rooms, etc.), it has the characteristics of an area suited to host visitors to the sanctuary even prior to their initiation.

The Eastern Hill, especially the space above the southern perimeter of the theatral area (Fig. 3:25), might also have been a good place for displaying records of initiates. Inscription **123**, a small fragment, was found there, but since a fragment of the frieze of dancing maidens from the Hall of Choral Dancers was found nearby,[17] **123** may likewise have traveled quite a distance from its original location. Numerous marble bases are also preserved in this area.[18] Some originally held a stele with a decree next to the statue, while others might have held stelai with lists of initiates, but no stele with such lists has been found. A fragment of **63** was found built into a retaining wall along the Sacred Way (between the theatral area and the center of the sanctuary), and its other fragments were excavated nearby in the Sacred Way; but all are light enough to have been carried from a distance. Thus convincing evidence is lacking for the display of initiation records around the theatral area or along the Sacred Way.

Inscription **55** was found alongside the path from the Propylon of Ptolemy II to the ancient city—probably not far from its original location, given its enormous size. It was originally created as a statue base for a gymnasiarch, and may have served that function throughout antiquity. But on at least two of its other sides, at dates later than the original inscription, lists of initiates were inscribed. These are examples of the parasitic lists mentioned above, which were placed on monuments that were not originally designed to hold records of initiates.

Inscription **39**, a very substantial block not built into a later structure, was found well within the the ancient city, at a considerable height above sea level. The initiate lists on it are probably parasitic. Given the large size of the block, it probably has not traveled far from its original location, and therefore demonstrates that monuments in the ancient city received inscriptions of initiation records. We have a parallel monument in **76**, a substantial statue base that carries a dedication by the demos of Samothrace in honor of Pythokles, son of Apollophanes, and has on its right side a parasitic list of initiates. It was found in the ancient city; Fraser assumed that it was moved there from the sanctuary, but it is far more probable that, like **39**, it was originally set up in the ancient city and remained there, providing at a later date a suitable surface for a list of initiates. When systematic excavations of the ancient city are undertaken, we can probably expect many more such monuments to come to light.

Some inscriptions have been found in or near the following buildings in the sanctuary (see Fig. 3): the Sacristy (**34, 48, 101, 154**), the Anaktoron (**42, 155, 169**), the Rotunda of Arsinoe (**40, 100, 137, 141, 162**), and the Hieron (**81, 165, 168**). Of the inscriptions found in the Sacristy, **48** was found in the Late Roman floor in secondary use; **34** (of A.D. 113), according to Lehmann, was built into the interior wall of the building (or intended for that purpose), presumably in the early-4th-century repair;[19] and **101** and **154**, relatively small fragments, were found nearby. Thus no clear case can be made for original display within this structure, and in any case such

17. Diary 1965, p. 266.

18. Publication of the Eastern Hill is currently being prepared by Bonna Wescoat.

19. For the date of the building and the repair, see Lehmann 1998, p. 61.

a display would not be consistent with the public purpose of these records. The few fragments of records found near the Anaktoron, the Rotunda of Arsinoe, and the Hieron are small and easily movable, and therefore insufficient to support an argument for original location in these areas.[20]

Thus the locations attested with most probability for the display of initiation records are the area in and around the Stoa on the Western Hill, the road from the ancient city to the sanctuary, and the ancient city itself. The shared characteristic of these areas is apparently the fact that they were located outside the sanctuary, that is, outside the specific sacred area that was prohibited by **168** and **169** to those who had not undergone *myesis*.

EDITORIAL ARRANGEMENT OF RECORDS CONCERNING INITITATION

In Chapter 6 (**29–116**), the documents concerning initiates are arranged geographically, according to the ethnic of the initiates. If a document lists two or more ethnics, it is included only once, with a cross-reference under the other place(s) mentioned. Under "Roman initiates" are listed initiates with Roman names whose city of origin is unspecified or who are from Rome itself. Records of initiates whose ethnic is unknown are grouped together in Chapter 7 (**117–167**). Presumable records of initiation are indicated with a question mark after the word "initiate(s)." By "presumable records" I mean documents that do not preserve categories such as *mystai, epoptai*, slaves, freedmen, or sailors. It must be noted that the degree of probability within the presumable records varies: if we are dealing with blocks or stelai with non-Greek (mostly Roman or Thracian) names, then it is highly likely that these are lists of initiates; this is also true if we have a Roman date or a list of Greek names; but if only the Greek date is preserved, then there is considerable uncertainty.

Chapter 8 contains other documents concerning initiation at Samothrace: two prohibition inscriptions forbidding entry to the *amyetoi* (**168** and **169**); a Samothracian decree in honor of Hippomedon, a benefactor of the sanctuary who was eager to take part in the Mysteries (**170**); and a Samothracian copy of a decree of Odessos in Thrace, which refers to Odessitan participation in the Samothracian cult (**171**).

Appendix II comprises inscriptions from other sites relevant to initiation at Samothrace: **1** concerns initiates and Samothrakiasts from Rhodes, and **2** and **3** mention initiates from Greek colonies on the Black Sea, Tomis and Dionysopolis, respectively.

20. Inscriptions **168** and **169** are not records but prohibition documents; neither was found in situ. On the location of **169**, see Clinton 2003, p. 61 with n. 43.

INSCRIPTIONS CONCERNING INITIATES WHOSE ETHNIC IS KNOWN

The inscriptions below attest initiates into the Samothracian Mysteries from the following areas: Attica, the Peloponnese, Thessaly, Illyria, Macedonia, Thrace, the Aegean islands, Asia Minor, Rome, and Egypt.

ATTICA

29 Epitaph for a Samothracian initiate   Fig. 26

Two joining fragments of a pedimental stele of white (now grayish) marble, preserved on all sides except below, rough-picked on back. The letters bear traces of red paint. At ca. 0.05 m below the text are visible three small round holes, which must have held an elongated metal ornament, perhaps a branch, staff, or torch. Provenance unknown, possibly Amphipolis. The stele appeared in the Museum of Kavala during the German-Bulgarian occupation in World War II (1941–1944). Archaeological Museum of Kavala, inv. Λ 70 (old 465).

H. 0.925 m, W. 0.31 m, Th. 0.125 m (pediment), 0.10 m (field); L.H. 0.015–0.017 m (lines 1–3), 0.007–0.01 m (lines 4–22).

Ed. Karadima and Dimitrova 2003.

Cf. Lazarides 1969, pp. 87–88; Cole 1984, p. 113, n. 206 (mentioned); [*BullÉp* 1984 313].

2nd–1st century B.C.?

> Ἰσίδωρε
> Νικοστράτου
> Ἀθηναῖε χαῖρε
>
> ἀστὸν Ἀθηναίων ψαφαρὰ κόνις
> 5   ἅδε κέκευθεν ^v πολλάκις ὃς
> θυμέλας ἤροσε βακχεακὰς
> μιμικὸν ἐκφράζων ἱ<λ>αρὸν λό-
> γον ἐντρίτῳ ἤθ<ε>ι—^v τέρπων
> ταῖς φυσικαῖς μουσορύτοις
> 10 χάρισ{.}ι· ^v ἦν δὲ φίλοις ἐρατός, δί-
> καιος, πρὸς πάντας ἀληθής,
> εὐσεβὲς ἐν ψυχῇ κῦδος ἔχ[ων]

ἀρετῆς· ᵛ μύστης μὲν Σαμόθραξι ᵛ Καβίρου διχ᾽ ἱερὸν φῶς,
15 ἁγνὰ δ᾽ Ἐλευσῖνος Δηοῦς μεγάθυ-
[μο]ς ἴδεν· ᵛ οὕνεκεν εὐγήρως
[ὀκ]τὼ δεκάδας λυκαβάντων
[ἤ]νυσ᾽ ἀπημάντως Ἰσιόδωρος
[ἄ]νηι· ᵛ ἀλλ᾽ Ἀΐδα σκοτιοῦχε, βα-
20 [ρ]υσθενὲς ἕρκος ἀνάγκης,
[χῶρ]ον ἐς εὐσεβέων τόνδ᾽ ἀ-
[γ]αγὼν κάθισον.
vacat

Karadima and Dimitrova. **8** *vel* ἐν τρίτῳ. **19,** *fin.*–**20** Burkert (pers. comm.),
σκοτίου χέ<ρ>, ἀ[γ]ασθενὲς Karadima and Dimitrova.

Verse arrangement:
ἀστὸν Ἀθηναίων ψαφαρὰ κόνις ἅδε κέκευθεν ᵛ
    πολλάκις ὃς θυμέλας ἤροσε βακχεακὰς
μιμικὸν ἐκφράζων ἱ<λ>αρὸν λόγον ἐντρίτῳ ἤθ<ε>ι— ᵛ
    τέρπων ταῖς φυσικαῖς μουσορύτοις χάρισ{.}ι ᵛ
ἦν δὲ φίλοις ἐρατός, δίκαιος, πρὸς πάντας ἀληθής
    εὐσεβὲς ἐν ψυχῇ κῦδος ἔχ[ων] ἀρετῆς· ᵛ
μύστης μὲν Σαμόθραξι ᵛ Καβίρου δὶχ᾽ ἱερὸν φῶς,
    ἁγνὰ δ᾽ Ἐλευσῖνος Δηοῦς μεγάθυ[μο]ς ἴδεν· ᵛ
οὕνεκεν εὐγήρως [ὀκ]τὼ δεκάδας λυκαβάντων
    [ἤ]νυσ᾽ ἀπημάντως Ἰσιόδωρος [ἄ]νηι· ᵛ
ἀλλ᾽ Ἀΐδα σκοτιοῦχε, βα[ρ]υσθενὲς ἕρκος ἀνάγκης,
    [χῶρ]ον ἐς εὐσεβέων τόνδ᾽ ἀ[γ]αγὼν κάθισον.

Translation:
Isidoros | Nikostratou | of Athens, farewell.| This light earth has
covered |5 an Athenian citizen, who frequently | tilled at the Bac-
chic altars,| recounting merry speech as a mime | in the third part, |
delighting with his natural, Muse-flowing |10 graces. He was loved
by his friends, | a just man, truthful to all, | with reverent renown |
for the virtue in his soul. | As an initiate, great-hearted, | he saw the
doubly sacred light | of Kabiros in Samothrace,[1] |15 and the pure
rites of Demeter in Eleusis.[2] | Because of this, bearing his old age
well, | Isidoros completed eighty years | without pain and trouble.
But you, gloomy Hades, |20 extremely powerful bastion of necessity,
| lead this man to the Region of the Reverent | and place him there.

Epigraphical Commentary
The letters are inelegant and hard to read.
    Line 7: The second letter of ἱ<λ>αρὸν looks more like a delta.
    Line 8: ΕΝΤΡΙΤΩΗΘΙ *lapis*. The last letter looks like a combination of
epsilon and iota. Presumably the stonecutter omitted the epsilon and carved
iota first, then tried to correct it. At the place where the final iota of ἤθ<ε>ι
should have been, i.e., the space between ἤθ<ε>ι and τέρπων, there is now
only an upper horizontal. It is conceivable that the stonecutter exchanged
the places of the iota and the epsilon, and then just painted the correct
sequence. Another possibility would be to interpret the upper horizontal

1. Literally, "among the Samothracians," with poetic omission of the
preposition ἐν.
2. Literally, "the pure rites of Demeter of Eleusis."

Figure 26. Epitaph for a Samothracian initiate (29). Courtesy C. Karadima-Matsa

as an interpunct, denoting the verse end, but this is not very likely, since the other verse ends are marked only with a vacant space.

Line 10: χάρισ{.}ι: The dot represents what looks like a crossed-out sigma. The stonecutter must have started to carve a second sigma, and then changed his mind.

Line 14: The circle of the theta can be made out; the beta of Καβίρου is poorly cut: it looks like a delta, but narrower.

Line 18: First preserved letter: left vertical.

Line 20: The first letter is upsilon, whose right diagonal and middle vertical are visible; there are scratches to the right of it, which create the appearance of an alpha, as was incorrectly assumed in the *editio princeps.*

Commentary

Although this document is not from Samothrace, it is included here, and not in Appendix II, due to its extraordinary importance. The commentary is largely reprinted from the *editio princeps,* with some additions and corrections. The inscription is an epitaph for the Athenian citizen Ἰσίδωρος Νικοστράτου, a man of admirable qualities and a curious fate, described below. The letters, and especially the broken-bar alpha, are consistent with a date in the Late Hellenistic period. The 2nd century B.C. is the suggested terminus post quem, since the theophoric name Isidoros is apparently unattested in Attica before the 2nd century B.C.[3]

Lines 4–22 represent a poem, written in elegiac distich.

Lines 6, 9, 18: βακχεακὰς instead of βακχειακάς, μουσορύτοις instead of μουσορρύτοις, and the form Ἰσιόδωρος must be *metri causa*. Isiodoros occurs rarely; it is attested in *IMT* 1011; *I.Mylasa* 632–635, 803, etc., as the name of a Mylasean priest of Isis.

Lines 6–8: μιμικόν indicates that Isidoros must have been a mime, which is consistent with the idea that he brought joy to his audience. This is emphasized in lines 7–8 by ἱ<λ>αρὸν λό|γον and τέρπων, and brings to mind Quintilian's discussion (6.2.13) of the good speaker's ethos: *non solum mite ac placidum, sed plerumque blandum et humanum, audientibus amabile atque iucundum.*

θυμέλας ἤροσε βακχεακάς: The "Bacchic altars" are to be understood as a metonymy for "orchestra." Θυμέλη was the altar of Dionysos, which stood in the orchestra, and the orchestra was the place where mimes usually performed; cf. Suda, s.v. σκηνή.

A helpful parallel for the use of the word θυμέλη in an epitaph for a mime is provided by an inscription from Aquileia, *IG* XIV 2342 (= *GVI* 567, ca. 220 B.C.), commemorating the glorious mime Basille, who was called by the author of the poem "the tenth Muse":

Τὴν πολλοῖς δήμοισι πάρος πολλαῖς τε πόλεσσι
δόξαν φωνάεσσαν ἐνὶ σκηναῖσι λαβούσῃ
παντοίης ἀρετῆς ἐν μίμοις, εἶτα χοροῖσι
πολλάκις ἐν θυμέλαις, ἀλλ᾽ οὐχ οὕτω δὲ θανούσῃ
5   τῇ δεκάτῃ Μούσῃ τὸ λαλεῖν σοφὸς Ἡρακλείδης
μιμάδι Βασσίλλῃ στήλην θέτο βιολόγος φώς·
ἢ δὴ καὶ νέκυς οὖσα ἴσην βίου ἔλλαχε τιμήν,
μουσικὸν εἰς δάπεδον σῶμ᾽ ἀναπαυσαμένη . . .

It is noteworthy that in both poems the word πολλάκις is associated with θυμέλαι. This helps to explain the somewhat unusual metaphor "plowed the Bacchic altars" in line 6 as most likely meaning "tilled at the Bacchic altars," in the sense of performing repeatedly in the orchestra.

Isidoros might be the same as the mime mentioned in Cicero, *In Verrem* 2.3.34.78, 2.5.12.31, 2.5.31.81, as John Jory pointed out to me.[4] Our Isidoros, in any case, was well traveled, and the location of his epitaph in northern Greece presumably indicates the place where he settled in old age.

A possible explanation of the crux ἐντρίτῳ / ἐν τρίτῳ ἤθ<ε>ι ("in a threefold/third character") was recently suggested by Jory, who drew my attention to the fact that the parts played by mimes were sometimes designated by numerical notations; cf. Latin *tertiarum, secundarum,* and *quartarum.*[5] The phrase can be translated as "in the third part," thus

3. Parker (2000, p. 74) confirms Dow's conclusions (1937) that the cult of Isis was established in the 2nd century B.C., and adds that the two firmly datable names derived from Isis (a Thasian Isigonos, attested in 350 B.C., and a Rhamnousian Isigenes, attested in 325 B.C.) are questionable since they "are known from defective transcripts of stones now lost."

4. Pers. comm.

5. *CIL* VI 10103, VI 10118, X 814, XIV 4198; Val. Max. 9.14.4; Cic. *Div. Caec.* 48. For ranks in the mimes' hierarchy, see Jory 1963, esp. p. 75; Beacham 1992, p. 132, with nn. 52, 53. I am very grateful to John Jory for this information.

referring to a grade in the mimes' hierarchy. Horace, for instance, compares the subservient man to the mime playing the "second part" (*Epistulae* 1.18.10–14). A problem with this interpretation, as noted by Nicolay Sharankov,[6] is that it would be unusual to mention in an inscription containing mostly praise for Isidoros that he was a "third-part" actor. Yet a Latin inscription (*CIL* X 814) mentions the dedication of a statue in honor of the archimime Sorix, who is called *secundarum,* that is, "of the second part,"[7] without any unflattering connotations.

Another interpretation would be to translate ἐντρίτῳ / ἐν τρίτῳ ἤθ<ε>ι as "in a threefold way"; that is, Isidoros was able to play several characters within one performance, which was an alleged quality of mimes, as we see, for instance, in Cicero ("He jumped for joy like a character in a mime, starving one moment, then suddenly rich," *Phil.* 2.65)[8] and Choricius of Gaza ("Who would not give up an attempt to enumerate all [mimes] imitate? Master, servants, merchants, sausage sellers, bakers, restaurateur, banqueters, contract makers, stammering child, youth in love, another one angry, another quieting the other's anger," *Apology for Mimes* 110). Accordingly, the phrase "in a third character" might indicate a canon of parts or characters that the mimes performed, as Mr. Sharankov suggested to me.[9]

The fact that Isidoros was an actor bears upon the importance of theatrical performance in Samothracian cult; see Chapter 4. We do not know whether he performed at Samothrace, but his visit to the island is paralleled by the visits of musicians and Dionysiac artists (**10, 11, 35, 121**).

Line 12: εὐσεβές: Religious terminology is abundant in the poem. εὐσεβές and εὐσεβέων in line 21 immediately bring to mind the typical phrase applied to Samothracian initiates, μύσται εὐσεβεῖς. The adjective ἁγνὸς (line 15) belongs to the cultic vocabulary of the Eleusinan Mysteries, and is a frequent epithet of Demeter and Kore. Its substantivized use, however, is very rare: apparently the only parallel is *I.Ephesos* 27C, lines 383–384 (καὶ τὰ ἁγ]νὰ κ[αὶ] τὰ κοινὰ τ[ῆς μεγίστης] καὶ | ἐπισ[ημοτάτης ὑμῶν πόλεως).

Lines 13–14: Among the most important features of this text are the use of the word Κάβιρος at Samothrace and the information that viewing sacred light was central to the initiate's experience there.

The only appellations that otherwise occur in inscriptions for the gods of the Samothracian Mysteries are Θεοὶ Μεγάλοι, Θεοὶ Σαμόθρᾳκες, or simply Θεοί.[10] The name Kabiri appears in literary sources[11] and in inscriptions recording related cults in other places (notably Delos[12]), but never in inscriptions referring to the cult in Samothrace. A possible explanation for this is to assume that the title Kabiri was applied informally (hence its use in literature or in the present epigram), and that the appellation "Great Gods" was established by the Samothracians as the official title.

6. Pers. comm.

7. I owe this reference to Karin Schlapbach.

8. Csapo and Slater 1995, pp. 376–377.

9. Pers. comm.

10. See Cole 1984, pp. 1–2.

11. E.g., Hdt. 2.51; Stesimbrotos, *FGrH* 107 F10 = Strabo 10.3.19–20; Dion. Hal. *Ant. Rom.* 1.23.5; Euseb. *Praep. evang.* 1.10 (on the last, see *Samothrace* 1 140, 163, 168). Burkert

(2002, p. 45) points out that since Stesimbrotos wrote a book on the mysteries, and since he was from the neighboring island of Thasos, he probably knew well who the Samothracian gods were.

12. Cf. Bruneau 1970, pp. 390–399.

In Καβίρου δὶχ᾽ ἱερὸν φῶς, "the doubly sacred light of Kabiros," the adverb δίχ(α) must modify ἱερὸν. One way to understand Καβίρου is to assume that a single god Kabiros was worshipped at Samothrace, as, for example, in Thebes,[13] Pergamon,[14] and Thessaloniki.[15] The problem with this interpretation, however, is that no source known to us mentions a single Kabiros in Samothrace.[16] Moreover, in Pergamon, for instance, we have solid evidence for worship of the Kabiri in the plural, in addition to the mention of Kabiros in the singular.[17] Even in the Theban cult, the most notable example of a single Kabiros, the plural form is sometimes used.[18] The Samothracian Kabiri are always referred to in the plural. According to some authors (e.g., Nonnos, *Dion.* 14.17–22; 29.193–196),[19] they were two; according to Mnaseas (Scholia Parisina to Ap. Rhod. *Argon.* 1.917),[20] two, three, or four; according to Strabo (10.3.20), three.[21] Presumably this discrepancy implies that sometimes the title was used to refer only to a couple of central male divinities, and sometimes to the whole group of deities worshipped in the Samothracian Mysteries. Thus it has been inferred that there were two central Kabiri, frequently equated with the Dioscouri.[22] The lack of precision in using the name Kabiri may have been an additional reason for the adoption of the title Theoi Megaloi, which must have included the entire group of divinities.

Therefore it seems right to interpret "the doubly sacred light of Kabiros" as a poetic way of saying "the sacred light of the two Kabiri." I understand δίχα, "doubly," not in the sense of "twice," but in the sense of "in two parts," the basic meaning of the word. It is unclear how literally one should interpret this phrase, but it is conceivable that the initiates saw illuminated twinlike statues of the Kabiri, possibly the two statues that were set up in the Anaktoron, according to ancient testimony (Hippol. *Haer.* 5.8–9).[23] It has long been known that light played a significant role in the Samothracian cult, as is clear, for instance, from the remains of monumental marble torches;[24] from the depiction of torches on stelai with records of initiates;[25] and from the evidence of Nonnos, who describes sailors rejoicing at seeing the sleepless flame of the Samothracian torch (*Dion.* 3.43–44),[26] the nocturnal festive torch of Samothrace (*Dion.* 4.185),[27] or statues holding blazing torches before banqueters (*Dion.* 3.169–171[28]).[29] In the epitaph for Isidoros we learn for the first time that viewing "sacred light" constituted a central act of the initiates' experience, as in the Eleusinian Mysteries.

13. Hemberg 1950, pp. 184–186.

14. Hemberg 1950, pp. 176–178.

15. Hemberg 1950, pp. 205–210.

16. The only possible indication of a Kabiros on Samothrace is an early coin, whose image Schwabacher (1952) has interpreted as that of Kabiros.

17. Hemberg 1950, pp. 172–175.

18. Paus. 4.1.7, 9.25.5–10; cf. Hemberg 1950, pp. 184, 204.

19. *Samothrace* 1 167.

20. *Samothrace* 1 150a.

21. *Samothrace* 1 163.

22. See, most recently, Clinton 2003, p. 69.

23. *Samothrace* 1 148. Cf. the discussion in Clinton 2004; see also Clinton 2003, p. 75.

24. *Samothrace* 3, pp. 135–138; cf. Parisinou 2000, pp. 200–201, nn. 114, 115.

25. *IG* XII.8 188, 189, 190.

26. Cf. *Samothrace* 1 73.

27. Cf. *Samothrace* 1 151.

28. Cf. Cole 1984, pp. 36–37; *Samothrace* 1 67.

29. Cf. also Cole 1989, p. 1576, with n. 45.

Line 21: [χῶρ]ον ἐς εὐσεβέων: The restoration is fairly certain, since the expression is typical of epitaphs in which the deceased either abides in the χῶρος εὐσεβέων or a wish is expressed that he/she may be sent there.[30] The Region of the Reverent has long been identified with Elysium and the Isles of the Blessed, where heroes and even gods dwell.[31] The χῶρος εὐσεβέων is in the underworld;[32] thus, for example, *IG* XII.5 304 (Roman period) and XII.3 1190 (undated) suggest that the χῶρος εὐσεβέων is located in the house of Persephone. *IG* XII.5 310 (2nd century A.D.) also associates the place with Persephone: Ἀλλὰ σὺ παμβασίλεια θεά, πολυώνυμε Κούρα,| τήνδ᾽ ἄγ᾽ ἐπ᾽ εὐσεβέων χῶρον, ἔχουσα χερός.

Pseudo-Plato's account, [*Ax.*] 371c–d (Late Hellenistic period), is especially illuminating. Discussing Plouton's kingdom, Socrates describes an idyllic place reserved for those whose lives were inspired by a good *daimon*:

> ὅσοις μὲν οὖν ἐν τῷ ζῆν δαίμων ἀγαθὸς ἐπέπνευσεν, εἰς τὸν τῶν εὐσεβῶν χῶρον οἰκίζονται, ἔνθα ἄφθονοι μὲν ὧραι παγκάρπου γονῆς βρύουσιν, πηγαὶ δὲ ὑδάτων καθαρῶν ῥέουσιν, παντοῖοι δὲ λειμῶνες ἄνθεσι ποικίλοις ἐαριζόμενοι, διατριβαὶ δὲ φιλοσόφων καὶ θέατρα ποιητῶν καὶ κύκλιοι χοροὶ καὶ μουσικὰ ἀκούσματα, συμπόσιά τε εὐμελῆ καὶ εἰλαπίναι αὐτοχορήγητοι, καὶ ἀκήρατος ἀλυπία καὶ ἡδεῖα δίαιτα· οὔτε γὰρ χεῖμα σφοδρὸν οὔτε θάλπος ἐγγίγνεται, ἀλλ᾽ εὔκρατος ἀὴρ χεῖται ἀπαλαῖς ἡλίου ἀκτῖσιν ἀνακιρνάμενος. ἐνταῦθα τοῖς μεμυημένοις ἐστίν τις προεδρία·

The last sentence is important in pointing up the connection between initiation and blissful afterlife. Since initiates had a privileged position in the χῶρος εὐσεβέων, they must have been inspired by a good *daimon*, that is, their lives must have been marked by good deeds and pursuits.[33] This is consistent with Diodorus's statement that initiation in the Samothracian Mysteries made people morally better, εὐσεβεστέρους καὶ δικαιοτέρους.[34] It is difficult not to connect Diodorus's εὐσεβεστέρους with χῶρος εὐσεβέων and μύσται εὐσεβεῖς. Initiates were perceived as more reverent than non-initiates, and therefore worthy of a *prohedria* in the Region of the Reverent.

It is well known that initiates in the Eleusinian and certain other Mysteries deserved a better place in the afterlife.[35] Early on, initiates at Eleusis

30. Cf. Gow and Page 1965, 1199–1202; *ISE* 115; *SEG* XIII 206 (= *IG* II² 13088); *Corinth* VIII.1 130; *SEG* XXXIV 325; *IG* XI.2 313.a; *EAM* 193; *EKM* I 404; *IG* XII.7 115; *IG* XII.8 38; *IG* XII.5 304, 310; *TAM* 470; *IG* XII.3 1190, etc. On εὐσεβής as an epithet of the deceased, cf. Erhardt 1999, p. 274, with n. 9.

31. On the χῶρος εὐσεβέων, see the detailed discussion by Graf (1974, pp. 79–94); cf. *Etym. Magn.*, s.v. Ἠλύσιον, where the χῶρος εὐσεβέων is equated with Ἠλύσιον and the νῆσοι

μακάρων. See also Nilsson II², pp. 231–242.

32. See Graf 1974; [Plut.] *Cons. ad Apoll.* 120 B also places the χῶρος εὐσεβέων in Hades: Λέγεται δ᾽ ὑπὸ μὲν τοῦ μελικοῦ Πινδάρου | ταυτὶ περὶ τῶν εὐσεβῶν ἐν Ἅιδου· | τοῖσι λάμπει μὲν σθένος ἀελίου τὰν ἐνθάδε νύκτα κάτω . . . (Pind. fr. 129).

33. Cf. Nilsson II², pp. 241–242. On *agathos daimon* here in the sense of good spirit—and not, for instance, in the sense of good fortune or a tutelary deity (a good genius) that accompanied

a person's life—see Hershbell 1981, p. 67, n. 68. The context of the dialogue makes it clear that those inspired by a good *daimon* are morally better people, since they are further contrasted with the evildoers, who were led to the χῶρος ἀσεβέων ([*Ax.*] 371e).

34. Diod. Sic. 5.49.6. With regard to this passage, Rohde (1987, p. 235, n. 34) comments that the *mystai* did not appear to have any moral obligation, but were made better "without effort on their part by a pure act of grace."

35. Cf. Burkert 1987, pp. 21–29.

are distinguished as receiving a good lot, while non-initiates receive a bad lot.[36] When belief in the χῶρος εὐσεβέων was well developed, this was felt to be their proper place, but their special status, at least according to the *Axiochus,* now demanded *prohedria* as well.

The relation between mystery cult and χῶρος εὐσεβέων is nicely illustrated in an epigram of Posidippos that parallels both the *Axiochus* passage and our document:[37]

14 ἦλθεν ἐπ᾽ εὐσεβέων Νικοστράτη ἱερὰ μυστῶν
15   ὄργια καὶ καθαρὸν πῦρ ἔπι Τριπτολέ[μου
16 ἦν ἂψ ἡ φ. . [. . . . .] . . . Ῥαδαμάνθυος [
17   Αἰακὸς ε[. . . . . .] . δῶμα πύλας τ᾽{ε} [Ἀΐδεω
18 τέκνων [πλῆθος] ἰδοῦσαν· ἀεὶ δ᾽ ἀπα[λώτερο]ς οὕτω
19 _ ἀνθρώπ[οις λυγρ]οῦ γήραος ἐστι λιμή[ν.

It is likely that the reason the Samothracian initiates are referred to as μύσται εὐσεβεῖς has to do precisely with the χῶρος εὐσεβέων; the present epigram is the only documentary piece of evidence to support this supposition, since Isidoros was a Samothracian initiate. οὕνεκεν in line 16 implies a causal connection between the previous and following thoughts, and may be interpreted as an indication that initiation was believed to make a person more prosperous in life and more hopeful about death—an alleged benefit to those initiated into the Eleusinian Mysteries.[38] Up to this point there has been no certain evidence that the Mysteries of the Great Gods at Samothrace assured a happy life and afterlife;[39] the current epigram is the first document to tell us that both the Eleusinian and the Samothracian Mysteries provided this benefit.

30   Record of initiates from the Athenian cleruchy on Imbros   Fig. 27

Stele of Thasian marble, broken above and below, with molding, rough-picked on back. The inscription was found in secondary context and brought to Paris by Champoiseau, after his mission to Samothrace in 1891. Musée du Louvre, inv. Ma. 4191. I saw the stone in July 2001.

H. 0.85 m, W. 0.38 m (above)–0.44 m (below), Th. 0.06 m; L.H. 0.015 m.

Edd. Reinach 1892, p. 201, no. 4; Fredrich, *IG* XII.8 216; Dittenberger, *Syll.*³ 1054; Cole 1984, p. 150, no. 19, pl. V:b.

Cf. Kern 1893, p. 372, no. 15.

A.D. 160–180

```
          θ    ε    ο    ἱ.
      βασιλεύοντος Σαβείνου οἵδε
        Ἀθηναίων ἐμυήθησαν·
      ὁ ἀπ᾽ ἄστεως στρατηγὸς Ἀθηναίων τῶν
5     ἐν Ἴμβρῳ Σωκράτης Ἀρχελάου Πειραι-
        εύς
      vacat
      Φιλοκράτης ὁ καὶ Εἰσίδωρος Φιλο-
        κράτους Ὄηθεν
      Ἀσκληπιάδης Μηνοδώρου Φλυεύς
10    Εὐσχήμων Χρυσέρωτος Πειραιεύς
      Κορνήλιος Ἀδείμαντος Ἀναφλύστιος
```

36. *Hym. Hom. Cer.* 480–482: ὄλβιος ὃς τάδ᾽ ὄπωπεν ἐπιχθονίων ἀνθρώπων· | ὃς δ᾽ ἀτελὴς ἱερῶν, ὅς τ᾽ ἄμμορος, οὔ ποθ᾽ ὁμοίων | αἶσαν ἔχει φθίμενός περ ὑπὸ ζόφῳ εὐρώεντι; Soph. fr. 837: ὡς τρισόλβιοι | κεῖνοι βροτῶν, οἳ ταῦτα δερχθέντες τέλη | μόλωσ᾽ ἐς Ἅιδου· τοῖσδε γὰρ μόνοις ἐκεῖ | ζῆν ἔστι, τοῖς δ᾽ ἄλλοισι πάντ᾽ ἔχειν κακά.

37. Bastianini and Galazzi 2001, no. VII.14–18. I understand lines 14–15 as "Nikostrate went to the sacred rites of reverent initiates and the pure fire of Triptolemos." On p. 160 the editors list this translation as a possibility, but prefer to take εὐσεβέων with an omitted noun (χῶρος, *vel sim.*). The use of εὐσεβέων with μυστῶν creates better parallelism, however: ἐπὶ is used once with ἱερὰ ὄργια and a second time with πῦρ; not a third time to modify yet another, omitted, accusative.

38. Cf. Cic. *Leg.* 2.36: *initiaque ut appellantur, ita re vera principia vitae cognovimus; neque solum cum laetitia vivendi rationem accepimus, sed etiam cum spe meliore moriendi;* Isoc. *Paneg.* 28: τὴν τελετήν, ἧς οἱ μετασχόντες περί τε τῆς τοῦ βίου τελευτῆς καὶ τοῦ σύμπαντος αἰῶνος ἡδίους τὰς ἐλπίδας ἔχουσιν.

39. Previously, the only known benefit for Samothracian initiates was safety at sea; cf., most recently, Burkert 2002, p. 61.

Figure 27. Record of initiates from
the Athenian cleruchy on Imbros
(30). Photo © C. Larrieu, courtesy Musée
du Louvre, Department of Greek, Roman,
and Etruscan Antiquities

Κορνηλία Ἀλεξάνδρα Κορ(νηλίου) Ἀδειμάντου θυ(γάτηρ)
Κορνηλία Φιλότροφον ἐξ Ἀζηνιέων
Σωτᾶς Βότρυος Δαιδαλίδης
vacat
15   ἐπόπται
Πό(πλιος) Ἐρέννιος Λεοντεὺς Ἀζηνιεύς
Κλᾶρος Κλάρου Αἰξωνεύς
Ἰούλιος Ἕρμιππος
in corona:
          Θεοῖς
20   Μεγάλοις
          Σαμόθρα-
           ξι.

Fredrich.

Epigraphical Commentary

The letters are clear, with a characteristic rectilinear shape, especially sigma.
They resemble the hand(s) of **36** (except for the omega), **41**, inscription iii,
45, 116, 166, and perhaps **44**.

    Line 16: The omicron of Πό(πλιος) is above the pi and much smaller
than the other letters.

Commentary

The inscription is a record of Athenian initiates from Imbros, dated by Dittenberger to A.D. 160–180 since several of the names mentioned in the inscription are attested elsewhere. The initiates were members of the Athenian cleruchy on Imbros. Reinach (p. 203) concludes from the expression ὁ ἀπ᾽ ἄστεως στρατηγὸς Ἀθηναίων in line 4 that at the end of the 2nd century A.D. Imbros was still an Athenian cleruchy, and that the *strategos* in the present inscription (unattested otherwise) was sent by Athens, and not elected by the cleruchy.

Line 2: The eponymous official is otherwise unknown. The formula βασιλεύοντος + name is common throughout the Greek world, but atypical of Samothrace. The only other example of βασιλεύοντος possibly occurs in **104**.

Lines 2–3: οἵδε . . . ἐμυήθησαν is unattested as a formulaic expression. The verb μυέω is used in one other Samothracian inscription (**126**), but in the aorist active, and the participle μυηθέντες occurs in **61** and **63**.

Line 5: For Archelaos, father of the Socrates mentioned here, see Traill, no. 209755.

Line 7: See Traill, no. 384110. A certain Eisidoros, son of Philo-, of Oe, was an ephebe in A.D. 155/6 (Traill, no. 384180), but it is unclear whether he is the same person or a relative.

Line 9: A certain Ἀσκληπιάδης Μηνοδώρου of Phlya is attested in an ephebic catalogue of A.D. 154/5 (*IG* II² 2967.67). It is likely that he is the same person, as Dittenberger points out. This consideration as well as the probable identification of Πό(πλιος) Ἐρέννιος (see *ad* line 16) were the reasons for Dittenberger's dating of the inscription to A.D. 160–180. On Ἀσκληπιάδης Μηνοδώρου and his family see Traill, nos. 219840, 219825, 219830.

Line 14: Sotas's brother, Νείκων Βότρυος Δαιδαλίδης ν(εώτερος), is mentioned in *IG* II² 5964, dated to the 2nd century A.D.; see Traill, no. 267930. On the semantics of the name Botrys, cf. **34**, line 11.

Line 16: Πό(πλιος) Ἐρέννιος Λεοντεὺς Ἀζηνιεύς (Traill, no. 401480) is well known from other inscriptions, as Dittenberger points out (see above, *ad* line 9): he served as an ephebe in A.D. 142/3 (*IG* II² 3740.B.21), as a gymnasiarch (*IG* II² 2049.25), and as a *bouleutes* in A.D. 152/3 or 153/4 (Attica, *Agora* XV 336.II.17).

Line 18: It is interesting that Ἰούλιος Ἕρμιππος has no demotic.

Lines 19–22: The document is both a list of initiates and a dedication to the Great Gods. The dedicatory formula is inscribed within a laurel crown.

PELOPONNESE

31 Greek record of initiates(?) from Alexandria, Tegea,   Fig. 28
Thera, Torone, and Aspendos[40]

Fragment of a stele of Thasian marble, broken above and below. Provenance unknown. Archaeological Museum of Samothrace. No inv. no.

40. For material pertaining to Elis, see **16**.

Figure 28. Greek record of initiates(?) from Alexandria, Tegea, Thera, Torone, and Aspendos (31)

H. 0.21 m, W. 0.255 m, Th. 0.065 m; L.H. 0.01 m.
Unpublished.

Date?

```
[- - - - - - - - - - ᶜᵃ·²⁰ - - - - - - - - -]
[- - - - - - - - - - ᶜᵃ·²⁰ - - - - - - - - -]
[- - - - - - - - - - ᶜᵃ·²⁰ - - - - - - - - -]
[- - -⁵- -] . . . [- - - - -ᶜᵃ·¹² - - - -]
```

5   vacat Ἀλεξανδρεύς vacat
       [- - - -ᶜᵃ·¹⁰ - - - -]Ἀπολλωνίου[-?-]
       vacat Τεγεάτης   vacat
       Θεμισταγόρας Ἀπολλοδώρου
       vacat Θηραῖος   vacat
10   Κρατίδαμος Ἀπολλοδώρου
       · Ρ . . ΤΩ . . . ΔΚ . . . ΙΤΟΥ
       [Το]ροναῖος Ἱεροκλῆς Δ . . . ΟΥ
       [Εὐπ]ορίων Κυαίου Ἀσπέν[διος]
       -

Epigraphical Commentary
The inscription is now badly worn.

Commentary
This probably was a list of Greek initiates, who came from various cities—Alexandria, Tegea, Thera, Torone, and Aspendos. All except Alexandria are hitherto unattested as ethnics of initiates.

THESSALY

For material pertaining to Azorion/Azoros, see **35**.

ILLYRIA

32   Record of initiates from Epidamnos

Fragment of Thasian marble. Found in Palaiopolis, now lost. Its dimensions are unknown.

Edd. Blau and Schlottmann 1855, p. 619, no. 9; Fredrich, *IG* XII.8 196; Cabanes and Drini 1995, 515 (*SEG* XLV 696).

Cf. Conze 1860, p. 62.

Date?

```
        μύσται εὐσ[εβεῖς]
          Ἐπιδαμνίω[ν·]
        Φίλων[. . .]ΑΣΤ[- -]
        Λυσίων Ε[- - -]
   5    Σωσί[. .]ος Παρμενίω[νος]
        ΑΤΕΙΡΙΟ[. . . .]ΧΡΗ[- -]
        - - - - - - - - - - - - - - -
```

Fredrich. **3** [Ἀδρ]άστ[ου?] Fredrich. **5** Σωσί[λα]ος Fredrich. **6** Ἀτείριο[ς? Θεο]χρή[στου?] Fredrich.

Commentary

Lines 3, 5, 6: The restorations proposed by Fredrich are not the only possibilities.

Line 4: Λυσίων is a relatively rare name. It occurs mostly in Epidaurian and Rhodian documents.

Line 6: Ateirios apparently is not attested. Ἀτέριος is attested in Attica (see *LGPN* II) and in Macedonia (*SEG* XXXVIII 701). Ἀτῆρις (genitive Ἀτήριος) occurs occasionally in papyri.

MACEDONIA

For material pertaining to Styberra, see **53**—which also has a probable initiate from Sirrhai; for Herakleia apo Strymonos, see **36**, and for Torone, **31**.

33   Record of an initiate from Sirrhai   Fig. 29

Block of Thasian marble, with a raised right edge, broken below. There is a lip on the left and anathyrosis on the back. A clamp hole is visible on the top, near the back edge, and it is roughly centered. Found in Chora on June 25, 1939. Archaeological Museum of Samothrace, courtyard, inv. 39.83.

H. 0.61 m, W. 0.18 m, Th. 0.26 m; L.H. 0.02 m (lines 3–6), 0.025–0.03 m (lines 1–2, 7–10).

Edd. Lehmann-Hartleben 1940, p. 358, no. 4; Fraser, *Samothrace* 2.1 (1960) 46.

Cf. Robert and Robert, *BullÉp* 1944 151a; Walton 1963, p. 99; Robert 1963, p. 65, n. 7.

Figure 29. Record of an initiate from Sirrhai (33)

2nd century A.D.?

[ἀγ]αθῆ[ι]
τύχηι
ἐπὶ βασι-
λέως Κλ.
5 Διονυσίου
μύστης
εὐσεβὴς
Παρά-
μονος
10 Ζωίλου
Σιρραῖος.
vacat

Fraser. 4 Κλ. Fraser. 8 Παράμονος Fraser. 8–9 Παρά|μονος Walton.

Epigraphical Commentary

The lettering, dated by Fraser to the 2nd century A.D., resembles that of **34**, with lunate epsilon and sigma. Ligatures of omicron and upsilon are used (lines 5, 10).

Line 1: First preserved letter: right oblique stroke followed by a circle.

Line 4: The lambda is clear.

Commentary

It is possible that the block belonged together with **67** and **97**; see *ad* **67**. According to Fraser, it was first used in a structure where it lay horizontally, in light of the anathyrosis on the back, and was then reused in a vertical position, as the clamp hole above, predating the inscription, shows.

Lines 8–10: A certain Zoilos, son of Paramonos, is attested in another inscription from Macedonia (*SEG* XXXVIII 679.42–43, A.D. 74/5). It is impossible to prove a connection, however, as both Paramonos and Zoilos are very common Greek names. Paramonos occurs as the name of a slave from Beroia in another Samothracian document (**34**).

Line 11: Most likely the same ethnic occurs in **53**; see Robert, p. 65.

34   Record of initiates from Beroia   Fig. 30

Stele of Thasian marble, preserved on all sides, with a tenon below for insertion. The back is rough-picked. Found in the Sacristy on July 5, 1939. Archaeological Museum of Samothrace, courtyard, inv. 39.332.

H. 0.74 m, W. 0.37 m, Th. 0.10 m; L.H. 0.02–0.025 m.

Edd. Lehmann-Hartleben 1940, p. 345, with p. 493; Fraser, *Samothrace* 2.1 (1960) 47.

Cf. Robert and Robert, *BullÉp* 1944 151a; Robert 1963, pp. 70–76; Walton 1963, p. 100; Robert and Robert, *BullÉp* 1964 377; Lehmann 1998, p. 61.

A.D. 113

        ἐπὶ βασιλέως
        Θεοδώρου τοῦ ϛ′
        μύσται εὐσεβεῖς
        · Βεροιαῖοι
5   · Τι. · Κλαύδιος Εὔλαιος
        · Οὐλπία · Ἀλεξάνδρα
        · ἡ γυνὴ αὐτοῦ
        · Γα · Ἰτύριος Πούδης
           · δοῦλοι
10   Κλαυδίου Εὐλαίου
          Στάχυς
           Παράμονος
          Θηβαΐς
        ἔτους   αξϛ   *era-date 261*

Fraser. **8** Γαι. Τύριος Πούδης Robert.

Epigraphical Commentary

The letters are very similar to those of **33**, except that there are no ligatures. It is possible that they were executed by the same hand.

Commentary

This is a record of Roman initiates from the Macedonian city Beroia and of their slaves. It is dated to the year 261 of the Macedonian era, which began when Macedonia became a Roman province in 148 B.C. (see Fraser, p. 100, n. 1; Samuel 1972, p. 247).

Figure 30. Record of initiates from
Beroia (34)

Line 2: Fraser corrects Lehmann's reading Θεοδωροῦτος to Θεοδώρου τοῦ ϛ΄, following Robert's suggestion about the numeral ϛ΄, "six." The ancestors of the eponymous king Theodoros had the same name for six generations (Robert, p. 70, n. 1). Other eponymous kings whose first name or patronymic is Theodoros are attested in **1, 17**, inscription iii, **46**, inscription ii, and on coins; see *IG* XII.8, p. 41.

Line 5: Robert (pp. 71–76) discusses the name Eulaios in great detail, refuting the traditional view that the tutor of Ptolemy Philometor who was called Eulaios was of oriental origin. The conclusion that the name is Macedonian is richly supported by epigraphical evidence; see *IG* X 2.1 243.I (1st–2nd century A.D.); *SEG* XXIV 505 (2nd–3rd century A.D.); *SEG* XXXVIII 679, line 40 (A.D. 74/5), 680, line 52 (A.D. 74/5); *SEG* XXXIX 627 (Roman period).

Line 6: Robert (p. 70) points out that cities stopped bearing the name Ulpia early in the reign of Hadrian, while the personal name remained in use long thereafter.

Line 8: Fraser comments that "Pudens, who alone of those present has the 'tria nomina,' is sandwiched between the Beroians and their slaves," but there is no indication that he was not a Beroian himself, as Robert remarked (p. 70; cf. also Walton, who writes: "There is no reason to question the explicit statement on the stone that Eulaios, his wife, and Pudens are one and all Beroians."). Robert also draws attention to the fact that

Tiberius Claudius Eulaios has three names, while Ulpia is not supposed to have three names, being a woman.

Iturius is a rare name, bringing to mind the Iturius mentioned in Tacitus, *Annales* 13.19–22, as Fraser notes. The name Ituria occurs in *CIL* VI 35503 (see Robert), and also in an early Christian epitaph from Italy, *ICUR* IX 26070 (undated). In view of the name's rarity, Robert suggests that we might be dealing with the common name Turius instead, and proposes to read Γαι.Τύριος Πούδης. The medial dot after the alpha looks certain, however. Another problem with this reading is the fact that in Greek inscriptions the name Gaius is very seldom abbreviated after the iota; of the examples known to me, *I.Cos* 228, *NSER* 563, and *I.Ephesos* 267 and 458, only the last two have unproblematic readings. Γα. is a much more common abbreviation.

Pudens occurs frequently in Greek inscriptions both as a cognomen and a first name. In Macedonia it occurs in, e.g., *SEG* XXXVIII 680, line 42 (A.D. 74/5), and XL 557 (Imperial period).

Line 11: Robert (p. 70, n. 2) discusses the semantics of the name Στάχυς. He cites an epitaph from Thessaloniki, in which two men with the remarkable names Botrys (grape cluster) and Stachys (corn ear) set up a monument in memory of their brother (*IG* X 2.1 401, 2nd century A.D.). The name is not infrequent throughout the Greek world in Hellenistic and Roman times (ca. 50 examples).

Line 13: The personal name Θηβαΐς is very rare.

35   Records of initiates from Azorion and Kassandreia   Fig. 31

Fragment of a statue base of Thasian marble, broken only on top. Found built into the church of St. Andrew, now in the Archaeological Museum of Samothrace, courtyard. No inv. no.

H. 0.07 m, W. 1.62 m, Th. 0.49 m; L.H. 0.015 m (inscription i), 0.012 m (inscription ii).

Edd. Conze 1875, p. 42, no. 19, pl. 71:19; Fredrich, *IG* XII.8 178.

Cf. *SEG* II 504; Hiller von Gaertringen, *IG* XII Suppl. (1939), p. 149; Salviat, Chapouthier, and Salač 1956, p. 144, with n. 5; *BullÉp* 1958 261; Collini 1990, p. 261.

2nd century B.C.?

```
      -----------------------------------------------------------------------
i     [--------------------------------]          ii     [. . . .] μύστις εὐσεβής· Μένυλλα
      ἀπὸ Ἀζωρίου στρατηγὸς Τριπολιτ[ῶ]ν καὶ            5  Ἱπποστράτου Κασσανδρεῖτις
      ὁπλοφόρος Παρμενίσσκος· ἀκόλουθος Μένανδρος.          κιθαρίστρια ἀκόλουθος Εἰρήνη.
```

Fredrich.

Epigraphical Commentary

It is unclear how many lines are missing above the two inscriptions. The hands of i and ii are <u>different</u> in size and shape, dated by Fredrich to the 2nd century B.C.

Commentary

The base contains two records of initiation, i and ii. It is impossible to say whether the inscriptions were original or secondary. Both i and ii list individual initiates with their accompanying servants, *akolouthoi*.

Figure 31. Records of initiates from Azorion and Kassandreia (35): left end of statue base *(top)*, central portion *(middle)*, and right end *(bottom)*

Line 2: Ἀζώριον, also known as Azoros, is a city in Thessaly, as Fredrich notes (Polyb. 28.11; *IG* X.2, p. 265). He also remarks that *strategos* is the title of the eponymous magistrate of the Tripolitai (i.e., the citizens of Ἀζώριον, Δολίχη, Πύθιον).

Line 3: The name Παρμενίσσκος seems to be recorded with double sigma only in the present inscription and in *Gonnoi* II 261 (undated). The suffix -ίσσκος, however, occurs with two sigmas all over the Greek world.

Line 4: The name Μένυλλα is very rare, as opposed to its rather frequent masculine counterpart Μένυλλος. Apart from the present inscription, it is attested, to my knowledge, only in *I.Delos* 298.A, line 10 (240 B.C.).

The name Ἱππόστρατος occurs elsewhere in Macedonia, but is attested in Kassandreia for the first time.

Line 5: Fredrich prefers to punctuate after Κασσανδρεῖτις, while Wilhelm after κιθαρίστρια. I refrain from expressing a definite opinion on Menylla's occupation, but tend to support Wilhelm's conjecture. Moreover, the first record too has *akolouthos,* followed by the name it modifies.

Line 6: Salviat interprets the mention of the *kitharistria* as evidence for musical performance at the Samothracian festival. Although there is no evidence that this particular musician participated in any Samothracian performance, the mention of her profession may be related to the importance of theatrical performances for the Samothracian cult (cf. the Dionysiac artists in **10** and **11**).

Figure 32. Record of initiates from Thessaloniki and Herakleia apo Strymonos (36)

36 Record of initiates from Thessaloniki[41] and Herakleia apo Strymonos   Fig. 32

Stele of Thasian marble, broken at top and bottom. The back is rough-picked. A piece is broken off at the top left corner. Acquired in 1926 by Chapouthier from Chrysostomos Nimorios.[42] Archaeological Museum of Samothrace, courtyard, inv. 49.438.

H. 0.225 m, W. 0.29 m, Th. 0.055 m; L.H. 0.02–0.025 m.

Ed. Fraser, *Samothrace* 2.1 (1960) 58.

Cf. Chapouthier 1935, p. 234, n. 4; Robert 1936, p. 53; Hiller von Gaertringen, *IG* XII Suppl. (1939), p. 149, under no. 195; Hemberg 1950, p. 209, n. 6; Salviat 1962, p. 269; Robert 1963, pp. 76–77; *BullÉp* 1964 378.

2nd–3rd century A.D.?

- - - - - - - - - - - - - - - - - -

[. ?]ΙΟΣ Θεσσαλονεικεύς,
Μ. Ὀρφίδιος Ἀγησίλαος
Ἡρακλεώτης ἀπὸ Στρυμόνος,
Κλαύδιος Σύμφορος
5   Θεσσαλονεικεύς,
Μάρκιος Μυρισμός
Θεσσαλονεικεύς.
[δ]οῦλοι εὐσεβεῖ[ς]

- - - - - - - - - - - - - - - - - -

Fraser. 1 ΙΟΣ Fraser. 3 Στρυμόνος Fraser. 8 Dimitrova, δ]οῦλοι Εὐσεβ[ίου?] Fraser.

Epigraphical Commentary

The rectilinear hand, consistent with a date in the 2nd and 3rd centuries A.D., resembles that of **30** (except for the omega), **41**, inscription iii, **45**, **116**, **166**, and perhaps **44**. Fraser must have not seen a photograph of **30**, since he concludes that the hand is quite different from that of any other Samothracian inscription, but resembles the style of inscriptions from Thessaloniki

41. See also **37**, line 7, for a Thessalonikian initiate, and **166** for possible initiates from Thessaloniki.

42. Cf. Salviat 1962, p. 269.

(p. 108, n. 1). He suggests that the carver was trained in that style (p. 108). It seems to me that such a connection would be hard to prove, in view of the above examples of Samothracian documents with rectilinear lettering.

Line 1: There is space for one or two letters before the dotted vertical. First letter: bottom part of vertical stroke. NE are in ligature.

Line 2: ΗΣ are in ligature.

Line 3: TH and TP are in ligature. The omicron of ἀπὸ and the letters μονο are much smaller than the other characters; see Commentary.

Line 8: Top part of a circle; upper part of upsilon; apex of a triangle; top part of a circle; top vertical; top left vertical joined with top horizontal; upper part of upsilon; top left vertical joined with top horizontal; top left vertical joined with top horizontal; top part of beta or rho; top horizontal followed by the top part of a vertical.

Commentary

Although the title *mystai eusebeis* is missing, the listing of slaves in line 8 makes it highly probable that the monument is a record of initiates, since the typical layout of such documents has at first *mystai*, followed by freed-men or slaves.

Line 1: There must have been at least one letter (or a ligature) before the first preserved letter. It is unclear whether a complete name was in-scribed there or whether it was transferred from the line above. It is more logical to expect a full name, since all other names in the inscription are kept within a single line.

Line 2: The nomen Orfidius is relatively rare, as Fraser notes. He cites the names of C. Orfidius Benignus (*legatus leg. I Adiutr.* in A.D. 69) and P. Orfidius Senecio (*consul suffectus* in A.D. 148), but it is impossible to establish a connection with the M. Orfidius in the present document.

Line 3: Robert (p. 77) points out that Fraser's reference to his article in *RPhil* 1936 is incorrect, since the article in question does not refer to the so-called Herakleia ἀπὸ Στρυμόνος. The Herakleia in question is identified by Collart[43] and Honigmann[44] with the town of Zervochori, as Robert notes. He draws attention to the fact that the usual appellation of the town is Σιντική, while "of the Strymon" is attested only in Hierocles (639.9), and suggests that Σιντική was probably inscribed originally in the present document, and then corrected to "of the Strymon," which can explain the discrepant letter size. It has to be noted, however, that Σιντική does not appear in inscriptions, while "of the Strymon" occurs also in a grave epigram from Dion for a renowned doctor from Ἡρακλεία Στρυμωνίς (*SEG* XXXI 630.8, Roman date). It is curious that in this inscription Στρυμωνίς is spelled with omega. This unusual feminine adjective is attested in Stephanus of Byzantion (s.v.), spelled Στρυμονίς.

Line 6: Robert comments on the curious semantics of the name My-rismos. He mentions that names deriving from words denoting ointments are typical of the Imperial period and cites several parallels, listed in *BullÉp* 1939 171, 1953 194, and 1954 159. The last reference contains five examples of the name Myrismos, given in Kallipolitis 1953.

Line 8: Fraser suggests that a name in the genitive singular, e.g., Εὐσεβίου (of the slaves' master), should be expected after δοῦλοι. He also allows for the possibility δοῦλοι εὐσεβεῖς, but prefers to restore a

43. Collart 1937, pp. 503–507.
44. Honigmann 1939, p. 15.

personal name because the expression is unparalleled. On the other hand, the remains on the stone are consistent with restoring εὐσεβεῖς. Fraser is not convinced that the horizontal mark after the beta is a letter at all, but I see clear traces of a top horizontal and a top vertical.

37   Record of initiates from Thessaloniki, Amphipolis, and Beroia

Marble stele, broken on top, with a tenon for insertion below. The text was copied by Dionysios Markopoulou παρὰ τῷ ἐν Δαρδανελίοις κ. Δημητρίῳ Ξανθοπούλῳ. Part of the Froehner collection. *Non vidi.*

H. 0.60 m, W. 0.35 m, Th. 0.07 m; L.H. ca. 0.015 m.

Edd. Markopoulou, Μουσεῖον καὶ βιβλιοθήκη (Smyrna) II, 2–3, (1876–1878) 17, 219 *(non vidi);* Fredrich, *IG* XII.8 195; Robert 1936, p. 52, no. 44, ph.; Hiller von Gaertringen, *IG* XII Suppl. (1939), p. 149.

Cf. *BullÉp* 1938 309; Robert and Robert, *BullÉp* 1958 270, p. 256; Robert 1963, pp. 67–69.

38 B.C.–A.D. 43

```
           [ἐπὶ βασιλέως]
           [Ἀν]τιμέδοντος τοῦ [. . . .]
           ΛΕΙΔΟΥ · vac. ἀγορανομοῦν[τος]
           Φιλεταίρου τοῦ Δημητρίο[υ] ·
    5      ὡς δὲ Μακεδόνες ἄγουσιν
   Φιλέ-   ἔτους Α κ[αὶ .] καὶ Ρ, μηνὸς        era-date 1(?)1
   ρως     Ἀρτεμισίου · vac. Θεσσαλονικεύ[ς]
   Βιθυ-   μύσται εὐσεβεῖς · Ἀρχέπολι[ς]
   ος      Νικοπόλεως · Ἀμφιπολῖτα[ι] ·
   10      [Γ]λαυκίας Ἀπολλοδώρου,
           Κλεοπάτρα Θεοδότου,
           Γλαυκίας Γλαυκίου · Διο-
           νύσιος Μαντας · ἀπελεύθε-
           [ρ]οι · Βιθυς Γλαυκίου, Κοτυς
   15      Γλαυκίου, Ἀπολλώνιος Γλαυ-
           [κ]ίου, Μητρόδωρος Βιθυος,
           [Ἀ]θηνίων Βιθυος vacat
           Βεροιαῖος vac. Περίτας Μενά-
           νδρου, Διονύσιος Ἀρχε-
   20      πόλεως · vac. Ῥουφίων <Λ>έοντος,
           Ἄλυπος Λέοντος.
```

Fredrich, Robert. **3** Ἀγίδου Fredrich, ... |λείδου Robert; *vac.* Robert. **6** [Α καὶ Ι] Fredrich, [Α' καὶ .] Robert. **7** *vac.* Robert, Θεσσαλονικε[ῖς] Fredrich, Θεσσαλονικεύ[ς] Robert. **8** Ἀρχεπόλεως Fredrich, Νικοπόλεως Robert. **13** Μαντα<ς> Fredrich, Μαντᾶς Robert. **17** Ἀθηνίων Fredrich, [Ἀ]θηνίων Robert, *vacat* Robert. **18** Πέρσας Fredrich, *vac.* Περίτας Robert. **20** *vac.* Robert, Ο . . . . . Λ Fredrich, Ῥουφίων <Λ> Robert.

In latere sinistro: Ῥῶς *vel* Τρώς Fredrich, Φιλέ|ρως Βίθυος Robert.

Epigraphical Commentary

The letters are clear and elegant; see the photograph in Robert's edition.

Line 6: I see a clear alpha, followed by kappa in the photograph.

Commentary

This is a record of initiates from Thessaloniki, Amphipolis, and Beroia. The initiates from Thessaloniki and Beroia must have accompanied those from Amphipolis and their freedmen.

Line 3: On the *agoranomoi* see **3**, *ad* line 13.

Line 6: If iota is to be restored in the brackets, then the date of the inscription would be 111 years after 148 B.C. (the start of the respective Macedonian era; see *ad* **34**), i.e., 38 B.C., as Fredrich calculates. Yet any number between 1 and 9 seems possible, so the era date could be 191, 181, 171, 161, 151, 141, 131, 121, or 111, and the date of the inscription would fall in any of the following years: 38, 28, 18, 8 B.C., or A.D. 3, 13, 23, 33, 43.

The name on the left side, Phileros Bithyos, was omitted initially.

Line 7: Θεσσαλονικεύ[ς] was added later in the vacant space, as the ethnic of Ἀρχέπολι[ς] Νικοπόλεως; see *IG* XII Suppl. (1939), p. 149.

Line 11: A Κλεοπάτρα Θεοδότου is attested in an epitaph from Egypt (*SEG* VIII 384), but no additional information is available.

Lines 13–14: Robert assumed that the freedmen are Dionysios and Mantas; see *IG* XII Suppl. (1939), p. 149. There are difficulties with this interpretation, however. First, the name Mantas occurs primarily in its feminine form, Manta. It is also possible that Διονύσιος Μαντας is a single person. Another difficulty with understanding Dionysios and Mantas as the freedmen is the position of the title ἀπελεύθε|[ρ]οι. It normally precedes the names it modifies (cf. **41**, side B, **46**, **53**, and **63**), and so I prefer to connect it to the names that follow.

Lines 14–16: Kotys and Bithys are among the most common Thracian names. For Bithys, see *ad* **78**, line 18. The men with patronymics Glaukiou may be brothers.

Lines 16–21: Presumably Metrodoros, Athenion, and Phileros Bithyos (lines 6–9, left side) are brothers (possibly sons of Bithys in line 14). Rhouphion and Alypos may also be brothers. The ethnic Beroiaios modifies the name (or names) that follows, as Robert noted. Moreover, all of the ethnics in this inscription precede the names they refer to.

THRACE

For other material pertaining to Thrace, see **137**. On the importance of the Samothracian cult there, see *ad* **19** and Chapter 9. See **39** and **53** for certain initiates from Byzantion and **67** and **134** for possible initiates from there.

38   Records of initiates from Philippi and Chios, and   Fig. 33
   of Roman initiates of unknown provenance

Stele of Thasian marble, broken above and on the left, rough-picked on back. Found in Palaiopolis, now in Paris, Musée du Louvre, inv. Ma. 4190. I saw it in July 2001.

H. 0.29 m, W. 0.18 m, Th. 0.07 m; L.H. 0.015 m (lines 1–2), 0.025–0.03 m (line 3), 0.02–0.025 m (line 4), 0.01–0.015 m (lines 5–9).

Edd. Reinach 1892, p. 203, no. 6; [Mommsen, *CIL* III Suppl. I.3 (1893) 12319]; Fredrich, *IG* XII.8 209; [Lommatzsch, *CIL* I² (1918) 666].
    Cf. Kern 1893, p. 373, no. 17.

2nd–1st century B.C.?

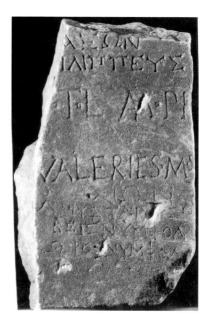

Figure 33. Records of initiates from Philippi and Chios, and of Roman initiates of unknown provenance (38). Photo © C. Larrieu, courtesy Musée du Louvre, Department of Greek, Roman, and Etruscan Antiquities

i   - - - - - - - - -
          [- - - - - -]ΑΞΩΝ
          [- - - - -Φ]ιλππεύς
ii   [- - - - - -]· T(iti) · l(ibertus) · m(ystes) · pi(us)
iii   [- - - - - -]Valeries *(sic)* · m(ystes) *leaf*
iv   5   Χίων
          vacat μύσται [εὐ]σε-
          vacat βεῖς Νυμφόδ-
          vacat ωρος Νυμφοδ[ώ]-
          [ρου].
          vacat

Fredrich. **1** [Πρ]άξων Fredrich. **4** *fortasse* Valerie *(sic)* s(ervus)? Dimitrova, m(yste)s Fredrich, m(ystes) Reinach.

Epigraphical Commentary

Fredrich notes that the lettering of lines 1–2, 3, and 4 differs from that of 5–8. He dates lines 1–2 to the 2nd century B.C. and lines 5–8 ("pessime scripti") to the 1st century B.C., whereas lines 3 and 4 must have been written at different times between the 2nd and 1st centuries B.C.

Line 4: The final s, represented by previous editors in the reading m(yste)s, is a leaf.

Commentary

The fragment contains four separate inscriptions. Inscription i is a record of an initiate from Philippi, ii and iii are of two Roman initiates, and iv is of an initiate from Chios.

Line 1: [Πρ]άξων, though plausible, is not the only possible restoration, since there are various other names ending in -άξων, e.g., Anaxon or Phylaxon.

Line 4: It is unclear whether Valeries is a misspelled name or an ethnic, as Reinach noted.

Lines 7–8: The name Νυμφόδωρος is attested elsewhere on Chios (e.g., *I.Chios* 408.1).

39   Records of initiates from Byzantion and Perinthos   Fig. 34

Base of Thasian marble, preserved on all sides, inscribed on front and top; two dowel holes with pour channels are visible on top, one near the right edge, the other ca. 0.30 m from the left edge. The inscription on the top (side B) is near the left dowel hole. Found in 2004 by the workmen of the Ephoreia of Prehistoric and Classical Antiquities, on the eastern bank of the eastern streambed of the lower part of the ancient city, at an elevation of ca. 43 m, ca. 120 m southwest of the southeast tower of the Gattilusi fortification. Its long axis lies in a north-northwest to south-southeast direction. Ephoreia inv. 68.

Ed. Matsas and Dimitrova 2006, pp. 128–129.

H. 0.26 m, W. 1.35 m, Th. 0.667 m; L.H. 0.022 m (side A), 0.01 m (side B).

1st century B.C.–2nd century A.D.

Side A

Ἀγαθῆι τύχηι
ἐπὶ βασιλέως Νικοστράτου
μύσται εὐσεβεῖς Βυζάντιοι
Πο. Καστρίκιος Ἀπφοῦς
5   Κάρπος Παπᾶ
Περίνθιος Ἀσκληπιόδοτος Βασιλείδου
Μύρων Πρόκλου τρόφιμος Ἀσκληπιοδότου
δοῦλος

Side B

ἐπὶ βασιλέως Μουσωνίου τοῦ Διογένους
ΤΟ . Β . μύστης εὐσεβής . . . . [. ^{ca. 5} .]
[. . . . . . ^{ca. 15} . . . . . .]ΡΟΣ[. . . . . . ^{ca. 15} . . . . . .]
- -

B.2 *fortasse* τοῦ Β.ʼ

Figure 34. Record of initiates from Byzantion and Perinthos (39): side A *(above)*, side B *(below)* (not at same scale)

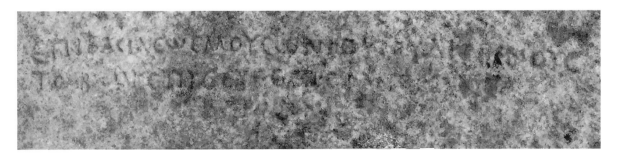

Epigraphical Commentary
The inscription on top of the base is very worn, and displays lunate letter shapes.

Commentary
The inscriptions on the front (A) and top (B) are records of initiation. That on side B may be later than that on A, judging by the letter style. Both inscriptions most probably represent a secondary use of the base; the dowel holes suggest that a block stood on top, which may have held the original inscription. Initiate lists are frequently inscribed on reused surfaces.[45] This is the first record of initiation definitely found in the ancient city: other monuments have been found between the city and the sanctuary. So far most of the initiate lists found in ancient contexts have come from the sanctuary, and especially the area around the Stoa. Both eponymous kings are hitherto unknown.

The Roman name Castricius is attested from the 1st century B.C.; hence the terminus post quem. The name Publius Castricius is attested for several family members mentioned in an epitaph from Ephesos (*I.Ephesos* 2266), but a clear connection with the Castricius in the present monument cannot be established. None of the Castricii listed in *PIR²* has the praenomen Publius.

The names Apphous and Papas are sometimes accented on the first syllable. Karpos may have been a freedman, judging by the semantics of his name.

Lines A.6–7: The singular Περίνθιος refers to Asklepiodotos, although naturally his household slave must have come from Perinthos too.

Line B.2: τοῦ Βʹ is a frequent expression in Greek documents and would make good sense as referring to the patronymic of the eponymous king.

40   Records of Roman initiates of unknown provenance and   Fig. 35
          of initiates from Maroneia, and a record of an *epoptes*

Stele of Thasian marble, broken on top and on the left, badly damaged. Found near the Rotunda of Arsinoe. Its present location is unknown.
H. 0.56 m, W. 0.25 m, Th. 0.08 m; L.H.?
Edd. Conze 1875, p. 39, no. 3, pl. 71:3; [Mommsen, *CIL* III Suppl. I.1 (1889) 7368]; [Cagnat, *IGR* I.4 (1905) 849]; Fredrich, *IG* XII.8 215.

A.D. 64? (*vss.* 1–17), A.D. 65 (*vss.* 18–21)

i   [C. Laecanio Basso, M. Licinio Crasso]
         [Frugi co(n)s(ulibus) ?]
              [- -dies- -]
              [mysta]e pii
     5   [- - - - - -]Q · Clodius Longus
         [- - -]IAΛNDRVSSAPAMONI
           - -]Leontiscus [L]eon[t]isci
ii   [eis]dem co(n)s(ulibus)
              [-?- id]us Maias *May 8–14*

45. Cole 1984, p. 41.

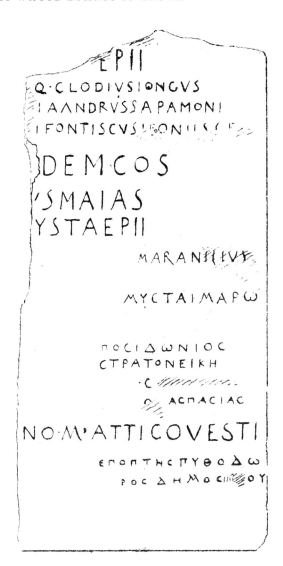

Figure 35. Records of Roman initiates of unknown provenance and of initiates from Maroneia, and a record of an *epoptes* (40). Conze 1875, pl. 71:3

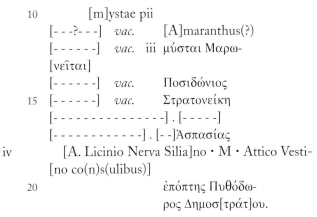

10   [m]ystae pii
       [- - -?- - -]   *vac.*   [A]maranthus(?)
       [- - - - - -]   *vac.*   iii μύσται Μαρω-
       [νεῖται]
       [- - - - - -]   *vac.*   Ποσιδώνιος
15   [- - - - - -]   *vac.*   Στρατονείκη
       [- - - - - - - - - - - - - -] . [- - - - -]
       [- - - - - - - - - - -] . [- -]Ἀσπασίας
iv   [A. Licinio Nerva Silia]no · M · Attico Vesti-
       [no co(n)s(ulibus)]
20   ἐπόπτης Πυθόδω-
                             ρος Δημοσ[τράτ]ου.

Fredrich. **1–4, 8, 18** Hirschfeld (*apud* Fredrich). **6** [- - -Eu]andrus [P]aramoni *correxit* Wil. (*apud* Fredrich). **7** *correxit* Wil. (*apud* Fredrich). **11** MARAŇIIIVI Mommsen, M. Aranteius Wil. (*apud* Fredrich), M. Aranplius, M. Aratrius, Fredrich.

Epigraphical Commentary

The stele is now lost, but one can get an idea about the letter forms from Conze's facsimile.

Line 6: IAΛNDRVSSAPAMONI, facsimile.

Line 7: I FONTISCUS, facsimile.

Line 11: MARAN I I IVS, facsimile.

Line 16: Either a lunate sigma or an omicron.

Line 17: The top part of a circle is visible on the facsimile.

Commentary

The stele contains three records of initiates and one of an *epoptes*, dated according to the Roman consuls. Greeks from Maroneia and Romans are listed together.

Lines 1–2: The reason for Hirschfeld's restoration is the assumption that the consuls of the previous year, A.D. 64, must have been listed. Of course, this is only a conjecture.

Line 5: A Q. Clodius is also mentioned as an initiate in **14**. He was a freedman of a certain Q. Clodius, but it is unclear whether his master might be related to the initiate in the present document.

Line 6: [Ev]andrus is not the only possible restoration, and it does not match the remains on the stone: the facsimile shows a vertical line before the first preserved letter. As for his patronymic, <P>a<r>amoni is indeed a probable conjecture, since the name is extremely common, while there is no known name that contains the letters SAPAMONI or APAMONI. In fact, Παραμόνου occurs as a patronymic in the next document, **41**, line 6.

Line 9: There must have been a numeral before Id]us, since for the the day of the Ides we would expect the ablative; any day between May 8 and 14 is possible; cf. Clinton 2001, p. 35.

Line 11: Amaranthus is a well-attested name (unlike Aranteius and Aranplius); cf. *CIL* II 178, 2432, 4970.360, 6257.13, *CIL* III 1770, *CIL* V 4722, etc.

Lines 12–17: It is unclear whether the Greek initiates were part of the same record as the Roman initiates. Perhaps they were, because there is no separate date for their listing in either record ii or iii.

Line 13: Hirschfeld assumed that the letters -[νεῖται] were on another stone, but Fredrich advanced the counterargument that this is a stele, not a block. Presumably the ethnic was continued in the beginning of line 13 (Fredrich) or on the side of the stele.

41   Records of initiates from Thasos and Maroneia   Fig. 36

Two joining fragments of a block of Thasian marble, inscribed in front (side A) and on the right side (side B). Broken on top, back, and on the left. Found in "the bigger tower" (Conze). Paris, Musée du Louvre, inv. Ma. 4192. I saw the stone in July 2001.

H. 0.61 m, W. 0.44 m, Th. 0.23 m; L.H. 0.025 m (fragment *a*, except line 10, 0.01 m), 0.02 m (fragment *b*).

Edd. Conze 1860, p. 63; Fredrich, *IG* XII.8 220.

Cf. Collini 1990, p. 261; *SEG* LX 748; Salomies 1996, p. 118 (*SEG* LXVI 1186).

End of 1st century A.D.–beginning of 2nd?

Side A

i   -

[μύστις εὐσ]εβὴς Βαιβία Φ . . [. ^{ca. 5} .]

vacat spatium unius versus

ii   [ἐπὶ β]ασιλέος *(sic)* Τι. Φλαουίο[υ]

[Τίτ]ου υἱοῦ Κτησιφίλου

μύστις εὐσεβὴς

5   Θασία·

[. ^{ca. 5} .]τειμία Παραμόνου

[ἡ] καὶ Ζωσίμη

iii   [. ^{ca. 5} .]δοτος Ἀπολλωνίου.

iv   [ἐπὶ β]ασιλέως Μ. Ῥ(ουβίου) Φρόν-

10   Ἰκ[έ]σιος Ἀντιόχου

[τω]νος μύσται εὐσεβεῖς

[Μαρω]νεῖται· Ἀπολλόδωρος ΤΟΛ-

[^{ca. 3}]ου, Εὐβούλα Διονυσίου, ΣΕΙ

[^{ca. 3}] Διονυσικλείου, Τιουτα

15   Ἐντίμου.

Side B

v   [. .]ΙΑΔΙ[.^{1–5}.]

ὁ καὶ Παλ[. . .]

ἀπελεύθ[εροι]

Νεικόστ[ρ]ατο[ς]

20   Γλαφυρ[ί]δ[η]ς

Γάμος

vacat

Εἰσίδωρος

Ἐπαφρόδε[ιτος]

   ʋ   *vacat spatium unius versus*

   ο   *vac.* Παίζ<ω>ν

   ᴴ

   ⟨

   ∾

   ·ο

Fredrich. **1** Βαιβία Φρό[ντωνος?] Fredrich. **3** *init.* Dimitrova, [Τιβερί]ου Fredrich. **6** [Φιλο]τειμία Fredrich. **12–13** Τολ|[μαί]ου? Dimitrova. **13–14** Σει|[ληνὶς] Fredrich. **14** Τιθύτα Fredrich, Τιουτα Dimitrova.

Epigraphical Commentary

The hands of the five records are different (note especially the shape of the sigma: in inscription i it is four-bar, in ii lunar, in iii rectilinear, in iv rectilinear, and in v four-bar).

Line 10: The name is carved in smaller letters. Presumably Ἰκέσιος Ἀντιόχου was omitted from the record below.

Line 14: ΤΙΟΥΤΑ *lapis.*

Line 24: A bottom horizontal precedes the pi of Παίζ<ω>ν. The penultimate letter is an omicron.

There might be traces of erased letters below the vertical ὁ δῆμος.

Commentary

The block contains records of initiates from Thasos (inscription ii) and
Maroneia (iv), dated to different years. Inscriptions i, iii, and v are presumably also records of initiation, but no details are preserved. The thickness
of the block matches that of the theoroi blocks, but its preserved height
(0.61 m) is too great. The vertical upside-down inscription in the lower left
part of the document (side B) seems unrelated to the records of initiation,
but it can provide a clue about the nature of the monument. It predates
the initiation records, given its layout, and forms part of a dedication by
the demos. This means that the block was part of a base, which held the
letters ὁ δῆμος horizontally, in the upper left corner.

    Line 2: Α Φλ. Κτησίφιλος was *agoranomos* in the year when M. Ῥούβιος
Φρόντων was eponymous king, as **45** testifies (on the *agoranomoi* see above,
3, *ad* line 13). Most probably he is the same person, and in this case record
ii should be dated to approximately the same time as iv. The name Φρόντων
is also attested for the eponymous king in **97**. It is possible that the two
people are related.

    Line 3: [Τίτ]ου suits the space better, and is more commonly attested
as the praenomen of Flavius. As for the abbreviation in line 2, it regularly
represents the name Titus in Greek inscriptions. A certain Titus Flavius is
also attested as *basileus* in **95**. He may well be the same person, given the
similar lettering and the spelling βασιλέος, present in both records.

    Line 6: The name Φιλοτειμία/Φιλοτιμία is apparently not attested epi-
graphically except for ships (e.g., *IG* II² 1631.d.484). There are numerous instances of the name Παράμονος on Thasos, and no identification is possible.

    Lines 9–10: On Φρόντων, see also **45**, line 2.

    Line 13 end: There are many possibilities for restoration.

    Line 14: The name Τιθύτα is apparently unattested. Τιουτα, however,
is a common Thracian name.[46]

Figure 36. Records of initiates from
Thasos and Maroneia (41): side A
(left), side B *(right)*. Photos © M. and
P. Chuzeville (A), C. Larrieu (B), courtesy
Musée du Louvre, Department of Greek,
Roman, and Etruscan Antiquities

46. See Detschew 1957, p. 507; cf.
IGBulg 1005, 1348.

Figure 37. Record of initiates from Ainos (42). *Samothrace* 2.1, pl. XVIII:42

42   Record of initiates from Ainos   Fig. 37

Fragment of stele of Thasian marble, preserved on the right, with double molding above. The back is reworked, perhaps close to the original surface. A dowel hole is visible on top, at 0.065 m from the right edge. A caduceus is engraved in the lower right part of the stone (cf. **104, 156, 169**). Found near the Anaktoron on June 30, 1953. Archaeological Museum of Samothrace, courtyard, inv. 53.84.

H. 0.48 m, W. 0.19 m, Th. 0.13 m; L.H. 0.015–0.018 m (lines 1–5, 9), 0.025 (line 6), 0.02 m (line 7).

Ed. Fraser, *Samothrace* 2.1 (1960) 42.

1st century B.C.–1st century A.D.?

        [ἐπὶ βασιλέω]ς Φρυνίχου
        [τοῦ - - - - - -]οδώρου
        [μύσται εὐσ]εβεῖς Αἴνιοι
        [- - - - - - Φ]ιλώτου
    5 [- - - - - - Δ]ημητρίο[υ]
        [- - - - - - - - - - -]ΗΝΟΣ
        [- - - - - - - - - - - -]ΙΟΣ *vacat*
        vacat spatium 0.05 m
        [- - - - - - - - - - - -]ΥΛΟΣ[- -]
        - - - - - - - - - - - -

Fraser. **2** [τοῦ Δι]οδώρου Fraser.

Epigraphical Commentary
The inscription is now badly defaced. The letters are squarish.

Commentary
This is a record of initiates from Ainos. The date is unknown, possibly early Imperial, judging by letter forms, as Fraser suggests.

The eponymous official may be numismatically attested as ΦΡΥΝΙ; see *IG* XII.8, p. 41.

Line 2: [τοῦ Δι]οδώρου is not the only possible restoration.

Line 6: Fraser suggests that -ηνος is a patronymic rather than an ethnic, but such patronymics are extremely rare as opposed to ethnics ending in -ηνος (see, e.g., **46**, col. I, line 11, Ἀβυδηνός). The only well-attested example of such a patronymic that I know of is the genitive Ἕλληνος. Given the ending -ιος in the following line, I consider it likely that both lines 6 and 7 contained ethnics.

43   Record of initiates(?) from Ainos

A fragment of Thasian marble, found in Chora, transferred from the church Παναγοῦδα into the house of Phardys. The inscription is now lost. It is unclear whether the fragment is preserved on any side.

H. 0.30 m, W. 0.15 m, Th. 0.08 m; L.H.?

Edd. *Tachydromos* (newspaper, Istanbul) May 29, 1898 *(non vidi);* Fredrich, *IG* XII.8 217.

Cf. *BullÉp* 1900, p. 129.

1st–3rd century A.D.?

> [ἀγαθ]ῆ̣ τύ[χη]
> [ἐπὶ βασιλέως- -]ασίωνος[-?-]
> [μύσται εὐσεβ]εῖς Αἰν[ίων *vel* -ιοι]·
> [- - - - - - Ῥο?]ύφου[-?-]
> 5 [- - - - - - - -]ΟΣΙ[- - - -] .

Fredrich. 2 Ἰ]ασίωνος Fredrich. 4 Αἰν[ίων] Fredrich, Αἰν[ίων *vel* -ιοι] Dimitrova. 6 - - -οσί[ου?] . Fredrich.

Epigraphical Commentary
The letters, judging from Fredrich's majuscule copy, look rounded, with lunate epsilon and sigma; hence the tentative date.

Commentary
This probably is a record of initiates from Ainos, in view of the likely restoration in line 3. Fredrich's publication is based on Phardys's copy.

Line 2: Ἰασίων is an extremely rare name, although it is tempting to imagine a Samothracian king with the name of the mythical figure Iasion. I know of only one inscription, however, that mentions this name, and it is far from providing a certain reading (*IG* XII.3 1504: κα[ὶ Ἰα]σί[ω]ν[?]). Θασίων, on the other hand, is relatively common, and is attested for a Samothracian king; see **87**. Another problem with Fredrich's restoration is that usually both the first name and the patronymic of the king are given. Θασίων Θαλασίωνος is possible, in which case the inscription is to be dated to A.D. 14. Unfortunately this is only a hypothesis, since the remains of the inscription do not allow for any cross-references to be made.

Line 4: Both the genitive and nominative plural are possible.

Line 5: Ῥοῦφος is a very common name in the Roman period, and Ῥο?]ύφου seems to be the most likely conjecture.

44   Record of *mystides* from Ainos

Fragment of Thasian marble. Discovered in "the lower part of the castle" (Conze), but now lost. I saw a squeeze in the Berlin Academy in May 2004.

H. 0.18 m, W. 0.22 m, Th. 0.10 m; L.H. 0.01 m.

Edd. Blau and Schlottmann 1855, p. 621, no. 14; Fredrich, *IG* XII.8 218.

Cf. Conze 1860, p. 65; *SEG* LX 748.

Roman?

> [μ]ύστιδες εὐσεβεῖ[ς]
>   Αἰνίαι·
> Κυϊντία Μίλωνος
> [Ἰ]ουλία Γηπαιπυρον
> 5   [- - - -]ΙΑ Καλλικράτου
> [- - - - - -]ΠΗ Νίκωνος
> [- - - - - -]ΙΟΝ [Ἀ]ντιφῶν[τος]
> [- - - - - -]ΙΟΝ Διονυσίου.

Fredrich. 4 [Ἰ]ουλία Γηπ[αι]πύρο<υ> Mordtmann, Γηπαιπυρον Dimitrova. 5 [Ἰουλ]ία Fredrich. 6 [Καλλιό?]πη Fredrich. 7 *legit* Hiller (*apud* Fredrich).

Epigraphical Commentary

The lettering is rectilinear; for Samothracian parallels, see *ad* **30**.

Line 4: Γηπαιπυρον: the squeeze shows faint traces of alpha and iota and a clear nu.

Commentary

The inscription represents a record of female initiates from Ainos, dated to the Roman period on account of the names Κυϊντία and [Ἰ]ουλία. It is noteworthy that they were initiated as a group and therefore must have arrived together as a group. Presumably they were accompanied by an entourage of servants.

Line 4: Γηπαιπυρου is not attested. Γηπεπυρις, on the other hand, is a Thracian feminine name.[47] *IGBulg* 1346 has Γηπεπυρις Μοντανοῦ, where Gepepyris can be a feminine or a masculine name—although the latter is less likely, for lack of good parallels. It is possible that Iulia's cognomen was modified to resemble Greek feminine names in -ον (cf. the names in -ον in lines 7–8) or was recorded incorrectly on the stone.

**45   Record of Roman initiates of unknown provenance and   Fig. 38
of an initiate from Ainos**

Base of Thasian marble, preserved on all sides, rough-picked on back. A clamp cutting is visible on top at the right edge. Six laurel crowns are

47. Cf. Detschew 1957, p. 106; *IGBulg* 2343.

carved above the inscription. Two of them, the ones on the right, are not fully preserved. Paris, Musée du Louvre, inv. Ma. 4193. I saw the stone in July 2001.

H. 0.695 m, W. 0.62 m, Th. 0.14 m; L.H. 0.02 m (line 1), 0.012–0.017 m (lines 2–6).

Ed. Fredrich, *IG* XII.8 221.

Cf. *BullÉp* 1911, p. 321; Robert and Robert, *BullÉp* 1958 270, p. 256; Robert 1963, pp. 67–69; Salomies 1996, p. 118 (*SEG* XLVI 1186).

End of 1st century A.D.–beginning of 2nd

corona	*corona*	*corona*
corona	*corona*	*corona*

ΕΓ

ἐπὶ βασιλέως · Μ · Ῥουβίου Φρόντω-
νος · ἀγορανομοῦντος Τ̣(ίτου) Φλαβίου
Κτησιφίλου μύσται εὐσεβεῖς· Γ. · Ἰούλιος
5   Νίγερ, · Τ. · Ῥουτειλίου Ποτείτου οἰκονόμος
Ἀ. Προύσιος, *vacat* Νεικόλαος ΟΛΙ . ΟΥ Αἴνιος.

Fredrich. **3** Τ̣(ίτου) Dimitrova, Φλαβίου Fredrich. **5** Οἰκονόμος Fredrich, οἰκονόμος Dimitrova. **6** Προύσιος, Ὀλίου Fredrich.

Figure 38. Record of Roman initiates of unknown provenance and of an initiate from Ainos (45). Photo © M. and P. Chuzeville, courtesy Musée du Louvre, Department of Greek, Roman, and Etruscan Antiquities

Epigraphical Commentary

The rectilinear letter style resembles that of **41**, inscription iii, except for the shape of the phi and the more elegant layout. Given the fact that the eponymous king is the same (**41**, inscriptions iii and iv), it is conceivable that the cutter might have been the same, too. For other Samothracian documents with rectilinear lettering, see *ad* **30**.

Line 1: Apparently the stonecutter began writing the text on this line, but then changed his mind because the text would have been too close to the crowns, as Fredrich points out. This proves that the crowns are older than the text.

Line 3: The oblique stroke of what Fredrich took as an interpunct resembling the digit 7 seems to be a stray mark.

Line 6: Προύσιος: the dotted letters are almost illegible now.

Commentary

This is a record of Roman initiates and an Ainian initiate. The height of the block is comparable with that of **41**, if one assumes that not much is missing from the latter. Given the crowns, it is likely that the block belonged to a monument base, which was reused. At least one other block must have been attached to the right, and it probably held the original inscription.

Lines 1–3: For the names of the officials and the date of the document, see *ad* **41**.

Line 2: The name Rubius, attested also as Rubbius and Roubius (see Fredrich), is relatively rare. Salomies suggests that the person in the present inscription and in **41** may be related to Ῥουββία Μάρκου ἀπελευθέρα Ῥηγίλλα at Thessaloniki.

Lines 4–5: A person with the name of Gaius Iulius Niger is recorded as a hierophant in a catalogue of Cyzicene officials, (*IMT* 1459.A.II.19), dated to the reign of Trajan. The same name appears in *AÉ* 1975 284 and 1979 35, and *ILAlg.* I, 3279. People with the name Gaius Iulius Niger are rather frequently attested in papyri from the middle of the 2nd century A.D. Given the popularity of the name Gaius Iulius Niger, it seems impossible to identify the person in the present inscription with any of his homonyms.

Line 5: Fredrich takes οἰκονόμος to be a personal name, but given the genitive of the name Titus Rutilius Potitus (which seems complete by itself, and not in need of a second cognomen), it seems more probable that it was the title of Niger or Prusius.

Line 6: The form Προύσιος is not attested, while Προυσίας occurs frequently. It is possible that the ending of the name was Latinized, especially in view of the person's praenomen. Prusius may be attested in *ILJug.* 1365 and *IMS* II 19, but the endings in both documents are restored.

46   Record of initiation of Thracian royalty, Romans,   Fig. 39
      Odessitans,[48] and a citizen of Abydos

Nine fragments of a stele of Thasian marble, broken in the upper right corner. The back is rough-picked and largely reworked; several holes were cut through it secondarily. A rebate of ca. 0.01 × 0.013 m running along the bottom edge in front evidently marks the upper end of a tenon,

48. For material pertaining to Odessos, see also **171**.

now missing. Found on August 2, 1971, east of the Stoa on the Western
Hill, in the northeastern corner of room D. Archaeological Museum of
Samothrace, inv. 71.961.

H. 0.67 m, W. 0.47 m, Th. 0.07 m; L.H. 0.014–0.015 m (line 1),
0.032–0.033 m (lines 2–3), 0.025 m (lines 4–6), 0.015 m (line 6, last word),
0.011–0.013 m (lines 7–8, except beta, 0.020 m), 0.009–0.011 m (lines 9–19,
except rho), 0.009–0.012 m (lines 21–24), 0.013–0.017 m (line 25).

Ed. Clinton, forthcoming.

Cf. Cole 1984, p. 120, n. 356.

Ca. A.D. 40–45?

i   ἐπὶ βασιλέως Ἀγησάρχου τοῦ Ἀγη[σάρχου ?]
        Γ α ῖ ο ς ᾿Ι ο ύ λ ι ο ς Ρ α σ [κ ο ς]
        Ρ ο ι μ η [τ α λ] κ ο υ [. . . ⁸ . . . .]
        [Ἀ]ντων[ία Τρύφαι]να βα[σιλέως Πο]-
   5   λέμωνος [θυγάτ]ηρ κα[ὶ βασιλίσσης]
        [Πυ]θοδωρίδ[ος] ᵛᵛ μύ[στ]αι
        vacat spatium unius versus

                    Col. I   Col. II

        [Κοίν]τος Ὀκτάβᵛιος Ἀπε . [- - - - - - - - - - - - - -]   [- - - - - - - - -]
        [. . . .]ος Μαικίλιος Τίτου υ[ἱ]ὸς [- - - nomen - - - -]   [- - - - - - - - -]
                                                                     [- - - - -]δου
        [. . . .] Καιρέλλιος Γάλλος ᵛᵛᵛ [- - - - - -]πος
   10   [Κ]ο[ί]ντος ῾Ραπίλλιος Κοίντου υ[ἱ]ὸς [nomen   5 - - - - - - -]λευς
                                                                     [- - - - -]ΕΣ[.]ΟΣ
        [Θεο]δόσιος 〚Μενοικέως Ἀβυδηνό[ς]〛
                                                                     [- - - - - - - - - - -]ς
        [. . . . .]ν Ἀγαθήνορος Ὀδησσείτης
                                                                     [- - - - - - - - -]
        Ποσιδώνιος Τειμοκράτου[ς Ὀ]δησσείτ[ης]   [- - - - - -]ος ᵛᵛ της
                                                              10 [- - - -]ευς κυβερνή-
        ἀπελεύθεροι ᵛᵛ [- - - - - - - - - - - - - - -]
   15   [Μ]ᾶρκος Ἀντώνιος [- - - - - - - - - - - - - -   Σ]τέφανος
        [Ὀ]πτάτα PAN[- - - - - - - - - - - - - - - - -]   - - - - - - - - - - - - - - -
        [Ἀ]ντωνία [- - - - - - - - - - - - - - - - - - -]
        [Ἀ]ντωνία [- - - - - - - - - - - - - - - - - - -]
        [Ἀ]ντων[ι- -]
   20   [- -]
        vacat
ii   ἐπὶ βασιλέως Θεοδώρ[ου? τοῦ]
        Μητρώνακτος μύσται ᵛ εὐσεβε[ῖς]
        Γάιος Αὐρήλιος Μάρκου υἱὸς Ἰφ[ι - - - - - -]
        Ἀγαθώνυμος Σωσιδάμου ᵛ Ὀδη[σσείτης]
   25   συνμύστης.

        Clinton.

Epigraphical Commentary
I have reprinted Clinton's epigraphical commentary, after collating it with
the stone.

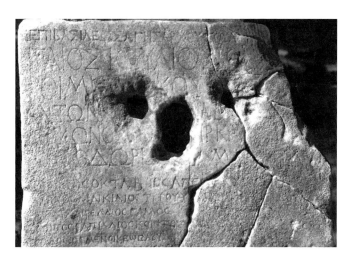

Figure 39. Record of initiation of
Thracian royalty, Romans, Odessitans, and a citizen of Abydos (46)

Line 1: Next-to-last letter before break: bottom part of a vertical stroke
at the left. Last letter: two vertical strokes.

The lacuna on the right is 0.13 m long and could have contained nine
letters at most.

Line 2: Next-to-last letter before break: apex and right oblique stroke
of the alpha.

The lacuna on the right is 0.095 m long and could have contained
three or at most four letters.

Line 3: The lacuna on the right is ca. 0.198 m long and could have
contained seven or at most eight letters.

Line 4: Next-to-last letter: vertical stroke on the left; the horizontal
attached to its lower end seems to curve upward on the right; a short stroke
joining the center of the vertical seems to slant upwards. Last letter: on the
left the lower tip of a stroke, apparently oblique.

The lacuna on the right, including the last preserved stroke, is ca.
0.17 m long and could have contained eight or at most nine letters (if one
was an iota).

Line 5: First letter: an upper apex.

The right-hand lacuna is approximately 0.14 m long, enough for approximately eight letters; the restoration would have completely filled the
space, with perhaps a little crowding.

Line 6: Letter before last break: the upper tip of the left oblique stroke and perhaps the bottom tip of the vertical of upsilon.

Following line 6 there is a vacant space of approximately the same height as line 7.

Line 7: Last letter (following epsilon): only an upper serif, apparently over the center of the letter, perhaps lambda.

Clearly a second column of names was inscribed, presumably starting at the level of column I, line 7; its first preserved line does not align with column I, line 8; other lines in this column are similarly out of alignment with column I.

Line 11: The second text in the erasure is apparently by a different hand, employing rectilinear epsilon and sigma instead of lunate. The original text is illegible.

Line 13: Of the first letter the bottom parts of two verticals can be made out in the photograph; of the second a circle; of the third the left half of a circle.

Lines 21–25 may be by a different hand. The distorted character of line 25 undoubtedly reflects the difficulty that the cutter had in carving these lines after the stele was erected, especially this last one.

Line 21: The rho is quite faint.

Line II.7: Apparent traces of letters, but they are difficult to distinguish.

Lines II.9–10: Having run out of space at the end of line 10, the cutter put the last syllable on the line above.

Commentary

See Clinton's commentary for a detailed discussion of this document. The stone contains two records of initiation, i and ii. Inscription i provides our first evidence that Thracian royalty took part in the Mysteries of the Great Gods. The only other mention of Thracian kings occurs in **53**, where freedmen of king Rhoimetalkes are listed as initiates. Gaios Ioulios Rhaskos, a hitherto unknown member of the Thracian dynasty, is the most prominent initiate in this list, judging by the size and spacing of the letters of his name. Antonia Tryphaina (*PIR²* A 900), daughter of Polemon I, king of Pontus, and wife of Kotys VIII, king of Thrace, is listed second.

Clinton concludes that Rhaskos was most likely the son of Rhoimetalkes II (*PIR²* I 517), and adds other arguments for dating the inscription to A.D. 40–45. Rhaskos was probably the last member of the Thracian royal line before Thrace became a Roman province.

Most of the *liberti* have the same *gentilicium* as Antonia Tryphaina, and were presumably her freedmen, as Clinton observes. The people listed in column II may have been members of the ship's crew (cf. line 10).

Line 1: The eponymous king is unknown, as Clinton notes.

Line 8: Possibly [Μᾶρκ]ος Μαικίλιος Τίτου υ[ἱ]ὸς [Ῥοῦφος], proconsul of Achaia before A.D. 67 (*PIR²* M 44), who was honored with an equestrian statue at Olympia before A.D. 67 (*IvO* 334).

Lines 12–13: For connections between Odessos and Samothrace, see also **171**.

Agathenor is a very popular name at Odessos.

Lines 21–25: This is a different record of initiates, added later, as Clinton notes. Eponymous kings with the name or patronymic Theodoros are attested in **1, 17**, inscription iii, and **34**, and with the name or patronymic Metronax in **6**, inscription ii, and **89**; for Theodoros and Metronax as attested on Samothracian coins, see *IG* XII.8, p. 41.

Lines II.9–10: The name of the *gubernator* was probably added later, and the final syllable of κυβερνήτης was written on the line above, as Clinton remarks.

47   Record of Roman initiates of unknown provenance, and records of initiates from Alopekonnesos and Tralles

Stele of Thasian marble, broken above and apparently below. The back is smooth. It was inscribed on both the left and right sides, but the letters are now badly damaged. Found in Chora, in the house of Phardys, after being reused in the church Ayios Stephanos. A round building with a door, flanked by a snake-entwined torch on either side, is carved on the front. Archaeological Museum of Samothrace, Hall B, inv. 68.55.

H. 0.51 m, W. 0.44–0.445 m, Th. 0.115 m; L.H. 0.01 m.

Edd. Reinach 1892, p. 200, no. 3; [Mommsen, *CIL* III Suppl. I.3 (1893) 12323]; Kern 1893, p. 360, no. 6.A; Fredrich, *IG* XII.8 190.

Cf. Lehmann and Lehmann 1973, pp. 25–47, esp. pp. 32–33, with photograph of front, fig. 24; Roux, *Samothrace* 7, pp. 32, 115–116, with photographs, figs. 31, 79 (front).

1st century B.C.

Side A *(in latere dextro)*   Side B *(in latere sinistro)*

i
[myst]ai [piei]
M. Livius
Pamplus,
Babullius
5   [P]amphilus M. l.
[A]stymeno[s]
ii   [ἐ]πὶ βασιλέω[ς]
[Δ]ημοκλείου[ς]
[το]ῦ Πυθογέ-
10   [ν]ου Ἀλωπε-
[κον]νήσιος
[μ]ύστης εὐ-
[σ]εβὴς
Ἀττινᾶς
15   Διογένου
[κ]αὶ μύστη[ς]
[Ἀ]νδρόμαχ[ος]
Κρ]ατέρου,
Ἀπολλών[ιος *vel* -ίδης]
20   Μηνοφαν[- -].
[μ]ύστης εὐσ[εβὴς]
['Έ]νδημος?

iv   [ἐ]πὶ βασιλέ-
ως Δημο-
κλείους
τοῦ Πυθο-
35   γένους·
Τραλλιανο[ί]·
μύστης
[ε]ὐσεβὴς
[ὁ] κατα<γ>γε[λ]-
40   εὺς τοῦ [ἱ]-
 εροῦ καὶ στ[ε]-
φανείτου
ἀγῶνος
τῶν Πυθ[ί]-
45   ων καὶ ἱε-
ραγωγὸς
Αματοκος
[Δ]ημητρί[ου],
. . . .
50   [- - - - - - - - - - -]
- - - - - - - - - - -

μύστης εὐσε[βὴς]

[. .]ΙΚΟΣ ΤΟΜ[. ³⁻⁴.]

vacat spatium 3 vss.

iii   25   ἐπὶ βασιλ[έως]

[Δη]μοκλέου

[τ]οῦ Πυθο[γένου]

[μύστ]αι [εὐσε]-

[βεῖς - - - - - - -]

30   [- - - - - - - - - -]

- - - - - - - - - -

Fredrich. **11** [κο]νήσιος Fredrich. **19** Dimitrova, Ἀπολλών[ιος] Fredrich. **20** Μηνοφάν[ους] Fredrich.

Epigraphical Commentary

The inscription is now badly defaced, and I have mostly reprinted Fredrich's text.

Line 49: Third and fourth letters: apparently a triangle and a circle.

Commentary

The right side of the stone contains three records of initiates, one in Latin (inscription i) and two in Greek (ii, iii), of which ii mentions two initiates from Alopekonnesos. The left side contains one record of Greek initiates (iv) from Tralles. The ethnics of the other initiates are unknown. All of the Greek lists are dated to the same year, but the date of the Latin list is unclear.

Perhaps the most striking feature of this stone is the relief with the round building. There are three other such stelai (**56–58**). They all mention Cyzicene initiates, and Phyllis Lehmann concluded that the building represented is a symbol of Kyzikos: a round building is depicted on Cyzicene coins (p. 37, fig 26) and on a funerary stele from Kyzikos (p. 43, fig. 27). The present inscription, however, does not mention Cyzicene initiates. This might mean that the text is not contemporary with the relief or that Cyzicene initiates were mentioned on the part of the stone that is now lost (on any side of the stele), including the upper part of the front face. The other possibility would be not to assume a definite connection between the relief and Kyzikos; see also *ad* **56**.

Lines 14–15: A certain Ἀττινᾶς Διογένους is mentioned in *IOSPE* I² 394, found at Chersonesos on the north coast of the Black Sea and dated to A.D. 140. It is unlikely that he was the same person.

Lines 19–20: A certain Ἀπολλώνιος Μηνοφάντου occurs in an Ephesian list of *kouretes eusebeis* (*I.Ephesos* 447, undated), but no identification is possible for lack of further information. Moreover, the names matching the remains of the stone are quite common.

Line 24, end: Perhaps an ethnic like Τομίτης.

Lines 34–35: The abbreviations ΠΥΘ and ΠΥΘΟ are numismatically attested for Samothracian officials; see *IG* XII.8, p. 41.

Lines 39–46: Ἀματοκος Δημητρίου was announcer of the *Pythia* celebrated in Tralles; cf. Fredrich, *ad* line 44). The term *katangeleus* is synonymous with *theoros* as a festival announcer (cf. *Syll.*³ 635.32; *OGIS* 456;

Boesch 1908, p. 11, cited by Fredrich; and above, Chap. 1, pp. 13–15). Apart from festival announcer, Ἀματοκος Δημητρίου was also *hieragogos*. This I take also to be synonymous with *theoros*, as an envoy sent to a sanctuary to perform a sacred mission; see below, *ad* **50**. The name Amatokos is Thracian, better attested as Amadokos (Detschew 1957, pp. 14–15).

AEGEAN ISLANDS

With regard to Kos see **120**, and possibly **122**, line 1. A new record of initiates found in 2005 provides information that initiates from Andros visited Samothrace; its publication is in preparation.

48   Record of initiates from Thasos[49] and Philippi   Fig. 40

Plaque of Thasian marble with incised akroteria and cornice, broken below. The back is rough-picked. A rectangular cutting is visible on top. Found in the Late Roman floor of the Sacristy on July 10, 1939, secondarily used as a pavement slab. Archaeological Museum of Samothrace, inv. 39.547.

H. 0.55 m, W. 0.40 m, Th. 0.08 m; L.H. 0.035 m (line 1), 0.025–0.03 m (line 2), 0.025 m (lines 3–5), 0.02 m (lines 6–13).

Edd. Lehmann-Hartleben 1940, pp. 346–348, fig. 25; Fraser, *Samothrace* 2.1 (1960) 59.

Cf. *BullÉp* 1944 151a; Robert 1963, pp. 67–69; Robert and Robert, *BullÉp* 1964 378.

2nd–3rd century A.D.?

Figure 40. Record of initiates from Thasos and Philippi (**48**)

in cornice:	ἀγαθῇ τύχῃ
below cornice:	ἐπὶ βασιλέως Ἰου-
	νίου Ἡρώδου μύσται
	εὐσεβεῖς Θάσιοι
5	Ἀρισταγόρας Εἰσιδώρου
	Μ. Ἀντώνιος Ὀπτᾶτος Φιλιπ<π>εύ-
	ς
	vacat 0.035 m
	δοῦλοι Ἀρισταγόρου
	Φιλούμενος
	Μαγιανός
10	Φιλόστοργος
	[Ν]υμφικός *leaf*
	[- - - - - -]Ρ
	[- - - - - -]ΙΣ
	[- - - - - - - - - - - - - -]

Fraser. 7 Ἀρισταγόρα Fraser, Ἀρισταγόρου *lapis.*

Epigraphical Commentary
The lettering is highly decorated. Fraser notes (p. 110, n. 1) that the style is typical of northern Greece, and is found in 3rd-century A.D. Thasian inscriptions.

49. For other material pertaining to initiates from Thasos, see **41**, **51**, **53**, **62**.

Line 6: The second pi of Φιλιπ<π>εύς is omitted. Lehmann-Hartleben (p. 348; see also Fraser, p. 110, n. 4) thinks that the letters of this line are "sloppier," but Fraser sees no difference in style. I tend to agree with Fraser's conclusion. The cutter left out a letter and squeezed the final sigma below the upsilon, but this may have been due to lack of space.

Commentary

This is a list of initiates from Thasos and Philippi.

Lines 2–3: Fraser remarks that the eponym is otherwise unknown.

Line 4: Fraser thinks that the plural form Θάσιοι is illogical, since there is only one Thasian initiate. Lehmann-Hartleben (p. 348) believes that the stele was originally meant for a Thasian, but M. Antonius Optatus from Philippi was "later added to the stone (probably by a lucrative trick of the administration)." It seems to me that we need not assume that Optatus was added later (see Epigraphical Commentary, *ad* line 6), but the form Θάσιοι can be explained by the fact that both Ἀρισταγόρας and his slaves were Thasians who were initiated.

Lines 8–end: None of the slaves' names are attested elsewhere on Thasos.

Fraser notes that this is the only list of Thasian *mystai* (p. 110), but **41, 51, 53,** and **62** record other Thasian initiates.

49   Records of initiates from Chios[50] and Rome

Stele of Thasian marble, preserved on all sides, with two Greek inscriptions on the front side, another Greek inscription on the left, and one in Latin on the right side. The inscription was found in Solinari, on the north shore of Samothrace, some 4 km east of the sanctuary. Archaeological Museum of Samothrace, courtyard, Ephoreia inv. C 81.2.

H. 0.94 m, W. 0.315 m, Th. 0.12 m; L.H. 0.013–0.017 m (side A, inscription i, lines 1–11), 0.01 m (side A, inscription i, lines 12–36; side A, inscription ii; side B), 0.022–0.025 m (side C).

Ed. Skarlatidou 1993, with photograph (*SEG* XLI, 717; *AÉ* 1992 502).

Cf. *BullÉp* 1994 456; Clinton 2001, p. 32, n. 22.

2nd–1st century B.C.?

Side A

```
i     - - - - - - - - - - 3–4 lines - - - - - - - - - -
          [- - - - - - - - - - - - - - -]
          [- - - - - - -]ΤΑΤ.[- - - -]
          [- - - - - - - - - - - - - - -]
          στε[φανῶσ]αι τοὺς δι-
    5     κ[αστὰς ? Λ[- - -]ΤΙ . Ο [- -]
          Μενά[νδρου κ]αὶ Σάτυρ[ον]
          Σατύρου χρυσῶι στε-
          φάν[ω]ι ἀρετῆς ἕνεκ[α]
          καὶ φι[λο]τιμίας τῆς εἰς ἑ-
    10    αυτοὺς· μύσται καὶ ἐφό-
          πται εὐσεβεῖς
```

50. For other material pertaining to initiates from Chios, see **38, 49, 89.**

vacat ca. 1 vs.

	Ἀθήναιος	Δημῶναξ
	Διοσκουρίδης	Μητρόδωρος
	Διονυσόδωρος	Ἀρτέμων
15	Φιλόδημος	Ἀντίπατρο[ς]
	Ἀθήναιος	Νέων
	Ἀπολλώνιος	Ἀγγελῆς
	Διονύσιος	Θεόδοτος
	Φίλων	Δημήτριος
20	Ἀπολλώνιος	Ἀγγελῆς
	Διονύσιος	Νουμήνιος
	Φιλό[ξε]νος	Οὔριος
	Νικήρατος	Ἀγγελῆς
	Εὐριπίδης	Ἀσκληπιάδης
25	Διονύσιος	Θόας
	Ἀναξίδοτ[ο]ς	Θεοφάνη[ς]
	Μένων	Θεόκριτος
	Ξένων	Θεοφάνης
	Ἀγγελῆς	Κράτων
30	Ἀντίπατρος	Νικίας
	Δημέας	Γοργίας
	Τιμησίπολις	Στέφανος
	Μενεκράτης	Ἀπελλικῶν
	Ἀγγελῆς	Φιλιστῆς
35	Ἡρακλέων	Θέων
	Σωσίβιος	*vacat ca. 1 vs.*

vacat ca. 1 vs.

ii   Χίων

Οἱ στρατευσάμενοι ἐν τοῖς ληστο-
φυλακικοῖς πλοίοις τὸ δεύτερον ὑπὸ
ἄρχοντα Ἡράκλειτον τὸν Δωροθέου

5 [γ]ονῆ δὲ Ἴωνος μύσται εὐσεβεῖς

Θεοφάνης	ἐφόπται
Διοσκουρίδης	Ν[ι]κίας
[. ᶜᵃ·⁵ .]ιος	Ἡρακλεώτης
[...⁷⁻⁸...]δης	[Συ?]νήθιος

10 [- - - - - - - - - - - - - - - - -]

Side B *(in latere dextro)*

iii   Χίω[ν]

[Οἱ σ]τρατευ[σά]-
[με]νοι ἐν τοῖς
[λη]στοφυλακ[ι]-
5 [κο]ῖς πλοίοις ὑ[πὸ]
[ἄ]ρχοντα Ἡρά-
[κ]λειτον Δω[ρο]-
[θ]έου γονῆι δ[ὲ]
[Ἴ]ωνος
10 [μ]ύσται εὐσε-
[βε]ῖς ὑπὸ δεκά-

[τ]αρχον Σαραπ[ί]-
[ω]να καὶ οἱ ὑπὸ δ[ε]-
[κά]ταρχον Μηνᾶν
15   Θασίων, [Ἀ]γγελῆ[ς]
Ἀγγελῆς, Ἀγγελῆς
[Σ]ωσίστρ[ατο]ς
Σωσίστρατος
[Θ]ευδᾶς, Ἡρακλέω[ν]
20   Μύρμηξ, Διονύσι[ος]
Πάνταυχος, Ἡρακ[λ . . .]
[Κ]αλλικλῆς, ΜΑΝ[. . .]
Παρμενίσκος
[Ἀ]πολλοφάνης
25   . ΟΜ[. . .⁵⁻⁸. . .]Σ
[.]Α[. . .⁵⁻⁸. . .]ΟΣ
[Δ]η[μήτ]ριος
[Ἀ]σκληπιάδης
[Ἡ]ρακλέων
30   [Π]ραξαγόρας
Μεν[. . .]ος, Ἡρακ[λῆς?]
[Ἐ]ξήκεστος
Διοσκουρίδης
[Ἐ]πόπται
35   Ἡράκλειτος
Σαραπίων
Ἡρακλέων
Ἀθηνίων
Πουλυδάμας
40   Δημήτριος
Ἀνδρόμαχος
Μηνόφιλος
Θεοφάνης
            vacat
Ἐπίγονος

Side C *(in latere sinistro)*

iv   [- - - -^ca. 10^ - - - -]Vol(tinia) · eq(ues) · m(ystes) pius
[*v.*?]C · Aninius(?) C. · f. · eq(ues) Sab(atina) m(ystes) · pius
[. . .].DUS · s(ervus) · m(ystes) pius

Skarlatidou. **i.4** στε[φ]α[vo]ῦσι Πυτ[- -] Skarlatidou. **i.5** [- - - - - - - - -]ο[. . .] Skarlatidou. **ii.8** Ἡρακλέων Skarlatidou, Ἡρακλεώτης Dimitrova. **ii.9** [- - - -]ν . θιος Skarlatidou, [Συ?]νήθιος Dimitrova. **iii.15** Θάσων Skarlatidou, Θασίων Dimitrova. **iii.20**
ΕΥΡΥ[- -] Skarlatidou, Μύρμηξ Dimitrova. **iii.21–22** Dimitrova. **iii.27** [-]η[.^ca. 4^.]ης
Skarlatidou, [Δ]η[μήτ]ριος Dimitrova. **iv.2** [1–2] Caninius Skarlatidou.

Epigraphical Commentary

Lines 1–6 on side A are badly worn. The lettering of the Greek records
is similar, consistent with a date in the 2nd or 1st century B.C. Horizontal
lines are drawn between lines, as Skarlatidou notes (p. 155).

Lines A.10–11: The letters of the heading μύσται καὶ ἐφόπται εὐσεβεῖς are somewhat crowded and less regular than the preceding text.

Line B.20: First letter: The mu is damaged, with only its left diagonal visible; a narrow bottom horizontal is discernible below the level of the line.

Commentary

See Skarlatidou's commentary for a detailed discussion of the document and its historical context. The stele contains one decree and four lists of initiates, three Greek and one Latin. The precise relation between the decree and the first record of initiation is unclear. Judging by the crowding of the rubric in lines 10–11 it would seem that the decree was original, and the record was added later. Skarlatidou considers the first list to be the earliest on the basis of its lettering, and she dates it to the second half of the 2nd century B.C. The other two Greek lists enumerate Chian initiates, who fought in anti-pirate ships, *lestophylakika ploia*. These records are dated by Skarlatidou to 80–60 B.C., the time of the Mithridatic wars, when Greek cities joined Rome in her actions against the pirates. The editors of *BullÉp* suggest that the anti-pirate patrol may have consisted of light and swift ships, presumably *triemioliai* (small war galleys), and compare their function with that of the *phylakides* ships of Athens and Rhodes (cf. Robert, *Hellenica* 2, pp. 123–126). The commander of a ship is called *archon* (side A, inscription ii, line 4; side B, inscription ii, line 6) and *dekatarchos* (side B, inscription ii, lines 11–14). The *archon* is the chief officer, attested also in Rhodes as a commander of small units and light ships, as the editors of *BullÉp* note. The term *dekatarchos*, commander of 10, is more difficult to define in this context. We only know that he was a junior officer in the Rhodian fleet, who probably replaced the *pentakontarchos* in smaller units (Casson 1995, p. 309). Furthermore, the term *dekatarchos* is attested in a Rhodian document (*IG* XII Suppl. [1939] 210, as Skarlatidou notes), which probably refers to the crew of a *triemiolia*, as Casson remarks (p. 309, n. 39). Thus it is possible that the anti-pirate patrol ships in question were indeed *triemioliai*.

The first list may have included Chian initiates as well, in view of the prominence of the name Ἀγγελῆς, which is extremely typical of Chios. Its initial part is a decree in honor of certain benefactors, one of whom is named Σάτυρος Σατύρου. It is curious that all of the Greek initiates are listed with a single name, perhaps in order to save space.

Line ii.4: Both Ἡράκλειτος and Δωρόθεος are well-attested names in Chios.

Line B.14: The name Μηνᾶς is not attested in Chios, to my knowledge, but is otherwise common in Ionia.

Line C.2: I see a medial dot between C and Aninius, but this implies that there was a vacant space before it. Caninius cannot be excluded. Both C. Aninius, C. filius, and Caninius, C. filius, are commonly attested and no identification is possible. As far as the date of this list is concerned, it is possible that it was inscribed before the right side of the stele was, and therefore the terminus post quem would be around the middle of the 2nd century B.C., the approximate terminus post quem of side A, inscription i.

50   Record of initiates from Rhodes,[51] Xanthos, and Ephesos   Fig. 41

Stele of Thasian marble, inscribed on front and back, preserved on the right (with respect to the front, side A). Found in Chora, now in the Archaeological Museum of Samothrace, courtyard. No inv. no.

H. 0.25 m, W. 0.22 m, Th. 0.05 m; L.H. 0.011 m.

Edd. Rubensohn 1892, p. 233, no. 3; Kern 1893, p. 365, no. 9; [Michel 1900, no. 1142]; van Gelder 1900, pp. 466, nos. 107, 108; Fredrich, *IG* XII.8 186; [Dittenberger, *Syll.*³ 1052a–b]; Hiller von Gaertringen, *IG* XII Suppl. (1939), p. 149; *I.Perinthos* (1998) 15.

Cf. Robert 1963, p. 67.

Early 1st century B.C. (side A), ca. 137–134 B.C.? (side B)

Side A

```
        [ἐπὶ βασιλέως]
        Πυθίωνος τοῦ Ἀριδήλου
        Ῥοδίων ἱεροποιοὶ
        μύσται καὶ ἐπόπται
  5       εὐσεβεῖς·
        Σωσικλῆς Εὐκράτευς
        Πεισικράτης Τιμαράτου
        Δαμάτριος Ἀμφοτεροῦ
        συνέγδαμοι·
 10     Καλλικράτης Δαματρίου
        Ἀναξικράτης Ἀναξικράτε[υς]
        Θεύδωρος Ἡραγόρ[α]
        Ἰσίδοτος [- - - - - - - - -]
        Δαμασα[- - - - - - - - -]
 15     Ἀγασ[- - - - - - - - -]
        - - - - - - - - - - - - - - - - - -
```

Side B

```
        ἐπὶ βα[σιλέως- - - - - - - - - - - - - -]
        ὡς δὲ ἐν Ῥόδ[ωι ἐπὶ ἱερέως]
        τοῦ Ἁλίου [Ἀριστ?]άκου
             Ῥ ο δ ί ω ν
 20     ἱεροποιοὶ [μύσται ε]ὐσεβε[ῖς·]
        Δαλι[άδας Ἀντιπά]τρο[υ]
        Ἀριστο[γένης Νικομ]άχο[υ]
             ν[αῦται]
        Διον[ύσι]ος Ἐφέσιος
 25     Θήρων Ξάνθιος
        Εὐσύης Ἐφέσιος
        [Ἀγ]αθάνγελος
        [. . ᶜᵃ·⁶ .]ιος ἐν Ῥόδωι
        [ἀγορανομ]οῦντος
 30     [- - - - - - - - - - - - - - - -]
```

Fredrich. **18** *supplevit* Hiller, cf. *IG* XII.1 1089 (*apud* Fredrich). **25** Περίνθιος Fredrich, Ξάνθιος Dimitrova.

51. With regard to Rhodes, see also **51** for certain initiates and **57** for possible initiates.

Figure 41. Record of initiates from
Rhodes, Xanthos, and Ephesos (50):
side A *(left)*, side B *(right)*

Epigraphical Commentary

The lettering of both sides is somewhat inelegant. Side A is almost entirely
obliterated: only the letters that are not underlined are now barely discernible.
Fredrich believes that the inscription on side B, written in even less elegant,
larger letters, is later than that on A, but it may be earlier; see *ad* line 18.

   Line 25: Ξάνθιος *lapis*.

Commentary

Both inscriptions represent lists of Rhodian *mystai* and *hieropoioi*, accompanied by *synegdamoi* in the list on side A and *nautai* in that on side B. The
officials listed on side A are both *mystai* and *epoptai*. This has bearing upon
the issue of the interval between the two stages of initiation. Other inscriptions (**56**, **67**, **89**, and **155**) also record people who are both *mystai* and *epoptai*.
None of these documents, however, provides indubitable proof that *myesis*
and *epopteia* took place on the same day; see Chapter 9, pp. 246–248.

   As for the office of *hieropoios*, the same title is also recorded for Cyzicene
initiates in **56** and **58**. Fraser assumes that the *hieropoioi* in **58** are Cyzicene
cult officials (*ad* no. 29, p. 82). Robert, on the other hand, in discussing the
examples of *hieropoioi* on Samothrace, concludes that their duty corresponds
to that of sacred envoys, elsewhere called theoroi or *synthytai*. He points
out that parallels for this usage are found in *IG* XII.1 701 and *Delphinion*
141. This hypothesis seems rather plausible. Moreover, two of the Cyzicene
hieropoioi appear in **10**, a list of presumable theoroi-proxenoi; see Commentary. The preferred terminology in documents issued by Samothracian
officials was apparently theoroi, while the designation of sacred envoys in
individual records of initiation was given according to the terminology
used in their respective cities (see also above, pp. 13–15, 120–121. This is
consistent with the fact that the title *hieropoios* is only found in individual
records of initiates, never on blocks recording theoroi-proxenoi. The term

used for an envoy from Tralles in **47** is *hieragogos;* this seems to be yet another way that a home city designated a sacred envoy; see *ad* **47**.

Line 2: The same eponymous official may be attested in **13**, inscription ii.

Line 6: Σωσικλῆς Εὐκράτ[ε]υς is attested in *Lindos* II 294.II.40, dated to 85 B.C. He served as a *hierothytes.* Presumably he is the same person, since the name is not attested elsewhere. This gives an approximate date for the inscription in the beginning of the 1st century B.C.

Line 9: συνέγδαμοι should be understood as private "fellow travelers," as attested in literary texts, cf. LSJ, s.v. συνέκδημος. They too were presumably *mystai* and *epoptai,* but are contrasted with the official delegates. This may be taken as additional evidence in support of interpreting the meaning of *hieropoioi* as "sacred envoys." The hierarchy exhibited in this inscription is paralleled in **14**, where only the first few of the *mystai* are *theoroi,* and the rest are *symmystai* and *akolouthoi.*

Line 14: In view of the rarity of names that would fit the remains on the stone, a plausible restoration would be Δαμασα[γόρας], attested partially in another Rhodian inscription, *NSER* 5.I.6.

Line 18: There are numerous other examples of dating Rhodian inscriptions by the priest of the Sun. The cult of the Sun was celebrated at Rhodes with a festival by the name of Ἁλίεια. Hiller von Gaertringen's restoration of the name [Ἀριστ?]άκου is based on *IG* XII.1 1089, which has the same eponymous official; cf. also *IG* XII.1 1247. *SEG* XXXIX 747 provides additional information:

Ἀρίστακος Χαριδάμου
   καθ᾽ υοθεσίαν δὲ
Ἀγήνακτος
   ἱερατεύσας
Ἁλίωι.

Finkielsztejn (2001, p. 195) dates Aristakos I to ca. 137/6–135/4. If this date is correct, then either the inscription on side B should be dated before that on side A, to the second half of the 2nd century B.C., or one has to assume that the priest of Helios with the name Aristakos mentioned on B is a different person, perhaps a descendant of the one in *SEG* XXXIX 747.

Line 24: A Διονύσιος Ἐφέσιος is attested as a Rhodian metic in *ASAtene* 22 168.21 B.I, line 4, tentatively dated to the early 1st century B.C. It is possible that he was the same person.

Line 25: This is the first instance of the ethnic Xanthios attested in Samothrace.

Line 28: An ethnic modifying Ἀγαθάνγελος is to be expected; cf. *Tit. Cam.* 282, 22, line 3, [Ἀρ]ιστομέδ[ης Θηβ?]αῖος ἐν Ῥόδ[ωι. Presumably ἐν Ῥόδ[ωι refers to all of the sailors listed above.

51   Record of initiates from Rhodes, Antioch, Priapos,   Fig. 42
        Thasos, and Arsinoe

Stele of Thasian marble, inscribed with uneven letters. It was built into the church of St. John in Loutra. The inscription is now lost.

H. 0.41 m, W. 0.23 m, Th. 0.05 m; L.H.?

Edd. Conze 1880, p. 96, no. 12; Fredrich, *IG* XII.8 184.

Figure 42. Record of initiates from Rhodes, Antioch, Priapos, Thasos, and Arsinoe (51). Conze 1880, p. 96, no. 12

Cf. Robert and Robert, *BullÉp* 1958 270, p. 256; Robert 1963, pp. 62, 67–69.

Date?

[μύστ]αι εὐσεβε[ῖς]·
[- - - -]κλῆς Φιλάγρου Ῥόδ[ιος]
[- - - -]ς Ἱέρωνος Ἀντιοχεύς
[- - - -]ος Ἀφροδισίου Ἀντιοχεύς
5   [- - - -]ς Διογένους Πριαπηνός
[- - - -]τόμαχος καὶ
[- - - -]ος καὶ
[- - - -]ς Στρατοκλέους
[- - - -]ίων Μίκα.
10   [μύ]σται εὐσεβεῖς·
[- - - -]Μίκα Θάσιος,
[- - - -]ς Ἀριστοδάμο[υ]
[Ἀ]ρσινοεύς
[ἀγοραν]ομοῦντος
15   [- -?- -Ἀρ]χικλέους
- - - - - -?- - - - - - - -

Fredrich. 1 εὐσεβεῖς Fredrich. 2 Ῥόδ[ιος] Fredrich. 5 Πριαπηνός Fredrich. 14 [ἀγορανο]μοῦντος Fredrich.

Epigraphical Commentary

Conze's facsimile gives an idea of the lettering of the inscription. He reports that the first five lines have large uneven letters, the following eight even larger letters, and the last two the smallest letters, but he gives no dimensions. Judging by the facsimile, the letters were probably carved by the same cutter.

Lines 1, 2, 5: The upsilon, omicron, and delta, dotted in Fredrich's text, seem unambiguous, though damaged.

Line 6: First letter: top horizontal.

Line 8: First letter: bottom horizontal.

Line 10: First letter: top and bottom horizontal.

Line 13: First letter: part of an upper circle.

Line 14: First letter: medial circle, with the right position for omicron.

Commentary

It is unclear how many records of initiates this document contains. The headings *mystai eusebeis* are probably attested in lines 1 and 10, though line 1 may have had *epoptai eusebeis* as well. If so, those listed may have been part of the same record. The initiates are from Rhodes, Antioch, Priapos, Thasos, and Arsinoe. Fredrich was uncertain about the identification of Antioch and Arsinoe, but Robert favors Antioch-on-the-Meander and Arsinoe near Patara.

Line 9: The name Mikas is characteristic of Thasos, as Robert notes.

Line 15: Since the inscription is lost, we do not know how much is missing to the left and below, and whether Ἀρ]χικλέους is the official's first name or his patronymic.

ASIA MINOR

For material relating to Aspendos, see **31**; to Keramos, **13**, inscription ii; to Magnesia, **53**; to Pergamon, **89**; to Sardis, **17**, inscription iii. For a list of possible Kalchedonian initiates, see **134**. For probable initiates from from Aigai in Cilicia, **53**; from Antioch-on-the-Meander, **51**; from Arsinoe near Patara, **51**. For Stratonikeia, see **17**, inscription ii for certain initiates and **166** for possible initiates. For initiates from Smyrna, see **63**; from Xanthos, **50**.

52   Record of initiates from Abydos

The text of the inscription is based on a copy made by the Swedish diplomat and orientalist Johan D. Åkerblad (1763–1819). Its dimensions are unknown.

Edd. [Boeckh, *CIG* II.1 (1832) 2160, with add. p. 1021]; [Fredrich, *IG* XII.8 183]; [*IMT* 77].

Cf. Fraser, *Samothrace* 2.1 (1960), p. 34, n. 1 (lines 1–3).

Date?

```
       ναυαρχοῦντος Λεόντιδος
       τοῦ Λεόν[τι]δος· Ἀβυδηνῶν
       μύσται εὐσεβεῖς·
       Ἀπολλοφάνης Διοδώρου
   5   Μενέδημος Μενεδήμου
       Φιλῖνος Φιλίνου νεώτερος
       Ἀν[τί]μαχος Ν[εί]κωνος
       Ἀπολλ[ών]ιος Δη[μ]έου
       Ἀνδρόνικος Ἀπολλωνίου
  10   Θέων Δημητρίου
       [Ἕ]ρμων Δημητρίου
       Κέρδων [Ἀ]ν[τ]ιμάχου
       Εὐήμερος Λεόν[τ]ιδος
       Βι[θ]υς Λεόντιδος
  15   Ποσίδεος Λεόντιδος
       Ὀπ[τ]ης? Μενίσκου
       ΓΗΡΟΥΣ? - - - - - -
       - - - - - - - - - - - - - - -
```

Fredrich.

Commentary

This is a list of initiates from Abydos (for Abydos see also **46**). It is possible that the initiates listed in lines 10–11 and in lines 13–15 were related, perhaps as brothers. The latter group may be related to the *nauarch*.

53   Record of Roman initiates of unknown provenance,   Fig. 43
         and of initiates from Ilion, Thasos, Byzantion, Sirrhai,
         Magnesia, Alexandria, Styberra, Aigai, and Thrace

Fragment of a block of Thasian marble, broken at top and bottom. The back was cut off and smoothed for shipping purposes in the 19th century. Found in secondary context, now in Paris, Musée du Louvre, inv. Ma. 4189. I saw the stone in July 2001.

Figure 43. Record of Roman initiates of unknown provenance, and of initiates from Ilion, Thasos, Byzantion, Sirrhai, Magnesia, Alexandria, Styberra, Aigai, and Thrace (53). Photo © M. and P. Chuzeville, courtesy Musée du Louvre, Department of Greek, Roman, and Etruscan Antiquities

H. 0.34 m, W. 0.48 m, Th. 0.08 m; L.H. 0.01–0.015 m.
Ed. Fredrich, *IG* XII.8 206.
Cf. *BullÉp* 1911, p. 321; Robert 1963, p. 65, with n. 7; Robert and Robert, *BullÉp* 1964 395; Robert 1966, p. 79, n. 6; Cole 1984, pp. 99–100; Habicht 1986, p. 97; Tacheva 1995, pp. 459–467 (*SEG* XLV 831); *SEG* LI 2094.

1st century B.C.–1st century A.D.

[. . .^{ca. 8}. . .Τιβέ]ριος Ἰούλιος [Εὐφ]ρόσυνος,
Σαλλούστιος Ῥοῦφος, Γάϊος Ἰούνιος Λυσίμαχος,
Γάϊος Ὀκταούιος Βάσος, Τίτος Λέπιδος Νύ[μ]-
φιος· Ἀντιφάνης Ἀπολλωνίου Ἰλιεύς, Κάδμος Θάσιο[ς],
5 Ἀπολλώνιος Ἀντιφάνου Ἰλιεύς, Ἀντίφιλος Ἀντιφίλου
Βυζάντιος· Δίδυμος Διδύμου Ἀλεξανδρεύς, Κρόν[ι]-
ος Ἡλιοδώρου Ἀλεξανδρεύς, Μενέμαχος Μητροδώρου Βυζάντιος· Βοιωτὸς Βριαρέως Σειραῖος,
Ἀλέξανδρος Ἰκεσίου Μάγνης· Δημήτριος Ἀπολλωνί-
10 ου Ἀλεξανδρεύς, Πρεῖμος Ἀπολλωνίου Ἀλεξανδρε[ύς],
Κόλλις Κόλλιδος ὁ καὶ Μάρεις· Ἀντιφάνης Διοσκουρ[ί]-
δου Στυβερραῖος, Διονύσιος κυβερνήτης Αἰγαῖος, Μᾶρκος Ἀντώ-
[ν]ιος Ἡγησίας, ἀπελεύθεροι Ῥοιμητάλκου β[ασι]λέ[ως]
vacat Πειθ[. . .^{ca. 10}. . . .]νικος, Διογένης[- - - - -^{ca. 10–15}- - - - - -]
15 [- -]ίου, Σκο[- - - -^{ca. 10}- - - -]
- -

Fredrich. **1** [Εὐφ]ρόσυνος praenomen Fredrich. **12** Ἀντ[ώ]- Fredrich.

Epigraphical Commentary
The letters are uneven and inelegant.
    Line 1: There are no traces of a praenomen in the end of this line.
    Line 2: Last letter: unclear traces.
    Line 7: Last letter: top left part of a circle.
    Line 12: Last letter: clear omega.

Commentary

The inscription records the names of Romans, Greeks from various cities (notably Alexandria, Ilion, and Byzantion), and a group of freedmen of the client king Rhoimetalkes of Thrace. The Samothracian gods were certainly worshipped at Ilion, but their sanctuary is not positively identified.[52] Although the title *mystai eusebeis* is missing, it is almost certain that the people listed in this text were initiates. The heading *apeleutheroi* lends considerable probability to this assumption, since names of slaves and freedmen are attested in numerous records of initiates. It is unclear which Rhoimetalkes is meant, as Fredrich observes. For members of the Thracian royal family, cf. **46**.

Line 1: Fredrich assumes that the praenomen of Sallustius Rufus must have been written at the end of this line. The remains on the stone, however, do not confirm this assumption. Moreover, the name Sallustius Rufus occurs also in an inscription from Aphrodisias (Cormack 1962, no. 517, Imperial period), without a praenomen; the inscription honors the daughter of a senator named Sallustius Rufus. It is unclear whether he is related to the Samothracian initiate.

Line 3: A certain Gaius Octavius Bassus, son of Gaius, is attested in an undated Delian inscription (*I.Delos* 2488), but no identification is possible.

Lines 6–7: Robert assumes that Egyptian Alexandria is meant since the names Δίδυμος, Κρόνιος, and Ἡλιόδωρος are frequently attested in Egypt. Κόλλις and Μάρης in line 11 are also typical of Egypt, as Fredrich notes.

Line 8: Presumably Σειραῖος is to be understood as referring to Macedonian Sirrhai, as Hiller von Gaertringen (*apud* Fredrich) and Robert remark. Robert notes, moreover, that the rare name Βοιωτός occurs in another document from Sirrhai (*SEG* XXX 590). Βριαρέως is a hapax.

Lines 9–10: Habicht notes that Demetrios, son of Apollonios, from Alexandria, may be the same as the homonymous sculptor from Alexandria, attested in two Messenian dedications, roughly dated to the 1st century B.C.–1st century A.D. (*IG* V.1 1461 and *Praktika* 1962, p. 112 [= *SEG* XXIII 225]; cf. *SEG* XXXVI 789.

Line 12: Robert suggests that Aigai in Cilicia is meant, since it was an important port.

54   Record of initiates from Alexandria Troas

Fragment of Thasian marble, found in Palaiopolis, now lost. The inscription was on the left side of the stone; the right side was still in the ground at the time of Fredrich's edition.

H. 1.00 m, W. 0.96 m, Th. 0.22 m; L.H.?

Edd. Kern 1893, p. 373, no. 19; Fredrich, *IG* XII.8 223; [*IMT* 446]; [Ricl, *I.Alexandreia Troas* (1997), p. 224, no. T 117, 2].

41/30–27/12 B.C.

> ἐπὶ βασιλέω[ς]
> Μητροδώρ[ου]
> τοῦ Μητρ[ο]-
> δώρου μ[ύσ]-

52. This is the current opinion of Brian Rose, the director of the excavations at Troy (see Rose 2003). Cf. the recent discussion by Mark Lawall (2003).

5   ται εὐσεβ[εῖς]
    Τρωαδεῖς
    Ἰουλ[ι]ε[ῖ]ς·
    - - - - - -

Fredrich.

Commentary

The eponym is otherwise unattested. The date of the inscription is based
on the fact that Alexandria Troas was named Colonia Iulia (line 7) between
41/30 B.C., when the Roman colony was founded, and 27/12 B.C., when
Augustus sent additional colonists and changed the city's appellation to
Colonia Augusta; see *I.Alexandreia Troas*, pp. 224–225.

55   Records of Greek and Roman initiates from Alexandria   Fig. 44
       Troas

Block of white marble, broken on top, inscribed on the front (side A),
left (side B), and back (side C). The right side might have been inscribed,
too, but is now very worn. Found alongside the path from the Propylon of
Ptolemy II to the city, about 10 m inside the back gate to the sanctuary.
Archaeological Museum of Samothrace, courtyard, Ephoreia inv. C 81.3.
      H. 0.51 m, W. 0.71 m, Th. 0.55 m; L.H. 0.04 m (side A), 0.02–0.025 m
(sides B, C).

Unpublished.

Middle of 2nd century B.C.–1st century A.D.?

                         Side A

      - - - - - - - - - - - - - - - - -
      [- - - - - - ^{15(?)} - - - - - -] . . . . καὶ
      γυμνασίαρχον γενόμενον
      ἐν ἑνὶ καιρῶι μεγαλοψυχίας
      ἕνεκεν καὶ τῆς περὶ πάντα
5   τὸν βίον ἀρετῆς.
            vacat

                         Side B

      - - - - - - - - - - - - - - - - -
      [Ti(berio) Plautio Aeli-]   *September 11(?), A.D. 45*
      ano Tauro Statilio Corvino co(n)s(ulibus) III Idus Se[pt.]
      mistae . . . . . . ^{ca. 15} . . . . . . OR . . Heraclid . . ^{ca. 6} . .
      Metronacte Metro[nactis(?) rege(?)- - - - - - -]
5   L. Comenius L. f. . . . M . . . anus Troadensis
      C. Decimius C. f. Felix Troadensis
      Thimotheos, Μειλάσιος
      [- - - - - - - - - -] ΔΙΟΝΥΣΙΟ .
      [- - - - - - - - - -] ΙΣΕΥ [- - - -]
10   Λ. Σεπτείμιος Κράσος *(sic)*, ὁ καὶ [. . . .]
      ΝΑΙΟΣ
                              Side C
      - - - - - - - - - - - - - - - *illegible traces* - - - - - - - - - - - - - - -
      -

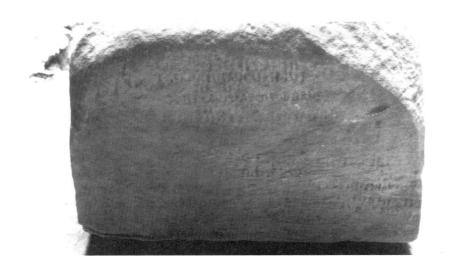

Figure 44 *(opposite)*. Records of
Greek and Roman initiates from
Alexandria Troas (55): side A *(top)*,
side B *(middle)*, side C *(bottom)*

```
        - - - - - - - - - - - - - - - - - - - - - - - - - - - - - - - - - - - - - - -
        - - - - - - - - - - - - - - - - - - - - - - - - - - - - - - - - - - - - - - -
   5  [- - - - - - - - - - - - - - - -?- - - - - - - - - -  Μ]ατρώνακτος
      [- - - - - - - - - - - - - - - - -?- - - - - - - - - - -] . . . . ιου μύστις
      Θεόξενος Α . ΟΥ[- - - - - - - - - -?- - - - - - - - -] . . . .^(ca. 10) . . .
      [- - - - - - - - - - - - - - -?- - - - - - - - - - -Μα]κεδόνος
```

Epigraphical Commentary

The letters of side A are even and somewhat narrow, suggestive of a late
Hellenistic date; the broken-bar alpha favors a date after the middle of the
2nd century B.C. Sides B and C, inscribed later, are badly worn.

Commentary

This is a statue base in honor of a gymnasiarch, whose name is not preserved.

The Latin document, inscribed on side B, is the first hitherto attested
list of initiates of the year A.D. 45.

Line B.4: If Metronacte is correct, then it prompts the restoration
[rege(?), which would be the first documentary instance of the dating
formula in Latin.

Line B.7: Meilasios, derived from the ethnic Milesios/Milasios, is very
rare as a personal name; cf. *MAMA* 5 228.3, which has Meilasia.

Line C.8: Μα]κεδόνος could be an ethnic or a name.

56   Record of initiates from Kyzikos[53]

Two joining pieces of a stele of Thasian marble, preserved on all sides.
It was found in Palaiopolis, later moved to Athens, and is now built into
a wall in Bignor Park, Sussex, England. The upper part of the stele contains a relief of a round building, flanked by snake-entwined torches, and
crowned with a pediment enclosing a circular object; the text is inscribed
below. *Non vidi.*

H. 0.79 m, W. 0.33–0.37 m, Th.?; L.H. 0.017–0.02 m.

Edd. Boeckh, *CIG* II.1 (1832) 2158; Conze 1880, pp. 113–114;
[Rubensohn 1892, 158, 171, 216]; Fredrich, *IG* XII.8 188, with add. p. vii;
Fraser, *Samothrace* 2.1 (1960), p. 112, appendix IV, pl. III.

Cf. *BullÉp* 1929, p. 196; Robert 1936, p. 60, n. 4; Hiller von Gaertringen, *IG* XII Suppl. (1939) 149; Robert and Robert, *BullÉp* 1958 270; *SEG*
XIX 593; *BullÉp* 1964 392; Robert 1963, pp. 67–69; Lehmann and Lehmann 1973, pp. 30–47; Cole 1984, pp. 45–46; 1989, p. 1580, n. 71; Roux,
Samothrace 7 (1992), pp. 223–226; *SEG* XLII 1100*bis*; [*IMT* 1568].

2nd–1st century B.C.?

```
            ἐπὶ βασιλέως Δείνωνος τοῦ
                    Ἀπολλωνίδου,
            [ἀ]γορανομοῦντος Ἑρμοκρά[του]
                    τοῦ Πυθονείκου
       5  [ὧ]ς δὲ Κυζικηνοὶ ἐπὶ Ἑταιρίω-
          [ν]ος τοῦ Εὐμνήστου ἱππάρχ[εω]
          μύστης εὐσεβὴς καὶ ἐπόπτη[ς]
          [Ν]ῖκις Μνησισ[τρ]άτου, φύσει δ[ὲ]
          Ἀσκληπιάδης Ἀττάλου Κυζικη-
```

53. See also **59** for *hieropoioi* and
possible initiates from Kyzikos.

```
10   νός, ἀρχιτέκτων, ἀποσταλεὶς
     παρὰ Κυζικηνῶν [κα]τὰ τὴν
     πρεσβείαν τοῦ δήμου τοῦ
     [Σ]αμοθρᾴκων ἕνεκα τῆς Ι[- -]-
     ποΐας καὶ τῶν ἱερῶν εἰκόνων (?)
15   - - - - - - - - - - - - - - - - - - - - - - -
     - - - - - - - - - - - - - - - - - - - - - - -
     - - - - - - - - - - - - - - - - - - - - - - -
     - - - - - - - - - - - - - - - - - - - - - - -
     - - - - - - - - - - ΟΝΟΣ- - - - - - -
20   - - - - - - - - - - - -ας Ἀσκληπιάδου
     - - - - - - - - - -Σαμ . λου?- - - - - - - - -
     [Μα- - - - - - - - - - - - - - - - - - - -(?)]
     <Θ>ράσων- - - - - - - - - - - - - - -ΟΥ
     <Β>άκχιος- - - - - - - - - - - - - - - - -
     - - - - - - - - - - - - - - - - - - - - - - -
```

Fraser. **1** Δίνωνος Fredrich, Δεί̱νωνος Fraser. **2** Ἀπολλωνίδου Fredrich, Ἀπολλω̱νίδου Fraser. **3** Ἑρμο- - Fredrich, Ἑρμοκρά[του] Fraser. **4** τοῦ Ἀ[γα]θοκ[λ]ε[ί]ου[ς]? Fredrich, τοῦ Πυθο̱νείκου Fraser. **5** [ἐ]πὶ Fredrich, ἐπὶ Fraser. **6** Εὐμνήστου ἱ[ππά]ρ[χεω] Fredrich, Εὐμνήστο̱υ ἱππάρχ[εω] Fraser. **7** μύσ[τ]ης εὐσεβὴς καὶ ἐ[π]όπτ[ης] Fredrich, μύστη̱ς εὐσεβὴ̱ς καὶ ἐπόπτη[ς] Fraser. **8** [Ν]ῖκις Μνησισ[τρ]άτου, φύσει δ[ὲ] Fredrich, Μῖκις Μνησισ[τρ]άτου, φύσει δ[ὲ] Fraser. **9** Ἀσκληπιάδης Ἀττάλου Κυ[ζικη] Fredrich, Ἀσκληπιάδης Ἀττάλου Κυζικη Fraser. **10** νός, ἀρχιτέκτων, [ἀποσ]ταλ[εὶς] Fredrich, νός, ἀρχιτέκτων, ἀποσταλεὶς Fraser. **11** παρὰ Κυζικηνῶν [κα]τὰ τὴν <κ . . > Fredrich, παρὰ Κυζικηνῶν [κα]τὰ τὴν Fraser. **12** πρεσβείαν τοῦ δήμου τοῦ <Σ> Fredrich, πρεσβείαν τοῦ δήμου τοῦ Fraser. **13** [τ]ῆς ν[εω] Fredrich, τῆς ἱ[ερο] Fraser. **14** ποΐ[α]ς [καὶ] τ[ῶ]ν ἱερ[ῶ]ν Ἑρμῶν Fredrich, ποΐας καὶ τῶν ἱερῶν εἰκόνων Fraser. **19** ΟΝΟΣ Fredrich, ΟΝΟΣ Fraser. **20** - - -ας Ἀσκληπιάδου, Μν- - Fredrich, - - - -ας Ἀσκληπιάδου Fraser. **21** - - - -Σαμ[ύ]λου?, Μα- - Fredrich, - - - -Σαμ . λου?- - Fraser. **22** [- - - -, Θ]ράσων? [- - - - - - -] Fredrich, [Μα- - - - - - - -(?)] Fraser. **23** ου, [Β]άκχιος- - - - Fredrich, <Θ>ράσων- - - - - - - -ΟΥ Fraser. **24** <Β>άκχιος- - - - - - - - Fraser. **25** - - - - - - - Fraser.

Epigraphical Commentary

I have not seen the stone, which had badly deteriorated by the time of Fraser's copy. Lines 16–24 are now missing, judging by his photograph.

Commentary

The date is based on comparison with **58** and the letter forms. This is a record of a Cyzicene *mystes* and *epoptes,* Ἀσκληπιάδης Ἀττάλου, and possibly of other Cyzicene visitors, as the names in lines 19–end imply. The inscription, recorded initially by the fourth Earl of Aberdeen in Fauvel's Athenian house in 1803, had been lost and was later rediscovered at Bignor Park in Sussex.[54] The relief connects the document with a series of Samothracian stelai representing a round building with a snake-entwined torch on either side (**47, 57, 58**). Fauvel had noticed a figure, which he interpreted as Kybele, in the rectangular area below the pediment, as Phyllis Lehmann notes (p. 34, with n. 67). As noted in the Commentary on **47**, it is uncertain whether this relief should be connected exclusively with Kyzikos—though such an idea is very tempting, especially in view of Phyllis Lehmann's illuminating discussion of iconographic parallels in

54. See *Samothrace* 2.1, pp. 112–113, for a detailed account of the document's unusual fate.

INITIATES WHOSE ETHNIC IS KNOWN

137

a Cyzicene context. Some issues remain unresolved, however, such as the possible impact of the Rotunda of Arsinoe on the relief and the fact that the other Cyzicene images of round buildings are very few: two coins, discussed by Phyllis Lehmann (p. 37), and a funerary stele of Attalos, possibly Asklepiades' father, that depicts, *inter alia,* a female figure carrying a miniature round building. This stele (*I.Kyz.* 100) was recently discussed by Roux (pp. 223–225), who remarks that the inscription was carved on top of an older text that had been deleted, and therefore Attalos may not be associated with the round building on the relief at all. (I did not notice any evidence for a deleted text, however, when I saw the stone on exhibit in the Louvre in 2004.) The other Cyzicene reliefs that I know of have no bearing on round buildings. The inscriptions on three out of the four stelai with reliefs of round buildings (**47, 56, 58**)[55] mention people who were sent to the sanctuary on a sacred mission of some sort (*hieropoioi, hieragogos, katangeleus*). It is possible that the reliefs with round buildings represent the Rotunda of Arsinoe, and that the names of sacred envoys were inscribed on stelai with such reliefs because the Rotunda was connected with their activities (e.g., as the place where they were entertained at a festive dinner). So few reliefs are preserved on Samothracian stelai, however, that it is also possible that the depiction of a round building (perhaps the Arsinoeion) was a popular design at the sanctuary workshop, and that more prominent visitors had their names inscribed on such monuments.

Line 2: The name Ἀπολλωνίδης is attested for another Samothracian king; see **17**, inscription iii.

Lines 5–6: The *hipparch* is the usual eponymous official of Kyzikos.

Line 7: This should be taken not as evidence that Asklepiades received both stages of initiation within a single ceremony, but rather as his honorary titles; cf. **58**, line 24, where he is only *mystes.*

Line 8: Μικις (the type and place of accent are unclear) is a very rare name, attested only in Egypt, *Delta* 1–3 681.396 (6th–5th century B.C.), accented on the last syllable, and in *SEG* LX 1568, line 56 (220 B.C.), with an acute accent on the first syllable. Νῖκις, on the other hand, is a well-attested Greek name, and so I prefer Fredrich's reading.

Lines 11–12: For the phrase κατὰ πρεσβείαν, cf., for instance, *I.Delos* 1517.21 (ca. 154 B.C.).

Lines 13–14: On the office of *hieropoios,* see *ad* **50**. Fraser's restoration ἕνεκα τῆς ἱ[ερο]|ποΐας, "on account of *hieropoïa,*" has no parallels, and is hard to accept.

It is unclear what is meant by "sacred images." The expression seems to be unattested in inscriptions.

Lines 19–end: Possibly names of initiates; cf. **58**, though secure information is missing.

Of the names mentioned in the document, only Βάκχιος, Ἄτταλος and (rather frequently) Ἀσκληπιάδης are attested in Kyzikos.

57 Records of Roman initiates of unknown provenance, Fig. 45
and of initiates from Maroneia, Rhodes(?), and Kyzikos

A fragment of a stele of Thasian marble, inscribed on front (side A), back (side B), and on the left (side C), preserved in the upper left part (with respect to side A). The front shows traces of a relief with a round building

55. It is possible that the fourth inscription, **57**, listed such officials, too, on the missing parts of the stone.

flanked by snake-entwined torches. The inscription was found by Phardys
built into a Byzantine wall in the ancient city near the Gattilusi Towers, and
had been brought to Chora, when Fredrich published it. Its present location
is unknown. I saw a squeeze in the Berlin Academy in May 2004.

H. 0.33 m, W. 0.22 m, Th. 0.07 m; L.H. 0.035 m (side A, line 1), 0.02
m (side A, lines 2–10), 0.01 m (side B), 0.04 m (side C).

Edd. [Rubensohn 1892, pp. 227–231]; [Mommsen, *CIL* III Suppl.
I.3 (1893) 12322]; Kern 1893, pp. 356–357, no. 5 (with drawing, fig. 46);
BullÉp 1894, p. 389; [Cagnat, *IGR* I.4 (1905) 844]; Fredrich, *IG* XII.8
189; [*IMT* 1567].

Cf. Lehmann and Lehmann 1973, p. 32 (with drawing, fig. 23).

2nd–1st century B.C.?

Side A

i   K   υ   ζ[ι   κ   η   ν   ο   ι   *vel*   ν   ῶ   ν]
       MV[- - - -]
       M. PI / . . .   *snake-entwined*   *round*
       vac. M. . . .   *torch*   *building*
    5 MV[- - - -]
       . AMAS,
       [m]us[tes]
       [M]arone[ys]
       Seleucys
   10 . P I / I T I\I

Side B

i   [- - - - Ὀ]βρίμου
              [- - - -]κίου
              [- - - -]όδας
ii   [ἐπὶ - - - - - - - - - - - -] . , ἐπὶ βασιλέως δὲ ἐν Σα-
   15 [μοθράκηι τοῦ δεῖνος παρῆσα]ν οἱ στρατευσάμενοι
       [μετὰ - - - - - στρα]τηγοῦ ἀνθυπάτου
       [καὶ ναυάρχου τοῦ δεῖνος καὶ - -] . τάρχοντος Ἀνδρία καὶ τρι-
       [ηραρχοῦντος τοῦ δεῖνος μύστα]ι εὐσεβεῖς·
              [Ῥόδι?]οι Δαμαγόρας Φιλίσκου,
   20 [- - - -]ιοντος,   Διοκλῆς Εὐάνδρου
       [- - - -]άτωνος   Μελάνιππος   iii
       [μύσ]ται   Μέντωρ   ἐπὶ βασι-
       [ε]ὐσεβ[εῖς]·   [Μοι?]ραγένης   λέως
                               . . . . κράτης   35 Ἀριδήλου
   25   . . . . αχος   τοῦ Φιλο-
                               . . . μαχος   ξένου·
                               . . . . . δρος   μύστας
                               . . . . κλῆς   εὐσεβὴς
                               . . . . ανίας   40 Πυθαγό-
   30   . . . ων   ρας Ṭ
                               . . . ικλῆς
                               [- - - -]ς
              Side C
         42 C. Cestius.

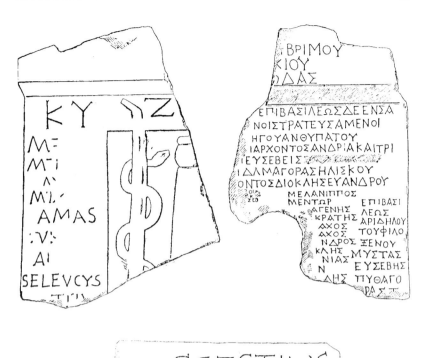

Figure 45. Records of Roman initiates of unknown provenance, and of initiates from Maroneia, Rhodes(?), and Kyzikos (57): side A *(upper left)*, side B *(upper right)*, and side C *(below)*. After Kern 1893, p. 356

Kern, Fredrich. **2** μύ[στης] Fredrich. **5** μύσ[της] Fredrich. **6** AMAS Fredrich *in maiusculis*, [Δ]αμᾶς *in minusculis*. **7** [μ]ύσ[της] Fredrich. **9** Seleycys Fredrich, Seleucys Kern. **14** ἱππάρχε?]ω Fredrich. **17** πρ]ω?τάρχοντος Fredrich, τάρχοντος Kern. **19** [Ῥόδι?]οι Dimitrova.

Epigraphical Commentary
Kern's facsimile and the squeeze are the only basis for picturing the layout and the letter forms of the document. Judging by the squeeze, there is no reason that lines 2–10 should all be in the Greek alphabet, and not the Latin.

Line 14: First preserved letter: right bottom horizontal; sigma is possible.

Commentary
The date is based on analogy with **56** and **58** and is consistent with the lettering and the possible identification of Damagoras Philiskou in lines 19–22. Side A contains one record of Roman (and possibly Greek) initiates, presumably from Kyzikos, if the names in lines 2–10 are contemporary with the heading in line 1; if they are later than the heading, then the names of the Cyzicene initiates were probably written below the relief. Side B includes at least two Greek records. Inscription ii on side B is a list of initiates from a naval crew, possibly from Rhodes. Fredrich thinks that B was the first side inscribed, then A, then C. If this is correct, then the relief was carved on the back side of the original stele. It is unclear whether the names written on the pediment are part of a separate record (side B, inscription i), but such a supposition seems likely. The right side lists one Roman name, C. Cestius, written vertically; cf. **66**, side B.

On the interpretation of the relief, see **56**, Commentary.

Lines 2–10: As mentioned above, it is possible that all of the names and titles listed here were inscribed in Latin.

Line 9: Seleucys has been interpreted by previous editors as the personal name Σέλευκος, not as the ethnic Σελευκεύς.

Lines 14–32: Apparently the crew of a warship; cf. **49**.

Line 16: The title *strategos anthypatos* corresponds to Roman proconsul.

Line 17: The title *protarchon* apparently does not occur for a naval officer. A word like [δεκ]ατάρχοντος is possible; cf. **49**, side B, lines 13–14.

Lines 19–22: A certain Δαμαγόρας Φιλίσκου is attested in a Rhodian document (*Chiron* 23, 83.12, shortly after 85 b.c.). He could be the same person, and if so, then the ethnic before his name should be *Rhodioi*. Fredrich's restoration [ἐπὶ - - - - - ἱππάρχε?]ω in line 14 led to the assumption that the initiates must be Cyzicene, since the eponymous *hipparch* is a Cyzicene, and not a Rhodian, official. Another argument in favor of supposing that the ship in question was Rhodian is the fact that the name Damagoras is extremely frequent in Rhodes, but unattested in Kyzikos, to my knowledge. The names Euandros, Diokles, Melanippos, and Mentor are also well attested in Rhodes.

Line 38: The Doric form *mystas* proves that the records of initiates must have been written by the initiates themselves before being inscribed on stone, as Clinton suggests.

Line 42: A C. Cestius was a consul in a.d. 35, but it is unclear whether he is related to the person in the present document.

58   Record of initiates from Kyzikos, and records of Greek   Fig. 46
and Roman initiates of uncertain provenance

The upper part of the monument (lines 1–8) is known only from a copy made by Cyriacus of Ancona. The lower and middle parts are two nonjoining fragments of a stele of Thasian marble. A round building with crown-shaped bands on either side is carved on the stone. Fredrich connected the lower part of *b* (*b²*) with the text of *a*, which was confirmed by the discovery of *a¹⁻²* in 1938 in the Byzantine chapel of St. Demetrios in Chora. Fragments *b¹* and *a³* are also known only from Cyriacus's manuscript. Archaeological Museum of Samothrace, Hall B, inv. nos. 39.16 *(a)*, 39.23 *(b)*.

a¹⁻²: H. 0.33 m, W. 0.28 m, Th. 0.08 m; L.H. 0.013 m (lines 1–4), 0.018 m (line 5), 0.016 m (lines 6–9).

b²: H. 0.20 m, W. 0.23 m, Th. 0.13 m; L.H. 0.016 m.

Edd.: Line 3, Latin: [Muratori 1739–1742 III, p. 1720 (after Cod. Ambros. *A* 55), no. 13]; [Mommsen, *CIL* III (1873) 721]; [Fredrich, *IG* XII.8, p. 39].

Lines 3–8, Greek: [Muratori 1739–1742 II, p. 650, no. 2 (under "Roma")]; [Franz, *CIG* III (1850) 6182b (under "Roma")]; [Kaibel, *IG* XIV (1890), p. 776]; [Ziebarth 1906, p. 413, no. 7]; [Fredrich, *IG* XII.8 259].

a¹: [Muratori 1739–1742 III 1636, no. 16]; [Franz, *CIG* III (1850) 5926a]; [Mommsen, *CIL* III (1873) 719]; [Fredrich, *IG* XII.8 211 (lines 1–4)].

a²⁻³: [Muratori 1739–1742 I 156, no. 1]; [Franz, *CIG* III (1850) 5927]; [Rubensohn 1892, 172]; [Michel 1900, no. 1141]; [Kern 1893, p. 364]; [Ziebarth 1906, p. 414, no. 10]; [Fredrich, *IG* XII.8 191].

b[1]: [Muratori 1739–1742 III 1670, no. 1]; [Franz, *CIG* III (1850) 5926b]; [Mommsen, *CIL* III (1873) 718]; [Ziebarth 1906, p. 414, no. 10]; [Fredrich, *IG* XII.8 212, lines 1–7)].

b[2]: [Kern 1893, p. 363, no. 7]; [Fredrich, *IG* XII.8 192].

a[1–2], *b:* Lehmann-Hartleben 1943, pp. 117–123, with photograph and reconstruction of the monument by S. M. Shaw; Fraser, *Samothrace* 2.1 (1960) 29.

Fragments *a*[2] + *b*[2], *a*[3]: [*IMT* 1570 + 1571].

Cf. Kerényi 1955, p. 151, esp. n. 1; Robert 1963, p. 67; Walton 1963, p. 99; *BullÉp* 1964, pp. 375, 393; Bodnar and Mitchell 1976, facs. fig. 13, 23; Cole 1984, p. 96; 1989, p. 1580, n. 71.

2nd–1st century B.C.?

Κυζικηνῶν
<ἱεροποιοί?> *vel* <[μύσται εὐσεβεῖς]?>

M · Oppius · Ne<p>os   ΜΥΣΙΛΛΑΣ τριήραρχος
Δημήτριος Δημητρίου
5   Μόσχος Μενεκράτου
Ζήνων Ζήνωνος
Ἀπολλώνιος
Διονυσίου

a[1] *vss. 9–12 in corona sinistra:*   *b*[1] *vss. 9–15 in corona dextra:*

Ἀνδρό-   ἐφό[π]της
10   μαχος   ΘΕΟΣΑΣ
Δημητρί-   {μο}ἱ<ε>ρ<ο>ποιός,
ου *vacat*   ΖΗΓΙΝΤΟΣ
Ῥοδοκλήου,
Ῥόδω-
15   ν.
PREGE [mystes(?)]

Q. Visellius L. · f.   pius

a–b[3]   [Κ]υζικηνῶν ἱεροποιοὶ καὶ μύσται
εὐσεβεῖς, ἐπ᾽ Ἀντιγένου
20   τοῦ Ἑρμαγόρου ἱππάρχεω
[ὡς δὲ] Σαμόθρακες ἐπὶ βασιλέως Ἀριδήλου
a[3]   [τοῦ - - - - - -]ίχου· Παρμενίσκος Ἀριστέω[ς],
[Φιλό]ξενος Φιλοξένου *vacat*
<μύσ>ται εὐσεβεῖς· Ἀσκληπιάδης Ἀ<ττ>άλου
25   Θερσίων Ἡρογείτ-<ονο>ς *vel* -<ου>, Κυβερνήτης Μηνοφίλου.

Fraser, Muratori, Cyriacus. **2** Clinton, Dimitrova. ΕΥΙΕΡΟΙ Cyriacus. **3** Neeos Cyriacus, Nepos Muratori. **10** ΘΕΟΣΑΣ Cyriacus, Θεο[λ]α[ς] Mommsen, Θεο[φ]α[ς] Fredrich, Θε<ωτ>α[ς] Boeckh, Θεο<ζ>ᾶ<ς> Fraser. **11** Dimitrova, ΜΟΙΡΑΠΟΙΟΣ Cyriacus, Μοιρα<γ>ό<ρ>ο<υ> Fraser. **12** ΖΗΓΙΝΤΟΣ Cyriacus, Ζ<ακυν>τος Boeckh, Ζή<λω>τος, Ζή<νοφαν>τος Fredrich, Ζή<λω?>τος Fraser. **17** pius Fraser. **20** ἱ|ππάρχεω Fraser, ἱ|ππάρχεω Walton. **24** ΑΙΤΑΙ, ΑΓΑΛΟΥ Muratori (Cod. Ambros., Ashm.), ΑΙΤΕΑΙ, ΑΓΑΔΟΥ Hamb., <μύσ>ται, Ἀγ[λ]άου Fredrich, Ἀ<ττ>άλου Boeckh, Fraser. **25** Θερσίων Cyriacus, Θέρσων Fraser, ΗΡΟΓΕΙΤΗΣ, ΜΕΝΟΦΙΛΟΥ Cyriacus, Ἡρογείτ[ονο]ς Boeckh, Fredrich, Fraser, Μηνόφιλο[ς]? Fredrich, Μηνόφιλο<ς> Fraser.

Epigraphical Commentary

The lettering, as far as it is possible to assess it from the scarcity of the preserved text, is consistent with 2nd–1st-century B.C. documents.

Line 17: Two lower verticals, followed by lower parts of a barely visible V and a clear S.

Line 20: The first letter of ἱ|ππάρχεω is not preserved, as Walton notes.

Line 24: Asklepiades is recorded only as *mystes* here, while in **56** he is *mystes* and *epoptes*.

Commentary

The main text (lines 18–end) represents a list of Cyzicene initiates and *hieropoioi*. It is unclear what the precise relation between the texts in the wreath-shaped bands and the main inscription is, as Fraser observes, though he agrees with Lehmann that the inscription coheres and all its parts are contemporary. Lehmann believes that the bands represent "the purple scarf which the initiated wore around the abdomen for protection from evil" and that the people listed within them are probably *epoptai*, as opposed to the *mystai* and *hieropoioi* recorded below (pp. 122–123). Only one of the people whose names are inscribed within the bands, however, is called *epoptes* (fragment *b*, lines 1–3). It is possible that the names within the bands are a continuation of another record of Cyzicene visitors, preserved in the manuscript, since lines 18–19 seem to be the beginning of a record. Therefore, I have printed the entire text of the stele as recorded by Cyriacus, although it is not completely certain that lines 1–8 render Samothracian inscriptions. Muratori attributes the Greek record in lines 3–8 to Rome, whereas Fredrich lists it under Samothrace but notes that its Samothracian provenance is not obvious (*IG* XII.8, *ad* 259). It seems likely, however, that the heading *Ad marmoream & ornatissimam basim Graecis & Latinis litteris epigrammata* (see facsimile in Fig. 46) refers to the entire page, even lines 1–2. The inscription on the previous page in the manuscript is from Thasos (*CIG* III 5901).

For the office of *hieropoios*, see *ad* **50** and Chapter 1, p. 14.

Line 2: The adjective εὐίερος, attested in the manuscript, is never applied to people. One would expect a title of some sort, such as the one in lines 18–19, [Κ]υζικηνῶν ἱεροποιοὶ καὶ μύσται|εὐσεβεῖς.

Line 3: The name ΜΥΣΙΛΛΑΣ is not attested. A name of the type Pausillas is possible.

On the office of the *trierarch*, see *ad* **61**.

Line 4: Two people with the name Δημήτριος Δημητρίου are recorded in a Cyzicene inscription (*IMT* 1456.I, line 46, and II, line 16), but it is unclear whether either of them is the same person, in view of the name's frequency. A Δημήτριος Δημητρίου τοῦ Δάμωνος is attested in *IMT* 1462, line 18 (pre-Roman).

Lines 7–8: A Διονύσιος Ἀπολλωνίου is attested in a Cyzicene epitaph of the Roman period (*IMT* 1594.4), but it is unclear whether he is related to the person in the present inscription.

Lines *a*.9–12: A certain Δημήτριος Ἀνδρομάχου is recorded in a Cyzicene inscription (*IMT* 1456, line 71), but the name is too common to allow further speculations on the possible relation between the two men.

Figure 46. Record of initiates from Kyzikos, and records of Greek and Roman initiates of uncertain provenance (58): facsimile of the monument as recorded by Cyriacus *(above)*, and actual fragments of the stele *(below)*. *Samothrace* 2.1, pl. XIV:29, and courtesy Samothrace Excavations, respectively

Line 10: The trouble with Fraser's conjecture, which best fits the manuscript reading, is that the form seems to be unattested.

Lines 16–17: *Prece pius* is an awkward phrase, which seems to be unattested. It is possible that PREGE was the name of another initiate (e.g., P. Rege[inus]), as Clinton suggests, or the continuation of the name below the left crown.

Line 17: It is unclear whether the Latin name was inscribed at the same time as the Greek text. Fraser notes that the Visellii of Brundisium were "active as wine-growers and exporters in the 1st century B.C. (See *CIL* X 545)." The person mentioned here might be connected with the consul of A.D. 24, L. Visellius Varro. A certain Κόιντος Οὐισέλλιος Γαίου- - -, is attested in an undated Delian inscription, *I.Delos* 1741.

Lines 22–23: The same people are attested in **10**, lines 17–18, dated on the basis of its hand to the 2nd–1st century B.C.

Line 25: Neither Ἡρογείτων / -ης nor Θερσίων is attested in Kyzikos. It is unclear why Fraser prints Θέρσων: the manuscript has Θερσίων, which is a more common name. Although Ἡρογείτωνος is a much better known form (and the name Herogeiton much more frequent), the genitive Ἡρογείτου is attested as well, which better fits the manuscript, so I keep the possibilities open. As for the last initiate mentioned, I prefer the reading Κυβερνήτης Μηνοφίλου, since the manuscript confirms it and since Κυβερνήτης is a well-attested name. Of course, κυβερνήτης Μηνόφιλος cannot be excluded as a possibility.

59   Greek record of initiates(?) and *hieropoioi* from Kyzikos   Fig. 47

Fragment of Thasian marble, broken at bottom and possibly on top. It is unclear how the back looks or whether the fragment belongs to a block or a stele. Found 'ς τὲς Μυρσίνες, in the northeastern part of the island. Its present location is unknown.

H. 0.69 m, W. 0.58 m, Th. 0.15 m; L.H.?

Edd. Conze 1875, p. 43, no. 21, pl. 71:21; Fredrich, *IG* XII.8 194; [*IMT* 1572].

Cf. Rubensohn 1892, pp. 171–172; Fraser, *Samothrace* 2.1 (1960), p. 116, n. 19; Robert 1963, p. 67.

1st century B.C.?

<pre>
      ἐ]πὶ βασιλέως
      Εὐμάχου τοῦ
      Τημένου, ὡς δὲ
      Κυζικηνοὶ ἄγου-
  5   σιν ἐπὶ Ἱππονίκου
      τοῦ Λυσαγόρου
      ἱππάρχεω, ἱεροποιο[ὶ]
      οἱ ἀποσταλέντες
      ὑπὸ τοῦ δήμου
 10   [τ]οῦ Κυζικηνῶν
      [Νικ?]ογένης Ἀττάλου
      [. . .] . ος Θεοχάρου
      - - - - - - - - - - -Ο . . .
      - - - - - - - - - - - - -
</pre>

Fredrich. **11** [Δι]ογένης Fredrich, [Νικ?]ογένης Dimitrova.

Epigraphical Commentary
Conze's facsimile gives an idea of the lettering and layout.

Line 12, beginning: Top horizontal followed by top part of a circle.

Commentary
This is a list of Cyzicene *hieropoioi*, who were presumably initiates. The preserved part of the stone does not contain the title *mystai*, but all other

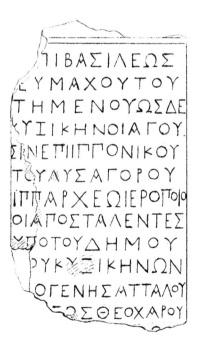

Figure 47. Record of initiates(?) and *hieropoioi* from Kyzikos (**59**). Conze 1875, pl. 71:21

hieropoioi mentioned in Samothracian documents were initiates. It is interesting that there is no relief of a round building preserved.

For the office of *hieropoios*, see *ad* **50** and Chapter 1, p. 14.

Lines 2–3: The eponymous king is unknown.

Lines 5–6: The name Hipponikos is well attested in Kyzikos, e.g., *IMT* 1459.A.II, line 12 (Hadrianic), 1460, line 17 (Hadrianic), 1461.3, line 42 (undated), 1486 (4th c. B.C.); and so is Lysagoras, e.g., *IMT* 1452 (undated), 1542 (1st century B.C./1st century A.D.).

Line 11: On the possible identification of [Nik]ogenes, son of Attalos, with the Cyzicene *theoros* listed in **9**, see *ad* **9**.

Line 12: The name Θεοχάρης is not otherwise attested in Kyzikos.

60 Record of initiates from Kaunos[56]

Block of Thasian marble, of which the left part was visible and the right side was hidden in the ground, "by the stream between the plane trees" in Palaiopolis, when Kern copied it. Its present location is unknown.

H. 0.39 m, W. 0.28 m, Th. 0.25 m; L.H.?

Edd. Kontoleon 1891, p. 299, no. 4; Reinach 1892, p. 203, no. 5; Kern 1893, p. 373, no. 18; Fredrich, *IG* XII.8 222.

1st–3rd century A.D.?

   Καυνί[ων]
   μύσται
   εὐσεβῖς· *(sic)*
   Ἀθηναΐς
  5 Περδίκας
   Ἀνδρόμαχος
   Φιλάργυρο[ς].

Fredrich.

Epigraphical Commentary
Judging by Reinach's majuscule copy, the epsilon and sigma are lunate.

Commentary
The initiates in this inscription may have been slaves, since they have just a single name. None of the names is attested otherwise in Kaunos. Fredrich (following Kontoleon) dates the inscription to the 3rd century A.D. on the basis of the lettering. An earlier date is also possible.

61 Record of initiates from Knidos and Rome   Fig. 48

Stele of Thasian marble, preserved on the left and on back, which is rough-picked. Found in July 1971 at 17.80–21.00 m east and 33.50–37.50 m south of the northeastern inner corner of the Stoa. Archaeological Museum of Samothrace, courtyard, inv. 71.962.

H. 0.56 m, W. 0.28 m, Th. 0.075 m; L.H. 0.02–0.025 m (lines 1–5), 0.015 m (lines 6–18), 0.02–0.025 m (lines 19–20), 0.015 m (line 21), 0.02–0.025 m (line 22).

Ed. McCredie 1979, pp. 16–17 (*SEG* XXIX 799).

Cf. *BullÉp* 1980 357; Cole 1989, p. 1580, n. 71, p. 1589, n. 131.

56. See also **133** for probable initiates from Kaunos.

2nd century B.C.?

i 　　　- - - - - - - - - - - - - - - - - - - -
　　　　　Κνιδίων
　　　μύσται καὶ ὑφόπ[ται] *(sic)*
　　　　　εὐσεβεῖς
　　　ναύαρχος Εὔβουλο[ς]
　5　　　Ἀρχιπόλιος
　　　τριήραρχοι Ἀγάθινος Εὐβ[ούλου]
　　　Ἱππόδαμος Ἀναξάνδριδ[ος]
　　　καὶ ἐπίπλοι τριήραρχοι ΚΛΕΥ[- - - - - -]
　　　Νικασιβούλου, Σωσθένης ΘΕΥ[- - - - - -]
　10　γραμματεὺς Ἀσκληπιάδη[ς]
　　　　　Διοκλέυς
　　　καὶ τοὶ συμπλεύσαντες
　　　καὶ μυηθέντες
　　　καὶ ὑποπτεύσαντες *(sic)*
　　　　　vacat
　15　ἐπὶ βασιλέως Μνησισ[τράτου]
　　　　　τοῦ Κλεοβούλου
　　　ὡς δὲ Κνίδιοι ἐπὶ δαμιο[υρ]-
　　　γοῦ *v* Πυθονίκου
ii 　　　mystae · piei
　20　qum · Cn. · Lentul[o]
　　　venere · initiatei · A · D [- - - -]
　　　P · Aninius · P · 1 · SA|.[- -]
　　　　　- - - - - - - - - - - -

Figure 48. Record of initiates from Knidos and Rome (**61**)

McCredie. **2** ὑπόπ[ται] McCredie, ὑφόπ[ται] *lapis*. **10** Ἀσκληπιάδη[ς] McCredie, Ἀσκληπιάδη[ς] *lapis*. **12** τοῖ McCredie, τοὶ Dimitrova. **20** Qu M · Cn · Lentulus McCredie, Qum Cn. Lentul[o?? Bingen (*apud SEG*), qum · Cn. · Lentul[o] Dimitrova. **22** l. Sai McCredie, 1 · SA|. Dimitrova.

Epigraphical Commentary
The letters are clear and carefully done. The Latin record shows republican letter forms, especially P.
　　Line 1: Lower part of a vertical stroke.
　　Line 2: Lower part of a left vertical.
　　Line 22: The L of l(ibertus) is clear.

Commentary
The inscription contains a fully preserved record of Knidian initiates in Greek (inscription i) and an incomplete record of Roman initiates in Latin (ii). The Knidian initiates were members of the crew of a war galley, as the titles of naval officers in lines 4, 6, 8, and 10 suggest. The *trier-arch*, commander of the trireme, was practically the captain in Hellenistic times (Casson 1995, p. 307), the *epiplous* was the vice-captain (Casson 1995, p. 307), and the *nauarch* was the commodore (Casson 1995, p. 307, n. 30). The *grammateus* was a high officer, the "trierarch's secretary and treasurer," as Casson defines it (p. 307). Lines 12–14 refer to the rest of the crew.

Line 2: The confusion of prefixes seen in the spellings ὑφόπ[ται] and ὑποπτεύσαντες in line 14 is noteworthy. The carver must have been thinking of ὕποπτος, as McCredie observed. The aspiration of the first pi is paralleled by ἐφόπται, which occurs in **49, 67, 71**, and *IG* XII.2 275.

Line 6: A certain Εὔβουλος Ἀγαθίνου of Knidos is honored in a decree issued by Chalcis, *IG* XII.9 900A, dated to the first half of the 2nd century B.C. It seems likely that he was related to the person mentioned in the present document, perhaps his father or son.

Line 7: The name Ἀναξανδρίδας is well attested in Knidos (e.g., in *I.Knidos* I 34, 76).

Line 9: The name Νικασίβουλος is attested elsewhere in Knidos (*I.Knidos* I 427). Σωσθένης is a common name, but unattested in Knidos.

Lines 17–18: Other Knidian inscriptions dated with the *damiourgos* are *I.Knidos* I 801, 7 (1st century A.D.?) and 802, 1 (ca. 100–150). The same official also occurs as eponym in Rhodes, Naxos, Samos, and Teos.

Lines 19–22: The spelling of the diphthong EI in the nominative plural of o-stems suits well a date in the 2nd century B.C.; see, e.g., Ernout 1935, pp. 50–51; Palmer 1961, p. 217.

Line 20: A Cn. Cornelius Cn. f. Lentulus was consul in 146 B.C., but it is unclear whether he is the same person or a relative.

For the spelling of the preposition *cum* as *qum*, cf., e.g., *CIL* I 1772, III 3908.

62 Records of initiates from Miletos and Thasos   Fig. 49

Block of Thasian marble, preserved on all sides. The left side has anathyrosis. The block is smooth-picked on the right, top, and bottom, rough-picked on back. Palaiopolis, Old School Lab of the Ephoreia of Prehistoric and Classical Antiquities. Ephoreia inv. C 80.105.

H. 0.35 m, W. 0.795 m, Th. 0.19 m; L.H. 0.03 m (inscripton i, lines 1–5), 0.025 (inscription i, line 6, and inscription ii).

Ed. Triantaphyllos 1985, pp. 312–313.

Cf. *SEG* XXXV 965; Touchais 1986, pp. 730–731.

2nd century B.C.?

i   ἐπὶ βασιλέως Φιλοξένου
          τοῦ Τισίου Μιλητοπολεῖται
          δικασταὶ μύσται εὐσεβεῖς
          Ἀρτεμίδωρος Ἀρτεμιδώρου
    5   τοῦ Ποσειδωνίου, Ζώπυρος
          Μενίππου
ii   Εὐσεβὴς Νικήφορος Μητροδώρου
          Θάσιος μύστης

Triantaphyllos. 2 Μιλητοπολεῖτ[αι] Triantaphyllos, Μιλητοπολεῖται Dimitrova.

Epigraphical Commentary

The letters of inscription i are more elongated and faded than those of ii, though sufficiently clear and legible. Inscription ii was added in the vacant space after i.

Line 2: The last two letters are faint, but visible.

Figure 49. Records of initiates from
Miletos and Thasos (62)

Commentary

The block must be from the building of theoroi, given its height and thickness. It contains two records of initiates, from Miletos and Thasos, dated
on the basis of the lettering.

Line 2: The name Τ(ε)ισίας is attested also in **16**, as the first name
of the eponymous official, and on Samothracian coins; see Ashton 1998,
pp. 131, 133, with nn. 16 and 17.

Line 3: On judges in Samothrace, see *ad* **17**.

63 Record of initiates from Rome, Pessinus, and Smyrna   Fig. 50

Four joining fragments of a stele of Thasian marble, with parts of
the top and the left and right sides preserved; the back is smooth-picked.
Archaeological Museum of Samothrace inv. nos. 93.47 (fragment *c*) and
93.48 *(b)* were found on June 30, 1993, in the excavation of the Sacred
Way on the Eastern Hill, just to the west of a rectangular structure that
protrudes southward from the north retaining wall of the Sacred Way
("the cement on the fragments suggests that they had been reused, either
in the adjacent structure or in the retaining wall," Diary 1993, p. 8). Inv.
93.49 *(d)* was found in the vicinity on the following day. Inv. 01.1 *(a)* was
removed from the retaining wall along the Sacred Way on June 26, 2001;
it had been built into the wall ca. 1.5 m east of the protruding structure.
The stele has a taper. Traces of mortar remain. Vertical border lines are
incised along the left and right edges.

H. 0.395 m, W. 0.466 m, Th. 0.052 m; L.H. 0.025–0.03 m (fragment
a), 0.010–0.014 m (fragments *b–d*).

Unpublished.

May–June A.D. 186

a   [ἀγαθῆι] τύχηι
        [πρὸ *vel* τῇ πρὸ- -ων Ἰου]νίων αὐτο-
        [κράτορι Μ. Αὐρ. Κομ]μόδωι τὸ Ε
        [καὶ Ἀκειλίωι]Γλαβρίωνι τὸ Β
    5   [ὑπάτοις οἵδε οἱ?] μύσται τοῖς

[σεμνοῖς? μυστ]ηρίοις μυη-
[θέντες κατὰ τ]ὴν πρόνοι-
[αν θεῶν μεγάλ?]ων· ἐπὶ βασιλέ[ως]
[- - - - - - - - - - - - - - - - - - -]ΑΠΟ[- - - - - - - - -]

10 [- - - - - - - - - - - -Π.] Ἰού[λιος   c

b [Γεμίνιος Μαρκι]ανὸς ἀνθ(ύπατος)

	Col. I	Col. II	Col. III
	[- - - - - - - - -]	[- - - - - - - - -]	Δ[- - - - - -]
	[- - - - - -] . . .	[- - - -]ίνιος[- -]	Σ[- - - - - -]
	[- -]ΑΡΧΙΟΣ[- -]	[- -]Ἐρατός	Φλα[- - - -]
15	[. . . .]Ἡράστρατο[ς?]	[- -]νέτιος Ῥηγεῖνος	Ἐπίλογος
	[. . . .]ῳ γυνὴ αὐτο[ῦ]	ΕΡ. [- - - -]	Φιλήσιος
	[.]Παπείριος Ἰοῦσ-	Οὐλ[. . . .ᶜᵃ·⁹. . . .]	Εὐπόριστος
	ᵛτο[ς Π]εσσινούντιο[ς]	. . . . παφος	Ἐπιτυγχάνω[ν]
	Αἴλ. Τειμαῖος Πεσ-	δοῦλοι	Σύμφορος
20	ᵛσινούντιος *vacat*	Πόντικος	Νεικήτης
	Γ. Περπέννα Φόσκος	[. .]ΝΟ[. .]Ν	Ο[- - - - - - -]
	Π . Αἴλ . Θαρσύνων	[- - - - - - - -]	[- - - - - - - -]
	ᵛᵉΣμυρναῖος	[- - - - - - - -]	[- - - - - - - -]
	ἀπελεύθεροι	[- - - - - - - -]	δοῦλ(οι) Ἰούσ[του]
25	Οὔλ Ἀλκιβιάδης	[- - - - - - - -]	Πεισαῖος
	Οὔλ Ἀρείων	[- - - - - - - -]	Θρέπτος
	Οὔλ Ἐιρκεῖνος	[- - - - - - - -]	Βούβαλος
	Αὐρήλιος Ἀχιλλεύς	[- - - - - - -]ιος	δοῦλ(οι)· Τειμαίο[υ]
	Κορνήλ(ιος) Πολύδωρ[ος]	[- - - - - - - -]	Σύρος
30	Παπείρ(ιος) · Ὑάκινθ[ος]	[- - - - - - -]ος	Μέμνων
	[Παπεί]ρ(ιος) Ἐλπίν[ικος]	[- - - - - - -]κος	δοῦλος Θαρσύν[οντ]ο[ς]
	[- - - - - - - -]Ι Ι Ι[- - -]	[- - - - - - - -]ς	Ἀλέξανδρος
	- - - - - - - - - - - - -	[- - - - - - - -]ς	Οὐλ· Εὐτυχιανό[ς]
		[- - - - - - - -]ς	Οὐλ· ΧειρΙ [- - - -]
		- - - - - - - - - -	- - - - - - - - - - - - -

Clinton, Dimitrova.

Epigraphical Commentary
The letters are elegant and somewhat rounded, with lunate epsilon and sigma, very similar to **133**.
    Line I.15: First letter: vertical stroke.
    Line II.16: Unclear traces; ẸP̣Ṃ is possible.

Commentary
This is the latest certainly dated list of Roman initiates, from late May (if the June Kalends are to be restored) or early June A.D. 186 (if the Ides or Nones are to be restored). Fragment *a* was built into the north retaining wall of the Sacred Way, so A.D. 186 is a terminus post quem for its construction.
    Line 2: πρὸ with the genitives Καλανδῶν, Εἰδῶν, Νοννῶν corresponds to Latin *pridie*, while τῇ [ἡμέρᾳ] πρὸ with the genitive of a number (e.g., τεσσάρων) followed by Καλανδῶν, Εἰδῶν, Νοννῶν corresponds to *ante*

Figure 50. Record of initiates from
Rome, Pessinus, and Smyrna (63)

diem, followed by the accusative of the relevant number and of the Kalends,
Ides, or Nones. A phrase containing a cardinal numeral in the dative (e.g.,
"on the first, second, third, fourth, day") with Καλανδῶν, Εἰδῶν, Νοννῶν
is also possible in Greek.

Lines 6–7: The phrase μυστ]ηρίοις μυη[θέντες is so far unparalleled
in Samothracian documents.

Lines 7–8: Versions of the expression κατὰ τὴν πρόνοιαν θεῶν appear in *Tit.Cal.* 69 (a little after 25 B.C.); *IOSPE* I² 42.e, line 12 (ca. A.D.
200–210); *IvO* 53 (A.D. 4); *LSAM* 69.I (end of 2nd century A.D.), *P.Oxy.*
XXVII 2477 (A.D. 289), etc.

Lines 10–11: The remains on the stone match the name of P. Iulius
Geminius Marcianus, proconsul of Asia around 186 A.D., and I find the
restoration likely.

Line 15: Herastratos is a rare form of Herostratos.

Lines 18–20, 23: These are the first initiates attested so far from Pessinus and Smyrna.

ROMAN INITIATES

64 Record of an initiate from Rome   Fig. 51

Fragment of a plaque of Thasian marble, broken on the right and perhaps on top. The back is rough-picked. Found near the Genoese Towers in early 1953. Archaeological Museum of Samothrace, courtyard, inv. 53.2.

H. 0.15 m, W. 0.23 m, Th. 0.03 m; L.H. 0.03 m.

Ed. Fraser, *Samothrace* 2.1 (1960) 25.

Cf. Cole 1984, pp. 134–135, n. 697; 1989, p. 1581, pl. 8; *SEG* XXXIX 927.

Beginning of 2nd century B.C.?

> L. Iu<v>entius · M [· f.]
> Thalna · my[stes]
> pius *vacat*

Fraser. **1** L. Fraser, P Edson (*apud* Cole), L. Dimitrova, IVENTIVS, *lapis*, M[fil.] Fraser, M [· f.] Dimitrova.

Figure 51. Record of an initiate from Rome (64)

Epigraphical Commentary

The letters are thin and relatively shallow.

Line 1: The first letter is a clear L, and the last letter a clear M.

Line 2: Last letter: upper left diagonal, suitable for Y or V.

Commentary

This is a record of a Roman initiate. The plaque contains only one name, Lucius Iuventius Thalna. Records of single initiates are relatively rare, as Fraser notes. Fraser dates the inscription to the 2nd century B.C., but thinks that identifying the initiate with the L. Iuventius Thalna known from Livy 38.4 and 39.31 is unlikely because this would require the inscription to be dated to the beginning of the 2nd century B.C. Charles Edson (*apud* Cole, pp. 134–135) thinks that the initiate in the present inscription is Publius Iuventius Thalna, who was sent to Macedonia in 148 B.C. to suppress Andriskos's revolt. The first letter is not a P, however, but a clear L. Lucius Thalna was active in 185/4 B.C., as Fraser notes. It seems likely to me that he is the initiate, although secure proof is missing. Plutarch mentions that Marcellus dedicated offerings at Samothrace as early as 211 B.C., as Cole observes (1989, p. 1570), so the early 2nd century B.C. may well have been a time when Romans were being initiated.

Line 1: The omission of the second V in Iu<v>entius is fairly typical. Fraser prints [fil.] in order to preserve symmetry, but this abbreviation is uncommon. Symmetry does not seem to be observed in the inscription: otherwise *pius* in line 3 would have been centered.

65 Record of Roman initiates(?)

The inscription is known from the copy made by Cyriacus of Ancona. Its dimensions and present location are unknown.

Edd. [Mommsen, *CIL* III Suppl. I.1 (1889) 7367]; [Kern 1893, p. 375, no. 23]; [Fredrich, *IG* XII.8, p. 38]; [Lommatzsch, *CIL* I² (1918) 662a–b].

Cf. Cole 1984, p. 93.

113 B.C.

> · C · Caecilio
> · Cn · Papirio
>   cos
> C · <M>arcello
> 5   proq

Mommsen. **4** AArcello, *codex.*

Epigraphical Commentary

Line 4: Presumably the M and A were in ligature, hence the spelling in
the codex.

Commentary

This probably was the beginning of a list of Roman initiates, dated to
113 B.C. The proquaestor (presumably in Macedonia) C. Marcellus has
been associated with C. Claudius Marcellus, who was praetor in 80 B.C.
(Broughton [1952] 1984, p. 55). It is possible that the latter was his son.
The ablative <M>arcello is unusual: it could be a mistake for <M>arcellus,
in which case he would have been an initiate.

66   Record of initiates from Rome and Catana   Fig. 52

Stele of Thasian marble preserved on all sides except above, rough-
picked on back, found in 1984 by D. Matsas at the site of Papa-Vounos, on
the southwestern shore of Samothrace, not far from Mikro Vouni, i.e., on the
side of the island opposite its original location in the sanctuary. The tenon
for anchoring the stele to a base is preserved below. There is a sharp taper
from bottom to top. Archaeological Museum of Samothrace. No inv. no.

H. 0.505 m (excluding tenon), W. 0.29 m (at line 1), 0.34 m (at last
line), Th. ca. 0.07 m; L.H. 0.032–0.038 m (line 2), 0.028–0.032 (lines
3–10), 0.032–0.036 (side B).

Ed. Clinton 2001, pp. 27–35 (*SEG* LI 1092).

September 4, 100 B.C.

Figure 52. Record of initiates from
Rome and Catana (66): side A.
Courtesy K. Clinton

                         Side A

> - - - - - - - - - -
> [- - - ^{ca. 8} - - -]II
> M · Fannius M · f.
> Cor(nelia) *vac.* praef(ectus)
> L · Tullius · M · f.
> 5 Cor(nelia) *vac.* praif(ectus)
> P · Petellius · Q · f.
>   Norba ^v eq(ues)
> P · Gadienus P · f.
>   Clu(stumina) ^{vv} eq(ues)
> 10 C · Menenius C · f · Ar(nensi)
>   Σικελὸς ^{vv} Καταναῖος
>   Ἀρτεμίδωρος Πανκράτου
>   L · Valer(io) C · Mar(io) · cos · pr(idie) n(onas) Sept.

Side B *(in latere dextro)*

[- - - -]ς *vv* A · Claudius C · f · Mass°

Clinton.

Epigraphical Commentary

The lettering and layout closely resemble those of **72**, and it is likely that the cutter was the same. I have reprinted Clinton's Epigraphical Commentary below, after checking it against the stone.

In addition to the inscription on the front side (A), one line is inscribed vertically on the right side (B).

Nearly all Latin words and abbreviations are separated by a midline dot or a vacant space.

Line A.1: Of the final letter the lower part of a vertical stroke is preserved, almost directly above the vertical stroke of the final F in the next line. Of the preceding letter the very bottom of a vertical stroke is preserved, centered over the M in the following line; it seems too distant from the next letter to be an I (cf. IF in line 5). The space seems too narrow to contain PR. (The narrow R at the end of line 10 is the result of crowding, but there is no reason to assume similar crowding in this line, which presumably holds only the tribal affiliation and a title.)

Lines A.11–12: These lines appear to have been carved by a different hand.

Line A.13: This seems to be by the same hand that carved the rest of the Latin text, but its uneven character suggests that it may have been inscribed after the stele had already been set in its base.

Line B.1: M and A are in ligature. The final O is very small, obviously because the cutter had run out of space.

Commentary

See Clinton's commentary for a detailed discussion of this monument. The document inscribed on the front, dated to September 4, 100 B.C., records Roman initiates, including Lucius Tullius, Cicero's uncle; M. Fannius, the praetor in 80 B.C. and plebeian aedile; and other prominent Romans. All were returning from the campaign of M. Antonius, the orator and grandfather of Mark Antony, against the Cilician pirates. The inscription informs us that L. Cicero stopped in Samothrace on the way back from Cilicia, and that he was initiated on September 4. On the other hand, Cicero writes that his uncle Lucius not only went to Cilicia with Antonius, but also departed together with him (*una decesserat, De or.* 2.2). This raises the question whether Antonius was also initiated, his name inscribed in the missing top part of the stone. There are various pro and contra arguments for this suggestion, which, as Clinton notes, "remains at best only a possibility" (p. 31).

Lines A.6–7: Petellius, in listing his city instead of his tribe, departed from the practice of the other Roman citizens in this list, as Clinton notes.

Lines A.11–12: This is the first citizen of Catana in Sicily known to visit Samothrace.

67   Records of initiates from Rome and Byzantion(?)

Block of Thasian marble inscribed on the front, left, and right. The back is smooth-picked. Dowel holes are visible on top and bottom, and there is a pi-shaped clamp hole on top, behind the dowel hole. Brought from the church of Ayios Demetrios in 1953, now in the Archaeological Museum Samothrace, courtyard, inv. 53.560.

H. 0.66 m, W. 0.28–0.32 m, Th. 0.18 m; L.H. 0.02–0.025 (side A), 0.015–0.020 (sides B, C).

Ed. Fraser, *Samothrace* 2.1 (1960) 28.

Cf. Robert 1963, pp. 66–67; *BullÉp* 1964 374; Cole 1984, p. 93; Sherk 1984, p. 26, no. 27.A; Cole 1989, p. 1580, with n. 71, p. 1589, with n. 131; Clinton 2001, p. 35.

2nd–1st century B.C.?

Side A *(June 13)*	Side B	Side C
. IVSO . . . . . [. . . .]	. . . OΛI	[Δ]ιον[ύσιος]
[*vv*?]ID · Iunieis · epop[ta *vel* -es]	[M]ύσται εὐσ[εβεῖς]	[Δ]ιονυσ[ίου]
[.] Cornelius · L · f · Lent[ulus]	[Σ]ώστρατο[ς]	['Η]ρακλῆ[ς]
leg · pro · pr. *vacat*	Προκλείο[υς]	['Η]ρακλέ[ους]
5 mustae piei	[.] . ιθόδημο[ς *vel* -υ]	[Γ]λαυκί[ας]
[L . C]ornelius · L · l. Phil[o]	['I]ερομαχο[ς *vel* -υ]	. όλωνος
[C .] Mutius · C · l · Erun[- -]	Ἀτ[τ]άλου	[.] . ολλᾶ[ς]
[. M]anius Demetr[ius]	[K]ροῖσος	['Ηρ]ακλέο[υς]
[P . .]allius · P · l · LICT[- -]	[Λ]υκόφρον[ος]	[Ἀπ]ολλώ[ς]
10 [. . .]Cor[. .]MITOR[- -]	ἀκόλουθοι	[Δι]οδότ[ου]
[- - - - - - - - -^ca. 20^- - - - - - - - -]	['Η]λιόδωρ[ος]	ἐφόπται · *vv*
[. . . .]US Cornel[ius- - · l ·]	[Π]τολεμα[ῖος]	[Χα]ρίδαμος
[- -^ca. 6^- -]R · Muti · C · [l . . . .]	[Ἀ]μφίδοχο[ς]	[Χα]ριδάμο[υ]
[. . . . .]O · Corne[lius- - · l ·]	Σώσαρχος	[. .]έων
15 [- - - - -]N[- - - - - - - -]	- - - - - - - - -	[Βο]σπορίχο[υ]
- - - - - - - - - - - - - -	*vacat*	[Γλα]υκίας
		[. . .]ντος
		[. . σ]θένης
		[. .]ENIO[Y]
20		. . . EIO . . .
		- - - - - - - - -

Fraser. **A.1** I . . A . OE . . . . . Fraser. **A.2** . . . Id. Fraser, [*vv*] Id. Clinton. **A.9** [P. M]allius · P · l · Lict[avius?] Fraser. **A.10** [. . .]Cor[. .]Matrod[orus] Fraser. **A.11** [. . . .]C[. . . . .]NU[. . . . .] Fraser. **A.13** Muti(us) Fraser, Muti Dimitrova. **B.4** Προκλείο[υ] Fraser. **B.12** [Π]τολεμᾶ[ς] Fraser. **B.13** [Ἀ]μφί<λ>οχο[ς] Fraser, [Ἀ]μφίδοχο[ς] Robert. **C.7** [Π]τολλᾶ[ς] Fraser, [Ἀ]πολλᾶ[ς] *fortasse* Robert. **C.12–13** [Ἀ]ρίδαμος . . . [Ἀ]ριδάμο[υ] Fraser, [Χα]ρίδαμος . . . [Χα]ριδάμο[υ] Robert. **C.14** [Λ]έων Fraser, [Κλ]έων Robert. **C.17** [Λέο]ντος Fraser. **C.19** [Φα]έννο[υ] Fraser.

Epigraphical Commentary

The lettering of the Latin record (side A) is best preserved. That on side C is more legible than that on B.

Line A.1: The remains on the stone seem compatible with restoring the name of Drusus as part of the consular date.

Line A.2: Clinton (p. 35) suggests a lacuna at the beginning of this line, since there is space for no more than two letters.

Line A.3: The NT of Lent[ulus] is in ligature, as Fraser notes.

Line A.11: Illegible traces.

Line B.13: [Ἀ]μφίδοχο[ς] has a clear delta, as Fraser notes.

Lines C.12–14: Two letters need to be restored in the lacunae before the names of the *epoptai,* as Robert notes (p. 64).

Commentary

The block on which the above records were inscribed must have been part of a large structure. Fraser comments on the fact that more than one line must be missing above all three inscriptions, although the top of the block can barely fit one line. He suggests, therefore, that the block was joined with other blocks and that the structure was inscribed vertically on three sides. This is supported by the clamp and dowel holes in the block's top and bottom, as Fraser notes. The block's architectural form is similar to that of **33** and **97**, and it is possible that they belonged to the same structure. The inscriptions on the front and the sides of the present block would suggest that it was part of an anta or a similar structure, but the other two blocks are inscribed on one side only. It seems possible to fit the beginning of the records on sides A and B on line 1 and the missing line above it, so perhaps only side C was inscribed while the block was still in place.

This document, dated by Fraser to the late 2nd or the 1st century B.C., contains three lists of initiates: one Latin in front (side A), and two Greek, side B on the left and side C on the right. The record on side C is probably one of initiates from Byzantion. The spelling EI in the Latin record *(Iunieis, piei)* is consistent with a Republican date. Record A should be dated to June 13 and not before, as Clinton observes.

It is impossible to identify Cornelius Lentulus, as Fraser notes. Many people bore the name Cornelius, Luci filius, Lentulus, including the consuls in 201, 199, and 162, but we have no information about a *legatus pro praetore* with the same name. Fraser also remarked that Lentulus was made *epoptes* on the same day that the *liberti* listed on side A were initiated.

Fraser notes a difficulty in the distribution of patronymics in the names of initiates in record B. The only securely recorded patronymic is Ἀτ[τ]άλου in line 7. Fraser considers also Προκλειο[- -] in line 4 to be a patronymic, because it is inset. It must be noted, however, that Σώσαρχος in line 14 is also inset, but is not a patronymic. Προκλειο[- -] may well have been a patronymic because the nominative Πρόκλειος is very rare, compared to the frequently attested Προκλῆς/Προκλέης. Προκλέ(ί)ους is the typical genitive of the name Προκλῆς/Προκλέης, while Προκλέ(ί)ου is extremely rare. Fraser restores the name in line 5 as a nominative, but it could also be a second genitive, modifying Σ]ώστρατος Προκλείο[υς. The name in line 6, on the other hand, could be a patronymic of the name in line 5. Hence the alternative endings in lines 5 and 6.

Line A.9: There are many possibilities for restoration before -]allius and after Lict[- -]. Lictavius is a very rare name. The title lictor is possible.

Line A.10: A name such as Numitorius is possible.

Line A.13: The abbreviation Muti(us) is uncommon. We may simply have the genitive Muti.

Line B.5: [.] . ιθόδημο[ς *vel* -υ] is a possibility.

Line B.10: On the *akolouthoi* see also **14, 15, 35, 71**. Fraser remarks that they were presumably slaves or people of humble origin, and probably lacked patronymics. I have accepted Fraser's restorations of their names' endings, as they have no patronymics in any of the other inscriptions that list them.

Line B.12: Fraser restores [Π]τολεμᾶ[ς] for lack of space, although he admits that [Π]τολεμα[ῖος] would be more natural. He interprets the hypocoristic as indicative of a lower status, but Robert (p. 64) questions the validity of this observation. It is possible to fit [Π]τολεμα[ῖος] into the lacuna. Moreover, Ptolemas seems to be attested not as a masculine name, but as the genitive of Ptolema, a woman's name.

Line B.13: Robert remarks (p. 64) that [Ἀ]μφίδοχο[ς] is regularly formed and cannot be excluded as a possibility.

Line C.7: The name Πτολλᾶς is very typical of Egypt, and a certain Ἡράκλειος Πτολλᾶ is attested in Egypt (*Portes du désert*, 10.19, 2nd century A.D.), but the poor legibility of the inscription does not allow us to determine whether Fraser's restoration is correct.

Lines C.12–13: Ἀρίδαμος is not attested, while Χαρίδαμος is fairly common, as Robert points out (p. 64).

Line C.15: The name Βοσπόριχος is to be connected with the city of Byzantion, as Robert clarifies. Thus it is likely that the document lists initiates from Byzantion.

Line C.19: Robert (p. 65) notes that [Φα]έννο[υ] is unlikely.

68 Record of initiates and an *epoptes* from Rome?   Fig. 53

Fragment of Thasian marble, broken on all sides. The right side may be close to the original edge. Found on June 17, 1949, in the *Ruinenviereck* north of the Stoa (cf. Lehmann 1998, plans III:5, IV). Archaeological Museum of Samothrace, courtyard, inv. 49.4.

H. 0.16 m, W. 0.08 m, Th. 0.05 m; L.H. 0.03 (line 1), 0.015 (line 2), 0.005 (lines 3–7).

Ed. Fraser, *Samothrace* 2.1 (1960) 30.

Cf. Sherk 1984, pp. 26–27, no. 27.B.

2nd–1st century B.C.?

```
         - - - - - - - - - -
        [C. Mar]tius · [- -]
        [ep]optes · piu[s]
                vacat?
        [- - - -] . NINI · C · Mart(i) · [- -]
        [- - - -]ILACI vacat
    5   [- - - -e]xaminantes vacat
        [- - - - - -] . ARI . [- - - - -]
        [- - - - - - - - -] . M vacat
         - - - - - - - - - - - - - - - -
```

Fraser. **1** . tius Fraser, rius Sherk, Mar]tius Dimitrova. **3** Dimitrova, [- - - -]ONINI · C · Mari Fraser. **5** Dimitrova.

Figure 53. Record of initiates and an *epoptes* from Rome? **(68)**. Courtesy Samothrace Excavations

Epigraphical Commentary

The letters are Republican, carefully done, but hard to make out in places. The difference in size between those in line 1 and the rest is noteworthy.

Line 1: First letter: clear T. What looks like a right diagonal, suitable for R, is damage to the stone.

Line 1: Last letter: bottom part of a left oblique stroke.

Commentary

This is a record of a Roman *epoptes,* C. Martius, and his entourage. Martius is a relatively rare name, which caused difficulties in deciphering line 3, where previous editors read C. Mari, looking for connections with the famous Marius.

69 Record of Roman initiates and of an *epoptes* of unknown   Fig. 54
provenance

Fragment of a stele of Thasian marble, preserved on the left. The back is smooth, inscribed with very faint Greek letters. Brought from the church in Chora on July 5, 1949. Archaeological Museum of Samothrace, courtyard, inv. 49.442.

H. 0.39 m, W. 0.19 m, Th. 0.065–0.067 m; L.H. 0.03 m (line 1), 0.015–0.02 m (lines 2–3), 0.02–0.025 m (line 4), 0.01–0.015 m (lines 5–8).

Edd. Chapouthier, *BCH* 49 (1925), p. 256; *AÉ* 1926 34; [Lommatzsch, *CIL* I² (1918) 2505]; [Degrassi, *ILLRP* I (1957) and I² (1965) 209]; Fraser, *Samothrace* 2.1 (1960) 31.

99 or 44 B.C.?

```
- - - - - - - - - - - - - - -      tree
    M. Anton[io] [A. Postumio vel P. Dollabella]
        co(n)s(ulibus) A. D. IV [- - - -]
        epoptes p[ius]
    Q · Luccius · Q · [f ·]
5   mystae · piei
    P. Antonius Cn · f · V [- - - -]
    M. Antonius Cn · f · [- - - - -]
    Antonia · M · l. [- - - - - -]
    [. . .] . SED[- - - - - -]
- - - - - - - - - - - - - - -
```

Fraser. **6** P. Antonius Chapouthier, P. Antonius Cn. f. V Fraser. **7** M. Antonius [Q.] · f · Chapouthier, M. Antonius C. f. Degrassi, M. Antonius Cn. f. Fraser. **9** ISED Fraser.

Epigraphical Commentary

The Latin text is inscribed on top of a Greek text, illegible letters of which are visible in the upper left part; they occupy ca. 10 lines. The lower part of the Latin inscription is defaced, but still legible.

Commentary

This is a list of Roman initiates and an *epoptes.* Chapouthier dated the inscription to either 99 or 44 B.C., when there were consuls with the name

Figure 54. Record of Roman initiates and of an *epoptes* of unknown provenance **(69).** Courtesy Samothrace Excavations

M. Antonius. Degrassi prefers the earlier date, since in 44 Caesar's name always preceded that of Antony.

The inscription is decorated with a relief above, representing a tree. Chapouthier connects the tree with the Kabiri because of their association with vegetation and their relation to Dionysos, while Lehmann (*apud* Fraser, *per ep.*) suggests that the tree may have simply been a setting. I would not venture to interpret the meaning of the tree in the particular context, for lack of parallels, though I tend to agree with Lehmann that it could have had a decorative function: the Latin inscription was written on top of a Greek one, and the relief does a good job of setting them apart.

Lines 6–8: The initiates listed here probably belonged to the same family, as Fraser comments.

70   Record of initiates from Rome

The inscription is known from the copy made by Cyriacus of Ancona, Cod. Vat. Lat. 5250, folio 20, verso. Its dimensions are unknown.

Edd. [Ritschl 1852, p. 28 = 1866–1879 IV, p. 149]; [Mommsen, *CIL* I (1863) 578; *CIL* III (1873) 713, with Suppl. I.1 (1889) 7367 (commentary)]; [Garrucci 1875–1877 934]; [Dessau, *ILS* II.1 (1902) 4053]; [Ziebarth 1906, p. 411, no. 1]; [Fredrich, *IG* XII.8, pp. 38–39]; [Lommatzsch, *CIL* I² (1918) 663]; [Degrassi, *ILLRP* I (1957) and I² (1965) 210].

Cf. Hatzfeld 1919, p. 60; Cole 1984, p. 95.

July, 92 B.C.?

> [C.?] Claudio · M · Perpenna cos · mens(e) · Quinc(tili) · muste *(sic)* · piei
> L · Lucceius · M · f · leg(atus) · P . Livius · M · l · Pal(atina)
> M · Lucceius · M · l · Artemidorus
> Q̣· Hortensius · M · l · Archelaos

Mommsen. **1** DIEI Cyriacus. **2**, *fin.* PVL Cyriacus.

Commentary

This list of initiates is probably to be dated to July 92 B.C., when the consuls were C. Claudius and M. Perpenna. Another possible date is 130 B.C., as Mommsen notes, when the consuls had the same names except for the praenomen of Claudius (Aulus). Scholars have preferred the later date in view of the initiates' cognomina, which they deemed more suitable for 92 B.C., and because of the expedition against the Thracians dated to that year (see Degrassi).

Line 1: Cyriacus must have taken the open P in PIEI for D, as Mommsen notes.

Line 2: The codex has PVL, corrected by Mommsen to Pal(atina). The listing of tribes for freedmen is relatively rare.

Line 3: It is possible that the person listed here was a freedman of the father of Lucceius in line 2.

71   Record of initiates and *epoptai* from Rome

Pedimental stele of Thasian marble, with molding, broken at bottom. Found at Chora, now lost. I saw a squeeze in the Berlin Academy in May 2004.

H. 0.28 m, W. 0.23 m, Th. 0.05 m; L.H. 0.01 m.

Edd. [Rubensohn 1892, pp. 231–233, no. 2]; Kern 1893, p. 367, no. 10; [Cagnat, *IGR* I.4 (1905) 851]; Fredrich, *IG* XII.8 205; [Dittenberger, *Syll.*³ 1053]; [Hiller von Gaertringen, *IG* XII Suppl. (1939), p. 149].

Cf. Cole 1984, p. 96; 1989, pp. 1585–1586.

After 90 B.C.

ἐπὶ βασιλέως Ἀπολλοφάνου
τοῦ Διοδώρου
ἐφόπται εὐσεβεῖς ·
Λεύκιος Σικίνιος Μαάρκου
5   Ῥωμαῖος
καὶ ἀκόλουθος Σέλευκος
μύσται εὐσεβεῖς ·
Αὖλος Σικίνιος Λευκίου
Ῥωμαῖος Ἀθηνίων
10 [Σπό]ριος Πέρσιος Κοΐντου
[Ῥω]μαῖος Λεωνίδης
[- - - - - -]ὑπηρετικοῦ
[- - - - - -δη]μοσί[ο]υ
- - - - - - - - - - - - - -

Fredrich. **12–13** [ἄρχων] ὑπηρετικοῦ [πλοίου δη]μοσί[ο]υ Hiller.

Commentary

This is a record of Roman initiates, including Σπόριος Πέρσιος Λεωνίδης, probably captain of a dispatch boat *(hyperetikon)* in state service, as Hiller von Gaertringen surmised in *IG* XII Suppl., p. 149. Fredrich dates the inscription to after 90 B.C., since the Greek names of the initiates listed serve as cognomina.

72   Record of Roman initiates of unknown provenance   Fig. 55

Fragment of a pedimental stele of Thasian marble, preserved on top and the left. There is a molding above. The back may be close to the original surface. Found near the Genoese Towers. Archaeological Museum of Samothrace, courtyard, inv. 57.856.

H. 0.27 m, W. 0.22 m, Th. 0.075 m; L.H. 0.01 m (line 1), 0.02–0.025 m (lines 2–6), 0.02 m (lines 7–9).

Edd. Fraser, *Samothrace* 2.1 (1960) 32; [Sherk 1984, p. 26, no. 27].

Cf. Cole 1984, p. 95.

76 B.C.

on molding: [ἐ]πὶ βασιλ[έως- - - - - -]
below molding: Cn · Oc[tavio M. f.]
                 C · Scrib[onio C. f. co(n)s(ulibus)]
                    A · D · X[- - - - - -]
   5 mustae [piei]
                 Q · Minuc[ius- - - -]
                    The[rmus]
                 C · Magul[- - - - -]
                 [. L?]aberi[us- - - -]
            - - - - - - - - - - - - - -

Figure 55. Record of Roman initiates of unknown provenance (72)

Fraser. **8** P. Magul[nius Fraser, C. Magul[- - Dimitrova. **9** [. L- *vel* . F]aberius Fraser.

Epigraphical Commentary

The letters are clear and squarish. Line 1 has much smaller lettering, as Fraser notes. The hand looks the same as that of **66**.

Commentary

This is a list of Roman initiates, dated by Fraser to 76 B.C., on the basis of the consuls' names.

Lines 6–7: I find likely Fraser's suggestion that this might be the same Q. Minutius Thermus as the governor of Asia in 52–50 B.C. The homonymous legate of 86 B.C. is another possibility (cf. Broughton [1952] 1984, p. 592).

Line 9: Laberius is a very common name, and a preferable restoration.

73   Record of initiates and *epoptai* from Rome

Fragment of marble stele with molding above, broken on the right and below. Found in Potamia, in the northwest of the island, in a church, then brought to the school. Now missing. I saw a squeeze in the Berlin Academy in May 2004.

H. 0.25 m, W. 0.25 m, Th. 0.08 m; L.H. 0.02–0.03 m.

Edd. [Mommsen, *CIL* III Suppl. I.3 (1889) 12318]; Kern 1893, p. 374, no. 22; [Dessau, *ILS* II.1 (1902) 4054]; Fredrich, *IG* XII.8, p. 39, no. 1; [Lommatzsch, *CIL* I² (1918) 665]; [Degrassi, *ILLRP* I (1957)and I² (1965) 213].

Cf. Cole 1984, p. 96.

Ca. 79 B.C.?

```
        Mystae · piei · s(acrum vel -acra acceperunt?)
        Epoptae
    L · Fourius · L · f · Ou[f(entina)]
        Crassupes
  5 P · Teidius · P · f · Pom[p(tina)]
        unclear traces

    - - - - - - - - - - - - - - - - -
```

Mommsen, Degrassi. **1** Pieis, *edd.,* piei · s(acrum *vel* -acra acceperunt?) Dimitrova.

Epigraphical Commentary

The letters are discrepant, but clear. Line 1 is separated by one horizontal line above and one below.

Commentary

The date is based mainly on the plausible identification of L. Fourius Crassupes (see *ad* lines 3–4). The spellings EI and OU are typical of the Republican period.

Line 1: Previous editors have assumed that the right edge is preserved, and have printed PIEIS, which does not make sense. The squeeze shows a medial dot between PIEI and S.

Line 3: The last U, read by previous editors, is not visible on the squeeze.

Lines 3–4: The Furii Crassupedes (also spelled Crassipedes) were a famous family, as Degrassi observes. L. Fourius Crassupes of the present inscription is probably the same as the one attested in an inscription from the Piraeus, *IG* II² 3218, dated to ca. 79 B.C. He must have been an official in Greece, since the inscription from the Piraeus mentions an ambassador sent to him (cf. Münzer, *RE* VII.1 1910, cols. 352–353). He may also be the *legatus* of 73 B.C., mentioned by Plutarch.[57]

Line 5: The name Teidius is common during the Imperial period, as Mommsen notes.

74 Records of Roman initiates(?) of unknown provenance   Fig. 56

Top left (with respect to side A) part of an opisthographic stele of Thasian marble. Found in July 1962 in the area of the Stoa, in the interior of a post-antique structure, 2.15 m west of the west foundation. Archaeological Museum of Samothrace, inv. 62.1464.

H. 0.16 m, W. 0.07 m, Th. 0.05 m; L.H. 0.02 m (side A, lines 1–2), 0.01 m (side A, line 3, and side B).

Unpublished.

67 B.C.

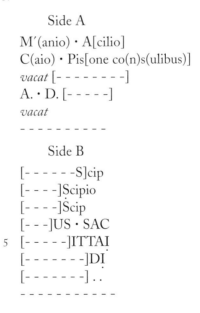

Side A

M′(anio) · A[cilio]
C(aio) · Pis[one co(n)s(ulibus)]
vacat [- - - - - - - -]
A. · D. [- - - - -]
vacat
- - - - - - - - - -

Side B

[- - - - - -S]cip
[- - - -]Scipio
[- - - -]Scip
[- - -]US · SAC
5   [- - - - -]ITTAI
[- - - - - -]DI
[- - - - - -] . .
- - - - - - - - - -

Epigraphical Commentary
The letters are carefully done.

Commentary
This may have been a list of Roman initiates, dated to 67 B.C. It is unclear whether the inscription on side B is a continuation of that on side A, but this seems likely in view of the lettering, which is consistent with a date in the 1st century B.C.

Figure 56. Records of Roman initiates(?) of unknown provenance (74): side A *(top)*, side B *(bottom)*

57. Thomasson 1991, p. 17, app. I, no. 146.

75   Greek record of Roman *epoptai*(?) of unknown provenance   Fig. 57

Fragment of a pedimental stele of Thasian marble, probably with crown-
ing molding, preserved on the left. The back is smooth-picked and inscribed
with stray letters. Found in August 1976 in a limekiln in the ancient city.
Archaeological Museum of Samothrace, storeroom, inv. 76.16.

H. 0.41 m, W. 0.145 m, Th. 0.071 m; L.H. 0.025–0.035 m (lines 1–3),
0.01–0.015 m (lines 4–10).

Unpublished.

Figure 57. Greek record of Roman
epoptai(?) of unknown provenance
(**75**)

62 B.C. or A.D. 78?

```
         Υ . . . ΩΙ[- - - - - - - - - - - - - -]
         Λευκίο[υ- - - - - - - - - - - - - - - -]
         Δέκ[μου- - - - - - - - - - - - - - - -]
         ἐπό[πται(?) - - - - - - - - - - - - -]
     5   Σκρειβω[νι- - - - - - - - - - - - - -]
         Σκρειβ[- - - - - - - - - - - - - - - - -]
         τοῦ Κ[- - - - - - - - - - - - - - - - - -]
         ΕΥΤ[- - - - - - - - - - - - - - - - - - -]
         Ε[- - - - - - - - - - - - - - - - - - - - -]
    10   ΛΕΥ[- - - - - - - - - - - - - - - - - - -]
         - - - - - - - - - - - - - - - - - - - - - -
```

Epigraphical Commentary
The letters are clear and carefully executed, similar to those of **79** (especially kappa).

Line 1: Unclear traces. ὑπάτων is possible.

Line 4: Third letter: a circle. Omega is possible, if the mark on the
left is part of the letter.

Commentary
This probably was a list of *epoptai* and initiates. The stone could belong with
79, but a secure join cannot be established. Two dates are possible if the
names Λεύκιος and Δέκμος are the consuls' praenomina: 62 B.C., when the
consuls were D. Iunius Silanus and L. Licinius Murena, and A.D. 78, when
the consuls were D. Iunius Novius Priscus and L. Ceionius Commodus. If
the stone belongs with **79**, then the earlier date is to be preferred since **79**,
inscription ii is dated to 46 B.C., and was inscribed after **79**, inscription i.

76   Record of Roman initiate(s) of unknown provenance   Fig. 58

Fragment of a base of Thasian marble, inscribed on the front and
right, broken on the left, above, and on the back. Found on July 18, 1950,
in the ancient city, just above the spring that fed the "Roman aqueduct."
Archaeological Museum of Samothrace, courtyard, inv. 50.632.

H. 0.22 m, W. 0.515 m, Th. 0.395 m; L.H. 0.03 m (side A, lines
1–4), 0.015 m (side A, line 5), 0.025 m (side B, lines 1–2), 0.03 m (side B,
line 3).

Ed. Fraser, *Samothrace* 2.1 (1960) 17.

Cf. Robert and Robert, *BullÉp* 1964 368, 400.

Figure 58. Record of Roman initiate(s) of unknown provenance (76): side A *(left)*, side B *(right)*

Hellenistic? (side A), 2nd–1st century B.C.? (side B)

Side A

[Σα]μο[θράικων]
ὁ δῆμος *vacat*
Πυθοκλῆν
[Ἀπ]ολλοφάνους
5 [- - - - - -ἐ]ποίη[σεν]

Side B

[- -]atello[- - mys]-
[tes?] pius . . . Regius[- -]
[- -] . PONTE[- - -]
[- - - -] . . [- - - - - -]

Fraser. **B.1** Atelli[us f. *vel* l. Fraser, - -]Metello[co(n)s(ulibus)(?) Dimitrova. **B.2** . . . NIO . NI Fraser. **B.3** epo<p>tes Fraser.

Epigraphical Commentary
The lettering of the Greek part suggests a Hellenistic date, as Fraser notes. The Latin part is defaced.
  Side B, first letter: Oblique stroke, as Fraser notes.
  Side B, dots: Unclear traces.

Commentary
The stone was originally a statue base, inscribed with the name Πυθοκλῆς Ἀπολλοφάνους when he was honored by the people of Samothrace. Then the stone was reused and a record of Roman initiates was inscribed on the right. The findspot of the base—the ancient city, above the spring that fed the Roman aqueduct—is curious; for the location of the spring, see Lehmann-Hartleben 1939, pp. 142–144. Fraser thinks that the base originally stood in the sanctuary and was transferred to the ancient city at a later date, but in view of the other inscriptions found in the ancient city (**39, 57**), such an assumption is no longer necessary.
  Pythokles, son of Apollophanes, is also known from an inscription on the base of a statue that he dedicated to the Great Gods. The monument

was found in the sanctuary, near the Milesian dedication (Salviat 1962, p. 270). It is possible that he was honored by the people of Samothrace because of the dedication that he made.

The tentative date of the Latin record is based on the lettering, especially the wide, open P, as Fraser notes. He dates the record before the middle of the 1st century B.C.

Line 6: A name such as Anatellon, relatively frequent in Roman inscriptions, is possible.

Line 8: Fraser reads epo<p>tes, but I find it unlikely that the carver inscribed N for a P. A name like Ponteius or Pontenius is possible.

77   Record of Roman initiates(?) of unknown provenance

Fragment of a pedimental stele of Thasian marble, broken on the left and below. Fredrich copied it in Chora, at the house of Phardys. Its present location is unknown. I saw a squeeze in the Berlin Academy in May 2004.

H. 0.24 m, W. 0.26 m, Th. 0.05 m; L.H. 0.012 m (lines 1–2), 0.025 m (line 3).

Edd. Kern 1893, p. 372, no. 16; [Mommsen, *CIL* III Suppl. I.3 (1893) 12320]; [Cagnat, *IGR* I.4 (1905) 846]; Fredrich, *IG* XII.8 208; [Lommatzsch, *CIL* I² (1918) 669].

50 or 49 B.C.

> [ἐπὶ] βασιλέως Νουμηνίου
> [τοῦ Ν]ουμηνίου
> [L. Paull- *vel* C. Lentul]o · C. Marce-
> [llo co(n)s(ulibus)]

Fredrich.

Commentary

This probably was the beginning of a list of initiates.

Lines 1–2: The eponymous official is otherwise unattested.

Line 3: Either name is possible, but the space is perhaps more suitable for a shorter name (e.g., [L. Paull]o), as Fredrich notes.

78   Record of Greek, Thracian, and Roman initiates from   Fig. 59
         Rome(?)

Stele of Thasian marble, found in Palaiopolis, then moved to Istanbul (Çinili Kiosk, Topkapı Palace), but Fredrich was unable to locate it.

H. 0.49 m, W. 0.16 m, Th. 0.08 m; L.H.?

Edd. Conze 1880, p. 92, no. 2; [Mommsen, *CIL* III Suppl. I.1 (1889) 7369]; [Cagnat, *IGR* I.4 (1905) 847]; [Fredrich, *IG* XII.8 207]; [Lommatzsch, *CIL* I² (1918) 668]; [Degrassi, *ILLRP* I (1957) and I² (1965) 212].

Cf. Robert and Robert, *BullÉp* 1958 270; Robert 1963, pp. 67–69; Cole 1984, p. 94.

59 or 48 or 46–44 B.C.

> sac[ra *vel* -um]
> C · Caes · [- -co(n)s(ulibus)]

Figure 59. Record of Greek, Thracian, and Roman initiates from Rome(?) (78). Conze 1880, p. 92, no. 2

A· D· V· I[dus- - -]
    must(ae) [pii]
5 T. Ofatulen[us - - -]
    Sabinus
Tertia · Dom[- - -]
    Πυθ[- - -]
T. Ofatulenus[- - -]
10 A. Furius [- - -]
T. Ofatulenu[s - - -]
T. Ofatulenus · S[abinus? - -]
P. Curtius · P. l(ibertus) I[- -]
Ἀντίγονος Τί[του?]
15 M. Baebius [- - -]
    Sabini · [servi?]
Philomusus, [- - -]
Beitus, Diodo[r *vel* -tus - -]
ἀγορανομοῦν[τος - - -].

Fredrich. 1 sa[cra acceperunt?] Hirschfeld [*apud* Fredrich], sac[ra *vel* sacrum] *vel* sacr[a (acceperunt?)] Dimitrova. 8 *omisit* Conze. 15 M. Baebius [- - - -Ofatuleni] Fredrich, M. Baebius [- - -] Dimitrova. 16 Sabini · [- - -] Fredrich, Sabini · [servi?] Dimitrova. 18 DION Conze, Diodo[*edd.*

Epigraphical Commentary

The lettering can be surmised from Conze's facsimile.
    Line 1: The C is visible on the facsimile.

Commentary

This is a list of Roman initiates, dated to one of Caesar's consulships.
    Line 1: The phrase *sacra acceperunt*, "received the sacred rites/things" is certainly paralleled in two other Samothracian documents (**100** and **169**), so the restoration would be likely, if it were not for the facsimile, which shows sac[r centered, with not enough space to add acceperunt. We see SACR in a similar position in **90**. Therefore, I have interpreted sac[r as an abbreviation for sacra (acceperunt). Of course, this is only a hypothesis, and simply sacra or sacrum is also possible.
    Line 16: Sabini is indented, probably marking a new category, most likely slaves. Hence my reluctance to restore [- - -Ofatuleni] at the end of the previous line.
    Lines 17–18: The slaves of Sabinus must be listed here. Beitus, Greek spelling Β(ε)ιθυς, is a well-attested Thracian name (e.g., *IGBulg* 738, 1283, 1398, 1419, 2322, 2337, etc.).[58]

79   Record of Greek and Thracian initiates, and record of   Fig. 60
       Roman initiates of unknown provenance

Two joining pieces of a stele of Thasian marble, broken only above. The back is smooth, inscribed with faint Latin characters. The lower part, in which a rectangular hole has been cut, has a rough surface below the inscription, but was smoothed at the bottom for insertion into a base. Found in Chora on June 20, 1939. Archaeological Museum of Samothrace, inv. 39.548.

58. Cf. Detschew 1957, pp. 66–68.

H. 0.62 m, W. 0.39 m, Th. 0.07 m; L.H. 0.01 m (Greek), 0.01–0.015 m (Latin).

Edd. Fraser, *Samothrace* 2.1 (1960) 33; *AÉ* 1947 5.

Cf. Lehmann-Hartleben 1940, p. 358; Cole 1984, p. 94; Clinton 2001, p. 35.

1st century B.C.? (inscription i), October 18, 46 B.C. (inscription ii)

i	Side A, Col. I		Side A, Col. II	
	- - - - - - - - - - -		- - - - - - - - - - -	
	. . ΩΝΕΩΣ		- - - - - - - - - - -	
	Ὠπηνεύ[ς]		- - - - - - - - - - -	
	Ἀριστοκλείους		Φιλ[- - - - - - - -]	
	Πυθίων		Δημ[- - - - - - -]	
5	Ἀριστοκλείους		Ε[ὐ]μέν[ης]	
	Θεόξενος		Σι . . . τας	
	Μητροδώρου		Πρόκλος	
	Μηνόφιλος		[- - - - - -]ΛΙ[- - - - - -]	
	Φιλίππου		Ἕλενος	
10	Διονυσοκλῆς		[- - - - - -]κου	
	Μητροδώρου		[- - - - - -]ΛΕ[- - - -]	
	Διζάσσκος	ii	[- - - - - -]ΟΝΕ	
	Ἀρίστων		[C.] I[ul]io Caesare	
	Ἀριστοθε[ί]ου		M · Lepido · cos · A.D.	*October 18, 46 B.C.*
15	Λεύκιος Ἄκαι[ο]ς		XV · K · Nov. musta	
	Διοφάνους		M · Paccius P · f ·	
	Περιγένης		Fal · Rufus · C · Pacciu[s]	
	Φιλοχάρους		C · l · Apollonides	
	Διονύσιος		Philodamus Pac[ci]	
20	Διοδότου		Antiochus Pac[ci]	
	Δίναρχος		[- -]MY[- - -]	
	Ἀγαθ[- - - - - -]		- - - - - - - - - - -	
	Ἐπιγένης			
	- - - - - - - - - - -			

Side B

- - - - - - - - - - -
[- - - - - -]IIV[- - - -]
[- - - - - -]ONIA[- - - -]
- - - - - - - - - - -
vacat?

Fraser.

Epigraphical Commentary
The inscription is now defaced, especially on the back.

Commentary
The lettering and physical properties of the stone are similar to those of **75**, but it is impossible to establish a secure join. The stone contains two lists of initiates, one Greek (inscription i) and one Latin (ii). The Latin list was inscribed in the blank space after the end of i, and Fraser suggests that it may have continued on the back. It is dated to October 18, 46 B.C.

Figure 60. Record of Greek and Thracian initiates, and record of Roman initiates of unknown provenance (79). Courtesy Samothrace Excavations

It is unclear from which city the Greek initiates came, as Fraser notes. Line 2: A genitive of the type Ἐτεωνέως is possible.

Line 12: Διζάσσκος must be a diminutive, formed after Greek models, of Dizas, a well-attested Thracian name; cf. *IGBulg* II 511, 523, 560, III 917, 1106, 1166, 1175, 1201, 1310, 1395, IV 2067, 2130, etc.[59] Fraser notes that he is the only person without a patronymic.

It is conceivable that the initiates listed in lines 3 and 5 and lines 7 and 11, respectively, were brothers, given their patronymics.

80 Record of Roman initiates of unknown provenance Fig. 61

Fragment of pedimental stele of Thasian marble, preserved on top and the left. The back is very close to the original surface, which was probably rough-picked. The fragment may belong together with **81**, though a secure join cannot be established. Found near the Genoese Towers on June 17, 1951. Archaeological Museum of Samothrace, inv. 51.98.

H. 0.226 m, W. 0.23 m, Th. 0.074 m; L.H. 0.008–0.012 m (lines 1–2, 5–7), 0.015 m (lines 3–4).

Edd. Lehmann 1953, pp. 12–13, pl. 6:d; Fraser, *Samothrace* 2.1 (1960) 34.

Cf. Walton 1963, p. 99; Robert 1963, pp. 67–69; Cole 1984, pp. 95–96; 1989, p. 1583 with n. 89; Clinton 2001, p. 35.

59. Cf. also Detschew 1957, pp. 133–134.

Figure 61. Record of Roman initiates of unknown provenance (80)

June 20, 35 B.C.

in pediment:	Hilarus Prim[us]
in cornice:	[ἀγ]ορανομοῦντος X[- - - -]
below pediment:	L · Cornuficio · Sex · Po[mpeio]
	cos · A · D · XII K · Iul(ias)
5	mustae p[i]ei
	M · Servilius · M · l(ibertus) · Philo
	[. .]E[. . . . .]S M · l(ibertus) Pamp[hilus]
	[- - - - - - -]‖[- - - - - -]
	- - - - - - - - - - - - - - - -

        Fraser. **6** M. Servilius Walton, [M. S]ervilius Fraser. **7** [M. S]e[rvilius] Fraser.

Epigraphical Commentary
The lettering and the physical features of the fragment are similar to those of **81**.

Commentary
This is a list of Roman initiates, dated to June 20, 35 B.C. The initiates whose names are preserved here were all freedmen.

    Line 1: Presumably this man was omitted from the list below and added later; cf. Cole 1984, p. 42.

81   Record of Roman initiates of unknown provenance   Fig. 62

    Stele of Thasian marble, preserved on the right and the rough-picked back. Found in 2002 in the stream near the Hieron, during cleaning operations in the area, now at Old School Lab of the Ephoreia of Prehistoric and Classical Antiquities in Palaiopolis. Ephoreia inv. 02.50.

    H. 0.23 m, W. 0.16 m, Th. 0.07 m; L.H. 0.01–0.015 m, 0.025–0.03 m (line 10), 0.02 m (line 11).

    Unpublished.

Figure 62. Record of Roman initiates
of unknown provenance (81)

1st century B.C.?

- -
      M · Aurelius M · l(ibertus) · O[- - - - -]
      Q · Masonius Sp · l(ibertus) · [- - - - - -]
      L · Ofalius M. l(ibertus) Oes .. iu[s- - - -]
      M · Considius Aristoni[cus- - - - - - - -]
  5 [.^{ca.4}.]philus · Theodot[us- - - - - - - - - -]
      C · M[arc]ellus C · l(ibertus) Herode[s- -]
      L (*vel* T) Petronius L (*vel* T) · l(ibertus) Persicu[s- -]
      L · Cornelius · L · l(ibertus) · Alypus I [- -]
      T · Annaeus · T · l(ibertus) · Gem[inus?- -]
      vacat 1 vs.
  10   SERVI ·
      vv Lepidus · D · s(ervus) [- - -?- -]
      vv Anteros · T · s(ervus) [- - -?- -]
- -

Epigraphical Commentary
The letters are elongated and clear, similar to those of **80**.
    Line 10: I-longa.

Commentary
This was a list of Roman initiates, tentatively dated on the basis of the
lettering to the 1st century B.C., though a later date cannot be excluded. It
is very similar to **80** in hand and layout, but the use of Y to render upsilon
(Alypus, line 8) and of I-longa (line 10) differentiate it from the orthography
of **80**, which has *mustae* (line 5) and does not employ I-longa.

82   Record of Greek initiates and of Roman *epoptai*(?) of   Fig. 63
      unknown provenance

Fragment of Thasian marble, preserved at the lower right. Brought from Chora, now in the Archaeological Museum of Samothrace, courtyard. No inv. no.

H. 0.19 m, W. 0.14 m, Th. 0.07 m; L.H. 0.04 m (line 4), 0.02 m (line 5), 0.015 (lines 1–4).

Edd. Conze 1875, p. 41, no. 11, pl. 71:11; [Mommsen, *CIL* III Suppl. I.1 (1889) 7370]; Fredrich, *IG* XII.8 210.

Cf. Clinton 2001, p. 35.

August 8, before 8 B.C.

Figure 63. Record of Greek initiates and of Roman *epoptai*(?) of unknown provenance (82)

```
        [- - - - - - - - - - - - -]
        [- - - - - - - -]μύστην
        [- - - - - - -]A . TPO[- - -]
        [- - - - - -e]phop[t? - -]
   5    [- - - -A. D.] VI · eid(us) · Sex(tiles)
        [- - - - - - -]Q. · f. co(n)s(ulibus)
```

Fredrich. 4 -phor[us] Fredrich, [- - -e]phop[t? - -] Dimitrova.

Epigraphical Commentary

The Greek in lines 1–2 is badly damaged, while the Latin letters are uneven and inelegant.

Commentary

The document contains an older Greek record of initiation and a Latin record, possibly of *epopteia*, dated by Mommsen before 8 B.C. because the name Sextilis went out of use when Augustus named the month after himself in 8 B.C. The date in lines 5–6 possibly indicates the beginning of a new record.

83   Record of Roman initiates(?) of unknown provenance   Fig. 64

Fragment of a pedimental stele of Thasian marble, broken below, rough-picked on back. Its findspot is unknown. Paris, Musée du Louvre, inv. Ma. 4196.

H. 0.15 m, W. 0.26 m, Th. 0.035 m; L.H. 0.02 m.

Ed. Fredrich, *IG* XII.8, p. 39.

8 B.C.

```
        [C.] Marcio C[e]nsorin[o]
        [C.] Asinio Gallo co(n)s(ulibus)
        - - - - - - - - - - - - - - - - -
```

1–2 Dimitrova, Marcio- - Fredrich.

Epigraphical Commentary

The inscription is nearly obliterated, and Fredrich could only read the name Marcio. The hand is similar to that of **84**.

Line 2: The Ls of Gallo are represented by two vertical lines.

Figure 64 *(above, left)*. Record of Roman initiates(?) of unknown provenance (83). Courtesy Musée du Louvre, Department of Greek, Roman, and Etruscan Antiquities

Figure 65 *(above, right)*. Record of Roman initiates(?) of unknown provenance (84)

Commentary

This probably was a list of Roman initiates; it is dated by consuls to 8 B.C.

84   Record of Roman initiates(?) of unknown provenance   Fig. 65

Fragment of Thasian marble preserved on the left; the back has mortar at places. Provenance unknown, now in the Archaeological Museum of Samothrace. No inv. no.

H. 0.09 m, W. 0.08 m, Th. 0.04 m; L.H. 0.02 m (lines 1–2), 0.015 m (lines 3–8).

Unpublished.

8 B.C.?

```
        - - - - - - - - - -
        [- - - - - -]U[- -]
        Verus vacat
        C · Axsius C[. F.- -]
        . Pomponi[us- -]
    5   C · Fictorius [- -]
        C · Rustius C · F[- -]
        M · Cusinius [- -]
        M · Licini[us- -]
        - - - - - - - - - -
```

Epigraphical Commentary

The letters are relatively broad and carefully done, with finials.

Lines 2, 6, 8: Dotted letters: unclear traces.

Line 4: First letter: unclear traces.

Commentary

This was probably a list of initiates, perhaps the continuation of **83**, in view of the similar layout and lettering.

85   Record of initiates from Rome   Fig. 66

Fragment of Thasian marble, broken on all sides. Provenance unknown. Archaeological Museum of Samothrace, courtyard. No inv. no.

H. 0.18 m, W. 0.27 m, Th. 0.06 m; L.H. 0.03 m.

Unpublished.

End of 1st century B.C.–middle of 1st century A.D.

```
- - - - - - - - - - - - - - - - - - - - - - -
            [myst]ae · leaf piei
    [- - - -] (.) . s · L · f · Ter(etina) · Proculus [-?- -]
    [- - -Ca]esaris Augusti ·  vacat [-?- -]
- - - - - - - - - - - - - - - - - - - - - - -
```

    3 [- - legatus(?)Ca]esaris Dimitrova.

Figure 66. Record of initiates from Rome (85)

Epigraphical Commentary

The letters are elongated, with finials.

   Line 2: The first letter is either U or a ligature of R and U. A ligature of RAS is also possible. The E of Ter(etina) is damaged, and may be confused with an F.

Commentary

This is a list of Roman initiates. The phrase [- - -Ca]esaris Augusti calls for an Imperial date, but the spelling *piei* makes dating the inscription after the middle of the 1st century A.D. unlikely. A certain Proculus, son of Lucius, of the tribe Teretina, is mentioned in an epitaph (*AÉ* 1908 218), but it is unclear whether he is the same person or related to the initiate listed here.

   Line 3: It is unclear whether [- - -Ca]esaris Augusti was part of Proculus's title or of the person listed after him, since we do not know the dimensions of the inscription. A plausible restoration would be [legatus Ca]esaris Augusti, an expression frequently attested with the name of the emperor Tiberius.

86   Record of Roman initiates(?) of unknown provenance   Fig. 67

   Two joining fragments of Thasian marble. The stele is preserved on the left and the top. The back is rough-picked. Fragment *a* was found at 17.00–21.00 m east and 33.00–37.50 m south, and fragment *b* at 17.85–21.15 m east and 32.70–37.50 m south, of the northeastern inner corner of the Stoa in July 1971. Archaeological Museum of Samothrace, inv. 71.954.

   H. 0.36 m, W. 0.16 m, Th. 0.06 m; L.H. 0.04 m (line 1), 0.03 m (line 2), 0.035 m (line 3), 0.015 m (lines 4–5), 0.02 m (line 6), 0.03 m (line 7).

   Unpublished.

A.D. 6

```
        D(is) ·          M(agnis)
    M(arco) · Aemilio [Lepido]
    L(ucio) · Arrun[tio consulibus]
             ἐπὶ β[ασιλέως- - - - - - - -]
  5  Ἀττάλου v [- - - -?- - - - -]
             in[itiati sunt?- - - - - -]
    C(aius) · Gavius[- - - - - - - -]
    . . [- - - - - - - - - - - - - - - - -]
    - - - - - - - - - - - - - - - - - - - -
```

Figure 67. Record of Roman initiates(?) of unknown provenance (86)

Epigraphical Commentary
The letters are elegant and clear.

Commentary
The phrase D(is) M(agnis) corresponds exactly to Θεοῖς Μεγάλοις, and is also attested in an unpublished dedication (see *ad* **93**, Commentary), where it is not abbreviated. This was probably a list of Roman initiates.

87   Record of initiates from Rome

The inscription is known from Codex Ambrosianus A 55, now lost.
Edd. [Muratori 1739–1742 I, p. 268, no. 6, and III, p. 1498, no. 9]; [Boeckh, *CIG* II.1 (1832) 2159]; [Mommsen, *CIL* I (1863), add. p. 558 = *CIL* III (1873) 717, with add. p. 990]; [Dessau, *ILS* II.1 (1902) 4055]; [Cagnat, *IGR* I.4 (1905) 848]; [Fredrich, *IG* XII.8 214.]
Cf. Ziebarth 1906, p. 414, no. 11; Cole 1984, p. 91; 1989, pp. 1583–1584; Clinton 2001, p. 35.

September 13, A.D. 14

    ἐπὶ βασιλέως Θασίων<ο>ς <τ>οῦ
        Θαλασίωνος
    Sex. Pompeio · et · Sex. Appuleio · co(n)s(ulibus)
    Idibus · Septembr(ibus) mystes · pius
5   P. Sextius · Lippinus · Tarquitianus · q(uaestor) · Macedoni(ae) · et · sym-
      mys<t>ae · pii *vacat* PO P I I S

Fredrich. **2** Θαλασ<σ>ίωνος Boeckh. **5–6** P. Sextius · Lippinus · Tarquitianus · Q. Macedon · [f.] et · sym|mys[t]ae · pii *vacat* p[r]o · piis Mommsen. **6** <e>popt<i>s Huebner (*apud* Fredrich).

Epigraphical Commentary
Line 1: ΘΑΣΙΩΝΙΣΙΟΥ codex.
   Line 5: MACEDONI codex.
   Line 6: MYSIAE, PO PIIS codex.

Commentary
This is a record of Roman initiates: P. Sextius Lippinus Tarquitianus (*PIR* S 470), quaestor of Macedonia, and his entourage. It dates to September 13, A.D. 14.
Line 2: Thalas(s)ion is a very rare name; cf. *LGPN* II. Thalasios, however, is fairly common. The abbreviation ΘΑΛΑΣΙ is visible on a Samothracian coin; see *IG* XII.8, p. 41, which may refer to the same king. The name Thasion or Thalasion may also be attested in **43**; see *ad* line 2.
Line 6: The expression *pro piis*, which appears in dedications (though relatively rarely), does not occur in Samothracian inscriptions.

88   Record of an initiate from Rome   Fig. 68

Fragment of marble, found near the long wall of the Stoa, now lost.
H. 0.135 m, W. 0.14 m, Th. 0.045 m; L.H.?
Edd. Conze 1880, p. 91, no. 1; [Mommsen 1884, no. 223]; [Mommsen, *CIL* III Suppl. I.1 (1889) 7372]; Fredrich, *IG* XII.8, p. 39.

A.D. 18?

    [- - - -]Rufus · praetorius
    [must]es · pius
    [san]ctissuma numina ves-
    [vene]ror precibus |tra

Conze, Mommsen.

Epigraphical Commentary
The layout can be surmised from Conze's facsimile.

Commentary
This is a record of initiation, along with a personal declaration of respect for the cult by the *praetorius* Rufus. As Fredrich notes, he may be the same as T. Trebellenus Rufus, whom Tiberius appointed in A.D. 18 as the guardian of the children of the Thracian king Cotys IV after the latter's murder by the former king Rhescouporis (Tac. *Ann.* 2.67).[60]

89   Record of initiates from Rome, Pergamon, Chios, and   Fig. 69
     of *epoptae* from Rome

    Limestone plaque, broken below and to the right. The back is smooth-picked, possibly inscribed. Acquired from Kamariotissa on July 30, 1939, where it had been reused as a step. Archaeological Museum of Samothrace, inv. 39.1072.

    H. 0.32 m, W. 0.32 m, Th. 0.08 m; L.H. 0.014 m (lines 1–3, 17), 0.012 m (line 4), 0.008 m (lines 5–16, 18–19).

    Edd. Lehmann-Hartleben 1940, p. 356; *BullÉp* 1944 151a; *AÉ* 1947 3; Fraser, *Samothrace* 2.1 (1960) 36.

    Cf. Lehmann, *Samothrace* 2.2 (1960), p. 24; Robert 1963, pp. 67–69; Cole 1984, pp. 98–99; Clinton 2001, p. 35.

June 6, A.D. 19

	Col. I	Col. II	Col. III
	[ἐ]π[ὶ βασιλέως . . . .]ου τοῦ		
	Μητρώνακτος		
	M · Iunio Silano · L · Norbano Bal[bo co(n)s(ulibus)]		
	VIII Idus Iunias, mystae pii		
5	C Marius L · f · Ste(llatina) · Schinas	servi Schinae	
	[R]upilia Q · f · Quinta	Cedrus	An[. ca. 4 .]
	Symmus[tae] · piI	Laetus	*vacat*
	L · Iulius · Sp · f · Pap(iria) · Niger	[. . .]mas	Opt[. ca. 4 .]
	[.] Aristopus Stephanius	Clenas	Sc[. ca. 4 .]
10	[.]Marius Fructus	Eoc[. . .]	To[. ca. 4 .]
	[. ca. 5 .]Y . RUS Pergamenus	Pho[e]bus	[. ca. 6 .]
	[Me]nander Chius	Paneros	[. ca. 6 .]
	[- - - - - -] Lusius	Epaphus	[. ca. 6 .]
	vacat	Paideros	Sp[. ca. 4 .]
		Tarula	Pa[. ca. 4 .]
15		Felix	Xys[. ca. 4 .]

Figure 68. Record of an initiate from Rome (88). Conze 1880, p. 91, no. 1

60. Cf. also *PIR* T 230, and Clinton, forthcoming (printed here as **46**, above).

Epoptae

[C] · Marius L · f · Ste(llatina) · Schinas

[Rupili]a Q · f · Quinta

[.] Marius Fructus

20 [ἀγοραν]ομοῦντος Ἀπολλ[- - - - τοῦ]

Διοδότου.

Fraser. 8 [Her]mas   Opt[atus] Fraser, [- -]mas   Opt[- - - -] Dimitrova.
9 [- - - - - -]asidius Stephaniu[s] Fraser, [- -]Pisidius Stephanius Dimitrova. 15
Xy[stus] Fraser, Xys[- -] Dimitrova.

Epigraphical Commentary

The letters are elongated and carefully done, though the inscription is now
badly defaced.

Line I.7: I-longa.

The slaves' names in columns II and III are rather narrowly spaced,
and do not align with the lines in column I.

Commentary

This is a list of Roman *mystae, symmystae* (including one person from Pergamon and one from Chios), *epoptae,* and slaves, dated to June 6, A.D. 19.
An eponymous official with the patronymic Μητρώνακτος is perhaps also
attested in **6** (2nd century B.C.?), but it is unlikely that the two are related.
It is possible that the eponymous *basileus* of **46**, Θεόδωρ[ος?] Μητρόνακτος,
was related in some way; for the name Metronax as associated with Samothracian eponyms, see also the numismatic evidence, *IG* XII.8, p. 41.

Figure 69. Record of initiates from
Rome, Pergamon, Chios, and of
epoptae from Rome (89). Courtesy
Samothrace Excavations

Marius Schinas and (presumably his wife) Rupilia (column I, lines 5–6) are the main initiates listed in this document. They were initiated together with six other people, (*symmystae,* column I, lines 7–13), and their household slaves (columns II and III, lines 5–15). It is unclear whether the main initiates and the *symmystae* formed one party, as Fraser notes. Three of the initiates became also *epoptae:* Schinas, Rupilia, and Marius Fructus (lines 16–19). This is usually taken as evidence that initiation and *epopteia* could occur on the same day; cf. Fraser, p. 91, and especially Cole 1984, p. 46. This is certainly a possible interpretation, and it cannot be ruled out, although it does not make sense from a ritual point of view (see Chap. 9, pp. 246–248).

I interpret the inscription somewhat differently. Although the hand is the same and there is no second date next to the listed *epoptai,* I see lines 16–19 as a later addition: the letters of the previous lines get progressively smaller, as if to leave space for a text that is to be inscribed later, and the rubric *Epoptae* infringes upon the end of column II. Moreover, if the headings *Mystae pii* and *Epoptae* were inscribed at the same time, then it would have been simpler to have the heading *Mystae et epoptae* above the relevant names, rather than to repeat them. Three other inscriptions mention people who were both *mystai* and *epoptai* (**50, 56,** and **67**), and all list the two titles together. Listing the *epoptae* with a separate heading below suggests that it was not known in advance who among the *mystae* would proceed to the second stage of initiation.

Lines 11–12: It is unclear whether the people from Pergamon and Chios belonged to the same group as the other initiates in this record. The inscription simply tells us that they were initiated together.

Line 14: Tarula is a Thracian name, a variant of Talouras, with metathesis of the liquids; see *ad* **19**, line 6.[61] On Thracian initiates, see Chapter 9, p. 244.

90   Record of Roman initiates of unknown provenance   Fig. 70

Fragment of marble stele with molding above, broken below and on the left. The back seems to be rough-picked. Found built into a church (*in ecclesia maiore*) in Chora, then brought to the "the school" (Fredrich). Archaeological Museum of Samothrace, courtyard. No inv. no.

H. 0.49 m, W. 0.36 m, Th. 0.16 m; L.H. 0.035 m (line 1), 0.05 m (lines 2–6), 0.055 (I-longa, line 4), 0.06 m (I-longa, line 3).

Edd. [Mommsen, *CIL* III Suppl. I.1 (1889) 12321]; Kern 1893, p. 374, no. 21; Fredrich, *IG* XII.8, p. 39.

Cf. Cole 1984, p. 182; Clinton 2001, p. 35.

Figure 70. Record of Roman initiates of unknown provenance (**90**)

June 7, A.D. 48

in pediment:	SACR *vacat*
in field:	[A.] Vitellio · L · F
	[L.] VIstano · Co(n)s(ulibus)
	VII · Idus · Iun(ias)
5	[fel]Iciter · myst-
	[es *vel* -ai] Philipp[us- -]

- - - - - - - - - - - - -

Fredrich. **1** Sacr[um] Fredrich, Sacr(a acceperunt? *vel* accepit?) *vel* Sacr(a) *vel* Sacr(um) Dimitrova. **6** [es] Fredrich.

Epigraphical Commentary

The letters are clear. I-longa is used in lines 3 (VIstano), 4 (Idus Iun.), and 5 ([fel]Iciter). The O and S of Co(n)s(ulibus) are inscribed within the C.

Commentary

This is a list of a Roman initiate or initiates.

Line 1: The restoration of the abbreviation is only hypothetical; cf. **78**.

Line 5: [fel]Iciter corresponds to Greek εὐτυχῶς; see *ad* **133**.

91   Greek record of Roman initiates of unknown provenance   Fig. 71

Fragment of stele of Thasian marble, broken on the left, below, and presumably above. The back is rough-picked. Provenance unknown. Archaeological Museum of Samothrace, courtyard, inv. 56.2.

H. 0.40 m, W. 0.24 m, Th. 0.09 m; L.H. 0.015–0.02 m.

Ed. Fraser, *Samothrace* 2.1 (1960) 41.

Cf. Robert 1963, pp. 67–69.

1st century A.D.?

```
        - - - - - - - - - - - -
        [- - - - - -]ΟΠ[- - - - - -]
        [- -Κορ]νήλιο[ς?] ΗΣΥ
        [- -]Σόσσιος[- -]
        Μύσται εὐσεβ[ε]ῖ[ς]
    5   [Λ]ούκιος [- - - - - -]
            Ἀθηνίων
        [Κόϊν]τος Φλάουειος
        [Ῥ]οῦφος Ἑρμ . . . . ιας
            δοῦλοι Ἀθηνίων[ος]
   10   [Χ]ρήσιμος[- - - -] . ΛΗΣΣ[- - - -]
        [ἐπὶ β]ασιλέως Ἀπολλο-
        [- -]ου τοῦ ΕΥ[- - - - - -]
        [ἀγοραν]ομοῦντος
        [- - - -] τοῦ [- - - -]
```

Fraser. **1** [ἐπ]όπ[- - - -εὐσεβ- - -] Fraser. **2** Dimitrova, [- - - -]ΛΗ . . . . ΗΣΥ Fraser. **3** Σόσσιος Fraser. **4** εὐσεβ[ε]ῖ[ς] Fraser. [Λ]ούκιος . Θ[- - - - - -] Fraser. **7** Φλάουιος Fraser. **8** Ἑρμ . . . . ιας (*fortasse* Ἑρμαγόρας) Fraser. **10** . ΛΗΣΣ[- - - -] Fraser.

Epigraphical Commentary

The lettering is relatively careless, with too little space between the lines. The right part of the stone is badly defaced, as Fraser observed.

Line 1: Circle, followed by a clear pi.

Line 2: I see nu and eta in ligature, followed by lambda, iota, and a faint circle. ΗΣΥ, read by Fraser, is now practically illegible.

Line 3: Both sigmas, dotted by Fraser, are clear.

Line 4: εὐσεβ[ε]ῖ[ς], read by Fraser, is now impossible to make out.

Lines 5, 8, 10: I see nothing clear after [Λ]ούκιος in line 5, [Ῥ]οῦφος in line 8, and [Χ]ρήσιμος in line 10.

Line 7: There is another letter between omicron and iota, of which a left vertical is visible.

Figure 71. Greek record of Roman
initiates of unknown provenance (91)

Commentary

This is a list of Roman initiates and their slaves, dated by Fraser to the
1st century A.D. on the basis of the hand. It is unclear whether an *epoptes*
is recorded in line 1.

92   Record of initiates from Rome   Fig. 72

Fragment of stele of Thasian marble, preserved on the left and on the
rough-picked back. Found in Chora, on August 13, 1939. Archaeological
Museum of Samothrace, courtyard, inv. 39.1071.

H. 0.33 m, W. 0.145 m, Th. 0.08 m; L.H. 0.02 m (lines 1, 5), 0.025–
0.27 m (lines 2–3), 0.03 m (line 4), 0.017–0.018 m (lines 6–7), 0.07 m (K).

Edd. Lehmann-Hartleben 1940, p. 356; *AÉ* 1947 2; Fraser, *Samothrace*
2.1 (1960) 40.

Cf. Clinton 2001, p. 35.

September 1, 1st century A.D.?

      [ἐπὶ?]
   βασιλ[- - - - -]
   L · Non[io-?-]
   M · Arru[ntio co(n)s(ulibus)?]
   K. Sept · M[ystae pii]
5 L · Arrunti[us- - - -]
   prómag[ister] *vel* -istri]
   Ti · Claudius · D[- - - - - -]
   Ṭi · Cḷ[audius(?)- - - -]
   - - - - - - - - - - - -

Fraser. **1** [ἐπὶ] Fraser, Lehmann, ἐπὶ *AÉ*, [ἐπὶ?] Dimitrova. **2** βασι[λέως Fraser, βασιλ[- -] Dimitrova. **4** Ṃ[ystae Fraser. **5–6** promag[ister] Lehmann, [- - - - magister] pro mag[istris], Fraser. **8** legatus Lehmann, Ti̭ · Cl̥[audius Fraser.

Epigraphical Commentary

The lettering is elegant, with cursive elements (M, A).

    Line 2: Clear iota, followed by the lower part of a left oblique stroke.

    Line 4: Last letter: left part of M.

    Line 6: The M is clear. The O is marked by an apex.

    Line 8: Unclear traces, followed by a clear C and a left vertical.

Commentary

This is a list of initiates from Rome dated to September 1 of an unknown year. The consuls (if consuls are listed in lines 3–4) are unknown, and the document cannot be dated precisely.

    Before line 1: I am hesitant about restoring ἐπὶ or anything else. The next line is indented, and it seems to be the beginning of the inscription. Therefore, we may have a different formula indicating the eponymous king, such as βασιλεύοντος (cf. **30**).

    Lines 5–6: Fraser restores [- - - - magister] pro mag[istris] and suggests (p. 95, with nn. 2–4) that the *magistri* in question may be "of the type found in Roman and Italian communities in the East, whose functions have been much discussed." He doubts the existence of such a community in Samothrace, however, and proposes that they came from elsewhere. I find Fraser's restoration difficult to accept, for lack of precise parallels. On the other hand, the title *promagister* is well attested as denoting a vice-*magister*—whatever meaning *magister* has, be it a priest of the *Fratres Arvales* or a provincial magistrate (usually in the phrases *promagister publicorum portuum* or *frumenti municipalis,* as in, e.g., *I.Ephesos* 761, 823, 824, 825, 826, 827, 1403).

    One wonders if *promagister* can also be a term related to teaching (though its precise translation in this context is unclear for lack of parallels), since one of the basic meanings of *magister* is "teacher." A document of the Claudian period from Xanthos in Lykia (*FdXanth* VII 64) mentions a certain Lucius Arruntius, who served as a teacher of emperors:

    [Μᾶρ]κον Ἀρρούντιον Ἀκύλαν
    [υ]ἱὸν Λουκίου Ἀρρουντίου
    Ἑρμ[α]κ̣ότου καθηγητοῦ αὐτο-
    κρατόρων, χειλίαρχον λεγε-
  5 ῶνος Κυρηναϊκῆς, ἐπίτροπον
    [Κ]α[ίσαρος] Π[αμφυλίας].

It is possible that the Lucius Arruntius is the same person in both documents, but we do not know whether the title of promagister refers to him or to the names that follow. A Marcus Arruntius was consul in A.D. 66 and possibly 77, as Fraser notes, but in neither year was the colleague named Lucius Nonius. On the other hand, a Lucius Nonius must have been a consul ca. A.D. 72 (see Degrassi 1952, s.v.; *PIR²*, N, no. 132; W. Eck, *RE Suppl.* 14, cols. 285–286, n. 8a).

Figure 72. Record of initiates from Rome (**92**)

Figure 73. Record of Roman initiates
of unknown provenance (93) *(above)*;
and dedication by Roman soldiers,
Archaeological Museum of Samothrace, inv. nos. 71.960 + 71.956
(below)

93   Record of Roman initiates of unknown provenance   Fig. 73

Fragment of pedimental stele of Thasian marble, preserved in the upper
left corner. The back is smooth. Found by the joint French and Czechoslovakian expedition in 1926 at the foundations of the Milesian dedication (cf.
Salviat). Archaeological Museum of Samothrace, courtyard, inv. 49.437.

H. 0.21 m, W. 0.155 m, Th. 0.07 m (stele)–0.085 m (pediment); L.H.
0.015 m (line 1), 0.015–0.02 m (lines 2–4).

Ed. Fraser, *Samothrace* 2.1 (1960) 39.

Cf. Salviat 1962, p. 270; Bouzek and Hošek 1995, pp. 83–85 (*SEG*
XLV 1198–1201, lemma 3).

1st century A.D.?

in pediment:	ἀγαθ[ῆ τύχη]
on molding:	mist[ae pii ?]
in field:	Afini[- - -?]
	M · AU.[- - -]
5	. . . [- - -]
	- - - - - -

Fraser. **3** . Afini[ụṣ- -?] Fraser. **4** Maur[us] Fraser. **5** Ṭ . Ụ[- - Fraser.

Epigraphical Commentary

The letters are clear and elegant.

Line 3: I cannot see any letter preceding Afini[.

Line 4: Top part of a left vertical joined with a top horizontal, suitable for R, F, or P. There seems to be a medial dot between M and A, in which case a name such as M. Aurelius or M. Aufidius is possible.

Line 5: Unclear traces.

Commentary

This is a record of Roman initiates. If Afini[- - -] is part of the consular date, then perhaps it is A.D. 62, when L. Afinius Gallus and P. Marius Celsus were consuls. The inscription possibly belongs together with two joining fragments of an unpublished dedication by Roman soldiers (Fig. 73), given the similar hand and physical features (thickness and smooth back). If this supposition is correct, then the entire text would read:

in pediment:	ἀγαθ[ῇ τύχῃ]
on molding:	mist[ae pii ?]
in field:	Afini[- - - - - - - - -?]
	M · AU ·[- - - - - - - -]
5	...[- - - - - - - - -]
	- - - - - - - - - - -

a   *b*

.. O . [- -]
. IA et Fl. Sabino Aur(elio) Hermo[...]
militibus coh(ortis) Cocceius Phoeb[us]
Cocceius Theodotus Cocceius
5 Celerinius ...⁶... Cocceius
Dracontius piei inorantes
Diis Magnis Samothraci-
bus votum libentes meri-
to solverunt *vacat*

94   Record of initiates from Rome

Fragment of pedimental stele of Thasian marble, preserved on the left and above. Salviat copied it at the house of Chrysostomos Nimorios. Its present location is unknown.

H. 0.185 m, W. 0.115 m, Th. 0.035 m; L.H. ca. 0.015–0.025 m.

Edd. Salviat 1962, pp. 278–279, no. 5; Šašel Kos, *ILGR* (1979) 251.

Cf. Cole 1984, pp. 97–98; 1989, p. 1587; Clinton 2001, p. 35.

A.D. 65

A. Lic[inio Nerva Silano]
M. Vis[tinio Attico co(n)s(ulibus)]
Mys[tae pii]
IV · Idu[s- - - - -]
5 Lutacius[- - - - - -]
C. Iulius Augu[rinus]
[- - - - - -]TIS[- -]

Salviat.

Epigraphical Commentary

The letters are relatively broad, especially M. They tend to get smaller toward the end of the inscription.

Commentary

This is a list of initiates from Rome, dated by Salviat to A.D. 65 on account of the consuls.

Line 6: Gaius Iulius Augurinus is perhaps the same as the knight involved in the Pisonian conspiracy of the spring of 65 (Tac. *Ann.* 15.50), as Salviat suggests (p. 279). He also remarks that the present document may indicate that Augurinus was sent into exile at Samothrace—a likely place, since the Aegean islands were a typical destination for deportees in the Roman empire. He notes that "the fourth day before the Ides" in line 4 may refer to the Ides of May, since the conspiracy was planned for April 19, and disclosed on April 18. On the basis of this date Cole concludes that if Augurinus was "exiled immediately, he would have had time to arrive at Samothrace by May 12" (1989, p. 1587). We need not assume, however, that the Ides of May are meant—the later months cannot be excluded, and may work better with respect to the interval between Augurinus's departure from Rome and his visit to Samothrace, if the identification is correct.

95   Record of Roman initiates(?) of unknown provenance   Fig. 74

Fragment of a block of Thasian marble, preserved at bottom. Said to have been found at the Genoese Towers. Archaeological Museum of Samothrace, inv. 68.858.

H. 0.23 m, W. 0.20 m, Th. 0.17 m; L.H. 0.02 m.

Unpublished.

End of 1st century A.D.–beginning of 2nd?

```
          - - - - - - - - - - -
        . vacat . . [- - - - - - - - - -]
        . vacat    POSI[- - - - -]
        [- - - -]OR · Labeont[- - -]
        [- - - -]US · African[- - - -]
     5  [- - - -]US · Success[- - - -]
        [- - - -]. US · Diadumen[- - - -]
        [ἐπὶ βασιλ]έος (sic) Τίτου Φ[λαουίου Κτησιφίλου(?)]
```

Epigraphical Commentary

The letters are narrow, elongated, and uneven, with cursive elements (especially M and A). The Greek text in line 6 seems to have been incised by the same hand.

Commentary

This probably was a list of Roman initiates. The *basileus* could be the same as the one in **41** (see *ad* lines 2–3), or related to him; I therefore suggest dating the inscription to the end of the 1st or the beginning of the 2nd century A.D.

Figure 74 *(above, left)*. Record of Roman initiates(?) of unknown provenance **(95)**

Figure 75 *(above, right)*. Record of Roman initiates(?) of unknown provenance **(96)**

96 Record of Roman initiates(?) of unknown provenance   Fig. 75

Fragment of Thasian marble, preserved on the left and bottom, possibly rough-picked on the back; traces of claw chisel at the bottom. Found in August 1969 near the Stoa. Archaeological Museum of Samothrace, inv. 69.556.

H. 0.17 m, W. 0.14 m, Th. 0.07 m; L.H. 0.008–0.01 m.

Unpublished.

1st century B.C.–1st century A.D.?

```
      - - - - - - - - - - - - - -
      [..] . . . [- - - - - - - -]
      Philoni[s? - - - - - - - - -]
      Mnesima[- - - - - - - - - -]
      Pilinus · A[- - - - - - - -]
   5  Memno · SE . [- - - - - - - -]
      Mnesima C. · s(erva?) · . [- - -]
      Heraclio · MUC I [- - -?- - -]
      Lucumo · Vateri · I[- - - - -]
      vacat
```

Epigraphical Commentary
The letters are clear and elegant, compatible with a date in the 1st century B.C. or A.D.

97 Greek record of a Roman initiate(?)   Fig. 76

Block of Thasian marble, broken above. Brought from Chora. Archaeological Museum of Samothrace, courtyard, inv. 49.418.

H. 0.51 m, W. 0.18 m, Th. 0.30 m; L.H. 0.015–0.025 m (except phi, 0.03–0.035 m).

Edd. Kern 1893, p. 374, no. 20; Fredrich, *IG* XII.8 219.

1st–2nd century A.D.?

    - - - - - -
    [. .] . ΘΑΝ[. .]
    vacat ca. 4 vss.
    Γ. Ἰούλιος
    Αὐφιδια-
    νός· Τι(βερίου)
5   ἀδε(λφός)
    ἀγαθῆ τ[ύχῃ]·
    ἐπὶ βασιλ[έ-]
    ως Φρόν[τ-]
    ωνος το[ῦ]
10 Σεκο̣ύν[δου?]

Fredrich. **1** . . . ΟΛΑ Fredrich. **10** *an* ἐκ Φρι- *an* Ἐ<κ>φρί[λλου] Fredrich, *fortasse* Σεκο̣ύν[δου] Dimitrova.

Epigraphical Commentary
The lettering is uneven and inconsistent, suggestive of a later date.

Line 6: τ[ύχῃ] must have been squeezed in at the end of the line.

Line 10: What was read by previous editors as phi does not have its central vertical project beyond the circle. Omicron should be considered as a possibility, especially since the central vertical resembles a stray mark.

Commentary
This probably was a record of initiation. For the possibility that the block may have belonged together with **33** and **67**, see *ad* **67**. The name Φρόντων occurs as the eponymous official's patronymic in **41** and **45**.

98   Record of initiates from Rome   Fig. 77

Two joining fragments of a stele of Thasian marble, broken below. The back and sides are rough-picked. Found in Chora on June 25, 1939. Archaeological Museum of Samothrace, courtyard, inv. 39.79.

H. 0.38 m, W. 0.315 m, Th. 0.135 m; L.H. 0.04 m (lines 1, 3, 6), 0.02 m (lines 2, 5, 8), 0.03 m (line 4), 0.025 m (line 7).

Edd. Lehmann-Hartleben 1940, p. 357; *BullÉp* 1944 151a; *AÉ* 1947 4; Fraser, *Samothrace* 2.1 (1960) 51.

Cf. Cole 1984, p. 92; 1989, p. 1584; Clinton 2001, p. 35.

April 22, A.D. 116

        L. Fundanio Lamia
            Aeliano
        Sex · Carminio Vet(ere)
            co(n)s(ulibus)
5   X · K · Mai. mystae pii
        L. Pomponius
        Maximus Flavius
        [Sil]vanus Q · propr
        [prov. Maced.]

        - - - - - - - - - - -

Figure 76. Greek record of a Roman initiate(?) **(97)**

Figure 77. Record of initiates from Rome **(98).** Courtesy Samothrace Excavations

Fraser. **3** Vet(ere) Fraser, Vet(ere) Dimitrova.

Epigraphical Commentary
The letters are clear and elongated.
Line 1: The AM of Lamia are in ligature.
Line 3: E and T are clear.

Commentary
This is a list of initiates from Rome, dated to April 22, A.D. 116.
Line 6: Fraser notes that Pomponius may be the son of L. Pomponius, *consul suffectus* in A.D. 121 (cf. Cole 1989, p. 1584). This would mean that he became *quaestor pro praetore* at an early age.

99 Record of Roman initiates of unknown provenance   Fig. 78

Fragment of stele of Thasian marble, preserved only on the left; the back may be close to original surface. Brought in by a local person in 1927 (cf. Salviat). Archaeological Museum of Samothrace, courtyard, inv. 38.380.
H. 0.28 m, W. 0.22 m, Th. 0.09 m; L.H. 0.035–0.04 m.
Ed. Fraser, *Samothrace* 2.1 (1960) 52.
Cf. Salviat 1962, p. 269; Walton 1963, p. 99.

2nd century A.D.?

Figure 78. Record of Roman initiates of unknown provenance (99)

```
        - - - - - - - - - - -
        SPME . . . . [- - - - -]
             Servi[- -]
        Eutychus Siger[us]
        Epaphroditus
     5  Tyrannu[s]
        - - - - - - - - - - -
```

Fraser. **1** . aspares Fraser, . spar(*vel* n?)es Salviat. **2** Se[rvi] Fraser, Servi [- -] Salviat. **3** Eutychus Fraser, Eutychus Siger[us] Salviat. **4** Epaphrodit[us] Fraser, Epaphroditus Salviat. **5** Tyranni[o Fraser, Tyrannu[s *vel fortasse* Tyranniu[s Dimitrova.

Epigraphical Commentary
The letters, dated by Fraser to the 2nd century A.D., have cursive elements, especially R, A, and D. Salviat's readings are based on a photo taken in 1927, after which a piece was apparently broken off on the right.
Line 1: I restore nothing before S, given the alignment of the names below (lines 3–4).
Line 5: R and A are in ligature. The last letter preserved consists of two top verticals, suitable for U. Tyrannus is likely, or perhaps Tyrannius, if the N and I are in ligature.

Commentary
This probably was a list of Roman initiates, as the heading *servi* in line 2 indicates.
Line 1: It is possible that we have the praenomen Sp(urius), folowed by a nomen beginning with Me-.

100   Record of initiates from Rome

Three fragments of a stele of Thasian marble, broken below; *a* and *b* join. The back is smooth-picked. Fragments *a* and *c*, now in the Kunsthistorisches Museum in Vienna, inv. III 167 *a* + *b*, were found near the Rotunda of Arsinoe. I saw these fragments in May 2007.[62] Fragment *b* was found in Chora in 1938. Archaeological Museum of Samothrace, courtyard, inv. 38.355.

a: H. 0.29 m, W. 0.17 m, Th. 0.075 m; L.H. 0.044 m (line 1), 0.03 m (line 2), 0.028 m (line 3), 0.024 m (line 4), 0.015 m (lines 5–7), 0.01 m (line 8).

b: H. 0.23 m, W. 0.13 (top)–0.14 m (bottom), Th. 0.075 m; L.H. as on fragment *a*.

c: H. 0.28 m, W. 0.15 (top)–0.16 m (bottom), Th. 0.075 m; L.H. 0.006–0.015 m.

Edd. *a, c,* Conze 1875, p. 37, pl. 62; Dürr 1881, no. 80; [Mommsen, *CIL* III Suppl. I.1 (1889) 7371]; [Dessau, *ILS* II.1 (1902) 4056]; *a* + *b, c,* Lehmann-Hartleben 1939, p. 145; *AÉ* 1939 4; Fraser, *Samothrace* 2.1 (1960) 53, 53*bis.*

Cf. Fredrich, *IG* XII.8, p. 39; Henderson 1923, pp. 289–290; *BullÉp* 1939 297; Oliver 1939; Robert, *Hellenica* 2 (1946), p. 57, no. 17, with n. 2; Hemberg 1950, p. 94, n. 1; Lewis, *Samothrace* 1 (1958), p. 92; Walton 1963, p. 99; Cole 1984, pp. 92, 100; 1989, pp. 1584–1585, 1587–1588, 1595–1596; McCredie et al., *Samothrace* 7 (1992), p. 47, n. 101; *SEG* XLII 780*bis;* Clinton 2001, p. 35.

November 9, A.D. 124

```
a      Régibus · Iov[e] et · Minerv(a)         b
       iterum · M · Acilió
       Glabrione, [C.] Bellició
       Torquato cos · mystae · pii
    5  [s]acra accépérunt . V · Idus · Novembr(es)
       [Q. Pla]nius · Sardus · Varius Ambibulus prócos ·
       prov[inci]ae Mac[e]doniae
       [- - - - - - - - -]us lég. [p]ró pr. próv. eiusdem
       - - - - - - - - - - - - - - -        c
       [- - - - - - - - - - - -] . . . o
       [- - - - - -]s · P. Curtilius · Commodus
       [- - - - - -]s lIctor C · Fádius Endymión
       [- - - - - -]alis Peregrinus C Maxsiminus
    5  [- - - - -]I
       [- - - - - -]órus Euanthés · Pretiósus
       [- - - - - -]hés · NIcéphorus · Callistión ·
       [- - - - - -]us · Euporus · Hermés ·
       [- - - - - -]Lacón · Auctus · Euprepé[s]
   10  [- - - - - -]tión · Restitutus
       [- - - - - -]NA .I . [- - -]
       - - - - - - - - - - - - - - -
```

Fraser. **8** [provinci]ae Fraser, prov[inci]ae Walton. *c.4, fin.* Amacil(ius)?? Isinis?? Fraser, Amacil Isianus Mommsen, Maxsiminus, Dimitrova. *c.1* clio Fraser. *c.3* lictor(es) Fraser. *c.5* [serv]i (*vel* [ministr]i) Fraser, [pedesequ]i Hiller.

62. I am very grateful to Alfred Bernhard-Walcher for his kind assistance and permission to examine these fragments.

Epigraphical Commentary

The lettering is elegant, with cursive elements; apices and I-longa mark long vowels. Fraser attributes fragment *c* to a different hand, but I agree with Conze and Mommsen that the hand is the same. I consider fragment *c* part of the same inscription as *a* and *b*, given the identical thickness and hand, though it is unclear how much is missing between the end of *a/b* and the beginning of *c*. It is possible that *b* and *c* join, but less likely than to assume a gap, in view of the different widths of *b* and *c*. These fragments show a gradual increase in width, consistent with the slant of the break.

Commentary

Fraser, following Conze, suggests that this may have been a block from the Rotunda of Arsinoe because it is slightly concave. The back, however, is straight, and the curve on the front cannot have belonged to a circle with a radius larger than 0.60 m (cf. *Samothrace* 7, p. 47).

This document has been the focus of much debate, mostly because of the dating formula "when Jupiter and Minerva were kings for the second time." As Oliver points out (p. 464), "in a year when no citizen is found to accept the financial burden of the public office, the town is forced to take money from a temple treasury, and the god concerned becomes eponymous." Oliver concludes that Jupiter and Minerva must be a Latin translation of the Kabiri (p. 465), since the Sanctuary of the Great Gods was the principal sanctuary of Samothrace, and must have paid for the expenses of the kingship, while on the other hand there is no example of two sanctuaries sharing such expenses. Cole rejects this interpretation for various reasons (1989, p. 1596), and suggests that the gods mentioned are local divinities, especially since the temple of Athena was the traditional place where documents of the city were set up. I find this suggestion highly plausible: the usual Latin appellation of the Great Gods was Di Magni, without specification of their actual names, so it is unlikely that they would be called Jupiter and Minerva in an official document set up at Samothrace. Even if Roman literary tradition likens the Great Gods to the triads Jupiter, Juno, Minerva, or Jupiter, Hermes, Minerva, this reflects the political effort to find the origin of the Penates in Samothrace, and is quite different from actually calling the Samothracian gods by the names of traditional Roman divinities.

The document is important for revealing that the cult of Zeus, in addition to the well-documented cult of Athena, was probably a principal one in the polis of Samothrace. The inscription may also indicate the relative poverty of Samothrace in the Hadrianic era, since there was no one to assume the financial burden of the eponymous magistracy.

Line 6: Ambibulus was consul in A.D. 128; see Degrassi 1952, s.v.

101   Record of initiates(?) from Rome   Fig. 79

Three joining fragments of a stele of Thasian marble, broken above and below; the back is rough-picked. Found near the Sacristy on July 6, 1939. Archaeological Museum of Samothrace, courtyard, inv. 39.348.

H. 0.40 m, W. 0.31–0.315 m, Th. 0.06 m; L.H. 0.03 m (lines 1–6), 0.02 m (line 7).

Edd. Lehmann-Hartleben 1940, p. 346, no. 3, with p. 493; *AÉ* 1947
1; Fraser, *Samothrace* 2.1 (1960) 50; Walton 1963, p. 99.
    Cf. Cole 1984, pp. 91–92; 1989, p. 1584.

Hadrianic?

- - - - - - - - - - -
    tinianus Q(uaestor) · prov · M̲[ac](edoniae)
    S̈ex · Palp[.]llius Candi-
        dus Tullittianus ·
    C · Modius Asclepiades
5   A · Vereius · Felix ·
        Bato · Batonis
        Purpurio
- - - - - - - - - - -

Fraser. 2 Palp[e]llius Fraser. 4 Walton, *omisit* Fraser.

Figure 79. Record of initiates(?) from Rome (**101**)

Epigraphical Commentary
The letters are elongated and carefully done, with finials.
    Line 1: First letter: bottom part of a vertical; second letter: lower part
of a vertical; last letter: lower part of a left barely slanting stroke.
    The Q of Q(uaestor) has a horizontal mark above, indicating ab-
breviation.
    Line 7: The smaller letters perhaps indicate that this is close to the
bottom of the stone.

Commentary
This was probably a list of initiates from Rome, including a governor of
Macedonia and his retinue.

102   Record of Roman initiates(?) of unknown provenance   Fig. 80
    Fragment of a stele of Thasian marble with incised pediment and
akroteria, preserved in upper left corner; the back is rough-picked. Found
in Chora in 1938. Archaeological Museum of Samothrace, courtyard, inv.
38.393.
    H. 0.5 m, W. 0.33 m, Th. 0.06 m; L.H. 0.015 m (line 1), 0.03–0.035 m
(lines 2–4).
    Edd. Lehmann-Hartleben 1939, p. 145, no. 3; *AÉ* 1939 3; Fraser,
Samothrace 2.1 (1960) 54.

A.D. 131

in pediment: ἀγαθῆι [τύχηι]
below pediment: · M · S · Le[na]
                        Ponti[ano]
                        M · An[tonio]
                        [Rufino]
5   [co(n)s(ulibus)]
                        - - - - - -

Figure 80. Record of Roman ini-
tiates(?) of unknown provenance
(**102**). *Samothrace* 2.1, pl. XXI:54

Fraser.

Epigraphical Commentary

The letters are clear, if a bit inelegant, suitable for the 2nd century A.D.

Commentary

This was probably the beginning of a record of Roman initiates, dated to A.D. 131.

The misspelling of the diphthong AE with E, attested in the name Laenas, occurs throughout the Roman empire following the 1st century A.D.

103   Record of Roman initiates of unknown provenance

Fragment of marble stele. Its dimensions and present location are unknown. It was brought by Behr to the Louvre, whence "venit ad Leblantium."

Edd. Lenormant 1857, p. 224; Conze 1860, p. 71, n. 1; [Mommsen, *CIL* I (1863) under no. 581]; [Mommsen, *CIL* III (1873) 720]; Ziebarth 1906, p. 413, no. 5; Fredrich, *IG* XII.8, p. 39; [Lommatzsch, *CIL* I² (1918) 664].

Cf. Conze 1875, p. 39; Cole 1989, p. 1568, n. 21; Pounder and Dimitrova 2003, p. 35.

A.D. 136

            [L · Ceioni]o · Com[mo]-
            [do · Se]xto · Vetu[leno]
            [civica . P]ompeiano [co(n)s(ulibus)]
            [. .⁵. .]XIII · XII · XI [K.- -]
      5   [m]ystae pii
            - - - - - - - - - - - - - - -

Mommsen. **4** [K. Aug. Mommsen.

Commentary

This is a list of Roman initiates, dated to A.D. 136. Cole (p. 1568, n. 21) cites this document as evidence for "the festival at Samothrace." Her reason must be the listing of at least three consecutive days in line 4. It should be noted, however, that this cannot be taken as secure evidence for a festival. It is possible that the people enumerated in the document were initiated during a sequence of days. It is also uncertain which month is to be restored in the lacuna at the end of line 4. Mommsen restored [K. Aug.] because he assumed that the festival took place in July, on the basis of **70**, which mentions the month Quintilis.

104   Record of initiates from Rome   Fig. 81

Two joining fragments of a stele of Thasian marble, preserved on all sides, rough-picked on back. The upper part is decorated with an incised pediment with corner akroteria; a caduceus, flanked by two snakes, is carved in the center of the pediment (cf. 42, 156, and 169). The surface of the stone is damaged in the upper left part, and a large cutting runs across the face of the upper fragment, from the middle to the right edge. Found in the southern room of a two-room structure, in a group of marbles west of

the west foundation and 77–78 m south of the northeastern inner corner of
the Stoa. Archaeological Museum of Samothrace, courtyard, inv. 62.885.

H. 0.92 m, W. 0.46 m, Th. 0.085–0.125 m; L.H. 0.02 m (line 1),
0.025–0.03 m (lines 2–5), 0.015–0.02 m (lines 5–42).

Edd. McCredie 1965, pp. 114–116, pl. 39; *AÉ* 1965 205; Oliver 1966;
AÉ 1967 444; Harris 1992; *SEG* XLII 780; *BullÉp* 1993 51.

Cf. Robert and Robert, *BullÉp* 1966 342; Weaver 1966, column II
19–20; Robert and Robert, *BullÉp* 1967 451; Šašel Kos, *ILGR* (1979) 250;
Cole 1984, p. 92; 1989, p. 1585; Clinton 2001, p. 35.

May 1, A.D. 165 or 166

```
              [Ἀγ]αθῆ[ι] τύχηι.
        [ἀγορανομοῦν- vel βασιλεύον]τος Αἰλίου Ἐπιμάχου
        [- -μη]νὸς Μουνυχιῶνος
        [Orfito vel Pollione] et Pudente co(n)s(ulibus) · K(alendis) Mais
  5     P. Anteius · Orestes · proco(n)s(ul) · prov(inciae) · Mac(edoniae)
              amic[i]              Iulius Lupercianus
        Septimius Tigr[a]nes
        Fl. Theodorus
        Marcius Felix Vic[tor? - -]
 10     Aurelius Verinus . I[- - - - - -]
        Clinias Pompeianus PI[. (.) .] vacat
        vacat    serr(vi) Orestis proco(n)s(ulis)
```

	Col. I		Col. II
	[- - - - - -]ius		Lydus
	. . . [- - -]		. V[- - - -]
15	Appius		Parthenopae[us]
	Dionysius		Abascantus
	Lycorus		Zoticus
	Zelotus		*vacat*
	Phileys		Felix Augustor(um)
20	. . . . . .		verna
	Philon · Scopus		Onesimus Verini
	Moschus		dec(urio?)
	THS must(- -) Euthyches servos Sep-		
	Menan[der] . .		t[imi] T[i]granis
25	Numenius S THS		Pasiphilus
	Pontius, Marcellus THS		
			A. · Fl(avius) Threptio
	Iunius M · F · SER		[- - - -]rius
	Gemi[nus]		

McCredie. **1** [Ἀγ]αθῆ[ι] McCredie, [ΑΓ]ΑΘΗΙ Harris. **2** [Ἀγορανομοῦν]τος
McCredie, [Βασιλεύον]τος Oliver, [ΒΑΣΙΛΕΥΟΝ]ΤΟΣ Harris. **4** [Orfito] McCredie,
Oliver, Harris. **5** P . Antipa[. . .]ristis McCredie, P. Anti(us) P. [f. O]ristis Oliver,
P. ANTEIV[S . O]RESTIS Harris, P. Anteius · Orestes Dimitrova. **6** I[. . .]us
McCredie, [V]ib[i]us Oliver, IV[LI]VS Harris, Iulius Dimitrova. **7** Tigr[a]nes
Oliver, TIGRINES Harris. **8** P. Theodosus McCredie, Fl. Theodo[.]us Oliver,
Theodorus Dimitrova. **9** lic[tores] Oliver, VIC[TOR or TORINUS] Harris.
10 Asc[. .]us Vennus Vic[McCredie, Asc[o]n[i]us Vennus vi[atores- - - -] Oli-
ver, AVRE[L]IVS VERINVS DI[- - - -] Harris, Aurelius Verinus VI[- - - -]
Dimitrova. **11** Dimitrova, CE[.]IA[. .]OMPEMNVS PIS McCredie, Cleinia,

Figure 81. Record of initiates from Rome (104)

Pompeianus, pi pr(ece) Oliver, C[- - - -] POMPEIANVS PI[- - -] *vacat* Harris.
12 SERRV[. . . . .]Procos McCredie, serrvi eus(dem) procos Oliver, SERR(i . e .
servi) O[RES]T[I]S PROCO(N)S(VLIS) Harris, serr(vi) Orestis proco(n)s(ulis)
Dimitrova. 15 MAPPIVS Harris. 18 Aucustor McCredie, autuitor Oliver,
AVGVSTOR(um) Weaver, Harris. 20 [.]AM[. .]SS[- - - -] McCredie, Pam[-
- - - - -] Oliver, AM[ ]SS[ ] Harris. 21 Philo[. . .]sedius, Vinni Oliver, Virin
McCredie, VERIN[I] Harris, Philon · Scopus, Verini Dimitrova. 23 milit(es)
Oliver, MVLT(itudo) Harris, must(ae?) Dimitrova. 24 T[- - -]eacranis McCredie,
T[I]CRANIS Harris, T[i]granis, Dimitrova. 25 THS McCredie, THS Harris. 26
Dominis [- - - -]C[- - - -]THS McCredie, Pothinus a(diutor) 7 XRC [- - - - -]
Ths Oliver, PO[- - - - - -]ACHI[V]S *vacat* THS Harris, Pontius Marcellus THS
Dimitrova. 27 Asethreptio McCredie, Atithreptio Oliver, Harris, A. Fl. Threptio

Dimitrova. **28** Dimitrova, *fortasse* mi(les) ep(istularius) Oliver, MI(stes) EP(optes) Harris. **29** Cim[- - - -] McCredie, CEM[- -] Harris.

Epigraphical Commentary
The letters are elegant, with cursive elements (M, R, A, V).

Line 5: The penultimate letter of Anteius and the O of Orestes are visible.

Line 7: I am doubtful with respect to Harris's TIGRINES. The fifth letter is illegible, and I find restoring A plausible, since the same name is mentioned in line 24 with a clear A.

Line 15: Nothing needs to be restored before A, given the alignment of the other names.

Line 20: I cannot make out the beginning of this line.

Line 21: There is a ligature of N and I in Verini.

Line 23: The S of MUST is clear. The faint letters THS at the beginning of the line were omitted by previous editors.

Line 28: Unclear traces.

Commentary
This is a list of initiates from Rome, dated to May 1 of either A.D. 165 or 166: in both years there was a consul with the cognomen Pudens (cf. *AÉ* 1965 205). The consuls in 165 were M. Gavius Orfitus and L. Arrius Pudens, and in 166 Q. Servilius Pudens and L. Fufidius Pollio. All previous editors have preferred 165, since in 166 Pudens is usually listed first. Harris (p. 74) thinks that the mention of a *verna Augustor(um)* in lines 19–20 is another argument in favor of the earlier year, since it "confirms the dating to a time when there were two or more Augusti in office." M. Aurelius's fellow emperor, Lucius Verus, died in 169, however, so he was still in office in 166. In addition, there is no reason someone should stop being called a *verna Augustorum* after the reign of the relevant Augusti.

Line 2: The eponymous official is otherwise unattested, as Oliver notes (p. 75). Although it is logical to expect a *basileus,* since this is the only Samothracian official referred to in this document (cf. Oliver, p. 77; Harris, p. 73), the formula βασιλεύοντος occurs only once in Samothracian inscriptions (**30**), in contrast with the frequent ἀγορανομοῦντος, and I prefer to keep the possibilities open.

Line 3: The mention of the month Mounychion is of crucial importance. It shows that the Samothracian calendar was influenced by the Athenian, since Mounychion is a typical Athenian month; on Samothracian months, see Pounder and Dimitrova 2003, p. 35, n. 15 (= **26**, Commentary). The only other known Samothracian month, Maimakterion, is also Athenian.

Line 5: P. Anteius Orestes is unknown. For other people with the name P. Anteius, see Harris, p. 74.

Line 15: Mappius is unattested, as Harris notes, but I read the common name Appius.

Line 23: The letters THS at the beginning are also found in lines 25 and 26. They must denote a rubric of some kind, and Harris (p. 78) suggests that THS be read as "Th(eodo- ri or ti) s(ervi)." The heading in line 23 must refer to the following three names, and THS in line 25 may go with Pasiphilus from column II, while THS in line 26 goes perhaps with

Marcellus, whose name appears to have been added later. It is also possible that the stonecutter was somewhat confused in copying the rubrics and their correct attributions.

Line 27: Atithreptio, read by Oliver and Harris, does not exist as a name. I propose A. Fl. Threptio: the stone confirms it, and Threptio is a well-attested name (cf. Harris, p. 78). His name is written in slightly larger letters, and it is likely that he was not a slave, but a Roman citizen.

Line 28: If the reading M · F · SER is correct, it must mean Marci Felicis servus, which would provide further support for Harris's suggestion about THS.

105   Record of Roman initiates of unknown provenance   Fig. 82

Fragment of Thasian marble, preserved only on the back, which is rough-picked. Found in August 1976 inside the fenced property of G. Glynias in the ancient city, now in the Archaeological Museum of Samothrace, storeroom, inv. 76.18.

H. 0.22 m, W. 0.29 m, Th. 0.10 m; L.H. 0.04–0.05 m.

Unpublished.

2nd–3rd century A.D.?

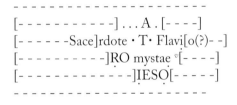

```
- - - - - - - - - - - - - - - - - - - - -
[- - - - - - - - - - -] . . . A . [- - - -]
[- - - - - -Sace]rdote · T· Flavi[o(?)- -]
[- - - - - - - - - -]RO mystae ᵛ[- - - -]
[- - - - - - - - - - - - -]IESO[- - - - -]
- - - - - - - - - - - - - - - - - - - - -
```

Figure 82. Record of Roman initiates of unknown provenance (105)

Epigraphical Commentary
The letters are elongated and carefully done.

Line 1: First letter: bottom part of a vertical; second letter: lower part of D, S, or B.

Line 2: Last letter: left vertical.

Line 3: First letter: right upper part of R is possible; last letter: E or I.

Line 4: First letter: vertical stroke; second letter: E or I; last letter: left top part of a circle.

Commentary
This is a list of Roman initiates, tentatively dated on the basis of the hand. [Sace]rdote in line 2 can be either a cognomen or a title. Consuls with the names Sacerdos are attested for A.D. 148 and 219, but none of them had a colleague T. Flavius; the title co(n)s(ulibus) does not occur after [Sace]rdote to indicate that T. Flavius was a different official. If the title "priest" is meant, it is possible that T. Flavius was the *sacerdos* himself, and that the]RO in line 3 is part of his name in the ablative.

106   Record of Roman initiates of unknown provenance

The inscription is known from the copy made by Cyriacus of Ancona, Cod. Vat. Lat. 5250, folio 20, verso. Its dimensions are unknown.

Edd. [Mommsen, *CIL* I (1863) 579 = *CIL* III (1873) 714]; Ziebarth 1906, p. 413, no. 5; Fredrich, *IG* XII.8, p. 39; [Lommatzsch, *CIL* I² (1918) 664].

Date?

>   CL · Lucci · C · F · EQ
>   C · Mispius · muste *(sic)*

Mommsen. **1** L. Q(uinctius?) Mommsen.

Commentary

This is a list of Roman initiates. Mommsen interprets the first line as C.
et L. Lucci, sons of Gaius. As for EQ, he considers it to be a name, such
as L. Quinctius. Eq(uites) is possible; cf. **49, 66**.

107   Record of Roman initiates of unknown provenance   Fig. 83

Fragment of a stele of Thasian marble, broken on all sides; the back
is smooth, however. Archaeological Museum of Samothrace, courtyard,
inv. 39.549.

H. 0.45 m, W. 0.31 m; L.H. 0.03 m.

Edd. Conze 1875, p. 42, no. 14, pl. 71:14; [Mommsen, *CIL* III Suppl.
I.1 (1889) 7373]; Fredrich, *IG* XII.8, p. 39, no. 7, with add. on p. vii.

Cf. Cole 1984, pp. 171, 173, 175, 177, 182.

Imperial period?

```
      - - - - - - - - - - - - - - - - - - - -
      [- - - - - -] . . paideuta CH[- - - - -]
      [- - - - -E]utyches RES a linteis[- - -]
      [- - - - - -]aris Litus cubicular[ius- -]
      [- - - - Di]onysides Chresimus[- - - -]
  5   [- - - -Pr]iamus Anthimius PIS[- - - -]
      [- - - - - -]Phaestas Asclas BA[- - - -]
      [- - - - - -]orarius Eros LECTIS[- - - -]
      [- - - -]cosmeta Dorus . [- - - - - - -]
      [- - ?]actator Fortuna[tus- - - - - - -]
 10   [- -Cle]mens velar[ius- - - - - - - -]
      [- - - -]OREXST[- - - - - - - - - - -]
      - - - - - - - - - - - - - - - - - -
```

Figure 83. Record of Roman initiates
of unknown provenance (**107**)

Fredrich. **1** N *vel* M [- - - -]IRFVIII H Conze, [- a]munerib . Eutyches
Fredrich, paideuta Dimitrova. **2** RESRLINTEIS Conze, ser. a linteis Fredrich. **3**
aris Litus cubicularius Fredrich. **6** PHRESTATASCIAS BA Conze, [Tym]phrestas,
Asclas, Ba- Fredrich, Phaestas Dimitrova. **7** l]orarius Eros lectis Conze, lectic[arius]
Fredrich, lectis[ternator?] Dimitrova. **9** Fortunus Conze, m]actator Fortuna[tus
Fredrich. **10** OENS Conze, Cle]mens velar[ius] Fredrich. **11** OAEX Conze, S]orex
St- - - Hiller (*apud* Fredrich).

Epigraphical Commentary

The letters are almost cursive, with practically no difference between R
and A.

Line 7: Last letter: upper part of S.

Line 10: Last letter: unclear traces.

Commentary

This document was probably a record of Roman initiates, since it lists
slaves of a fairly large and prosperous household, with their positions and

occupations. The date is based on the lettering, which is very similar to that of **108**; see **108**.

Line 1: *Paideuta,* "teacher"; the term is attested also in *CIL* III 14195, spelled paedeutes.

Line 2: I find Fredrich's emendation of RES to ser(vus) plausible, but the exact meaning of ser(vus) a linteis (perhaps "slave in charge of the linen materials") is unclear.

Line 3: The title *cubicularius,* "chamber servant," is relatively frequent; see, e.g., *AÉ* 1905 97, 1910 29, 1912 116, 1946 99, 1975 416, 1980 151b.

Line 6: The name Φαέστας occurs in *IG* XII.2 15, 268, as opposed to Tymphrestas, which, to my knowledge, is not attested.

Line 7: Fredrich restores l]orarius, but there are other possibilities, such as marm]orarius, eb]orarius, etc. Marmorarius is commonly attested in inscriptions. It is tempting to restore lectic?[arius], "litter bearer" or "chair bearer" (cf., e.g., *CIL* VI 966, 9509), but the letter before the brackets is S. A word like lectisternator is possible.

Line 8: *Cosmeta* (formed like paideuta in line 1) is a transliteration of Greek *kosmetes,* but its precise meaning in this context is unclear.

Line 9: Mactator, restored by Fredrich, is unattested in inscriptions, to my knowledge.

Line 10: The term *velarius,* "servant in charge of the curtains or sails," occurs elsewhere, e.g., *CIL* V 7966, XIII 8160, 8321.

Line 11: Hiller von Gaertringen's restoration seems plausible.

108   Record of Roman initiates(?) of unknown provenance   Fig. 84

Fragment of marble stele, brought from a church into "the school" (Fredrich). Its present location is unknown.

H. 0.23 m, W. 0.20 m; L.H.?

Edd. Conze 1875, p. 61, no. 13, pl. 71:13, and cf. p. 42; [Mommsen, *CIL* III Suppl. I.1 (1889) 7374]; Fredrich, *IG* XII.8, p. 39, no. 8.

Cf. Cole 1984, pp. 172, 180.

Imperial period?

```
    - - - - - - - - - - - - - - -
    [- - - - - - -]SCU[S- - - - - - -]
    [- - - - - - -]\NDE[R- - - - - - -]
    [- - - - -]Daphnus TH[- - - -]
    [- - -Pa]ntonicus TOH[- -]
5   [- - - -]rius IENE[- - - - -]
    [- - - - - -]E Eusebia[- - -]
    [- - - - - -]MIAIA[- - - -]
    - - - - - - - - - - - - - - -
```

Conze. 6 [- - - -]EEYXΠETIX[- - -] *edd.,* [- -]E Eusebia[- - -] Dimitrova.

Epigraphical Commentary
The hand closely resembles that of **107**, judging from Conze's drawing.

Line 6: Eusebia, facsimile.

Commentary
This may have been a Latin list of initiates. It likely belongs with **107**.

Figure 84. Record of Roman initiates(?) of unknown provenance (**108**). Conze 1875, pl. 71:13

109   Record of Roman initiates(?) of unknown provenance   Fig. 85

Fragment of a marble pedimental stele, preserved on the left, back, and top. The left akroterion is preserved, and the left side has moldings. The back is smooth. Found at 16.00–26.00 m east and 32.00–43.00 m north of the northeastern inner corner of the Stoa in July 1971, now in the Archaeological Museum of Samothrace, courtyard, inv. 71.953.

H. 0.24 m, W. 0.16 m, Th. 0.035 m (pediment 0.06 m); L.H. 0.01 m (line 1), 0.035 m (M, line 2), 0.03 m (line 2), 0.02 m (lines 3–6).

Unpublished.

Date?

in cornice:	[ἐπὶ βασιλ?]έως *vacat* [- - - - - -]
in field:	M(arco?) An[tonio?- - - - - -?- - - - - -]
	TRE[- - - - - - - - -?- - - - - - - - -]
	my[stae?- - - - - - -?- - - - - - - -]
5	I . [- - - - - - - - - - -?- - - - - -]

Figure 85. Record of Roman initiates(?) of unknown provenance (**109**)

Epigraphical Commentary

The letters are elegant and clear.

Line 1: The vacant space takes ca. 1–2 letters before the break.

Line 2: The M is bigger than the other letters.

Line 4: Second letter: diagonal preserved on the left, U or Y is possible.

Commentary

This probably was the beginning of a list of Roman initiates, but no additional information can be derived.

110   Record of Roman initiates of unknown provenance   Fig. 86

Fragment of an opisthographic stele of Thasian marble, broken on all sides, though the left and right side may be close to the original surface. Archaeological Museum of Samothrace, courtyard. No inv. no.

H. 0.30 m, W. 0.30 m, Th. 0.13 m; L.H. 0.03–0.035 m (side A).

Unpublished.

Date?

Side A

- - - - - - - - - - - - - -

[*vacat?*]mystae pii [*vacat?*]
[- -Iu?]ventius · P · f · Stel(latina) CE[- -]
[Epic?]TETUS Horatius S . [- -]
[- - -] . . *vacat* [- -]

- - - - - - - - - - - - - -

Side B

- - - - - - - - - - - - - -

[- - - - - - -]ΔΩΡΟΦ[- - - -]
[- - - -] *vacat* ΓΕΩ . [- - - - -]
vacat

2 Ce[lsus?] Dimitrova.

Figure 86. Record of Roman initiates of unknown provenance (**110**): side A

Epigraphical Commentary
The letters are elongated, with cursive elements. The hand of the inscription on side B looks Byzantine.

Commentary
Side A contains a list of Roman initiates.

Line 2: A certain P. Iuventius, P. filius, Celsus, is attested in *AÉ* 1978 292. His tribe is restored as [V]el(ina), but St]el(latina) is also possible, in which case he might be the person in the present inscription or related to him.

Line 3: Epictetus is a very common name, but there are other possibilities (e.g., Philoctetus or Theaetetus).

111   Record of Roman initiates(?) of unknown provenance

Fragment of marble, broken on all sides. Documentation found among Antonin Salač's papers after his death in 1960.

H. 0.185 m, W. 0.115 m, Th. 0.035 m; L.H. ca. 0.015–0.025 m.

Edd. Vidman 1965 *(non vidi); AÉ* 1966 377; Šašel Kos, *ILGR* (1979) p. 108, no. 252.

Date?

```
- - - - - - - - - - - -
[- - - - - - Au]fideius H [- - - - - -]
[- - - - - - P]ompo[nius- - - - - -]
[- - - - - -] . [- - - - - -]
- - - - - - - - - - - -
```

Vidman. **3** D *vel* P Vidman.

Commentary
This may have been a list of Roman initiates.

112   Record of Roman initiates(?) of unknown provenance

Fragment of unclear nature. Its present location and dimensions are unknown, except that Conze mentions that its width is ca. 0.09 m.

Edd. Conze 1860, p. 61, pl. 16, no. 9; [Mommsen, *CIL* III (1873) 722]; Fredrich, *IG* XII.8, p. 39.

Imperial period?

```
      [- - - - - - - - - - -]
      [- - - - -]I[- - - -]
      [A]polloni[u?]
      s
5    CENIS Pr . i-
      nus
      [- - - -]ωΠ[- - - -]
      [- - - - - - - - - - -]
```

Fredrich. **5** Pr̲u . . . |nus Fredrich.

Epigraphical Commentary
The palaeography can be surmised from Conze's facsimile.

Line 5: The penultimate letter looks like a small omega on Conze's drawing.

Commentary

This may have been a record of initiation, but too little is preserved to provide any significant information.

113   Greek and Roman records of initiates(?) of unknown   Fig. 87
         provenance

Fragment of Thasian marble, preserved below and perhaps on the right. The inscription was in Chora when Fredrich published it. Its present location is unknown.

H. 0.21 m, W. 0.22 m, Th. 0.060 m; L.H.?

Edd. Conze 1875, p. 42, no. 12, pl. 71:12; [Mommsen, *CIL* III Suppl. I.1 (1889) 7375]; Fredrich, *IG* XII.8 213.

Date?

Figure 87. Greek and Roman records of initiates(?) of unknown provenance (113). Conze 1875, pl. 71:12

i   [- - - - - - - - - - -]ΛΙΗ[- - -]
         [- - - - - - - - -]λης Ἀκ[- -]
         [καθ᾽ υἱοθεσία]ν δὲ Δημον[ίκου].
         vacat
ii   [- - -]DNSIS · SYR[- - -]

Fredrich. 4 *fortasse* ENSIS Dimitrova.

Epigraphical Commentary

Conze's facsimile gives an idea about the hand. The Greek letters are suggestive of a later date, while the Latin ones are discrepant in size and somewhat inelegant.

Commentary

This may have been a list of initiates. The Latin part was added later, as Fredrich notes. The abbreviation DNSIS is, to my knowledge, unattested. It is possible that we have]ENSIS instead.

114   Record of Greek and Roman initiates of unknown   Fig. 88
         provenance

Fragment of an opisthographic stele of Thasian marble, with molding, preserved at the top left corner, damaged on back. Said to have been found at the Genoese Towers. Archaeological Museum of Samothrace, inv. 68.857.

H. 0.17 m, W. 0.16 m, Th. 0.07 m; L.H. 0.008 m (side A, lines 1–3, and side B), 0.045 m (side A, line 4), 0.025 m (side A, line 5).

Unpublished.

Roman period

Side A

on molding: [ἐπὶ] βασιλέω[ς- - - -]
                          [- -]οφῶντος τοῦ [- -]
                               μύστα[ι εὐσεβεῖς- -]

Figure 88. Record of Greek and Roman initiates of unknown provenance (114): side A *(right)*, side B *(far right)*

below molding: C · NU[- - - -]
5 TIT . . [- - -]

Side B

[- - - - -]N[- - - - -]
[- - - -] . I . [- - - - -]
[- - -]σιν καὶ δὲ[- -]
O[- -]ηνίων O[- -]
5 . [- -]Π̣ΟΝΟΣ[- -]
- - - - - - - - - - - -

Epigraphical Commentary
Side B is almost illegible; its letters are not aligned with the edge of the stone.

Commentary
Side A was a list of Roman initiates. Side B may have been a decree.

115 Greek record of Roman initiates(?) of unknown   Fig. 89
provenance

Two joining fragments of a stele of Thasian marble, preserved on the left, rough-picked on back. Fragment *a* was found in July 1968, at 27.70–31 m east and 23.40–27 m south, and fragment *b* in July 1993, at 24 m east and 25–33 m south, of the northeastern inner corner of the Stoa. Archaeological Museum of Samothrace, inv. nos. 68.673 *(a)* and 93.576 *(b)*.
H. 0.18 m, W. 0.17 m, Th. 0.03 m; L.H. 0.02–0.025 m.
Unpublished.

Date?

- - - - - -
. [- - - - - -]
ΠΑΚΙ . [- - -]
ΣΕΡΜ . I[- - - - -]
Μάμιος[- -]
5 . . [. . .] . .

Figure 89. Greek record of Roman initiates(?) of unknown provenance (115)

Epigraphical Commentary
The lettering is rather exquisite, suggestive of a later date.

Commentary

This may have been a list of Roman initiates, given the name Mamios in line 4.

116   Greek record of Roman initiates(?) of unknown   Fig. 90
           provenance

Two joining fragments of a stele of Thasian marble, preserved on the left. Found in July 1974 at 24.00–28.00 m east and 34.00–39.00 m south of the northeastern inner corner of the Stoa. Archaeological Museum of Samothrace, inv. 74.83.

H. 0.195 m, W. 0.20 m, Th. 0.05 m; L.H. 0.02–0.025 m.

Unpublished.

2nd–3rd century A.D.?

```
        - - - - - - - - - - - -
        ΣΕΒ[- - - - - -]
        Γ. Αἴλιος[- - - - -]
        [- - - -]ΥΟ[- - - - -]
        [- - - - - - - - - - -]
   5    . . ΝΑ[- - - - - -]
        ΦΙΛΟ . [- - - - - -]
        . . ΙΠ[- - - - - - -]
        - - - - - - - - - - -
```

Figure 90. Greek record of Roman initiates(?) of unknown provenance (**116**)

Epigraphical Commentary

The letters are rectilinear, suggestive of a date in the 2nd–3rd century A.D., similar to those of **30**, **36**, **44**, **45**, and **166**, but less carefully executed.

Lines 6–7: Dots: unclear traces.

Commentary

This probably was a list of Roman initiates, as the name G. Ailios in line 2 suggests.

EGYPT

For probable initiates from Egyptian Alexandria, see **53**, lines 6, 7, 10, and possibly **31**.

CHAPTER 7

INSCRIPTIONS CONCERNING INITIATES WHOSE ETHNIC IS UNKNOWN

The following 52 documents attest initiates or presumable initiates of unknown ethnic, and eight also mention an *epoptes* or *epoptai*. All the texts are in Greek except for the occurrence of one Roman name in the Latin alphabet (**131**). Two of the inscriptions are on limestone and the remainder are on marble, primarily Thasian; one stone is lost.

117   Greek record of initiates(?)   Fig. 91

   Fragment of Thasian marble, preserved on back, severely damaged in its lower part. It is unclear whether the top is preserved or cut off. The left side has been cut off with a saw. The inscription was in Chora when Fredrich published it. Archaeological Museum of Samothrace, courtyard. No inv. no.
   H. 0.34 m, W. 0.225 m, Th. 0.09 m; L.H. 0.015 m.
   Edd. Kern 1893, p. 371, no. 14; Fredrich, *IG* XII.8 180.

2nd century B.C.?

```
        - - - - - -
        [- - -]Διονυσίου
        [- - -]ς Ἀρίστωνος
        [- - - -]νακωντος
        [- - -Μ]ενάνδρου
   5    [- - -]ος Ὀλυμπιοδώρου
        [- -Δ]ιονυσίου
        [- - -]Ἡρακλείδα
        [- - -]ς Ἀπολλω[νίου]
        [- - -]ς[- - - - - - - -]
  10    [- - - - - - -]ς[- - - -]
        [- - - -]ο[- - - - - - -]
        - - - - - -
```

Fredrich. **3** [- - -Ξε]νακῶντος *supplevit* Wilhelm (*apud* Fredrich).

Epigraphical Commentary
The inscription is severely defaced.

Commentary

This probably was a list of initiates.

Line 3: The typical genitive of [- - -Ξε]νάκων would be [- - -Ξε]νάκωνος. [- -Μη]νάκωντος (e.g., *I.Kios* 97; *I.Prusa* I–II 27) would be a more likely conjecture.

118   Greek record of initiates(?)   Fig. 92

Fragment of a stele of Thasian marble, preserved on the right and probably below. The back was inaccessible, perhaps rough-picked, judging by the surface around its edges. Paris, Musée du Louvre, inv. Ma. 4188. I saw the stone in July 2001.

H. 0.39 m, W. 0.25 m, Th. 0.10 m; L.H. 0.01–0.015 m.

Ed. Fredrich, *IG* XII.8 181.

Cf. *BullÉp* 1911, p. 321.

3rd century B.C.?

```
          - - - - - - - - - -
          . [- - - - - -]
          ΛΛΙ . .
          [Μέ?]νανδρος
          Μητροφάν[ης vel -όφαντος]
     5    [Ν]υμφόδωρος [- - - - - -]
          [Σ]ωκλῆς [- - - - - -]
          Θεόδωρος [- - - - - -]
          Μητρῶναξ [- - - - - -]
          Ἀριστοφῶν [- - - - - -]
    10    Θεογείτων Σατύρ[ου]
          [Ε]ὔνομος [- - - - - -]
          [.] . . ΟΙΗΣ Ἀντιδώρο[υ]
          [Π]ολύδωρος Ἀπολλ . [- -]
          [Θ]εόμνης Θεοδώρου
    15    [Δι]ογένης Διονυσίου
          Ἀβαῖος Ἀντιδώρου
          [.]άνθος Κυδί[μου]
          Θρασύμαχος Πολυδ . [- -]
          Σωκλῆς Οἰα[- - - -]
    20    [Ὀ]τρύας Στησικλέους
          [Ἀ]πολλόδωρος Εὐδ[- -]
          [Σ]ωσίβιος Πολυκλέου.
          - - - - - - - - - -
```

Fredrich. **4, 12, 16, 17, 20** *correxit* Hiller.

Epigraphical Commentary

The hand is slanting, suggestive of a later date. The letters are now difficult to read.

Line 1: Unclear traces.

Commentary

This probably was a list of Greek initiates.

Line 17: Κάνθος is a very rare name. Ξάνθος would be a more likely restoration, but it is not the only possibility.

Figure 91 *(above, left)*. Greek record of initiates(?) **(117)**

Figure 92 *(above, right)*. Greek record of initiates(?) **(118)**. Photo © C. Larrieu, courtesy Musée du Louvre, Department of Greek, Roman, and Etruscan Antiquities

119   Greek record of initiates(?)

The inscription is known from a copy made by Cyriacus of Ancona, which he made στὸ βασιλικό (Conze 1860, p. 50), Cod. Vat. Lat. 5250, folio 20, verso. Its present location and dimensions are unknown.

Edd. [Ziebarth 1906, p. 412, no. 3]; [Fredrich, *IG* XII.8 182].

Cf. Mommsen, *CIL* III (1873) under no. 713 (mentioned).

1st century A.D.?

Δημοκράτ[η]ς Οὐλιάδου
Μηνόδωρος Τέχνωνος
Διονύσιος Τιμο[κλ]είους
Ἀπολλωνίδης Ζεύξιδος
5   Πολύχαρμος Χάρμου
Ἀλέξανδρος Ἀρτεμιδώρου
Ἐπίγονος Μενεστράτου
Ἀρτεμίδωρος Πυθέου
Ἀσκληπιάδης Διονυσίου
10   Δημήτριος Ἀρτεμιδώρου
Ἀπολλώνιος Εὐδα[ί]μονος
Στράτων Ἐπικράτου
Ἀπολλώνιος Ἀπολλωνίου
Ἀκέστωρ Εὐκτήμονος
15   Ἀγαθ{ε}ος Ἀγάθου
Χαρίδημος Χαριδήμου.

Fredrich. **15** ΑΓΑΘΕΟΣ *lapis.*

Commentary
This probably was a list of initiates, the beginning of which was not preserved.

Line 12: A certain Στράτων Ἐπικράτου is attested in *IG* X.2 259.II, line 32 (= *SEG* XXX 622), 1st century A.D. He was a priest in the Dionysiac mysteries at Thessaloniki. He might be the same person, given the name's relative rarity; hence the tentative date.

Line 16: Individuals with the name Χαρίδημος Χαριδήμου are attested in *I.Ephesos* 450 and 520 and in *I.Priene* 508, but no identification seems possible here. Cf. also **67**, which lists a Charidamos, son of Charidamos.

120   Greek record of initiates(?) and *epoptai*

Fragment of a marble stele, preserved on the left and partially on the right, badly effaced. Provenance unknown, acquired in 1927. Its present location is unknown.

H. 0.22 m, W. 0.31 m, Th. 0.055 m; L.H. ca. 0.007 m (lines 3–14), ca. 0.013 m (line 15–end).

Ed. Salviat 1962, pp. 275–278, no. 4.

Cf. Robert and Robert, *BullÉp* 1964 400.

2nd century B.C.?

```
        - - - - - - - - -
     . . ⁵ . . [- - - - - - - - - - - -]
     Αἰσχίνας Α[- - - - - -]
     Θεύδωρος Θευδώρου
     Διότιμος Διοτίμου
  5  Ὡρομέδων Σαίνοντος
     Ἀρριδαῖος Ἱμέρου
     Παλαίστρικος Διοκλεῦς
     Ἀλέξανδρος Αὐτοφῶντος
     Θεότιμος Ἀριστοδάμου
 10  Ἡραῖος Ἀλεξάνδρου
     Ἐπόπται εὐσεβεῖς
     Ἱππίας Αἰσχυλίνου
     Πυθίων Πυθίωνος
     Ἀλέξανδρος Ἰκάρου
     vacat ca. 1 vs.
 15  [- - - -]Α Γεράνιος
     [- - - - - - - - -] . .
        - - - - - - - - - - -
```

Salviat. **12** Αἰσκυλίνου Salviat, Αἰσχυλίνου Dimitrova.

Epigraphical Commentary

The inscription is badly defaced, but Chapouthier's facsimile and the photograph of the squeeze in Salviat's edition allow us to describe the lettering as clear and carefully done. Lines 15–end have larger letters and were written later, as Salviat notes.

Salviat restores [μύσται εὐσεβεῖς] as a first line, but we do not know the exact placement of this heading.

Line 2: Unclear traces of letters.

Line 6: Unclear traces of letters.

Line 12: Αἰσχυλίνου squeeze.

Commentary

This is a list of Greek initiates, probably recorded in lines 1–10, and *epoptai*, recorded in lines 11–14. Salviat (pp. 276–277) discusses the prosopography of the inscription in detail and plausibly suggests a Doric origin for the initiates, presumably the islands near Kos or Kos itself. The most interesting name is Ὠρομέδων (line 5), since it brings to mind Theocritus's *Idylls* 7.46, which mentions the mountain Ὠρομέδων on Kos (Salviat, p. 276, and see also n. 5 for other references). See Salviat's detailed discussion; I add here a few, mostly prosopographical, comments.

Line 1: It is unclear how many lines are missing above line 2.

Line 3: A Θεύδωρος Θευδώρου is attested in *I.Cos* 235.A.I.6, but the name is too common to suggest a connection.

Line 4: A Διότιμος Διοτίμου is attested in *I.Teos* 103 (as a citizen of Magnesia-on-the-Meander) and another one appears in *I.Iasos* 135, but no identification is possible.

Line 5: It must be noted that the name Sainon is not securely attested. Its only example is *IG* XII.3 34, where its ending is restored: Σαίνο[ντος]. Σαίνιος, on the other hand, is quite common.

Line 7: The name Παλαίστρικος seems to be epigraphically unattested otherwise, but the feminine Palaistrike exists (*SEG* XXXIV 1226; cf. also *SEG* LXIII 1215).

Line 12: Αἰσκυλῖνος is unattested, while Αἰσχυλῖνος is a common name, and confirmed by the squeeze.

Line 13: A Πυθίων Πυθίωνος is attested in *I.Cos* 235.A.II.8, the same document that lists Θεύδωρος Θευδώρου. Even though it is impossible to ascertain whether he is the same person, the connection of the present inscription with Kos seems likely.

121   Greek record of initiates   Fig. 93

Fragment of Thasian marble, broken on the left, and damaged in the upper right part. The inscription was in Chora when Fredrich published it. Palaiopolis, Old School Lab of the Ephoreia of Prehistoric and Classical Antiquities.

H. 0.23 m, W. 0.41 m, Th. 0.05 m; L.H. 0.012 m.

Edd. Kern 1893, p. 355, no. 4; Fredrich, *IG* XII.8 185.

Cf. Robert and Robert, *BullÉp* 1958 270; Robert 1963, pp. 67–69.

Figure 93. Greek record of initiates
(121)

1st century B.C.?

> [ἐ]πὶ βασιλέως
> Ὀρθέως τοῦ Ἐπιχάρου
> [μύσ]τα[ι   εὐ]σεβε[ῖς]·
> Ἀσκλαπίων Μητροδώρου
> 5   ἀοιδοὶ Ἀπελλέους·
> Ἐπαφρᾶς, Εὐπορίων, Πρῶτος.
> ἀγορανομοῦντος Φιλοθέου το[ῦ- - -].

Fredrich.

Epigraphical Commentary
The inscription is now severely abraded.

Commentary
The inscription is dated by Fredrich to the 1st century B.C. on the basis of the lettering. It is a list of initiates, including three *aoidoi*, slaves of Apelles.

122   Greek record of initiates(?)

Fragment of Thasian marble, found at Xeropotamos, now lost. Its dimensions are unknown.

Ed. Hiller von Gaertringen, *IG* XII Suppl. (1939) 344.

Date?

> - - - - -
> [- - - -]Κώϊος ?
> . . . . . υίου
> [. .]νος Ἰσίω[νος],
> [Αὐ]τομέδων,
> 5   [Ζ]ωΐλος,
> [Ἑρ]μίας,
> [. .]ννων,
> [. .]ίων,
> [Τ]ίμαρχος,
> 10   [. .]είων,
> [. .]ίων,
> Σάτυρος
> Σκαμάνδρου,
> Δαλεῖνος,
> 15   Μητρόδωρ[ος]
> - - - - - - - - - - - -

Hiller. **7** [Τύ?]ννων Hiller. **14** Δαλεῖνος Croenert (*apud* Hiller), ΛΛΛΕΙΝΟΣ *lapis.*

Epigraphical Commentary
The inscription is now lost, and the readings cannot be checked.

Commentary
This probably was a list of initiates.

Line 1: The reading of the ethnic is uncertain. Initiates from Kos are otherwise unattested.

Line 7: [Τύ?]ννων, is reasonable, though there are other possibilities.

Figure 94 *(right)*. Greek record of initiates(?) **(123)**

Figure 95 *(far right)*. Greek record of initiates(?) **(124)**

123   Greek record of initiates(?)   Fig. 94

Fragment of a stele or plaque of veined pink limestone, decorated with an incised pediment, preserved on top and the left, smooth-picked on back. Found in August 1965 on the Eastern Hill, on the second step of the theatral area (Fig. 3:25). Archaeological Museum of Samothrace, inv. 65.981.

H. 0.11 m, W. 0.135 m, Th. 0.025–0.03 m; L.H. 0.015 m.

Unpublished.

2nd–3rd century A.D.?

in pediment:	Ἀγαθῆ[ι τύχηι]
below pediment:	ἐπὶ βασιλέω[ς - - - - - -]
	Διογένους · . [- - - - - -]
	Τ . [- - - - - - - - - - - - -]
	- - - - - - - - - - - - - - - -

Epigraphical Commentary
The letters are elegant, with lunate epsilon and sigma.

Line 3: The first omicron is much smaller than the other letters.

Commentary
This was probably a list of Greek initiates.

Lines 3–4: The eponymous official is otherwise unattested.

124   Greek record of initiates(?)   Fig. 95

Fragment of Thasian marble, broken on all sides except the smooth back; said to have been found at the Genoese Towers. Archaeological Museum of Samothrace, inv. 68.856.

H. 0.11 m, W. 0.11 m, Th. 0.025–0.03 m; L.H. 0.01–0.02 m.

Unpublished.

2nd–3rd century A.D.?

- - - - - - - - - - - - - - - - - - - -
[μύσται εὐσ]εβε[ῖς ?- - - - - - -]
[- - - -]. Σ Διογέ[ν - - - - - - - - -]
[- - - -]ΝΟΣΕ . [- - - - - - - - - -]
[- - - -] . [- - - - - - - - - - - - -]
- - - - - - - - - - - - - - - - -

Epigraphical Commentary
The letters have lunate shapes, hence the tentative date.

125   Greek record of initiates   Fig. 96

Two joining fragments of a stele of Thasian marble preserved on the left
and apparently on back, which has been worked with a claw-chisel. Found
in August 1971 in the southeastern room at 24.00 m east and 36.20 m
south of the northeastern inner corner of the Stoa. Archaeological Museum
of Samothrace, inv. 71.967.

H. 0.20 m, W. 0.225 m, Th. 0.04 m; L.H. ca. 0.015 m except phi
(0.05 m).

Unpublished.

1st–2nd century A.D.?

```
- - - - - - - - - - - - - - - - - - - - - - - - - - - - - - - - -
      Ἥρως δοῦλ[ος - - - - - - - - - - - - - - - - - - - - - - -]
      Ἀφροδίσιος δ[οῦλος - - - - - - - - - - - - - - - - - -]
      Εὐφρόσυνος[- - - - - - - - - - - - - - - - - - - - - - - -]
      Λοῦππος δο[ῦλος- - - - - - - - - - - - - - - - - - - - -]
   5  Κορινθία · ΕΝ[- - - - - - - - - - - - - - - - - - - - - -]
- - - - - - - - - - - - - - - - - - - - - - - - - - - - - - - - -
```

Epigraphical Commentary
The letters are clear and elegant.

Figure 96. Greek record of initiates
(125)

Commentary
This was probably a list of Greek initiates, as the title *doulos,* typical of such
documents, indicates. The Latin name Λοῦππος suggests a Roman date.

126   Greek record of *epoptai* and initiates   Fig. 97

Fragment of a marble stele, preserved on the left. The back is rough-
picked. Found in July 1968 in a trench 25–28 m south of the northeastern inner
corner of the Stoa. Archaeological Museum of Samothrace, inv. 68.354.

H. 0.20 m, W. 0.26 m, Th. 0.065 m; L.H. 0.02 m.

Unpublished.

Date?

```
- - - - - - - - - - - - - - - - - - - - - - - -
   . . . [- - - - - - - - - - - - - - - - - - - - - - - - -]
   ἱστοριαγράφ[ος? - - - - - - - - - - - - - - -]
   ἐμύησε τοὺς[- - - - - - - - - - - - - - - - - - -]
    ἐπόπται ἀπ[ελεύθεροι?- - - - - - - - - - -]
 5  Χρυσόπτερος[- - - - - - - - - - - - - - - - -]
   μύσται ἀπελ[εύθεροι- - - - - - - - - - - - -]
- - - - - - - - - - - - - - - - - - - - - - - -
```

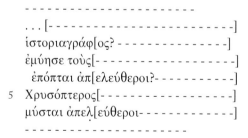

Epigraphical Commentary
The letters are clear and elegant.

Figure 97. Greek record of *epoptai*
and initiates **(126)**

Commentary
This is a list of *epoptai* and initiates, who were presumably freedmen.

Line 2: The term *historiographos* (or *historiagraphos*) occurs elsewhere
as a title following a name, e.g., in two decrees, from Delphi (*FdD* III.3
124) and Delos (*IG* XI.4 697).

Line 3: This is the only Samothracian inscription that uses the active form of the verb μυέω. Perhaps the form ἐμύησε is used in its causative meaning, "caused to be initiated," i.e., "paid for their initiation"; cf. Andoc. *De myst.* 132.5; Dem. *In Neaeram* 22.1.

127   Greek records of initiates   Fig. 98

Fragment of an opisthographic marble stele, broken on all sides. Found in Palaiopolis, at the house of Mr. Palamaroudes. Archaeological Museum of Samothrace, inv. 62.2.

H. 0.30 m, W. 0.25 m, Th. 0.07 m; L.H. 0.02 m (side A, lines 1–4), 0.015 m (side A, line 5), 0.010–0.015 m (side A, lines 6–end), 0.01–0.015 m (side B).

Edd. Salač and Frel 1968, p. 105, 2; Bouzek and Hošek 1995, p. 83, 1 (*SEG* XLV 1198).

Date?

Side A

```
- - - - - - - - - - - - - - - -
[- - - - - - - - - - -]ΛΚ Ι[- - - - - - - - -]
[- - - - - - - - - -] . ΣΑΝΤ . [- - - - - - - -]
[- - - - - - -] . ΟΥ γραμμα[τεύς- - - -]
[- - - - -]ΤΟΥ τριήραρχο[ς- - - - - - -]
5  [- - - -]ΔΩΡΟΥ γραμμα[τεύς- - - -]
[- - - - -]ΔΟΣΡ . . . Η[- - - - - - - - -]
[- - - -] . Δ . ΛΟ . . . ΟΤ[- - - - - - -]
[- - - - - - - - -]ΙΣΙ . . . ΟΝ ΓΙ[- - - -]
- - - - - - - - - - - - - - - -
```

Side B

```
- - - - - - - - - - - - - - -
[- - - - - - - - - - -] . [- - - - - - - - - - -]
[- - - - - - - - -]ΟΧΑ[- - - - - - - - - - -]
[- - - - - -Ἀ]νθίμι[ος?- - - - - - - - - -]
[- - - - - - - - - -]Ε[- - - - - - - - - - - -]
5  [- - - - - -]ναύαρχο[ς- - - - - - - - - -]
[- - - - -Ἀ]νδρόνικο[ς- - - - - - - - - -]
[- - - -τρι]ήραρχος ΜΛΙ[- - - - - - -]
[- - - - - -]ΛΑ. . . . ΟΥΤΟ . . [- - - -]
[- - - - - - -]ΙΟΥΜΑΣ[- - - - - - - -]
10 [- - - - - - - -]Ζώπυρος[- - - - - - - -]
[- - - - - - - -]ΠΑΝΔΙΟΥ ῬΥΘΜ[- -]
[- - - - - - - -]ΠΟΥ[- - - - - -]ΚΙѠΝ
[- - - - - - - -]ΝΙΚΟΜΙΚΟΣ[- - - -]
[- - - - - - - -]ΙΥΣ . [- - - - - - - - -]
15 [- - - - - - - -]ΙΝΙΣΣ . [- - - - - - - -]
[- - - - - - - -]ΟΥΤΟ . [- - - - - - - -]
- - - - - - - - - - - - - - - -
```

Figure 98. Greek records of initiates (**127**): side A *(above)*, side B *(below)*

Salač and Frel, Bouzek and Hošek. **A.2** Ἀντα[-Salač, Ἀρτα[- - Frel, Ἀντα [γόρας] Bouzek and Hošek. **A.6–8** Dimitrova. **B.1** *omiserunt edd.* **B.3** - -]Μ[- - *edd.* **B.10** ῥυθμικός Bouzek and Hošek. **B.12** Νικόμαχος Salač and Frel, νίκου Μίκος Bouzek and Hošek.

Epigraphical Commentary

The document on side A is written in larger letters and is better preserved, though in general it is badly damaged. The lettering and appearance are similar to those of **140**, and it is possible that they belonged together, namely, that **140** is to be placed near the lower part of A, given the similar letter heights.

Commentary

This document must have contained two lists of initiates, inscribed on front and back. The initiates were members of ship crews, as is evident from titles such as γραμματεύς, τριήραρχος, ναύαρχος; see *ad* **61**.

128   Greek record of initiates and an *epoptes*   Fig. 99

Fragment of a block of Thasian marble, broken on the left and the right; the top and bottom seem close to the original surface. The back may be close to the original surface; it has a cutting on the left, suitable for a pi clamp. Found in Palaiopolis in 1962, in the house of Marmoras, now in the Archaeological Museum of Samothrace, inv. 62.1.

H. 0.21 m, W. 0.255 m, Th. 0.07 m; L.H. 0.008–0.01 m.

Unpublished.

Date?

```
- - - - - - - - - - - - - - - - - - -
[- - - - - - - - - - - - - - - -]. .[- -]
[- - - - - - - -] . . . ΤΟΥ[- - - - -]
[- - - - - -]ΛΛ[- - - - - - - - - - -]
[- - - -]ΚΥΔΡΟΛ[.]ΟΥΣ [- - -]
5  [- - - - - - - -] . ΕΤ . [- - - - - - - -]
[- - - - -]νδρος Διονυσίο[υ?- -]
[ἐπ]όπτης εὐσεβ[ὴς- - - - - - -]
[- - - - -]ΩΝ Νικομήδ[ου?- - -]
               vacat
```

3 *fortasse* Κυδρο<κ>λ[έ]ους.

Epigraphical Commentary

The inscription is now badly damaged. The letters become larger at the lower part of the block.

Line 6: Last letter: apex of a triangular letter. The letters in this line are slightly larger.

Commentary

This is a record of an *epoptes*, whose name must have been preceded by those of initiates. It is unclear whence the block came.

Line 6: Νικομήδ[is more likely a patronymic, following a name ending in -ων, though the ethnic cannot be excluded.

129   Greek record of initiates and *epoptai*   Fig. 100

Stele of Thasian marble, broken only above, rough-picked on back. It was built into the wall of the church of St. Andrew, in the western part of the island, and inscribed with a Christian grave inscription (below a

Figure 99 *(above, left)*. Greek record of initiates and an *epoptes* (128)

Figure 100 *(above, right)*. Greek record of initiates and *epoptai* (129)

contemporary relief representing a cross within a circle) located above the ancient list of initiates. Archaeological Museum of Samothrace, courtyard. No inv. no.

H. 0.33 m, W. 0.26 m, Th. 0.07 m; L.H. 0.02–0.04 m (lines 1–3), 0.015 m (lines 4–10).

Edd. Conze 1875, p. 42, no. 20, pl. 71:20; Fredrich, *IG* XII.8 204.

1st century B.C.?

       relief
     ἐνθάδε κα-
     τακῖται *(sic)* Εὐή-
     θιν *traces occupying 1.5 lines*
     . . ΔΙΕΙ . ΑΠ . Λ . . . Ι . . .
  5 . . . . ΑΙ μύσται . .
     vacat ἐπόπται
     ΠΑΙΕΠ . . . . . Ι . . . . .
     . εοκλῆς . εοκλέους
     vacat μύστης *vacat*
 10 ἀκόλουθος Ἀσκλᾶς

Fredrich. 4–8 Dimitrova, - - - - - -Π- - - | 5 - - - - - -ΑΙ- - -| 6 - - -Ι- - - - - - -| 7 . . ΑΓΛΙ . . Σ| 8 - - -Λ- - - - - Fredrich.

Epigraphical Commentary

The original inscription, dated by Fraser to the 1st century B.C. on the basis of the lettering, is badly damaged. Lines 1–3 contain a Christian epitaph.

Line 6: The diagonal mark before ἐπόπται is damage.

Commentary

This was a list of initiates and *epoptai* (lines 5–6). Lines 8–10 record another initiate, accompanied by his *akolouthos*.

Line 8: Theokles, Neokles, *vel sim.*

130   Greek record of initiates(?) and *epoptai*   Fig. 101

Fragment of a stele of Thasian marble, broken on the left, below, and probably above; rough-picked on back. Found in 1924, below a fountain.[1] The surface of the stone is heavily damaged by water. Archaeological Museum of Samothrace, courtyard, inv. 49.444.

H. 0.19 m, W. 0.275 m, Th. 0.07 m; L.H. 0.007–0.01 m.

Ed. Fraser, *Samothrace* 2.1 (1960) 26.

Cf. Salviat 1962, p. 269; Robert 1963, p. 53; Robert and Robert, *BullÉp* 1964 373; Bouzek and Hošek 1995, pp. 83–85; *SEG* XLV 1198–1201.

2nd–1st century B.C.?

Col. I	Col. II
[- - - - - -]	[- - - - - -]
[- - - - - -]	[- - - - - -]
[- - - - - -]	Πο[- - - - - -]
[- - - - - -]	Νίνναρος
5 [- - - - - -]	Φιλοκτα[- -]
Ἐ π ό π τ α ι	Θεύδ[οτ]ος *vel* Θεύδ[ωρ]ος
[- -]ΥΠ[- -]	Διοφάνης
[- -]ΕΠ[. . . . . . .]Α	Κόνων
[- - - - - -]ΟΔΟΤΟΣ	ΔΙΟΝ[- - - - -]
10 [Ἀ]πολλόδωρος Β *vacat*	Α . . [- - - - - -]
[- - - - - - - - - -]	Ἀσκληπ[- - -]
[- - - - - -]Ε . Ν[- - - - - -]	[- - - - - -]
[- - - - - -]	[- - - - - -]

Fraser. **II.4** Μίνναρος Fraser, Νίνναρος Bouzek and Hošek.

Epigraphical Commentary
The stone is very hard to read. The hand suggests a date in the 2nd–1st century B.C.

Figure 101. Greek record of initiates(?) and *epoptai* (**130**). *Samothrace* 2.1, pl. XII:26

1. For details about the findspot, see Salviat 1962, p. 269. There is no information about the location of the fountain.

Commentary

The inscription, whose beginning is missing, represents a record of *epoptai* and probably initiates. It is interesting that the names that can be read have no patronymics except for [Ἀ]πολλόδωρος in line 5, if the following beta indicates that his patronymic was Ἀπολλοδώρου; such usage of Β as a numeral is quite common. According to Fraser, the patronymics must have been written on the lines below since there is insufficient space for them, at least in the second column. The preserved names, however, show that there were only single names listed.

Line II.4: The name Μίνναρος is otherwise unattested (cf. Robert, p. 53). Νίνναρος, however, is attested, and is confirmed by the stone.

Line II.6: Θεύδ[οτ]ος must have been one of the *epoptai*, although his name is inscribed on the same line as the heading, as Fraser notes.

131 Records of Greek and Roman initiates of unknown   Fig. 102
provenance

Round base of Thasian marble, with molding above, broken below. Found in 2003 in the Middle Byzantine ruins (inner dimensions 5.50 × 3.30 m) of the church of St. Georgios (Ai-Giorgis ston Katsamba), reused as the altar support, now at the Old School Lab of the Ephoreia of Prehistoric and Classical Antiquities in Palaiopolis. It must have held a tripod or a similar object. The top has a central hole, 0.16 m in diameter above and 0.085 m below, with a pour channel, and three smaller holes 0.07–0.08 m in diameter. Ephoreia inv. 69.

H. 0.45 m, Diam. (top) 0.46 m; L.H. 0.01–0.015 m.

Ed. Matsas and Dimitrova 2006, pp. 131–132.

Figure 102. Records of Greek and Roman initiates of unknown provenance (**131**)

1st century B.C.–2nd century A.D.?

i   ἐπὶ βασιλέως Ἀπελήους *(sic)*
      τοῦ Φιλοκράτους
      [. .²⁻⁵. .]ίνιοι
      μύσται εὐσεβεῖς
    5 Διονύσιος Διογένου
      Αὐτοκλῆς Συσίφου
      Λούκιος Μάρκου
      vacat 1 vs.
ii   ἐπὶ βασιλέως Ζωίλου
      τοῦ Ἀριστοξένου μύστης
   10 εὐσεβὴς A · | RA . . VS · | VR . . .
      [. . . . . .¹⁵⁻²⁰. . . . .]
      [. . .⁵⁻⁸. . .]σίππου [. . .⁵⁻⁸. . .]
      - - - - - - - - - - - - - - - - - -

Epigraphical Commentary

The stone is now very worn. The Greek hand of inscription ii is later, and less careful. The Latin hand of ii seems different from that of the Greek.

Commentary

The base has two records of initiates, probably not original. The names in lines 7 and 10 suggest a Roman date. The eponymous kings are apparently unknown, but the name Aristoxenos is numismatically attested for a Samothracian official; see Fredrich, *IG* XII.8, p. 41. This is the first base for a tripod-like object on which records of initiation have been found.

Line 1: The genitive of the name Apelles is spelled with an eta in several inscriptions, most of which happen to be from Ephesos (e.g., *I.Ephesos* 159, 552, 1406, 1407). Apeles with a single lambda seems to be epigraphically unattested, though simplification of double consonants is a widespread phenomenon.

Line 10: A Roman initiate's name is recorded in the Latin alphabet.

132   Greek record of an initiate

Fragment of Thasian marble, broken on both sides, now lost. It was copied by Phardys and Champoiseau, and later seen by G. Seure in Istanbul.

H. 0.25 m, W. 0.65 m, Th.?; L.H.?

Edd. Reinach 1892, p. 204, no. 1, under no. 6; Kern 1893, p. 375, no. 24, and cf. p. 373, under no. 17; Fredrich, *IG* XII.8 197; Hiller von Gaertringen, *IG* XII Suppl. (1939), p. 149; *I.Perinthos* (1998) 308.

Cf. Robert 1963, p. 65, with n. 6; Robert and Robert, *BullÉp* 1964 394; Fraser 2001, p. 183 (*SEG* LI 1092*bis*).

Date?

i   [- - - -]Ἰσιδώρου   iii   5 ἀγαθ[ῆι τύχηι]
ii   [- -]ΟΙ Περίνθιοι·   ἐπὶ βασιλέ[ως- - - - - -]
     [- - -]Μνησικλῆς   μύστης [εὐσεβὴς- -Ἀσκλη?-]
     [- - - - - - - - - - -]   πιάδου[- - - -]

Seure. **2** οἱ Περίνθιοι Seure. **8** ΤΡΙΑΔΟ Reinach.

Epigraphical Commentary

The letters of inscription iii are much bigger, according to Seure.

Line 1: The name was written within an erasure from Christian times, as Reinach observes.

Commentary

It is unclear what title the Perinthians mentioned in inscription ii had and whether the initiate in inscription iii was from Perinthos.

Line 2: I prefer to interpret OI not as the definite article, which is not typical in such documents, but as the ending of some word, possibly θεωροί.

133   Greek record of initiates   Fig. 103

Fragment of a marble stele, preserved on the right. The back is smooth-picked. Brought in during the winter of 1967, possibly from Chora. Archaeological Museum of Samothrace, inv. 68.56.

H. 0.21 m, W. 0.24 m, Th. 0.05 m; L.H. 0.02 m.

Unpublished.

End of 2nd century A.D.?

```
        - - - - - - - - - - - - - - - - - - -
       [- - - - - - - - -]A . [- - - - - -]
       [- - - - - - - -]Σ ἐ[πὶ] Στεφά-
       [νου vel -νηφόρων?- -]ου Ἀπελλοῦ
       [- - - - - - - κα]ὶ Μενεκλέ-
   5   [ους?- - - - Κα?]υνίων πρέσ-
       [βεις vel πρεσβευταί - -]μύσται
       [- - - - - - - - - - εὐ]τυχῶς
       [- - - - - - - - - -]ΟΣΟΙ[. . .]
        - - - - - - - - - - - - - - - - - - -
```

Epigraphical Commentary

The letter style closely resembles that of **63**. The upsilon has a decorative crossbar; the sigma and epsilon are lunate.

Line 5: First letter: right upper diagonal of upsilon.

Line 7: Last letter: left upper part of a circle.

Line 8: Dotted letters: right part of a circle, top part of a circle (cf. the last omicron in line 3); top vertical.

Figure 103. Greek record of initiates
(**133**)

Commentary

This is a record of ambassadors and initiates, possibly from Kaunos.

Lines 2–3: A name like Stephanos or the title *stephanephoros*. Parallels for the formula ἐπὶ στεφανηφόρων in the plural can be found in *TAM* V 542, line 12; *I.Didyma* 429, 515. *Stephanephoros* was the title of eponymous magistrates in various cities (e.g., Iasos).

Line 7: The adverb εὐτυχῶς is found in other inscriptions concerning mysteries, e.g., *I.Ephesos* 652, 1883; *I.Panamara* 245, line 41. A similar notion is expressed in **90**, line 5.

134   Greek record of initiates from either Byzantion or   Fig. 104
         Kalchedon

Fragment of pedimental stele of Thasian marble, preserved on the right and above; the back may be close to the original surface. The inscription was acquired by the excavators from a local person in 1926.[2] Archaeological Museum of Samothrace, courtyard, inv. 49.440.

H. 0.22 m, W. 0.15 m, Th. 0.08 m; L.H. 0.008 m (line 1), 0.012 m (lines 2–3), 0.015 m (lines 4–8).

Ed. Fraser, *Samothrace* 2.1 (1960) 27.

Cf. Salviat 1962, p. 269; Robert 1963, pp. 64–66; Robert and Robert, *BullÉp* 1964 373; Cole 1984, p. 40, with 110 (n. 330); Bouzek and Hošek 1995, pp. 83–85 (*SEG* XLV 1198–1201, lemma 5).

After middle of 2nd century B.C.–1st century A.D.?

in cornice:	[ἐπὶ βασιλέως - - - - - -]δώρου
below cornice:	[- - - - - - - - - ἐπὶ ἱερομ]νάμονος
	[- - - - - - - - - - - - - - -]ωνίου ·
	[μύσται εὐσε]βεῖς · *vacat*
5	[- - - - - - - - - - - - - Βε *vel* Με]νδιδώρο[υ]
	[- - - - - - - - - - - - - - - - - - -]ΟΥ *vacat*
	[- - - - - - - - - - - - - - - - - - - -]ΟΥΣ *vacat*
	- -

Fraser. 1 - -]κου Fraser, - -]δώρου Dimitrova. 4 βεῖς Fraser. 5 Βε]νδιδώρο[υ] Fraser, Βε *vel* Με]νδιδώρο[υ] Robert.

Epigraphical Commentary

The broken-bar alpha and the shape of the omega are consistent with a date after ca. 150 B.C. to some point in the 1st century A.D.

Line 4: Clear beta.

Commentary

This is a list of initiates from either Byzantion or Kalchedon.

Line 2: Fraser comments that *hieromnemones* are the eponymous officials of Byzantion, Perinthos, and Kalchedon. He is more inclined to attribute the document to Perinthos on the basis that "Perinthians outnumber Byzantines in Samothracian documents." It must be noted, however, that one of the initiates listed by Fraser as Perinthian (**50**, line 25 = *IG* XII.8 186.25) in fact has the ethnic Ξάνθιος. Perinthians are mentioned in **39**

2. See Salviat 1962, p. 269.

Figure 104. Greek record of initiates
from either Byzantion or Kalchedon
(134). Courtesy Samothrace Excavations

(one citizen and his household slave), **132** (at least one person, perhaps
a theoros), and possibly in **145**, but the remains on the stone allow other
restorations as well. On the other hand, Byzantines are recorded in **39**
(two people), **53** (one person), and perhaps in **67**, side C (nine people),
so the conclusion that Perinthians are more numerous than Byzantines in
Samothracian documents is incorrect. Even if they were more numerous,
this would still not be a decisive argument for the origin of the initiates
in the present monument (Robert, p. 65). What is more significant is
the Doric form of the title *hieromnamon*, which, as Robert points out
(p. 66), excludes the Ionic city of Perinthos as a possible candidate. He
further narrows the choice down to Byzantion because of the name Βε *vel*
Με]νδιδώρο[υ]; see *ad* line 5.

Line 5: Βενδίδωρος, derived from the name of Thracian goddess Ben-
dis, is also attested in the variant Μενδίδωρος; see Robert, p. 65. The name
Bendidoros/Bendidora occurs in Attica, Eretria, Thessaloniki, Lemnos,
and elsewhere.[3] Robert believes that the initiate in the present document
is from Byzantion, given the abundance of Thracian names there. It seems
to me that Kalchedon cannot be excluded as a possibility, in view of its
location and the Doric dialect spoken in it. Kalchedonians are honored in
IG XII.8 152 and are listed as theoroi in **22**.

135   Greek records of initiates

Fragment of Thasian marble, preserved at the upper right. The
inscription was in Chora when Fredrich published it. Its present location
is unknown. A basket is engraved in the middle of the stone, within which
inscription ii is cut.

3. See Robert 1963, pp. 64–65, for
the exact references.

H. 0.14 m, W. 0.31 m, Th. 0.10 m; L.H. 0.009–0.02 m.
Edd. Kern 1893, p. 371, no. 13; Fredrich, *IG* XII.8 201.

1st century B.C.?

i		ii		iii	
	[μύσται εὐσ]εβεῖς	ii	Τιμαγόρας	iii	Θε[- - - ·]
	[- - - - - - - -]ιοι·		Θεοκλείδου		Ἀρισ[- - -]
	[- - - - - - -] Ἄβρο-		καὶ Νικησίλε-		Παντε[- -]
	[- - -, - - - -]ΗΣ	10	ως	15	συνμύσ[ται]·
5	[- - -, - - -]ΜΙΣ		Σωτέλους.		Φανέα[ς]
	[- - - - - - -]οι Ὑ-				Σημ[- - -]
	- - - - - - - - - - - -				

Fredrich. **14** Παντέ[ως] Fredrich.

Commentary

This document contains three inscriptions. Inscriptions i and iii are lists of initiates, and ii may also be a record of initiation. Fredrich thinks that ii is the oldest, followed by iii and then i. He suggests a date in the 1st century B.C. on the basis of the letter style.

Lines 7–8: A certain Τιμαγόρας Θεοκλείδου is attested in an undated inscription from Naxos (*IG* XII.5 81). He may have been the same person, given the name's relative rarity, but the Naxian inscription contains no information other than the name.

Line 14: There are many possible restorations.

136   Greek record of initiates(?)   Fig. 105

Reused fragment of Thasian marble, with decorative molding at bottom and a rectangular cutting on the right, preserved on the left and below. Found in July 1971 at 17.85–21.15 m east and 32.70–37.50 m south of the northeastern inner corner of the Stoa. Archaeological Museum of Samothrace, inv. 71.958.

H. 0.26 m, W. 0.20 m, Th. 0.06 m; L.H. 0.01 m.
Unpublished.

Date?

```
         - - - - - - - - - - - -
         [. . .]ΑΛΟΣ[- - - -]
         [. . .]οδωρος[- - - -]
         [. . .]ΑΓΑ[- - - - -]
         [Ἀπο]λλοδ[- - -]
      5  [. . σ]θένης ΝΕΙ[-]
         [Μέ]νανδρος Μεν[- -]
         [Ἀλ]εξάν[δρου]
         [. . .]ΝΟΜΟΣ[- -]
         [. . .]ΜΩΝ Ἀπολλωνί[ου]
      10 [τ]οῦ Ἀρτεμιδώρου *vacat*
         *vacat*
```

Epigraphical Commentary

The inscription is now severely abraded.

Figure 105 *(above, left)*. Greek record of initiates(?) (136)

Figure 106 *(above, right)*. Record of Greek, Roman, and Thracian initiates(?) (137). *Samothrace* 2.1, pl. XII:37

137   Record of Greek, Roman, and Thracian initiates(?)   Fig. 106

Fragment of Thasian marble, broken on all sides. The back is rough-picked. Found on June 27, 1953, near the Rotunda of Arsinoe, to the west. Archaeological Museum of Samothrace, inv. 53.7.

H. 0.19 m, W. 0.165 m, Th. 0.03 m; L.H. 0.010–0.015 m.

Ed. Fraser, *Samothrace* 2.1 (1960) 37.

Imperial period

```
        - - - - - - - - - - - -
        [- - - - - -] Ι . Λ . [- - - - - -]
        [- - - - - -]ουπορις . . .
        vacat?    Ἀντίπατ<ρ>ος
        [Ἀλε]ξάνδρου
   5    [- - - - - -]τιανός
        [- - - - - -]πορεως
        vacat
        - - - - - -
```

Fraser. **2** Dimitrova, υπογισ Fraser. **5** Dimitrova, σιανός Fraser. **6** Dimitrova, νόρεως Fraser.

Epigraphical Commentary
Line 2: Part of a circle, followed by clear upsilon, pi, omicron, rho, iota, sigma.

Line 5: Clear tau.

Line 6: First letter: clear pi; what seemed to be the diagonal of nu is a stray mark.

Commentary

The names in *-poris* can be clearly identified as Thracian.[4] Unfortunately, too little is preserved to shed further light on this inscription. It is not certain whether it is a record of initiates, but the listing of Greeks, Thracians, and presumably a Roman (line 5) makes this a probable conjecture.

Line 5: The Latin suffix *-tianus* perhaps suggests a Roman Imperial date, but it is impossible to be more specific.

138   Greek record of initiates(?)   Fig. 107

Fragment of a block of Thasian marble, broken on the left. The back is rough-picked; the right side may have anathyrosis; the top and bottom are smooth-picked. Found in Apano Meria, in the ruins of a church known as "Treis Ekklisies st' Alonoudhi," now at the Old School Lab of the Ephoreia of Prehistoric and Classical Antiquities in Palaiopolis. Ephoreia inv. 25.

H. 0.17 m, W. 0.34 m, Th. 0.23; L.H. 0.014 m.
Ed. Matsas and Dimitrova 2006, pp. 130–131.

2nd century B.C.–2nd century A.D.?

```
         - - - - - - - - - - - - - - - - - - - - - - -
         [- - - - - - - - - - - - - - - - - - - -]
         traces of letters (ca. 10)
         [- - - - - - -] vacat? Δημοχάρης vacat
         [- - - - - -] vacat Λάμπωνος vacat
         [- - - - - -]. . vacat Διονυσίας vacat
    5    [- - - - - - -]Υ  vacat Ἐπικράτου vacat
         [- -] . ΙΟΙ        vacat
         [- -?-]            vacat
         [- -] . ΤΕΟΥ  vacat
         [- -] . ΠΟΙ ΟΥ       vacat
         - - - - - - - - - - - - - - - - - -
```

Epigraphical Commentary

The inscription is now badly damaged. The lettering is somewhat uneven and difficult to date.

Figure 107. Greek record of initiates(?) (**138**)

139 Greek record of initiates(?)

Fragment of Thasian marble, broken on all sides. The inscription was in Palaiopolis when Fredrich published it. Its present location is unknown.
H. 0.19 m, W. 0.22 m, Th. 0.055 m; L.H. 0.01 m.
Edd. Kern 1893, p. 379, no. 33; Fredrich, *IG* XII.8 179.

2nd century B.C.?

```
  - - - - - - - -
  [- - - - - - -]ΑΛΛ[- - -]
  [- -]ρέτη Ἀντιόχου
  [- -]Ι[- - - -]Η[- - - - - -]
  [- - - - - -]Λ[- - - - - - -]
5 [- - - - -]ΠΟ/[- -]ΑΙ[- -]
  [- - - - - - - - - -]ΑΠΟ
  [- - - - - - - - - -]ΠΟΥ
  - - - - - - - -
```

Commentary

Presumably this was a list of initiates, containing the name - -ρέτη Ἀντιόχου, but no further information can be surmised. Presumably the first name in line 2 was Arete or a compound of it, such as Nikarete or Mnesarete.

140 Record of Greek and Roman initiates(?) of unknown provenance   Fig. 108

Fragment of Thasian marble, broken on all sides. Found in July 1971 at 21.30–24.30 m east and 22.50–35.20 m south of the northeastern inner corner of the Stoa. Archaeological Museum of Samothrace, inv. 71.957.
H. 0.29 m, W. 0.22 m, Th. 0.10 m; L.H. 0.025 m.
Unpublished.

Roman period

```
  - - - - - - - - - - -
  [- - - -] . . . . . . [- - - - -]
  [-] . ΟΥΛΑΡΙΣ[- - - -] vel [- -] . ΟΥΛΙΑΡΙΣ[- - - -]
  [- -]ΟΥΕΝΤΟΣ Τ[- - -]
  [- -]Λλίστρατος [- -]
5 [- - - -]ΜΑΝΟΣ[- - - -]
  [- - - - - -]ΝΕΙΚΟΣ[- -]
  [- - - - - -]ΟΣ[- - - - - -]
  [- - - - - - - - - - - -]
  [- - - - - - - - - - - -]
10 [- - - - - - -]τιώτη[ς- -]
  [- - - - - - - - -]ΝΕΙΚΗ[- -]
  traces (3–4 vss.)
```

4 *fortasse* Κα]λλίστρατος.

Epigraphical Commentary

The inscription is badly defaced. The lettering and layout are similar to those of **127**.
Line 2: It is unclear if the vertical between lambda and alpha is a letter.

Figure 108. Record of Greek and Roman initiates(?) of unknown provenance (**140**)

Commentary

This may have been a list of Greek and Roman initiates from the Roman period, as the remains in lines 2 and 3 suggest.

Line 3: A name of the type Iuventus is possible.

141   Greek record of initiates(?)   Fig. 109

Fragment of Thasian marble, found near the Rotunda of Arsinoe, preserved on the right. Its present location is unknown.

H. 0.14 m, W. 0.19 m, Th. 0.05 m; L.H.?

Edd. Conze 1880, p. 95, no. 10; Fredrich, *IG* XII.8 199.

Cf. Robert and Robert, *BullÉp* 1958 270; Robert 1963, pp. 67–69.

Date?

Figure 109. Greek record of initiates(?) (141). Conze 1880, p. 95, no. 10

```
          - - - - - - - - - - - - - -
          Διαγόρα[ς] vacat [- - -]
          Διονύσιος vacat B[- - -]
          Ζηνοδώρα[- -]
             σίου
      5   ἀγορανο[μοῦντος- - -]
             τοῦ(?) [- - - -]
```

Fredrich. 6 τοξε Fredrich, τοῦ(?) Dimitrova.

Epigraphical Commentary

Conze's facsimile gives an idea about the lettering.

Commentary

This probably was a list of initiates, given the listed names and the mention of the *agoranomos;* on the *agoranomoi* see above, 3, *ad* line 13.

142   Greek record of initiates(?)   Fig. 110

Fragment of Thasian marble, preserved on the left and above, badly defaced. Its findspot and present location are unknown.

H. 0.29 m, W. 0.29 m, Th.?; L.H.?

Edd. Conze 1875, p. 41, no. 9, pl. 71:9; Fredrich, *IG* XII.8 224.

Cf. Robert and Robert, *BullÉp* 1958 270; Robert 1963, pp. 67–69.

Date?

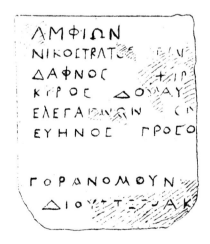

Figure 110. Greek record of initiates(?) (142). Conze 1875, pl. 71:9

```
          Ἀμφίων
          Νικόστρατο[ς] . . N
          Δάφνος          . IN
          Κῦρος         ΔΟ . ΑΥ
      5   ΕΛΕΓΑΙ Ν ω Ν   Ο Ν
          Εὔηνος, Γρόσφ[ος]
          [ἀ]γορανομοῦν[τος]
          ΔΙΟΥ . Τ . . . ΑΚ[- - - - -]
          - - - - - - - - - - - - - -
```

Fredrich. 5 ΕΛΕΓΑΓΝΟΝ Σ Ν Fredrich, ΕΛΕΓΑΙΝΩ Ν   ΟΝ Dimitrova. 6 Γρόσφ[ος] *supplevit* Wil. [*apud* Fredrich].

Epigraphical Commentary
The readings can be surmised from Conze's facsimile.
　　Line 6: Last letter: circle.

Commentary
This was probably a list of initiates. The lack of patronymics may indicate that the preserved names are those of slaves.
　　Line 5: A name of the type Meletainon is possible.

143　Greek record of initiates(?)　　　　　　　　　　　Fig. 111

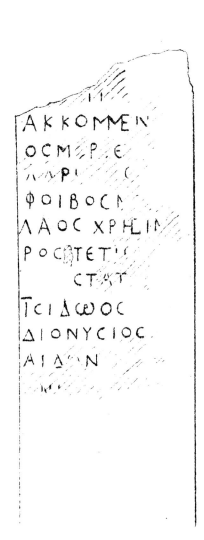

Figure 111. Greek record of initiates(?) (143). Conze 1875, pl. 71:16

　　Fragment of Thasian marble, preserved on the left and right, badly defaced. Its findspot and present location are unknown.
　　H. 0.60 m, W. 0.25 m, Th.?; L.H.?
　　Edd. Conze 1875, p. 42, no. 16, pl. 71:16; Fredrich, *IG* XII.8 225.

Date?

```
      - - - - - -
      [- -]. .[- - - - - -]
      ΑΚ Κομμέν[ι]-
      ος Μ . Ρ . Ε[- -]
      Ἀδρι[ανό]ς?
  5   Φοῖβος, Ν[ικό?]-
      λαος, Χρήσιμ[ος?]
      ΡΟΣ ΤΕΤ . . [- -]
      Στατ[ίλιος?]
      Ἰσίδωρος
  10  Διονύσιος
      ΑΙΔωΝ
      . . . [- - - - - - - -]
      - - - - - - - - - -
```

　　Fredrich. **2** ΛΚ Κομμέν[ι] Fredrich *in maiusculis*, ΑΚ Κομμέν[ι]- Dimitrova. **4** *supplevit* Hiller. **9** Ἰσίδω[ρ]ος Fredrich, Ἰσίδωρος Dimitrova. **11** ΑΙΔΟΝ Fredrich *in maiusculis*, ΑΙΔωΝ Dimitrova.

Epigraphical Commentary
Conze's facsimile gives an idea of the letter style.

Commentary
This was probably a list of initiates.
　　Line 1: Κομένιο[ς] (Latin Comenius), usually with a single mu, is a rare name, also attested in *IG* II² 6770 (1st century A.D.) and in *I.Leukopetra* 23, 25, 30.
　　Line 6: Ligature of eta and sigma.
　　Line 9: The rho of Ἰσίδωρος is in ligature with omega.

144　Greek record of initiates(?)　　　　　　　　　　　Fig. 112

　　Fragment of a stele of Thasian marble, preserved on the left, back, and below, with raised molding below; the back is rough-picked. Its findspot is unknown. Brought from Chora on July 5, 1949. Archaeological Museum of Samothrace, courtyard, inv. 49.441.

H. 0.246 m, W. 0.19 m, Th. 0.09 m; L.H. 0.025 m (lines 1–3), 0.015–0.017 m (lines 4–7).

Edd. Fraser, *Samothrace* 2.1 (1960) 19; Walton 1963, pp. 99–100; Salač and Frel 1968, p. 106, 4; Bouzek and Hošek 1995, p. 85, 2 (*SEG* XLV 1201).

Cf. Robert and Robert, *BullÉp* 1964 369.

2nd–3rd century A.D.?

Figure 112. Greek record of initi-
ates(?) (144). Courtesy Samothrace
Excavations

> [- - - - - - - - - - - - - - - -]
> τοῦ Εἰσ[ιδ[ώρου / -ότου ? οἱ ?]
> ἐν πλοίῳ ΔΙ[. ^{ca. 5} .]
> Β τοῦ Εἰσιδ[ώρου / -ότου]
> 5   καὶ σὺν α[ὐτ-ῷ / -οῖς]
> Θήρων Β τοῦ Μ[ενάνδ?]-
> ρου,
>
> Εὔνου[ς]

Fraser. **1–2** Dimitrova, [ἀνέθηκαν?] τὸ τέμ[ενος οἱ] Fraser, ΤΟΥ ΕΠ Walton.

Epigraphical Commentary

The lettering is uneven and inelegant, with rectilinear shapes. Line 7, which is only half of a line below line 6, may be by a different hand; it employs lunate epsilon. It is unclear how many lines are missing above.

Line 2: Third letter: clear upsilon; last letter: lower part of a left vertical, followed by another lower part of a vertical, which renders mu improbable, since the second vertical is too close to the first, thus suggesting that the first is a narrow letter, such as iota.

Commentary

The nature of this document, dated by Fraser to the 2nd–3rd century A.D., is unclear. Fraser thought that it was a dedication of a *temenos* by members of a ship's crew. I find the restoration of τέμ[ενος in line 2 unconvincing (cf. Walton), given the remains on the stone, and suggest that the document may have been a list of initiates.

145   Greek record of initiates(?)

Marble fragment found in Palaiopolis, at the "lower tower" (Conze). Its dimensions and present location are unknown.

Edd. Conze 1860, p. 64; Fredrich, *IG* XII.8 203.

Date?

> - - - - - - - - - -
> [Περιν?]θίων
> [- - - - - -]ΟΔΟΙ
> [- - - - - - -]Ν[- - - -]
> [- - - - - - -]Ο . ΟΥ[- -]
> - - - - - - - - - -

Fredrich. **2** [ἀ]ο[ι]δοί? Fredrich.

Commentary

This may have been a list of initiates. The restoration [Περιν?]θίων, and therefore the connection with Perinthos, is only hypothetical.

146   Greek record of initiates(?)   Fig. 113

Fragment of stele of Thasian marble, preserved on the left, rough-picked on back. Found in August 1988 on the Western Hill. Archaeological Museum of Samothrace, inv. 88.510.

H. 0.11 m, W. 0.11 m, Th. 0.06 m; L.H. 0.02 m (line 2), 0.04 m (line 3).

Unpublished.

1st–3rd century A.D.?

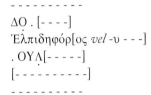

```
          - - - - - - - - - -
      ΔΟ . [- - - -]
      Ἐλπιδηφόρ[ος vel -υ - - -]
      . ΟΥΛ[- - - - -]
      [- - - - - - - - - -]
          - - - - - - - - - -
```

Figure 113. Greek record of initiates(?) (**146**)

Epigraphical Commentary

The lettering is uneven, with pronounced serifs, suggestive of a later date.

Line 1: Second letter: lower part of a circle; third letter: lower vertical.

Line 2: Cursive delta.

Line 3: First letter: right top horizontal (or an extended finial) joined with a barely slanting right stroke; third letter: triangle.

Commentary

This is may have been a list of initiates. It is possible to restore the heading *douloi* in line 1 or 3.

147   Greek record of *epoptai*   Fig. 114

Fragment of a pedimental stele of Thasian marble, broken below. Found on July 11, 1970, near the Stoa. Archaeological Museum of Samothrace, inv. 70.939.

H. 0.255 m, W. 0.26 m, Th. 0.045 m; L.H. 0.015–0.02 m.

Unpublished.

2nd century B.C.–2nd century A.D.?

```
        ἐπὶ βασιλέως . . . .
        . . νακτος Ἰ-
        εροκλέους ἐπόπται
        εὐσεβεῖς
    5   . . . .
        - - - - - - - - - -
```

Figure 114. Greek record of *epoptai* (**147**)

Epigraphical Commentary

The inscription is almost obliterated.

Commentary

This is a Greek record of *epopteia*. The eponymous official is so far unattested, but if his first name is to be restored as Metronax, then he might be related to the eponymous kings in **46**, inscription ii, and **89**.

148   Greek record of initiates(?)   Fig. 115

Block of Thasian marble, broken on top. There are vertical lines incised on both the left and right sides, presumably for decoration. Provenance unknown, perhaps brought from the Gattilusi Towers. The front surface was almost entirely covered with mortar. Archaeological Museum of Samothrace, courtyard. No inv. no.

H. 0.14 m, W. 0.54 m, Th. 0.33 m; L.H. 0.02 m.

Unpublished.

Figure 115. Greek record of initiates(?) (**148**)

Date?

- -

   . . οὑρου, Βάκχιος Πούδεντος(?)
   Βάκχιος Ἑρμέροτος, Ποσῆς Ἀπολ-
   λοφάνους, Τελεσφόρος Πάρμιδο[ς]
   Τυχέρως . . . . . Π . ΑΝ . . . .

Epigraphical Commentary

The letters are even and somewhat narrow, thus suggestive of a Late Hellenistic–Early Roman date.

Commentary

It is unclear whether the block belonged to a monument or to a building.

149   Greek record of initiates   Fig. 116

Fragment of a limestone block, broken below; the back seems to be smooth-picked. A rectangular hole is visible in front near the left edge. Found by Chapouthier. Brought from Chora on July 5, 1949. Archaeological Museum of Samothrace, courtyard, inv. 49.445.

H. 0.25 m, W. 0.48 m, Th. 0.21 m; L.H. 0.03–0.035 m (lines 1–2), 0.025–0.028 m (lines 3–4).

Edd. Chapouthier 1925, p. 254; *BullÉp* 1926, p. 275; Hiller von Gaertringen, *IG* XII Suppl. (1939) 346; Fraser, *Samothrace* 2.1 (1960) 60.

Cf. Salviat 1962, p. 268.

Figure 116. Greek record of initiates
(149). Courtesy Samothrace Excavations

2nd–4th century A.D.?

ἐπὶ βασιλέως
Καλλίππου · μύστ[αι]
εὐσεβεῖς · Ἥρων
Ὑγιαίν[ο]ν̣[τος], Η . ΡΕ̣
5 [- - - - - - - - - - - - -]
- - - - - - - - - - - - - - -

Fraser. 2 μύστ[αι](?) Fraser. 5 [- - - - - - - - - - - - -](?) Fraser.

Epigraphical Commentary
The lettering is late, with ligatures of mu upsilon (line 2), eta rho (line 3),
upsilon gamma (line 4).

Commentary
The eponymous official is unattested. This is a list of Greek initiates, but
no other information can be derived from it.

150 Greek record of initiates   Fig. 117

Fragment of Thasian marble, broken on all sides except the back (rough-
picked). Found near the Genoese Towers on June 21, 1939. Archaeological
Museum of Samothrace, courtyard, inv. 39.12.
H. 0.22 m, W. 0.23 m, Th. 0.07 m; L.H. 0.006–0.008 m.
Ed. Fraser, *Samothrace* 2.1 (1960) 35.

Figure 117. Greek record of initiates
(150). Courtesy Samothrace Excavations

Date?

```
- - - - - - - - - - - - - - - - -
[- - - - - - - - - - - - - -]ου
[- - - - - - - - - - -]ΟΤΟΣ
[- - - - - - - - - - - - -]ΑΜΟΥ
[- - - - - - - - - - - - - - - -]ω̣
5  [μύσται εὐσε]βεῖς
[- - - - - - - - - - - - -]ΟΥ
[- - - - - - - - - - - -]ΝΟΣ
[- - - - - - - - - - - -]δώρου
[- - - - - - - - - - - -]ΑΝΙΟΣ
10  [- - - - - - - -]Ο̣Υ . Σ[- - - -]
- - - - - - - - - - - - - - - - - -
```

Fraser.

Epigraphical Commentary
The inscription is badly damaged.

Commentary
Line 5 suggests that this was a list of Greek initiates, but no other information can be derived.

151   Greek record of an *epoptes*   Fig. 118

Fragment of Thasian marble, broken on all sides. Found in the area of the Stoa. Archaeological Museum of Samothrace, inv. 68.700.

H. 0.08 m, W. 0.14 m, Th. 0.035 m; L.H. 0.008–0.012 m.

Unpublished.

Date?

```
- - - - - - - - - - - - - - - -
[- - - - - -] . Ι . [- - - -]
vacat ΑΤΕ[- - - -]
[- -]ΑΣ ἐπόπτη[ς- -]
[- -] . . . . . .ᶜᵃ· ¹⁰. . . . . [- -]
- - - - - - - - - - - - - -
```

Epigraphical Commentary
Lunate epsilon and sigma are used.

Figure 118. Greek record of an *epoptes* **(151)**

Commentary

This is a record of an *epoptes*, but too little is preserved to gain further information from it.

152   Greek record of initiates   Fig. 119

Fragment of stele of Thasian marble, broken on all sides except the back, which is rough-picked. Found in Halonia on June 30, 1953. Archaeological Museum of Samothrace, inv. 53.74.

H. 0.13 m, W. 0.09 m, Th. 0.028 m; L.H. 0.025 m (lines 1–2), 0.01–0.015 m (line 3).

Ed. Fraser, *Samothrace* 2.1 (1960) 48.

Date?

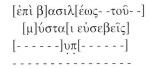

Fraser.

Figure 119. Greek record of initiates (152). *Samothrace* 2.1, pl. XIX:48

Epigraphical Commentary

Fraser notes the lettering, especially sigma, indicates a late Imperial date.

Commentary

This was the beginning of a list of initiates.

153   Greek record of an initiate   Fig. 120

Fragment of Thasian marble, with molding above, broken on all sides. It was found in Chora. Its present location is unknown. I saw a squeeze in the Berlin Academy in May 2004.

H. 0.20 m, W. 0.20 m, Th. 0.095 m; L.H. 0.013 m (line 1), 0.055 m (line 2).

Edd. Kern 1893, p. 364, no. 8; Fredrich, *IG* XII.8 193; [*IMT* 1573].

1st century B.C.?

μύστης εὐσε[βής]
ΚΥ[- - - -]
- - - - - - - - - - - -

Fredrich. 2 Κυ[ζικηνοί *vel* νῶν] Fredrich.

Figure 120. Greek record of an initiate (153). Kern 1893, p. 364

Epigraphical Commentary

The letters, dated by Fredrich to the 1st century B.C., are much larger on the second line, with a greater space between them, as Kern's facsimile shows.

Line 2: Left oblique stroke suitable for upsilon or chi.

Commentary

It must be noted that Κυ[ζικην- - ?] is not a certain restoration, since there are other ethnics beginning with kappa upsilon (e.g., Κυμαῖοι). Moreover, it is unclear whether Κυ[- -] is an ethnic at all. It is also unclear whether lines 1 and 2 belong to the same record.

154   Greek record of initiates   Fig. 121

Top right fragment of a stele of Thasian marble, with an incised pediment. The back is rough-picked, possibly broken toward the top. Found outside the Sacristy on July 7, 1939. Archaeological Museum of Samothrace, courtyard, inv. 39.338.

H. 0.208 m, W. 0.16 m, Th. 0.04 m; L.H. 0.01 m (line 1), 0.015 m (lines 2–4).

Edd. Lehmann-Hartleben 1940, p. 346, no. 2; Fraser, *Samothrace* 2.1 (1960) 49.

Cf. Lehmann, *Samothrace* 2.2 (1960), p. 30.

2nd–3rd century A.D.?

[ἀγα]θῆ τύχη
[ἐπὶ βασιλέω]ς Φλ. Ῥηγείνου
[τοῦ - -]ηλίωνος
[μύσται εὐσ]εβεῖς
- - - - - - - - - - - - -

Fraser. 3 Δ]ηλίωνος Fraser.

Figure 121. Greek record of initiates
(**154**). Courtesy Samothrace Excavations

Epigraphical Commentary
The letters are executed in a decorative style, with lunate epsilon and sigma, suggestive of a later date. Phi projects far beyond the restriction of the lines, which had been marked with guidelines before the text was inscribed.

Commentary
This was a list of Greek initiates, as is evident from line 4. The eponymous king is otherwise unattested.

Line 3: There are other possibilities for restoring the patronymic (for instance, Εὐμ]ηλίωνος, Τ]ηλίωνος, Ὠφ]ηλίωνος, etc.).

155   Greek record of initiates and *epoptai*   Fig. 122

Top right fragment of a stele of Thasian marble with molding; the back may be close to the original surface. Found near the south door of the Anaktoron on July 28, 1953. Archaeological Museum of Samothrace, inv. 53.616.

H. 0.12 m, W. 0.04 m, Th. 0.05 m; L.H. 0.015 m (lines 2–3), 0.01 m (lines 4–5).

Ed. Fraser, *Samothrace* 2.1 (1960) 55.

2nd–3rd century A.D.?

[ἐπὶ βασιλέως- - -τοῦ- -(?)]
[- - - - - - - - -] μύσται
[- -?- - - -] *vacat 0.02 m*
[- -?- - - - ἐπ]όπτα[ι]
[- - - - - - - - - -]ΤΙΟ[.]
5   [- - - - - - - - - -]Ṭ . [. .]
- - - - - - - - - - - - - - - -

Fraser. 3 [εὐσεβεῖς, καὶ ἐπ]όπτα[ι] Fraser. 4 [ης / αι- - - - - -]τιο[ι?] Fraser.

Figure 122. Greek record of initiates
and *epoptai* (**155**). *Samothrace* 2.1,
pl. XXI:55

Epigraphical Commentary

Line 1: There would be enough space for this line only if it is inscribed in smaller letters.

Line 2: Sigma, tau, and alpha are in ligature.

Line 3: Last letter: it is possible to discern traces of a triangular letter with a crossbar.

Commentary

This is a list of Greek initiates and *epoptai*. Fraser favors a date in the 2nd–3rd century A.D. on the basis of the lettering.

Line 4: Fraser suggests an ethnic, e.g., [Βυζάν]τιο[ι].

156   Greek record of an initiate, and Latin record of initiation(?) Fig. 123

Fragment of a stele of Thasian marble, preserved on the left and below, with molding at bottom. The back is smooth, inscribed with faint Latin characters. The lower part of a caduceus is barely visible above the text on side A; there may be another caduceus next to it (cf. **42, 104, 169**). Found in the church of Ayios Demetrios in Halonia on June 30, 1953. Archaeological Museum of Samothrace, courtyard, inv. 53.73.

H. 0.29 m, W. 0.19 m, Th. 0.065 m; L.H. 0.016 m (line 1), 0.020–0.025 m (lines 2–4), 0.01–0.015 m (side B).

Ed. Fraser, *Samothrace* 2.1 (1960) 56.

1st–3rd century A.D.?

Side A

ἐπὶ βασιλέω[ς- - - - - -τοῦ- - - - - -]
Κάστω[ρ]
  Ἐπικράτ[ους μύστης *vel* ἐπόπτης εὐ]-
σεβής

Side B

4–5 lines of Latin
[- -] . ERID . [- -]
- - - - - - - - - - -

Fraser. Side B Dimitrova.

Figure 123. Greek record of an initiate, and Latin record of initiation(?) (**156**): side A *(right)*, side B *(far right)*

Epigraphical Commentary
The letters are uneven and inelegant, suggestive of a later date. Side B is almost illegible.

Commentary
Side A is a record of a Greek initiate. Side B might have been a Latin record of initiation, but too little of it is preserved to be certain.

157   Greek record of an initiate   Fig. 124
      Block of Thasian marble with molding above, broken on right. Present location unknown. I saw a squeeze in the Berlin Academy in May 2004.
      H. 0.085 m, W. 0.31 m, Th. 0.14 m; L.H. 0.015 m.
      Edd. Conze 1875, p. 41, no. 10, pl. 71:10; Fredrich, *IG* XII.8 200.

Date?

μύστη[ς εὐσεβής]

Ἀγρεοφῶν Δη[- -]

- - - - - - - - - - - - -

Figure 124. Greek record of an initiate (157). Conze 1875, pl. 71:10

      Fredrich. **1** μύστη[ς Fredrich, μύστη[Dimitrova. **2** Ἀγρεοφῶν Δι- Fredrich, Ἀγρεοφῶν Δη Dimitrova.

Epigraphical Commentary
The readings can be surmised from Conze's facsimile.

Commentary
This is a record of a Greek initiate. Fredrich notes that the name Ἀγρεοφῶν is typical of Lykia and suggests that the initiate was from there, but the name is also well attested in Kaunos.

158   Greek record of initiates   Fig. 125
      Fragment of a stele of Thasian marble, broken on all sides. The back is rough-picked. Found in July 1970 at 33.50–34.50 m east and 19.50–22.00 m north of the northeastern inner corner of the Stoa. Archaeological Museum of Samothrace, inv. 70.771.
      H. 0.12 m, W. 0.12 m, Th. 0.07 m; L.H. 0.015 m.
      Unpublished.

Roman period?

- - - - - - - - - - - - - -

[- - - -] . . ΒΙΩ[- - -]

[- - -]ΑΔΕΣ μύ[σται]

[- -]ΟΥ Τιβ · ΟΥ[- -]

- - - - - - - - - - - - - - -

Epigraphical Commentary
The letters are highly decorated.
      Line 2: Epsilon and sigma are in ligature.

Commentary
This probably was a list of initiates from the Roman period, as the name Tib(erius?) in line 3 implies.

Figure 125 *(right)*. Greek record of initiates (158)

Figure 126 *(far right)*. Greek record of initiates (160)

159   Greek record of an initiate

Relief-decorated fragment of Thasian marble, found in Palaiopolis. Its dimensions and present location are unknown.

Edd. Blau and Schlottmann 1855, p. 619, no. 8; Fredrich, *IG* XII.8 202. Cf. Conze 1860, p. 62.

Date?

[μύστης] εὐσεβὴς
[- - - - - -]ος Δημητρίου
[το?]ῦ[- - - - - -]

Fredrich.

160   Greek record of initiates   Fig. 126

Fragment of stele of Thasian marble, broken on all sides, rough-picked on back; badly worn. Provenance unknown. Archaeological Museum of Samothrace, inv. 89.2.

H. 0.26 m, W. 0.14 m, Th. 0.08 m; L.H. 0.02–0.025 m.

Unpublished.

1st–3rd century A.D.?

- - - - - - - -
[- - - -]Ι ΦΘΙ . [- - -]
[- - - -]μύσται [- - - -]
[- - - -] . . . [- - - - - - -]
[- - - -] . . [- - - - - - -]
- - - - - - - -

Epigraphical Commentary

The lettering is elegant, with finials, suggestive of a later date. Sigma is lunate. Upsilon projects above the other letters.

Line 1: First letter: vertical stroke; last letter: left vertical.

Line 2: Last letter: faint vertical.

Lines 3–4: Unclear traces of letters.

Commentary

This is part of a list of initiates.

Line 1: τετράδ?]ι φθίνοντος is possible.

161   Greek record of an initiate   Fig. 127

Stele of Thasian marble, broken below. Found in Chora on June 20, 1939. Archaeological Museum of Samothrace, courtyard, inv. 39.545.
H. 0.72 m, W. 0.50 m, Th. 0.10 m; L.H. 0.025–0.03 m.
Ed. Fraser, *Samothrace* 2.1 (1960) 43.

1st century B.C.– 1st century A.D.?

    ἐπὶ [βα]σιλέως Ἀντι[γ]-
    όνο[υ τοῦ Μν]ησικλέου[ς]
    [μύστης] εὐσεβὴς
    ΕΠΤ[. . . .ᶜᵃ·⁸. . .] . πος
5 [- - - - - - - - - - - - - - -]
    - - - - - - - - - - - - - - -

Fraser. **5** M(N?) Fraser.

Figure 127 *(above, left).* Greek record of an initiate **(161)**

Figure 128 *(above, right).* Greek record of initiates(?) **(162).**
Samothrace 2.1, pl. XXII:57

Epigraphical Commentary
The inscription is badly defaced.
    Line 5: No letters visible.

Commentary
Fraser suggests an early Imperial date on the basis of the lettering.

162   Greek record of initiates(?)   Fig. 128

Fragment of a stele of Thasian marble, broken on all sides. Found southwest of the Rotunda of Arsinoe on July 30, 1949. Archaeological Museum of Samothrace, inv. 49.995.
H. 0.22 m, W. 0.12 m, Th. 0.15 m; L.H. 0.02 m.
Ed. Fraser, *Samothrace* 2.1 (1960) 57.
Cf. Robert 1963, pp. 67–69.

2nd–3rd century A.D.?

> *traces of letters*
> [ἐπὶ βασι]λέως[- - - - - -τοῦ- - - - - - -]
> [- - - - - -]ΑΝ[- - - - - - - - - - - - - - - - -]
> -

Fraser. 2 [ἀγορ]αν[ομοῦντος τοῦ δεῖνος- - - - -] Fraser.

Epigraphical Commentary
The lettering is inelegant, with a rectilinear sigma, suggestive of a date in the 2nd–3rd century A.D.

Commentary
This may have been the beginning of a list of initiates. The traces of letters above were perhaps remains of a previous document, as Fraser remarks.

163   Greek record of initiates(?)   Fig. 129

Top right fragment of a pedimental stele of Thasian marble, with a circular object in relief in the center of the pediment. Found near the Genoese Towers in August 1955. Archaeological Museum of Samothrace, courtyard, inv. 56.5.

H. 0.23 m, W. 0.18 m, Th. 0.09 m; L.H. 0.013 m (lines 1–2), 0.01 m (line 3).

Ed. Fraser, *Samothrace* 2.1 (1960) 61.

Cf. Robert 1963, pp. 53, 67–69.

Date?

> [ἐπὶ βασιλέω]ς Περ[ικ]λέο-
> [υς τοῦ- - - - -]αφάντου
> [ἀγορανομοῦντος - -]ΑΝΟΥ τοῦ
> [- - - - - - - - - - - -].....
> - - - - - - - - - - - - - - - -

Fraser. 2 Ἀγ]αφάντου Fraser.

Figure 129. Greek record of initiates(?) (163)

Epigraphical Commentary
The letters are now badly defaced.

Commentary
This probably was the beginning of a list of initiates.
    Line 2: Ἀγ]αφάντου is difficult to justify in view of the name's rarity, as Robert notes (p. 53).

164   Greek record of initiates(?)

Fragment of Thasian marble, preserved on the left. The inscription was in Chora when Fredrich published it. Its present location is unknown. I saw a squeeze in the Berlin Academy in May 2004.
    H. 0.23 m, W. 0.11 m, Th. 0.08 m; L.H. 0.015 m.
    Ed. Fredrich, *IG* XII.8 187.
    Cf. Robert and Robert, *BullÉp* 1958 270; Robert 1963, pp. 67–69.

Date?

```
        /[- - - - - - - - - - -]
        vacat
        ΟΝ[- - - - - - - - -]
        ἐπὶ βα̣[σιλέως- - -]
          Δω[- - - - - - -]
   5   ἀγοραν[ομοῦντος- -]
          Κλ̣[- - - - - - - -]
        - - - - - - - - - - - - - - -
```

Fredrich. **4** Δω[ροθέου?] Fredrich.

Epigraphical Commentary
Lines 3, 5: The nu's, dotted by Fredrich, are clear on the squeeze.

Commentary
This probably was the beginning of a list of initiates.

165   Greek record of initiates(?)

Fragment of Thasian marble, found near the "Doric Temple" (i.e., the Hieron), partially preserved on top. Vienna, Antikensammlung, inv. III 1202.
    H. 0.075 m, W. 0.12 m, Th. 0.035; L.H.?
    Edd. Conze 1875, p. 11; Fredrich, *IG* XII.8 198.

Date?

```
        ἀγαθ[ῆι τύχηι]
        [ἐ]πὶ βασ[ιλέως- -]
        - - - - - - - - - - - - -
```

Fredrich.

Commentary
This may have been the beginning of a list of initiates.

Figure 130. Greek record of initiates(?) (166)

166 Greek record of initiates(?) Fig. 130

Three joining fragments of a stele of Thasian marble, broken on all sides. The back is rough-picked. Inv. 71.950 was found in July 1971 at 17.00–17.80 m east and 37.50–38.80 m south, and inv. 71.963 at 17.00– 21.00 m east and 33.00–37.50 m south, of the northeastern inner corner of the Stoa. Archaeological Museum of Samothrace, inv. nos. 71.950 + 71.963A + 71.963B.

H. 0.18 m, W. 0.185 m, Th. 0.045 m; L.H. 0.02 m.

Unpublished.

Date?

```
        - - - - - - - - - -
        [- - - - - -]Δ vacat
        [- - - - - -]·
        [- - - - - -]νεικεῖς·
        [- - - - -]ΙΝΟΣ
    5   [- - - - - - - -]ΛΑΝΟΣ
        - - - - - - - - - -
```

Epigraphical Commentary

The lettering is rectilinear; see *ad* **30**.

    Line 4: First letter: top part of a vertical.

    Line 5: First two letters: two triangles.

Commentary

This may have been a list of initiates, probably from Thessaloniki or Stratonikeia, as the ending -νεικεῖς in line 3 suggests.

167 Greek record of an initiate(?) Fig. 131

Block of Thasian marble, broken on the right and on back, with a dowel hole and a pour channel at bottom, and raised molding above the text and at the back of the bottom surface. Found in June 1960 in "the lower town." Archaeological Museum of Samothrace, inv. 60.559.

H. 0.15 m, W. 0.25 m, Th. 0.32 m; L.H. 0.015–0.025 m.
Unpublished.

1st–2nd century A.D.?

       ἐπὶ β[ασιλέως - - - - - - - - -]
       τοῦ Ἀν[- - - μύστης εὐσε?]-
       βὴς Καλ[λ?- - - - - - - - - - -]
       [Ἡ]ρακλέ[- - - - - - - - - -]

Figure 131. Greek record of an initiate(?) (**167**)

Epigraphical Commentary

The letters are uneven, with lunate shapes, consistent with a date in the 1st–2nd century A.D.

    Line 3: First letter: top part of beta.

Commentary

This may have been part of a base, perhaps a dedication by an initiate. Presumably [Ἡ]ρακλέ[- was the patronymic of the initiate, though it is theoretically possible that it was part of a different name (e.g., that of an *epoptes*).

CHAPTER 8

OTHER INSCRIPTIONS
CONCERNING INITIATES

The following four documents that relate to initiates consist of two prohibition inscriptions, one in Greek and the other in Greek and Latin; the third and fourth inscriptions are decrees in Greek.

168　Greek prohibition inscription　　　　　　　　Fig. 132

　　Fragment of Thasian marble, preserved on the left and top. Found on July 10, 1951, ca. 4 m west of the pronaos of the Hieron. Archaeological Museum of Samothrace, Hall A, inv. 51.501.

　　H. 0.17 m, W. 0.38 m, Th. 0.09 m; L.H. 0.04 m.

　　Edd. Lehmann 1953, pp. 14–15, pl. 6:c; *SEG* XII 395; Fraser, *Samothrace* 2.1 (1960) 62; *SEG* XIX 593; Sokolowski, *LSS* (1962) 75.

　　Cf. Robert and Robert, *BullÉp* 1954 207; Lehmann 1955, pp. 33, 64, 78; Robert and Robert, *BullÉp* 1964 379; Lehmann, *Samothrace* 2.2 (1960), p. 276; Lehmann 1960, pp. 33, 65, 81; Cole 1989, p. 1575, with n. 41; Clinton 2003, pp. 61–62.

1st century B.C.?

　　　　ἀμύητον
　　　　μὴ εἰσιέναι
　　　　εἰς τὸ ἱερόν.

Fraser.

Figure 132. Greek prohibition inscription (**168**). *Samothrace* 2.1, pl. XXIV:62

Epigraphical Commentary

The letters are even and large, now slightly defaced, suggesting a date in the 1st century B.C., according to Fraser.

Commentary

This is a prohibition inscription ordering the *amyetoi* not to enter the sacred space. Lehmann interpreted τὸ ἱερόν as the name of the building near which the inscription was found. The document, however, was not in situ. Further, ἱερόν usually denotes a sanctuary and not a building, as Fraser observed (p. 117; see also Clinton). Numerous sacred laws prescribe how to enter a sanctuary, or prohibit entrance into it, and in none of them does τὸ ἱερόν denote a building; cf. *I.Priene* 205; *IG* XII 7220; *SEG* VI 775; Sokolowski, *LSCG,* nos. 50, 68, 69, 119, 128, 130, 136, 139, 158. Herodotus (3.37.9) provides a curious parallel from Egypt for prohibition of entry into a sanctuary of the Kabeiroi: Ἐσῆλθε δὲ καὶ ἐς τῶν Καβείρων τὸ ἱρόν, ἐς τὸ οὐ θεμιτόν ἐστι ἐσιέναι ἄλλον γε ἢ τὸν ἱρέα. Therefore, I find it likely that this document was set up at the entrance of the sanctuary (wherever the actual sacred space began), and that it refers to those who did not undergo *myesis* in the sense of preliminary initiation; see Clinton. This is consistent with the various cathartic requirements that regulate entry into a sanctuary or sacred space; the most recent discussion is by Eran Lupu (*NGSL,* Introduction).

169   Greek and Latin prohibition inscription   Fig. 133

Block of Thasian marble, preserved on all sides, rough-picked below (starting at ca. 0.40 m from the top), decorated with a caduceus and two snakes in the lower right corner (cf. **42, 104, 156**). The back is rough and irregular, with an oblique cutting close to the top. The surface below the text, 0.55 m high, is rough-picked. Found in June 1938 southwest of the entrance of the inner room of the Anaktoron. Archaeological Museum of Samothrace, Hall A, inv. 38.401.

H. 0.96 m, W. 0.52 m, Th. 0.26 m; L.H. 0.04 m.

Edd. Lehmann-Hartleben 1939, pp. 138–139, fig. 6; *AÉ* 1939 2; Fraser, *Samothrace* 2.1 (1960) 63; *SEG* XIX 593; Sokolowski, *LSS* (1962) 75a.

Cf. *BullÉp* 1939 296; Hemberg 1950, pp. 112–113; Lehmann 1955, p. 35, fig. 20, pp. 46, 79; Kerényi 1955, pp. 150–151; *BullÉp* 1964 379; Lehmann 1960, p. 82; Cole 1984, p. 89; 1989, p. 1575, with n. 42, p. 1591, with n. 143; Clinton 2003, pp. 61–62.

2nd–1st century B.C.

> deorum · sacra
> qui non accepe-
> runt · non intrant.
> ἀμύητον μὴ εἰ-
> 5 σιέναι

Fraser.

Figure 133. Greek and Latin prohibition inscription (**169**). *Samothrace* 2.1, pl. XXIV:63

Epigraphical Commentary

The letters are even and large, now slightly defaced.

Commentary

See the discussion of the previous inscription. This bilingual inscription is of identical type, set up primarily for the numerous Roman visitors. The rough-picked lower part implies that the stone may have been set into the ground. There is no compelling reason to assume that it was displayed inside the Anaktoron, as previously assumed; cf. Clinton, p. 61. The dimensions of the block and the rough-picked area below the text suggest that it was a reused building block.[1] The inscription was not found in situ, and given the numerous examples of sacred laws prohibiting entrance to a sanctuary (see **168**, Commentary), it was probably originally placed at an entrance to the sacred space.

170   Decree in honor of Hippomedon, an initiate(?)

Opisthographic stele of Thasian marble, broken above. A piece has broken off on the left since the publication in *IG* XII.8. Found in Chora, now in the Archaeological Museum of Samothrace, courtyard. No inv. no.

H. 0.48 m, W. 0.51m, Th. 0.09 m; L.H. 0.006–0.014 m.

Edd. Kern 1893, p. 348, no. 1; Fränkel 1894a, 1894b; [Michel 1900, no. 351]; Fredrich, *IG* XII.8 156; [Dittenberger, *Syll.*³ 502]; Robert 1935b, with pl. 27; Fraser, *Samothrace* 2.1 (1960), p. 39, app. I.[2]

228–225 B.C.

Side A

[. . . . βασιλεὺς Ἡγ]ησίστρατος Φι[. . . . εἶπεν· ἐπει]-
[δὴ Ἱππομέδων] Ἀγησιλάου Λακεδαι[μόνιος ὁ ταχ]-
[θεὶς ὑπὸ τ]οῦ βασιλέως Πτολεμαίου στρατ[ηγὸς]
[τοῦ Ἑλ]λησπόντου καὶ τῶν ἐπὶ Θράικης τόπων ε[ὐσε]-
5   [βῶ]ς διακείμενος πρὸς τοὺς θεοὺς τιμᾶι τὸ τέμ[ενος]
θυσίαις καὶ ἀναθήμασιν καὶ ἔσπευσεν παρα[γενό]-
μενος εἰς τὴν νῆσον μετασχεῖν τῶμ μυστ[ηρίων],
τῆς τε κατὰ τὸ χωρίον ἀσφαλείας πᾶσαν πρόνοιαν [ποιεῖ]-
ται ἀποστέλλων τοὺς διαφυλάξοντας ἱππεῖς [τε καὶ]
10   πεζοὺς στρατιώτας καὶ βέλη καὶ καταπάλτα[ς καὶ]
τοὺς χρησομένους τούτοις, εἴς τε τοὺς μισθοὺς [τοῖς]
Τράλλεσιν ἀξιωθεὶς προδανεῖσαι χρήματα ἔδω[κεν],
βουλόμενος ὑπακούειν πάντα τὰ ἀξιούμενα [ἀεὶ]
τῆι πόλει, διακείμενος δὲ καὶ πρὸς τὸν δῆμον [εὐνό]-
15   ως πᾶσαν ἐπιμέλειαν ποιεῖται καὶ κοινῆι τῆ[ς πό]-
λεως καὶ ἰδίαι τῶμ πρὸς αὐτόν ἀφικνουμένω[ν, ἀκό]-
λουθα πράττων τῆι τοῦ βασιλέως αἱρέσει, ἡ <δὲ> [βου]-
λὴ προβεβούλευκεν αὐτῶι περὶ ἐπαίνου καὶ καθότ[ι]
ἥ τε πολιτεία καὶ τὰ λοιπὰ τὰ δεδομένα παρὰ τ[ῶν πο]-
20   λιτῶν φιλάνθρωπα ἀναγραφήσεται εἰς στήλην κ[αὶ]
[ἀνατε]θήσεται ἐν τῶι ἱερῶι τῆς Ἀθ[ηνᾶς]· ἀγαθῆι τ[ύχηι]

Fraser.

Epigraphical Commentary

The stone is now severely damaged, especially side B. Only side A is included here, reprinted from Fraser's edition and based on his inspection of the stone.

1. I wish to thank Emil Nankov for bringing this to my attention.

2. The extensive bibliography on this inscription, mostly concerned with its economic aspects, is not included here.

Commentary

This is an honorary decree for Hippomedon, son of Agesilas, of Sparta, Ptolemaic governor of Hellespont and Thrace. The document has been discussed at length, mostly in connection with the export of grain (σίτου ἐξαγωγή, side B, line 15). Side A is presented here because of its relevance to initiation into the Samothracian Mysteries. Lines 6–7 imply that Hippomedon was initiated: "upon arrival on the island he was eager to participate in the Mysteria."

171   Decree of Odessos concerning the mysteries

Aedicula-shaped stele of marble, decorated with frieze and pediment. Found in 1927 in the joint French and Czechoslovakian excavations. Archaeological Museum of Samothrace, inv. 49.447.

H. 0.32 m, W. 0.32 m, Th. 0.06 m (stele), 0.12 m (pediment); L.H. 0.01 m (lines 1, 3–end), 0.025–0.03 m (line 2).

Edd. Salač 1928, p. 395, no. 3; Mihailov, *IGBulg* I¹ (1956), p. 53, under no. 42; Fraser, *Samothrace* 2.1 (1960) 6; Mihailov, *IGBulg* I² (1970), pp. 93–94, under no. 42.

Cf. Robert and Robert, *BullÉp* 1960 256; Robert 1963, pp. 57–58; Robert and Robert, *BullÉp* 1964 362.

Date?

in cornice:	ἐπὶ βασιλέως [τοῦ δεῖνος]
in metopes:	ψή φισ [μα Ὀδη σσ ιτ ῶν]
in field:	ὡς δὲ ἐν Ὀδησσῷ ἐπὶ [ἱερέω- - - - -τοῦ δεῖνος].
	ἔδοξεν τῇ βουλῇ ἐπιμηνιεύ[οντος τοῦ δεῖνος]·
5	[ἐπε]<ι>δὴ τοῦ δήμου διὰ προ[γόνων - - - -]
	[τῶν ἐν] Σαμοθρᾴκη μυστηρίῳ[ν μετέχοντος - -]
	[- - - - - -]τον ἀποδιδ[- - - - - - - - - - - - - - - - - - - -]
	[- - - - - -]δύναμιν [- -]
	[- - - - - - - - -]ΠΕΡΟ[- - - - - - - - - - - - - - - - - - - -]
	- -

Fraser. 5 διὰ πρό[τερον θεωριῶν Fraser, διὰ προ[γόνων Robert, Mihailov.

Epigraphical Commentary

The letters are slightly uneven. The words in line 2 are inscribed on the metopes; see Fraser for the spacing and word division.

Commentary

This is a copy of a decree of Odessos, concerning the Odessitans' participation in the Samothracian Mysteries (lines 5–6). It is possible that they sent theoroi to Samothrace, given the official nature of this document, but this is not explicitly stated.

CHAPTER 9

Conclusions, Part II

DATES OF THE RECORDS OF INITIATION

The earliest initiation record may date to the first part of the 2nd century B.C., if we accept the suggestion—to me, a highly probable one—that Lucius Iuventius Thalna (**64**) was indeed the person mentioned in Livy 38.4 and 39.31.4. He was active in 185/4 B.C., and I see no impediment to dating his initiation record to the 180s or so, since Romans were dedicating offerings at Samothrace as early as 211 B.C. (see *ad* **64**, Commentary). The latest precisely dated list of initiates is a new document, **63**, of May or June, A.D. 186. Of course, there must have been initiation records before ca. 180 B.C. and after A.D. 186, and the letter-shapes of a number of inscriptions are consistent with the earlier or later dates, but they do not provide a secure argument. Other new dates provided by hitherto unpublished monuments are 67 B.C. (**74**), 62 B.C. or A.D. 78 (**75**), A.D. 6 (**86**), September 11? A.D. 45 (**55**, side B), and presumably 8 B.C. (**83**).

PROSOPOGRAPHY

The documents in Part II add about 100 new names of initiates to the approximately 600 names collected by Cole.[1] Many of the previously published names have been corrected; see the Index of Names.

The list of eponymous kings has also been emended and supplemented with 14 hitherto unknown names (or parts of names); see **39, 46, 95, 114, 123, 131, 129, 135, 147, 156, 167**.

PROVENANCE OF THE INITIATES

The map of sites whence initiates came to Samothrace[2] has been changed on the basis of new or corrected evidence. Thus the certainly attested places are Abydos (**46, 52**), Aigai (**53**), Ainos (**42–45**), Alexandria (**31?, 53**, and see above, p. 4, n. 1), Alexandria Troas (**54, 55**), Alopekonnesos (**47**), Amphipolis (**37**), Andros (see above, p. 121, under Aegean Islands),

---

1. Cole 1984, appendix III.
2. See Cole 1984, pp. 43–44.

Antioch (**51**), Arsinoe (**51**), Athens (**29, 30**),[3] Azorion/Azoros (**35**), Beroia (**34, 37**), Byzantion (**39, 53, 67?, 134?**), Catana (**66**), Chios (**38, 49, 89**), Dardanos (**14, 15**), Dionysopolis (Appendix II.3), Elis (**16**), Ephesos (**50**), Epidamnos (**32**), Herakleia apo Strymonos (**36**), Ilion (**53**), Kassandreia (**35**), Kaunos (**60**), Keramos (**13.iii**), Knidos (**61**), Kyzikos (**56–59**), Magnesia (**53**), Maroneia (**40, 41.iv, 57**), Miletos (**62**), Odessos (**46, 171[?]**), Pergamon (**89**), Perinthos (**39, 132?, 145?**), Pessinus (**63**), Philippi (**38, 48**), Priapos (**51**), Rhodes (**50, 51, 57?**, Appendix II.1), Rome (**46, 49, 61, 63–67, 73, 78?, 85, 87–89, 92, 94, 98, 100, 101, 104**), Sardis (**17.iii**), Sirrhai (**33, 53**), Smyrna (**63**), Stratonikeia (**17.ii**), Styberra (**53**), Thasos (**41, 48, 51, 53, 62**), Thessaloniki (**36, 37**), Tomis (Appendix II.2), Tralles (**47**), and Xanthos (**50**). Likely cities of initiates are Aspendos (**31**), Kos (**120**), Tegea (**31**), Thera (**31**), and Torone (**31**); while Kos (**122?**), Kalchedon (**134?**), and Parion (**18?**) are only hypothetical cities of initiates. Roman initiates of unknown provenance are listed in **14, 15, 38, 40, 45, 47, 53, 57, 58, 72, 74(?), 75(?), 76, 77(?), 79–84, 86, 90, 91, 93, 95–97, 99, 102, 103, 105–116, 131, 137, 140, 156(?), 158**.

Although, as Cole observed (1984, p. 52), relatively few of the cities that sent theoroi are also represented in ethnics of initiates, the geographic distribution of the initiates' cities is very similar to that of the sacred ambassadors' cities (see Chap. 4), with one major difference: whereas about 50% of the initiates have Roman names, there are no Roman theoroi. Thrace is abundantly represented among initiates (as evidenced by the Thracian names in **19, 37, 41, 44, 46, 47, 78, 79, 89, 137**), including the noteworthy example of Rhaskos (**46.i**). This illustrates the long-standing interest of the Thracians in the Samothracian Mysteries, epigraphically attested as early as the 4th century B.C.[4]

CULTIC EXPERIENCE

With regard to initiation itself, Isidoros's epitaph (**29**) provides precious insight: "as an initiate . . . he saw the doubly sacred light of Kabiros in Samothrace and the pure rites of Demeter in Eleusis." This is the only documentary piece of evidence we possess about actual cultic experience in the Samothracian Mysteries and about the viewing of light as a central act in the initiation. Seeing light is a typical occurrence at the culmination of mystery rites; cf. Plutarch, *De anima*, fr. 178: "then one encounters an extraordinary light, and pure regions and meadows offer welcome, with voices and dances and majesties of sacred sounds and holy sights, in which now the completely initiated one becoming free and set loose enjoys the rite, crowned, and consorts with holy and pure men."[5] Furthermore, the phrase "doubly sacred light of Kabiros"—apparently a poetic expression for "the sacred light of the two Kabiri"—most probably implies that the Kabiri were two, and, even more importantly, provides the first attestation of the term *Kabiros* in documents concerning the Samothracian cult.

Isidoros's epitaph offers another valuable detail: "but you, gloomy Hades, extremely powerful bastion of necessity, lead this man to the Region of the Reverent and place him there." The crucial words here are

3. We have no way of knowing, however, whether the cosmopolitan mime Isidoros (**29**) is representative of Athens in the sense that he journeyed from Athens to Samothrace to be initiated; his initiation may have occured in the course of his travels or during his residence in northern Greece.

4. See Commentary to **19**, line 6.

5. Trans. Clinton 2003, p. 66; on light in the Eleusinian Mysteries, see above, p. 88. It is unclear how literally one should interpret the phrase "the doubly sacred light of Kabiros," but it is tempting to imagine that the initiates saw illuminated statues of the Kabiri, possibly the statues that were set up in the *anaktoron*, according to ancient testimony; cf. Clinton 2004.

choros eusebeon, "region of the reverent." This inscription is the only text, documentary or literary, that associates initiation at Samothrace with a privileged place in the underworld. Previously, the only benefit known to have come from the Samothracian Mysteries was safety at sea. The notion that Samothracian initiates went to the *choros eusebeon* may explain why their typical appellation was *mystai eusebeis.* Diodorus tells us (5.49.6 = *Samothrace* 1 142; *FGrH* 548 F1) that initiation at Samothrace made people *dikaioteroi* and *eusebesteroi.* Perhaps one reason so many records of *mystai eusebeis* were set up was to announce the initiates' *eusebeia,* with its implications both in life and after death.[6]

SOCIAL STATUS OF THE INITIATES

Initiation requirements at Samothrace were apparently quite liberal: there was no restriction on gender, origin, or social status. This is corroborated by the new documents published here, which provide further evidence that both men and women were initiated (though, naturally, far fewer women,[7] probably because of the practical difficulties of reaching the island), and that the social composition of the group was varied, including slaves, freedmen, ordinary citizens, high governmental or sacred officials, and royalty. In this respect the situation at Samothrace was the same as that at Eleusis.

STAGES OF INITIATION

The ritual of preliminary *myesis* is outlined above (p. 78). The prohibition inscriptions, **168** and **169**, which state that the *amyetoi* were not allowed into the sacred space, must imply that the *amyetoi* were those who had not undergone the preliminary *myesis.* Otherwise these prohibitions make little sense: excluding from the sacred space all those who had not undergone the main *myesis* would be tantamount to denying that ritual to everyone. Preliminary *myesis* is also attested at Eleusis, but in Samothrace it possibly took the form of *thronosis.* The *thronosis,* or "chairing," had purificatory aspects. It involved ecstatic dancing around the initiand, who was perhaps blindfolded and was sitting in a chair, presumably in the theatral area (Fig. 3:25) near the sanctuary's entrance.[8]

As Bengt Hemberg pointed out,[9] initiation at Samothrace (the main *myesis*) was apparently available throughout the sailing season. This was the case in the Roman period, at least, since the identified days and months we have are from Latin records, dated from April into November:[10]

98	(April 22, A.D. 116)
104	(May 1, A.D. 165 or 166)
40	(May 8–14, A.D. 64?)
63	(late May or early June, A.D. 186)
14	(June 3, 66 B.C.)
89	(June 6, A.D. 19)
90	(June 7, A.D. 48)

6. On the connection between mystery initiation and the promise of a happy life and afterlife, see Burkert 1987, p. 12.

7. Cf. Cole 1984, p. 42.

8. See Clinton 2003, p. 50.

9. Hemberg 1950, p. 108.

10. This is an updated version of the list in Clinton 2001, p. 35.

67	(June 13, 2nd–1st century B.C.?)
80	(June 20, 35 B.C.)
70	(July, 92 B.C.?)
82	(August 8, before 8 B.C.)
92	(September 1, 1st century A.D.)
66	(September 4, 100 B.C.)
55.B	(September 11?, A.D. 45)
87	(September 13, A.D. 14)
79.ii	(October 18, 46 B.C.)
100	(November 9, A.D. 124)

The most frequent month is June (5 or 6 out of 17 records), closely followed by September (4 out of 17). This may be due to the fact that the weather was, and still is, most favorable during these two months: warm, but not too hot, without etesian winds. It has therefore seemed logical to assume that initiation was available upon request,[11] after a sufficient number of people had arrived to participate in the initiation rite. Thus many initiation ceremonies would have taken place within a single year; in view of their large number, most of them (perhaps even all of them) probably did not take place in the context of a large-scale festival, as was the case at the Eleusinian Mysteries.

A special problem is the interval between the main *myesis* and *epopteia*, which at Eleusis was one year. Six inscriptions (**49.i, 50.A, 56, 61.i, 67, 89**) list people who were both *mystai* and *epoptai*.[12] These records are significantly fewer in number than the ones that mention *epoptai* separately (**30, 40, 49.ii–iv, 58, 61.i, 68–70, 72, 75, 82?, 120, 126, 128–130, 147**). Entries **56** and **58** are particularly instructive for the combination of *mystes* and *epoptes*. Both documents mention Asklepiades son of Attalos of Kyzikos. In **58** he is only *mystes*, while in **56**, in a list clearly issued in a different year, he is both *mystes* and *epoptes*, which suggests that he reached the second stage of initiation after the date of **58**. Document **56** is interesting in another respect. There Asklepiades son of Attalos of Kyzikos is at the head of a delegation from Kyzikos. After the year is given eponymously (according to the Samothracian *basileus* and *agoranomos* and the Cyzicene *hipparch*), the document announces: "*Mystes Eusebes* and *Epoptes* Nikis son of Mnesistratos, by birth Asklepidades son of Attalos of Kyzikos, architect, sent by the Cyzicenes according to the embassy of the demos of the Samothracians on account of the [- - -] and the sacred images(?)." "*Mystes Eusebes* and *Epoptes*" seems to be functioning as a title here, like "architect," the title that follows his name. Unfortunately, we have no information about the date of Asklepiades' *epopteia*.

Inscription **50** is similar to **56** in that it introduces a delegation, of *hieropoioi* in this case, as Ῥοδίων ἱεροποιοί, μύσται καὶ ἐπόπται εὐσεβεῖς; here, too, it is probably a question of a title, and no conclusion can be drawn about the date of the *epopteia*. It seems that in instances in which people were listed as both *mystai* and *epoptai*, this was understood as a title reflecting the fact that they had undergone both stages of initiation; but usually no inference concerning the interval between stages can be drawn. We may regard the designation μύσται καὶ ἐφόπται εὐσεβεῖς in **49**, incription i,

11. Cole 1984, p. 39.
12. Fraser's restorations in **155** are unlikely to be correct.

which refers perhaps to Chian sailors, in a similar way, as simply attesting to the fact that they are now both *mystai* and *epoptai*. The title appears again in **61**, incription i, but here we have a bit more information. The title stands at the head of a list of Knidian naval officers; it is followed by a mere reference (without a list of names) to the rest of the crew, as καὶ τοὶ συμπλεύσαντες | καὶ μυηθέντες | καὶ ὑποπτεύσαντες *(sic)*. The participles (instead of nouns) suggest activity, and we may surmise that the members of the crew received both stages of initiation during their recent stay on the island, or perhaps on a couple of recent stops during the same mission (the nature of which, if stated, is not preserved).

Inscription **73** is in a category different from the preceding examples: the first line, *Mystae · piei · s(acrum vel -acra acceperunt?),* is followed in the second line by the heading *Epoptae;* this is simply a list of initiates who underwent the *epopteia* (it is in effect equivalent to *mystae et epoptae*), without any indication of the interval between *myesis* and *epopteia.*

Only one of the records of initiates called both *mystai* and *epoptai* provides an apparent date, namely **89**, which has in lines 3–4 a date of June 6, A.D. 19. Three of the people listed under the heading *mystae* at the beginning of the document are also listed under the heading *epoptae* at the end. This has been taken to mean that *myesis* and *epopteia* could be available on the same day. We should note, however, that the original inscription was laid out in two columns, with the *mystae pii* and *symmustae pii* in the first column, and the *servi Schinae* in the second. This is followed by the title *epoptae*, in larger letters than the titles *mystae pii* and *symmustae pii* above, which introduces a list that intrudes upon the space below the second column: it clearly has a different layout from that of the two columns above, probably because it was not part of the original layout but a later addition. The *epoptae* (followed by the eponymous date of the Samothracian *agoranomos*) therefore have most likely been added later than the names of the *mystai.* Curiously, only three *epoptai* are listed, namely, the (only) two initiates listed above, and one of their six *symmustae.* We may therefore ask why their five other "fellow initiates" did not receive the *epopteia* at the same time—or, even more importantly, why, if these three initiates became *epoptai* on the same day, they were not simply called, at the outset, *mystae et epoptae* (instead of being listed separately as *epoptai* at the end of the document). The inscription of the stele was done, at the earliest, on the day after the ceremony took place, when it would have been known, had *myesis* and *epopteia* taken place on the same day, that these three initiates were both *mystai* and *epoptai.* At that point it would have been more economical to write *mystae et epoptae* above the relevant names, as is the case in the other examples of people who had both titles (**49.i, 50.A, 56, 61.i**), than to inscribe the names anew at the end of the document. Thus it is by no means clear that these three persons received the *myesis* and *epopteia* on the same day; it is more likely that they received *epopteia* at a later date in the same year. The precise interval between stages cannot be determined. The mason who carved the list of *epoptai* appears to be the same as the one who carved the rest of the document, but of course this does not preclude an interval of days or weeks between inscribings. Given the frequency of the celebration of the Mysteria during the sailing season (see above), it is conceivable that the three *mystai* of **89** became *epoptai* when the next celebration of the Mysteria took place—a few days later, or perhaps even (as **103** may indicate) the next day. If this was so, then the interval between *myesis* and *epopteia* precisely paralleled that at Eleusis, in that an initiate could become an *epoptes* only at the next performance of the Mysteria (which in the case of Eleusis would be a year later, at Samothrace sometimes perhaps just days later). Although at Eleusis the rule concerning the interval between stages was once broken, by Demetrios Poliorketes, it is nowhere attested that any *mystes* at Eleusis became an *epoptes* on the same day.[13] This is logical, since both *mystai* and *epoptai*, the "blinded" and the "viewers," were evidently present at the same nocturnal ceremony, with each class of initiate receiving a different experience. That a person could change roles within the same performance is difficult to imagine. Given the available evidence, the most reasonable hypothesis is that at Samothrace, as at Eleusis, a *mystes* could become an *epoptes* at the next performance of the Mysteria.

If initiates had to prolong their stay on the island for a certain period of time (even a short one) in order to achieve *epopteia*, this could explain why the records of *epoptai* are much fewer than those of *mystai*. Another reason for the scarcity of *epopteia* records may have been the imposition of some additional requirements (financial, at the least) that the *mystai* had to fulfill, but we have no secure evidence about such requirements.

ANNUAL FESTIVAL

Whether there was a special annual festival of the Mysteria in addition to the frequent celebrations attested in the epigraphical records cannot be inferred from the records themselves.

One document, **103**, seems to record at least three consecutive days on which people became *mystae pii*, and has been interpreted as evidence for an annual festival (see **103**, Commentary). This inscription, however, does not offer a definitive argument that these were the days of a grand festival, but simply tells us that people were initiated on these days—that is, celebrations of the Mysteria took place, and the initiates had their names listed together. The document is too fragmentary to yield a certain conclusion either about a special annual festival or whether the Mysteria could be performed on consecutive days, if necessary, which seems to be a valid alternative interpretation.

Cole proposed that June might have been the month of an annual festival, because at the time the majority of the documents preserving the name of the month were dated in June, and that *epopteia* could have been available only during the annual festival, since the few records of *epoptai* preserving the name of the month were also dated in June.[14] The new evidence discussed above, however, reveals that September is almost as well represented as June among the dates of initiation. As for dated *epopteia* records, we have only one (**89**), so its value as evidence is minimal.[15] None of the documents in this study provides definite proof for a special annual festival of the Mysteries at Samothrace.

13. Demetrios Poliorketes (Plut. *Demetr.* 26) did not want to wait a year to become an *epoptes*, and so the calendar had to be changed to suit his wishes, but we know only that in Boedromion he received both *myesis* and *epopteia*, not that he received both on the same day. For Roman emperors the Eleusinian Mysteria were performed at extraordinary times (for the *epopteia* of Augustus and the initiation of Lucius Verus), but there was an interval between ceremonies; see Clinton 1989, pp. 1508–1509, 1529.

14. Cole 1984, p. 39.

15. Inscription **67**.A is dated in June, but the *epoptai* appear on side C, which is not dated.

Literary evidence suggests the existence of a festival, though not necessarily an annual one. Plutarch (*Luc.* 13.2) writes that Voconius was delayed ἐν Σαμοθράκῃ μυούμενος καὶ πανηγυρίζων. This implies that initiation was separate, as we should expect, from the *panegyris,* a typical feature of a festival. A passage of Ephoros (*FGrH* 70 F120, quoted in a scholion to Eur. *Phoen.* 7) refers to the existence of a plurality of Samothracian festivals with a ritual characteristic of Mysteria: καὶ νῦν ζητοῦσιν αὐτὴν [sc. Harmonia] ἐν ταῖς ἑορταῖς, but the *heortai* should probably be taken as referring to the multiple performances of the Mysteria attested in the initiation records.[16] The testimony in the decree **170** that the general Hippomedon ἔσπευσεν παρα[γενό]μενος εἰς τὴν νῆσον μετασχεῖν τῶμ μυστ[ηρίων] ("upon arrival on the island he was eager to participate in the Mysteria") refers to his participation in one of these performances of the Mysteria. Thus there is no clear evidence that there was a special annual festival of the Mysteria, grander than any of the other celebrations; our information suggests that there were many celebrations of the Mysteria. Unfortunately, we do not know their frequency in a given year, except for the possibility apparently implied in **103** that they could occur over a three-day period. These celebrations were most likely regarded as ἑορταί, and there is no reason to think that each such festival was not accompanied by a *panegyris* of some sort, its size determined by the number of initiates and local participants. As a possible hypothesis we might consider the notion, from a practical point of view, that the celebration could be performed at approximately monthly intervals (every month from April into November is attested), the precise day of the month to be determined according to a formula not known to us, and it could extend over more than a single day if necessary.

The major annual festival of Samothrace, to which theoroi were invited and at which they were honored, could have been the Dionysia, as demonstrated by several pieces of evidence (see Chap. 4). In Part I we noted that there is no evidence securely connecting the theoroi with attendance at a special festival of the Mysteria. The Dionysia may have been the major festival at Samothrace that attracted a multitude of visitors from abroad. This festival was a venue at which performances of important Samothracian myths were put on, including myths that were connected with the Mysteria (see Chap. 4). The Iasian tragic poet Dymas, son of Antipatros, put on a tragedy about the exploits of Dardanos (Appendix I.4), and the Prienian epic poet Herodes, son of Poseidonios, wrote (and presumably recited in the Samothracian theater) an epic poem about the deeds of Dardanos and Eetion and the wedding of Kadmos and Harmonia (*I.Priene* 69).[17] Many performances at the Dionysia, evidently, highlighted the myths and cultic significance of the sanctuary at which the Theater of Dionysos was located. One can readily imagine that this great festival with its theatrical performances attracted many visitors, who might then stay on and take part in the Mysteria as *mystai* or *epoptai.*

16. On the search for Harmonia, cf. Clinton 2003, pp. 67–70, with bibliography.

17. Cf. Appendix I.5; Chaniotis 1988, no. E 60.

OTHER INSCRIPTIONS RELEVANT TO THEOROI IN SAMOTHRACE

These documents include information relating in some way to theoroi on Samothrace. The bibliography for each is restricted to the basic edition(s).

1 Koan decree mentioning theoroi on Samothrace

Edd. Herzog 1899, no. 87; Boesch 1908, pp. 28–29; Rigsby 2004.

Date?

```
     [- - - - - - - - - - - - - - - - - - - - - - - - - - - - - - - - - - - - - - - -]
     [- - - - - - - - - - - - - - - - - - - - - - -]κανοι[- - - - - - - - - - - -]
     [- - - - - - - - - - - - - - - - - - - - - -] αἱρεθέντες ἐς Ἴτωνον
     [- - - - - - - - - - - - - - - - - - - - - - -]τωι ἐπαγγελλόντω τὰ
  5  [Ἀσκλαπιεῖα - - - - - - - - - - - - - - ἐν] Θεσσαλίαι καὶ ἐν Ἄργει
     [- - - - - - - - - - - - - -τοὶ δὲ θεωροὶ τ]οὶ ἐς Σαμοθράικαν ἀποσ-
     [τελλόμενοι- - - -ἐπαγγελλόντω τὰ] Ἀσκλαπιεῖα ἐγ Χίωι καὶ
     [- - - - - - - - - - - - - - - - - - - - - - - - -]ομενοι θεωροὶ φορεύντω
     [- - - - - - - - - - - - - - - - - - - - -α]ἰτιευμέναν θεωρίαν
 10  [- - - - - - - - - - - - - - - - - -ἱεροφύλ]ακες, τοὶ δὲ
     [- - - - - - - - - - - - - - - - - - - - - - -] πανάγυρις
     [- - - - - - - - - - - - - - - - - - - - - - - - - - - - - - - - - - - - - - -]
```

Herzog.

Commentary

The theoroi in this document were supposed to announce the Asklepieia in Chios on their way to Samothrace. This means that *theoros* here was not a specifically defined term, if the same theoroi who were sent to Samothrace as sacred ambassadors acted as "announcing" theoroi on the way.

2 Koan copy of a Samothracian decree in honor of Πραξιμένης Πραξῆ Κῶιος

Edd. *a* Herzog 1899, no. 6; *a + b + e* Segre, *I.Cos* (1993) 28, 29 (*SEG* XLIII 549); *a + b + c + d + e* Hallof, Hallof, and Habicht 1998, pp. 134–136 (*SEG* XLVIII 1100); Hallof and Bosnakis 2003, pp. 210–211.

3rd century B.C.?

[vacat] Σαμοθράικων ψήφισμα.
[ἔδοξε] τῆι βουλῆι καὶ τῶι δήμωι· ἐ[πει]-
[δὴ Πρ]αξιμένης Πραξῆ Κῶιος πρ[όξε]-
[νος] ὢν τῆς πόλεως καὶ εὐεργέτ[ης κα]-
[τά] τε τὴν προξενίαν τοῖς παρα[γινο]-
[μέ]νοις τῶν πολιτῶν παρέχ[ων χρεί]-
[ας], καὶ τὰ πρὸς τὴν πόλιν κοι[νῆι ἀεὶ]
[φιλοτ]ιμούμενος κα[λὸς καὶ ἀγαθὸς καὶ]
[πρόθυμος ὢν διετέ]λει, π[άντα ἀεὶ λέ]-
[γων καὶ πράσσων] τὰ συμ[φέροντα τῶι]
[δήμωι, καὶ νῦν π]αραγεγέ[νηται εἰς]
[τὰ -ca. 5-6-]ια θε[ωρὸς ἀ]ποσταλεὶ[ς ὑπὸ τῶν]
[Κ]ώιων, οἱ δὲ ἄρχοντες προβεβο[ύλευ]-
[κα]σιν αὐτῶι π[ερὶ ἐπα]ίνου καὶ στ[εφάν]-
[ου] καὶ πολιτείας· ἐψήφισθαι τῶ[ι δήμωι·]
[ἐπ]αινέσαι μὲν Πραξιμένη ὧ[ν ἕνεκεν - - -]-
[. .]ται ἐνδ[ε]ίκνυται τῆι π[όλει - - - - - - - -]-
[- -, στεφ]ανῶσαι δὲ [αὐτὸν χρυσῶι στε]-
[φάνωι Διον]υσ[ίων τῶι ἀγῶνι τὴν ἀνάρ]-
[ρησιν ποιουμένους· ὁ δῆμος στεφανοῖ Πρα]-
[ξιμένην Πραξῆ Κῶιον πρόξενον ὄντα]
[τῆς πόλεως καὶ] εὐεργ[έτην χρυσῶι στε]-
[φάνωι εὐσ]εβείας ἕν[εκεν τῆς εἰς τοὺς]
[θεοὺς καὶ] εὐνοίας τῆ[ς εἰς τὸν δῆμον·]
[εἶναι δὲ] αὐτὸν καὶ τοὺς [ἐκγόνους πολί]-
[τας] μετέχοντας ὧν κα[ὶ οἱ ἄλλοι πολῖ]-
[ται]· δεδόσθαι δὲ αὐτῶι καὶ ἀτ[έλειαν]
ὧν ἂν εἰσάγηται ἢ ἐξάγη[ται εἰς τὸν]
[ἴ]διον οἶκον, καὶ προεδρίαν ἐν τ[οῖς ἀγῶ]-
σιν. εἶναι δὲ καὶ τοὺς ἀδελ[φοὺς αὐ]-
τοῦ Μενέστρατον καὶ Με[νεκράτη? καὶ]
Ὀνάσυλλον Κώιους προ[ξένους καὶ]
εὐεργέτας καὶ αὐτοὺς κ[αὶ ἐκγόνου]ς
καὶ ὑπάρχειν αὐτοῖς πάν[τα ἃ καὶ τ]οῖς
ἄλλοις προξένοις· ὑπά[ρχειν δὲ] αὐτοῖς.
[καὶ π]ροεδρίαν ἐν τοῖς ἀγῶ[σι, τὸν] δὲ πρεσ-
[βε]υτὴν τὸν κομίζοντα τ[ῆι πόλ]ει τῆι Κώι-
[ω]ν τὸν στέφανον τὸν [χρυσοῦ]ν ἀπενε[γ]-
[κεῖ]ν καὶ Πραξιμένει τ[ὸν ψηφισ]θέντα στ[έ]-
[φα]νον καὶ αἰτήσασ[θαι - -]Ο[- - - - - - - -]
[- - - -]Λ . ΝΤ . ΝΕ/[- - - - - - - - - - - - - - -]
[- - - - - -]ΙΛ[- - - - - - - - - - - - - - - - - - -]
- -

Herzog, Segre, Hallof, Hallof, and Habicht. **11–12** τὴν] | [νῆσον Segre,
τὸ] [ἱερὸν? Hallof, Hallof, and Habicht. **12–20** K. Hallof. **26–27** Hallof, Hallof,
and Habicht, μετέχου]|-[σι] Segre. **27–42** Hallof, Hallof, and Habicht.

Commentary

Praximenes was sent to Samothrace as theoros, as is evident from line 12. The remains of letters at the beginning of the line are compatible with restoring [Διονύσ]ια (cf. line 19) or perhaps [εἰς] | [τὰ Μυστήρ]ια, as K. Hallof suggests (2003, p. 211). There could be barely enough space to restore [εἰς] | [τὰ Διονύσ]ια, and perhaps not enough for [τὰ μυστήρ]ια, but in any case the question of space is not determinative. The Dionysia seem to make more sense in view of line 19. This is the first documentary association of theoroi in Samothrace with festival attendance; see Chapter 9. The inscription is interesting as an illustration of the honors granted by Samothrace to the theoroi, including προξενία, ἀτέλεια, and προεδρία ἐν τοῖς ἀγῶσι.

3 Iasian copy of a Samothracian decree in honor of theoroi from Iasos
Ed. Habicht 1994b.

Middle of 3rd century B.C.?

> Βασιλεὺς Ἰάσω[ν . . . .]ου εἶπεν, ἀγαθῆι τύχηι
> τῶν πόλεων ἀμφοτέρων, δεδόχθαι τῶι δήμωι· δέχεσθαι
> τὴν θυσίαν καὶ τὴν ἀπαρχὴν καὶ τὴν θεωρίαν τὴν παραγεγενη-
> μένην εἰς τὸ ἱερὸν παρὰ τοῦ δήμου τοῦ Ἰασέων κατὰ τὰ ἐψη-
> 5 φισμένα ἐπ᾽ εὐτυχίαι καὶ ὑγιείαι τῶν τε ἀποστειλάντων καὶ
> τῶν ἐν τῆι νήσωι, καὶ ἐπαινέσαι τὸν δῆμον τὸν Ἰασέων καὶ στεφανῶ-
> σαι χρυσῶι στεφάνωι Διονυσίων ἐόντων εὐσεβείας ἕνεκεν *vacat*
> τῆς εἰς τοὺς θεοὺς καὶ εὐνοίας τῆς εἰς τὸν δῆμον, ἐπαινέσαι δὲ
> καὶ τοὺς παραγεγενημένους θεωροὺς Γρύλλον Εὐκλείδου, Εὖκτον
> 10 Μενεκάρους καὶ εἶναι αὐτοὺς προξένους τῆς πόλεως μετ-
> έχοντας πάντων ὧν καὶ οἱ ἄλλοι πρόξενοι· ἀναγράψαι *vacat*
> δὲ αὐτῶν τὰ ὀνόματα εἰς τὴν στήλην καὶ καλέσαι αὐ-
> [τοὺς ἐπὶ] ξένια εἰς τὸ πρυτανεῖον· τὸ δὲ ἀνάλωμα δοῦ-
> [ναι τοὺς] ἀργυρολόλο[γους] ἐκ τοῦ κατατεταγμένου
> 15 [ἀργυρίου].

Habicht.

Commentary

The decree recommends acceptance of the sacrifice, first fruits, and *theoria* sent by Iasos to Samothrace, and praises the Iasian theoroi for their respect for the gods and benevolence toward the Samothracian demos. The Iasian demos and the theoroi are to be honored at the Dionysia. This is the second document that connects theoroi in Samothrace with festival attendance, though not with a special festival of the Mysteries.

Line 12: On the practice of inscribing names of theoroi on stelai, see *ad* 22.

4 Iasian copy of a Samothracian decree in honor of the poet Dymas Antipatrou
Ed. Blümel, *I.Iasos* (1985) I 153.
Cf. Chaniotis 1988, no. E 68.

2nd century B.C.

[ἔ]δοξεν τῆι βουλῆι· βασιλεὺς Θεοτέλης Ἀριφάντου εἶπεν· ἐπε[ιδὴ]

15 Δύμας ποητὴς τραγωιδιῶν τά τε πρὸς θεοὺς εὐσεβῶς δια[γό]-
     μενος καὶ τὰ πρὸς [τ]ὴμ πόλιν οἰκείως καὶ φιλανθρώπως ἀεί τι λ[έγων]
     καὶ γράφων καὶ πράττων ἀγαθὸν διατελεῖ περὶ τῆς νήσου, διὰ [παν]-
     [τ]ός τε ἀπόδειξιν ἐποιήσατο τῆς αὐτοῦ φύσεως καὶ πραγματείαν σ[υνέ]-
     ταξεν ἐν δράματι τῶν Δαρδάνου πράξεων τὰς μεγίστας μνημοσ[ύνας,]
20 ἡ δὲ βουλὴ προβεβ[ο]ύλευκεν αὐτῶι περὶ ἐπαίνου καὶ στεφάνου· [ὅπως]
     οὖγ καὶ ὁ δῆμος φαίνηται τοὺς εὐεργετοῦντας αὐτὸν τιμῶν ἀξίω[ς]
     διὰ παντός· ἀγαθῆι τύχηι· ἐψηφίσθαι τῶι δήμωι· ἐπαινέσαι Δύμα[ντα]
     ἐπὶ τῆι πρὸς τὴμ πόλιν εὐνοίαι καὶ στεφανῶσαι αὐτὸν χρυσῶι στε[φάνωι]
     Διονυσίων τῶι ἀγῶνι τὴν ἀνάρρησιν ποιουμένους· ὁ δῆμος στεφα[νοῖ]
25 Δύμαντα Ἀντιπάτ[ρ]ου χρυσῶι στεφάνωι ἀρετῆς ἕνεκεγ καὶ εὐν[οίας]
     τῆς εἰς αὐτόν· τῆ[ς] δὲ ἀναρρήσεως ἐπιμεληθῆναι τοὺς προέδ[ρους]
     [κ]αὶ τὸν ἀγωνοθέτην· εἶναι δὲ αὐτῶι καὶ ἄλλο ἀγαθὸν εὑρέσθαι ὅτ[ι ἂν]
     [β]ούληται παρὰ τοῦ δήμου· ἀναγράψαι δὲ τὸ ψήφισμα τὸμ βασιλέα [εἰς τὸ]
     [ἱε]ρὸν τῆς Ἀθηνᾶς· ἵν[α δ]ὲ φανερὸν ἦι καὶ Ἰασεῦσιν ὅτι ὁ δῆμος τιμᾶ[ι τοὺς]
30 [κα]λοὺς καὶ ἀγαθοὺς ἄνδρας ἀξίως τῆς αὐτῶν ἀρετῆς, δοῦν[αι τόδε]
     [τὸ] ψήφισμα τὸμ βασιλέα τοῖς πρώτοις παραγενομένοις θεωροῖς ἐ[ξ Ἰασοῦ]
     [καὶ] τὸ γραφὲν ἐπὶ Σωσιφάνους ἀνενεγκεῖν τῆι βουλῆι καὶ τῶι δήμ[ωι τῶι]
     [Ἰα]σέων, καὶ παρακε[κ]λῆσθαι Ἰασε[ῖ]ς ἐπιμεληθῆναι φιλοτίμως ἵνα [τὰ]
     [ψ]ηφίσματα ἔν τινι τῶν ἱερῶν ἀναγ[ρ]αφῆι καὶ οἱ στέφανοι ἀν[ακη]-
35 [ρυχ]θῶσιν ἐν Διο[νυ]σίοις εἰδότας δι[ό]τι ποιήσαντες τὰ ἠξι[ωμένα]
     [χα]ριοῦνται τῶι δ[ήμ]ωι.

    Blümel.

Commentary

The document contains two decrees in honor of the tragic poet Dymas
Antipatrou of Iasos, praised by Samothrace for his benevolence toward the
city and respect for the gods, but especially for his poem about Dardanos.
Only the second decree, lines 14–36, has been reprinted here, since it
concerns theoroi. Lines 30–31 recommend that the Samothracian *basileus*
give this decree to the first theoroi who arrive [from Iasos]. This expression
suggests that theoroi visited Samothrace on multiple occasions, and not
necessarily for a specific event.

5 Prienian copy of a Samothracian decree in honor of the poet
       Herodes Poseidoniou

       Ed. Hiller von Gaertringen, *I.Priene* (1906) 68.
       Cf. Chaniotis 1988, no. E 60.

Ca. 100 B.C.

    -
    [- -]δειν [. . . ᶜᵃ·⁷ . .]
    [- - - ᶜᵃ·¹⁵ - - -καὶ πρόσοδον πρὸς τὴν βουλὴν] καὶ τὸν δῆμον μετὰ τα
    [ἱερὰ πρώτωι καὶ εὑρέσθαι ἀγαθὸν ἐάν τι βο]ύληται τῶν δυνατῶν παρὰ
    [τοῦ δήμου· ἀναγράψαι δὲ τόδε τὸ ψήφ]ισμα εἰς στήλην καὶ ἀναθεῖναι
5   [εἰς τὸ ἱερὸν τῆς Ἀθηνᾶς· ὅπως δὲ καὶ] Πριηνεῖς εἰδήσωσιν τὴν τοῦ δήμου

[εὐχαριστίαν, ἣν ἔχει εἰς τοὺς προα]ιρουμένους τὴν ὑπάρχουσαν ταῖς πό-
[λεσι φιλίαν αὔξειν, ἀεί τι πράσσ]οντάς τ[ε] καὶ λέγοντας περὶ τούτων
[ὁ δ' ἡμέτερος δῆμος τοὺς ἀγαθοὺς] ἄνδρας τιμῶν ἀξίως φαίνηται, δοῦναι
[τόδε τὸ ψήφισμα τὸμ βασιλ]έα τοῖς πρώτοις παρεσομένοις θεω-
10   [ροῖς ἐκ Πριήνης καὶ ἀνενεγκεῖν αὐτὸ τῆ]ι βουλῆι καὶ τῶι δήμωι τῶι Πριηνέων καὶ
[παρακαλέσαι Πριηνεῖς φίλους ὄ]ντας καὶ οἰκείους ἐπιμεληθῆναι, ὅπ[ως]
[ἂν τὸ ψήφισμα τόδε ἀναγρα]φῆ ἔν τινι τῶν ἱερῶν καὶ ὁ στέφανος
[ἀναγορευθῆ ἐν Διονυσίοις, εἰδότας ὅτι ταῦτα] ποιήσαντες χαριοῦνται τῶι δήμωι.

Hiller.

Commentary

This document is a copy of a Samothracian decree (*I.Priene* 68) in honor
of Herodes, son of Poseidonios, of Priene, praised for writing about the
deeds of Dardanos and Eetion and the wedding of Kadmos and Harmonia,
as is clarified by the answer of Priene, which is inscribed on another fragment of the same stele (*I.Priene* 69, lines 6–8). The phrase τοῖς πρώτοις
παρεσομένοις θεω‖[ροῖς ἐκ Πριήνης ("the first arriving theoroi from Priene"), lines 9–10, closely resembles lines 30–31 of the decree honoring the
poet Dymas from Iasos; see Commentary *ad* Appendix I.4.

OTHER INSCRIPTIONS RELEVANT TO INITIATES IN SAMOTHRACE

These documents include information relating in some way to initiates on Samothrace. The bibliography for each is restricted to the basic edition.

1 Rhodes

  Ed. Carratelli 1942.

Date?

> [- - - - - - - - - - - - - -]α[. . . . .] Φίλωνος
> [τὸ κοινὸ]ν τὸ Σαμοθρα[ι]κιαστᾶν
> [Νικο?σ]τρατείων συνμυστᾶν
> [συνστρα]τευσαμένων ὑπὸ τριήραρχον
> 5 [- - - - - - -]ωνα Φ[ίλ]ωνος

Carratelli.

Commentary

This document was a dedication by the league of *Samothrakiastai* and presumably their fellow *mystai* from Nikostrateia, who fought under the command of a certain *trierarch*. The *Samothrakiastai* were apparently members of private clubs in the Aegean islands and along the coast of Asia Minor, honoring the Samothracian gods; cf. Cole 1984, p. 83, n. 670.

2 Tomis

  Edd. Točilescu 1883, pp. 8–9; Stoian 1962, pp. 75–79; Sokolowski, *LSCG* (1969) 87.

Date?

> [ἀγαθῆ τύχ]η· ὁ πριάμενος τὴν ἱερω-
> [σύνην τῶ]ν μυστῶν θεῶν τῶν ἐν
> [Σαμοθρά]κη ἱερήσεται διὰ βίο[υ καὶ]
> [Ἀπατου]ρεῶνος ἑβδόμη παρ[έξει εἰς]
> 5 [τὰ ἱερ]ὰ σχίζας καὶ ἐγχέει [σπον]-
> [δὴν τοῖ]ς μύσταις καὶ πομπε[ύσει]
> [. . . πα]ρ᾿ αὐτοῦ· στεφανωθήσεται
> [παρὰ] τῶν μυστῶν φιλοτιμίας ἕνε-

[κε]ν τῆς εἰς ἑαυτούς, ἐν ᾗ ἱερᾶται ἡμέ-
10 ρᾳ· συνθύσει δὲ καὶ τοὺς λιβάνους ἐμ
πάσαις ταῖς συνόδοις μετὰ τοῦ προ-
υπάρχοντος ἱέρεω τῶν μυστῶν καὶ
οἷς ἐπιβάλλει ἐκ τοῦ νόμου· κτλ.

Sokolowski.

Commentary

See Sokolowski's commentary. The document has two parts: column I is a fragment of an honorary decree, and column II, partly reprinted here, is a sacred law concerning the activities required of the person who purchases the priesthood of the initiates of the Samothracian gods. These activities include sacrifice, procession, and libation.

3 Dionysopolis

Mihailov, *IGBulg* I² (1970) 13 = V (1997) 5006.

Ca. 48 B.C.

   . . .   ἀναλαβ[ὼν]
[τὸν στέφανο]ν τοῦ θεοῦ τάς τε πομπὰς καὶ θυσίας [ἐπε]-
[τέλεσε καλ]ῶς καὶ μεγαλομερῶς καὶ τοῖς πολίταις μ?[ε]-
[τέδωκε κρε]ῶν ἀφθόνως, θεῶν τε τ[ῶ]ν ἐν Σαμοθρᾴκ[η]
20 [στέφα]νον ἀνειληφὼς διὰ βίου τάς τε πομπὰς κ[αὶ]
[τὰς θυσία]ς ἐπιτελεῖ ὑπέρ τε τῶν μυστῶν καὶ τῆς π[ό]-
[λεως, κτλ.

Mihailov.

Commentary

See Mihailov's bibliography and discussion. This is a decree honoring a priest of various deities worshipped at Dionysopolis. Lines 19–21 inform us that as a lifelong priest of the Samothracian gods he was organizing processions and sacrifices on behalf of the initiates and the city of Dionysopolis.

REFERENCES

AÉ = *L'Année épigraphique: Revue des publications épigraphiques relatives à l'antiquité romaine,* Paris.

Agora = *The Athenian Agora: Results of Excavations Conducted by the American School of Classical Studies at Athens,* Princeton

    XV = B. D. Meritt and J. S. Traill, *Inscriptions: The Athenian Councillors,* 1974.

    XVI = A. G. Woodhead, *Inscriptions: The Decrees,* 1997.

Aneziri, S. 2003. *Die Vereine der dionysischen Techniten im Kontext der hellenistischen Gesellschaft,* Stuttgart.

Ashton, R. 1988. "Pseudo-Rhodian Drachms from Samothrace," *NC* 148, pp. 129–134.

L'Association dionysiaque = *L'Association dionysiaque dans les sociétés anciennes: Actes de la table ronde organisée par l'École française de Rome (Rome, 24–25 mai 1984),* Rome 1986.

Axenidis, T. 1939. "Μία νέα θεσσαλικὴ ἐπιγραφή," *Hellenika* 11, pp. 263–271.

Bastianini, G., and C. Galazzi. 2001. *Posidippo di Pella: Epigrammi,* Milan.

Beacham, R. 1992. *The Roman Theatre and Its Audience,* Cambridge, Mass.

Bechtel, F. 1887. *Die Inschriften des ionischen Dialekts,* Göttingen.

———. 1898. *Spitznamen,* Göttingen.

———. [1917] 1964. *Die historischen Personennamen des griechischen bis zur Kaiserzeit,* repr. Hildesheim.

Blau, O., and K. Schlottmann. 1855. "25 Oktober: Gesammtsitzung der Akademie," *Monatsberichte der Königlich Preussischen Akademie der Wissenschaften zu Berlin* 20, pp. 601–637.

Bodnar, E. W., and C. Mitchell. 1976. *Cyriacus of Ancona's Journeys in the Propontis and the Northern Aegean, 1444–1445* (Memoirs of the American Philosophical Society 112), Philadelphia.

Boesch, P. 1908. *Θεωρός: Untersuchung zur Epangelie griechischer Feste,* Berlin.

Boethius, A. 1918. *Die Pythaïs: Studien zur Geschichte der Verbindungen zwischen Athen und Delphi,* Uppsala.

Bouzek, J., and R. Hošek. 1995. "Einige Inschriften aus Samothrake," in *Studia in honorem Georgii Mihailov,* ed. A. Fol, B. Bogdanov, P. Dimitrov, and D. Boyadziev, Sofia, pp. 83–88.

Boyadzhiev [Boïadjiev], D. 2000. *Les relations ethno-linguistiques en Thrace et en Mésie pendant l'époque romaine,* Sofia.

Bremen, R. van. 1996. *The Limits of Participation: Women and Civic Life in the Greek East in the Hellenistic and Roman Periods,* Amsterdam.

Broughton, T. [1952] 1984. *The Magistrates of the Roman Republic* 2, repr. Atlanta.

Bruneau, P. 1970. *Recherches sur les cultes de Délos à l'époque hellénistique et à l'époque impériale,* Paris.

Buck, C. D. 1953. "Theoros," in *Studies Presented to David Moore Robinson on His Seventieth Birthday* 2, ed. G. Mylonas and D. Raymond, St. Louis, pp. 443–444.

BullÉp = *Bulletin épigraphique* in *Revue des études grecques*

Burkert, W. 1987. *Ancient Mystery Cults,* Cambridge, Mass.

———. 1993. "*Concordia discors:* The Literary and the Archaeological Evidence on the Sanctuary of Samothrace," in *Greek Sanctuaries: New Approaches,* ed. N. Marinatos and R. Hägg, London, pp. 178–191.

———. 2002. "Greek Margins: Mysteries of Samothrace (Ελληνική Περιφέρεια: Τα Μυστήρια της Σαμοθράκης)," in *Λατρείες στην περιφέρεια του αρχαίου ελληνικού κόσμου,* ed. A. Avagianou, Athens, pp. 31–63.

Cabanes, P., and F. Drini. 1995. *Corpus des inscriptions greques d'Illyrie méridionale et d'Épire* 1: *Inscriptions d'Épidamne-Dyrrhachion et d'Apollonia,* pt. 1., *Inscriptions d'Épidamne-Dyrrhachion* (Études épigraphiques 2), Athens.

Carratelli, G. Pugliese. 1942. "Per la storia delle associazioni in Rodi antica," *ASAtene,* n.s., 1–2, 1939–1940, p. 153, no. 13.

Casson, L. 1995. *Ships and Seamanship in the Ancient World,* Baltimore.

Chaniotis, A. 1988. *Historie und Historiker in den griechischen Inschriften: Epigraphische Beiträge zur griechischen Historiographie,* Stuttgart.

Chantraine, P. 1968–1980. *Dictionnaire étymologique de la langue grecque,* Paris.

Chapouthier, F. 1925. "Inscriptions inédites de Samothrace," *BCH* 49, pp. 254–262.

———. 1935. *Les Dioscures au service d'une déesse: Étude d'iconographie religieuse,* Paris.

CIL = *Corpus inscriptionum latinarum,* Berlin 1865–.

CIRB = V. V. Struve, *Corpus inscriptionum regni bosporani,* Moscow 1965.

Clinton, K. 1989. "The Eleusinian Mysteries: Roman Initiates and Benefactors, Second Century b.c. to a.d. 267," *ANRW* II, 18.2, pp. 1499–1539.

———. 1992. *Myth and Cult: The Iconography of the Eleusinian Mysteries* (Acta Instituti Atheniensis Regni Sueciae 9), Stockholm.

———. 1993. "The Sanctuary of Demeter and Kore at Eleusis," in *Greek Sanctuaries: New Approaches,* ed. N. Marinatos and R. Hägg, London, pp. 110–124.

———. 2001. "Initiates in the Samothracian Mysteries, September 4, 100 b.c.," *Chiron* 31, pp. 27–35.

———. 2003. "Stages of Initiation in the Eleusinian and Samothracian Mysteries," in *Greek Mysteries: The Archaeology and Ritual of Ancient Greek Secret Cults,* ed. M. Cosmopoulos, London, pp. 50–78.

———. 2004. "Epiphany in the Eleusinian Mysteries," *Illinois Classical Studies* 29, pp. 85–109.

———. Forthcoming. "Thracian Royalty in Samothrace," in *Proceedings of the Symposium in Memory of E. Pentazos,* Komotini.

Cole, S. G. 1984. *Theoi Megaloi: The Cult of the Great Gods at Samothrace,* Leiden.

———. 1989. "The Mysteries of Samothrace during the Roman Period," *ANRW* II, 18.2, pp. 1564–1598.

Collart, P. 1937. *Philippes, ville de Macédoine, depuis ses origines jusqu'à la fin de l'époque romaine,* Paris.

Collini, P. 1990. "Gli dèi Cabiri di Samotracia: Origine indigena o semitica?" *Studi classici e orientali* 40, pp. 237–287.

Conze 1875 = A. Conze, A. Hauser, and G. Niemann, *Archäologische Untersuchungen auf Samothrake* I, Vienna.

Conze 1880 = A. Conze, A. Hauser, and O. Benndorf, *Archäologische Untersuchungen auf Samothrake* II, Vienna.

Conze, A. 1860. *Reise auf den Inseln des thrakischen Meeres,* Hannover.

Cook, J. M. 1968. "Coins from an Aeolic Site," *BSA* 63, pp. 33–40.

———. 1973. *The Troad: An Archaeological and Topographical Study,* Oxford.

Corinth VIII.1 = B. D. Meritt, *Greek Inscriptions, 1896–1927,* Cambridge, Mass., 1931.

Cormack, J. M. R., and W. M. Calder. 1962. *Monuments from Lycaonia, the Pisido-Phyrgian Borderland, Aphrodisias* (*MAMA* 8), Manchester.

Csapo, E., and W. Slater. 1995. *The Context of Ancient Drama,* Ann Arbor.

Degrassi, A. 1952. *I Fasti consolari dell' impero romano,* Rome.

Delphinion = G. Kawerau and A. Rehm, *Das Delphinion in Milet,* Berlin 1914.

Delta = A. Bernand, *Le delta égyptien d'après les textes grecs* 1, Cairo 1970.

Detschew [Dechev], D. 1957. *Die thrakischen Sprachreste,* Vienna.

Diary = annual Samothrace excavation notebooks.

Dillon, M. 1997. *Pilgrims and Pilgrimage in Ancient Greece,* London.

Dow, S. 1937. "The Egyptian Cults in Athens," *HTR* 30, pp. 216–223.

Dowden, K. 1980. "Grades in the Eleusinian Mysteries," *RHR* 197, pp. 407–427.

Dürr, J. 1881. *Die Reisen des Kaisers Hadrian,* Vienna.

EAM = T. Rizakis and Y. Touratsoglou, Ἐπιγραφές Ἄνω Μακεδονίας (Ἐλίμεια, Ἐορδαία, Νότια Λυγκηστίς, Ὀρεστίς), Athens 1985–.

EKM = L. Gounaropoulou and M. B. Hatzopoulos, Ἐπιγραφές Κάτω Μακεδονίας (Μεταξύ του Βερμίου όρους και του Αξιού ποταμού). Τεύχος Α΄: Ἐπιγραφές Βεροίας, Athens 1998.

Elvers, K. L. 1994. "Der 'Eid der Berenike und ihrer Söhne': Eine Edition von *IGBulg.* III 2, 1371," *Chiron* 24, pp. 241–266.

Erhardt, N. 1999. "Funde aus Milet, VII: Ein weiteres Zeugnis für die Menesthiden-Familie," *AA* 1999, pp. 273–275.

Ernout, A. 1935. *Morphologie historique du latin,* Paris.

FdD = *Fouilles de Delphes,* École française d'Athènes, Paris.
    III.2 = G. Colin, *Épigraphy: Inscriptions du trésor des Athéniens,* 1909–1913.
    III.3 = G. Daux and A. Salač, *Épigraphy: Inscriptions depuis le trésor des Athéniens jusqu'aux bases de Gélon,* 2 vols., 1932–1943.

FdXanth VII = A. Balland, *Inscriptiones d'Epoque impériale du Létôon,* Paris 1981.

Finkielsztejn, G. 2001. *Chronologie detaillée et revisée des éponymes amphoriques rhodiens, de 270 à 108 av. J.-C. environ: Premier bilan,* Oxford.

Fränkel, M. 1894a. "Die Hippomedon-Inschrift von Samothrake," *AM* 19, pp. 133–136.

———. 1894b. "Noch Einmal die Hippomedon-Inschrift," *AM* 19, pp. 395–397.

Fraser, P. M. 2001. Rev. of *I.Perinthos,* in *CR,* n.s., 51, pp. 182–183.

Frisk, H. 1960–1972. *Griechisches etymologisches Wörterbuch,* Heidelberg.

Gallis, K. I. 1980. "Νέα ἐπιγραφικὰ εὑρήματα ἀπὸ τὴ Λάρισα," *AAA* 13, pp. 246–262.

Garrucci, R. 1875–1877. *Sylloge inscriptionum latinarum aevi romanae rei publicae usque ad C. Iulium Caesarum plenissima,* Augustae Taurinorum.

Gelder, H. van 1900. *Geschichte der alten Rhodier,* The Hague.

Gow, A. S. F., and D. L. Page. 1965. *The Greek Anthology: Hellenistic Epigrams,* Cambridge.

Graf, F. 1974. *Eleusis und die orphische Dichtung Athens in vorhellenistischer Zeit,* Berlin.

Graham, A. J. 2001. "Thasian Controversies," in A. J. Graham, *Collected Papers on Greek Colonization* (Mnemosyne Suppl. 214), Leiden, pp. 384–402.

Günther, W. 1992. "Athenisches Bürgerrecht für Theoren aus Milet," *EA* 19, pp. 135–143.

GVI = W. Peek, *Griechische Vers-Inschriften* 1: *Grab-Epigramme,* Berlin 1955.

Habicht, C. 1972. "Beiträge zur Prosopographie der altgriechischen Welt," *Chiron* 2, pp. 110–113.

———. 1986. "Beiträge zur Prosopographie der hellenistischen Welt," *StClas* 24, pp. 91–97.

———. 1987. "The Role of Athens in the Reorganization of the Delphic Amphictiony after 189 b.c.," *Hesperia* 56, pp. 59–71.

———. 1994a. *Athen in hellenistischer Zeit,* Munich.

———. 1994b. "Iasos und Samothrake in der Mitte des 3. Jahrhunderts v. Chr.," *Chiron* 24, pp. 69–74.

Hallof, K., and D. Bosnakis. 2003. "Alte und neue Inschriften aus Kos I," *Chiron* 33, pp. 203–262.

Hallof, L., K. Hallof, and C. Habicht. 1998. "Aus der Arbeit der *Inscriptiones Graecae* 2," *Chiron* 28, pp. 101–142.

Hansen, E. 1971. *The Attalids of Pergamon,* 2nd ed., Ithaca.

Harris, W. 1992. "An Inscription Recording a Proconsul's Visit to Samothrace in 165 a.d.," *AJP* 113, pp. 71–79.

Hatzfeld, J. 1919. *Les trafiquants italiens dans l'Orient hellénique,* Paris.

Haussoullier, B. 1917. *Traité entre Delphes et Pellana: Étude de droit grec,* Paris.

Hellenica = L. Robert, *Hellenica: Recueil d'épigraphie de numismatique et d'antiquités grecques,* 13 vols., Limoges, 1940–1965.

Helly, B. 1995. *L'état thessalien: Aleuas le Roux, les tetrades et les "Tagoi,"* Lyon.

Hemberg, B. 1950. *Die Kabiren,* Uppsala.

Henderson, B. 1923. *The Life and Principate of the Emperor Hadrian, a.d. 76–138,* London.

Hershbell, J. P. 1981. *Pseudo-Plato: "Axiochus,"* Chico, Calif.

Herzog, R. 1899. *Koische Forschungen und Funde* XVI, Leipzig.

Herzog, R., and G. Klaffenbach. 1952. *Asylieurkunden aus Kos,* Berlin.

Holwerda, D. 1982. *Scholia in Aristophanem.* Part 2, *Scholia in Vespas, Pacem, Aves et Lysistratam,* fasc. 2: *Scholia vetera et recentiora in Aristophanis Pacem,* Groningen.

Honigmann, E. 1939. *Le synekdémos d'Hiéroklès et l'opuscule géographique de Georges de Chypre,* Brussels.

I.Alexandreia Troas = M. Ricl, *The Inscriptions of Alexandreia Troas,* Bonn 1997.

IC = M. Guarducci, *Inscriptiones creticae,* 4 vols., Rome 1935–1940.

I.Chios = D. F. McCabe and J. V. Brownson, *Chios Inscriptions: Texts and Lists,* 2 vols., Princeton 1986.

I.Cos = M. Segre, *Inscrizione di Cos* (Monografie della Scuola archeologica di Atene e della missioni italiane in Oriente 6), Rome 1993.

ICUR = I. B. de Rossi and G. Gatti, *Inscriptiones christianae urbis Romae, saeculo septimo antiquiores,* Rome 1861–.

I.Délos = *Inscriptions de Délos,* 7 vols., Paris 1926–1972.

I.Didyma = A. Rehm, *Didyma* II: *Die Inschriften,* Berlin 1958.

I.Eleusis = K. Clinton, *Eleusis: The Inscriptions on Stone. Documents of the Sanctuary of the Two Goddesses and Public Documents of the Deme* 1, Athens 2005.

I.Eleusis 2 = K. Clinton, *Eleusis: The Inscriptions on Stone. Documents of the Sanctuary of the Two Goddesses and Public Documents of the Deme* 2: *Commentary,* forthcoming.

I.Ephesos = D. F. McCabe, R. N. Elliott, A. Hilton, K. Na, and C. Redmond, *Ephesos Inscriptions: Texts and Lists,* 2 vols., Princeton 1991.

IG = *Inscriptiones graecae,* Berlin 1873–.

IG XII.8 = C. Fredrich, *Inscriptiones graecae,* fasc. 8: *Inscriptiones insularum maris thracici,* Berlin 1909.

IGBulg = G. Mihailov, *Inscriptiones graecae in Bulgaria repertae,* 5 vols., Sofia 1956–1997.

IGR = *Inscriptiones graecae ad res romanas pertinentes,* Paris 1911–1927.

IGUR = L. Moretti, *Inscriptiones graecae urbis Romae,* 4 vols., Rome 1968–1990.

I.Halikarnassos = D. F. McCabe, *Halikarnassos Inscriptions: Texts and Lists,* Princeton 1991.

I.Iasos = W. Blümel, *Die Inschriften von Iasos,* 2 vols., Bonn 1985.

I.Kios = T. Corsten, *Die Inschriften von Kios,* Bonn 1985.

I.Knidos = W. Blümel, *Die Inschriften von Knidos,* Bonn 1992.

I.Kolophon = D. F. McCabe, *Kolophon Inscriptions: Texts and Lists,* Princeton 1985.

I.Kyz. = E. Schwertheim, *Die Inschriften von Kyzikos und Umgebung,* Bonn 1980–.

ILAlg = *Inscriptions latines de l'Algérie,* Paris 1922–.

I.Leukopetra = P. M. Petsas, M. B. Hatzopoulos, L. Gounaropoulou, P. Paschidis, *Inscriptions du sanctuaire de la Mère des Dieux autochthone de Leukopétra (Macédoine),* Μελετήματα (Κέντρον Ελληνικής και Ρωμαϊκής Αρχαιότητος) 28, Athens 2000.

ILGR = M. Šašel Kos, *Inscriptiones latinae in Graecia repertae: Additamenta ad CIL,* Faenza 1979.

ILJug. = A. Šašel and J. Šašel, *Inscriptiones latinae quae in Iugoslavia inter annos MCMII et MCMXL repertae et editae sunt* (Situla 25), Ljubljana 1986.

ILLRP I = A. Degrassi, *Inscriptiones latinae liberae rei publicae,* Florence 1957.

ILLRP I² = A. Degrassi, *Inscriptiones latinae liberae rei publicae,* 2nd ed., Florence 1965.

ILS = H. Dessau, *Inscriptiones latinae selectae,* 3 vols., Berlin 1892–1916.

I.Magnesia = O. Kern, *Die Inschriften von Magnesia am Maeander,* Berlin 1900.

IMS = F. Papazoglou, *Inscriptions de la Mésie Supérieure,* Belgrade 1976–.

IMT = M. Barth and J. Stauber, *Inschriften von Mysia und Troas,* Munich 1993.

I.Mylasa = W. Blümel, *Die Inschriften von Mylasa,* 2 vols., Bonn 1987–1988.

IOSPE I² = B. Latyshev, *Inscriptiones antiquae orae septentrionalis Ponti Euxini graecae et latinae,* St. Petersburg 1916.

I.Panamara = M. Ç. Şahin, *Die Inschriften von Stratonikeia* 1, Bonn 1981.

I.Pergamon = M. Fränkel, *Die Inschriften von Pergamon,* 2 vols., Berlin 1890–1895.

I.Perinthos = M. H. Sayar, *Perinthos-Herakleia (Marmara Ereğlisi) und Umgebung: Geschichte, Testimonien, griechische und lateinische Inschriften,* Vienna 1998.

I.Priene = F. Hiller von Gaertringen, *Inschriften von Priene,* Berlin 1906.

I.Prusa = T. Corsten, *Die Inschriften von Prusa ad Olympum,* 2 vols., Bonn 1991–1993.

ISE = L. Moretti, *Iscrizioni storiche ellenistiche,* 2 vols., Florence 1967–1975.

ISM = D. M. Pippidi and I. Stoian, *Inscriptiones Scythiae Minoris graecae et latinae,* Bucharest 1980–.

I.Teos = D. F. McCabe and M. A. Plunket, *Teos Inscriptions: Texts and Lists,* Princeton 1985.

IvO = W. Dittenberger and K. Purgold, *Inschriften von Olympia,* Berlin 1896.

Jory, E. J. 1963. "Algebraic Notation in Dramatic Texts," *BICS* 10, pp. 65–78.

Kallipolitis, V. G. 1953. "Épigramme inédite en mémoire d'une musicienne de Beroia," in *Studies Presented to David Moore Robinson on His Seventieth Birthday* 2, ed. G. Mylonas and D. Raymond, St. Louis, pp. 371–373.

Karadima, C. 1995. "Αρχαιολογικές εργασίες στη Μαρώνεια και Σαμοθράκη το 1995," *Το Αρχαιολογικό Έργο στη Μακεδονία και Θράκη* 9, pp. 487–496.

Karadima, C., and N. Dimitrova. 2003. "An Epitaph for an Initiate at Samothrace and Eleusis," *Chiron* 33, pp. 335–345.

Ker, J. 2000. "Solon's *Theoria* and the End of the City," *ClAnt* 19, pp. 304–329.

Kerényi, K. 1955. "Das Werk des Skopas für Samothrake," *SymbOslo* 31, pp. 141–154.

Kern, O. 1893. "Aus Samothrake," *AM* 18, pp. 337–384.

———. 1894. "Theorenliste aus Samothrake," *AM* 19, pp. 397–400.

Koller, H. 1958. "Theoros und Theoria," *Glotta* 36, pp. 273–286.

Kontoleon, Al.-Emm. 1891. "Inscriptions grecques inédites, *RÉG* 4, pp. 297–300.

Kramolisch, H. 1978. *Strategen des Thessalischen Bundes vom Jahr 196 v. Chr. bis zum Ausgang der römischen Republik* (*Demetrias* 2), Bonn.

Larsen, J. A. O. 1968. *Greek Federal States: Their Institutions and History*, Oxford.

Laumonier, A. 1958. *Les cultes indigènes en Carie*, Paris.

Lawall, M. 2003. "In the Sanctuary of the Samothracian Gods: Myth, Politics, and Mystery Cult at Ilion," in *Greek Mysteries: The Archaeology and Ritual of Ancient Greek Secret Cults*, ed. M. Cosmopoulos, London, pp. 79–111.

Lazarides, D. 1969. Ὁδηγὸς Μουσείου Καβάλας, Athens.

Lefèbre, F. 1998. *L'Amphictionie pyléodelphique: Histoire et institutions*, Paris.

Lehmann, K. 1953. "Samothrace: Sixth Preliminary Report," *Hesperia* 22, pp. 1–24.

———. 1955. *Samothrace: A Guide to the Excavations and the Museum*, New York.

———. 1960. *Samothrace: A Guide to the Excavations and the Museum*, 2nd ed., New York.

———. 1998. *Samothrace: A Guide to the Excavations and the Museum*, 6th ed., rev. J. R. McCredie, Thessaloniki.

Lehmann, P. W., and K. Lehmann. 1973. *Samothracian Reflections*, Princeton.

Lehmann-Hartleben, K. 1939. "Excavations in Samothrace," *AJA* 43, pp. 133–145.

———. 1940. "Preliminary Report on the Second Campaign of Excavation in Samothrace," *AJA* 44, pp. 328–358.

———. 1943. "Cyriacus of Ancona, Aristotle, and Teiresias in Samothrace," *Hesperia* 12, pp. 115–134.

Lenormant, F. 1857. *Description des médailles M. Behr*, Paris.

LGPN = P. M. Fraser and E. Matthews, *A Lexicon of Greek Personal Names*, 4 vols., Oxford, 1987–2005.

Lindos = C. Blinkenberg, *Lindos: Fouilles de l'acropole* II: *Inscriptions*, Berlin 1941.

LSAM = F. Sokolowski, *Lois sacrées de l'Asie Mineure* (École française d'Athènes, Travaux et mémoires 9), Paris 1955.

LSCG = F. Sokolowski, *Lois sacrées de cités grecques* (École française d'Athènes, Travaux et mémoires 18), Paris 1969.

LSS = F. Sokolowski, *Lois sacrées de cités grecques: Supplément* (École française d'Athènes, Travaux et mémoires 11), Paris 1962.

MAMA = *Monumenta asiae minoris antiqua*, 9 vols., London 1928–1993.

Matsas, D., and N. Dimitrova. 2006. "New Samothracian Inscriptions Found Outside the Sanctuary of the Great Gods," *ZPE* 155, pp. 127–136.

McCredie, J. 1965. "Samothrace: Preliminary Report on the Campaigns of 1962–1964," *Hesperia* 34, pp. 100–124.

———. 1979. "Samothrace: Supplementary Investigation, 1968–1977," *Hesperia* 48, pp. 1–44.

———. 1990. "ΙΘ΄ Εφορεία Προϊστορικών και Κλασικών Αρχαιοτήτων," *ArchDelt* 41, Β΄ (1986), p. 184.

Merkelbach, R. 1984. *Mithras*, Königsheim.

Michel, C. 1900. *Recueil d'inscriptions grecques*, Brussels.

Müller, K. O. 1817. *Aegineticorum liber*, Berlin.

Münsterberg, R. [1911, 1912, 1914, 1927] 1973. *Die Beamtennamen auf den griechischen Münzen* (*Numismatische Zeitschrift* 4, 5, 7, 20), repr. Hildesheim.

Muratori, L. 1739–1742. *Novus thesaurus veterum inscriptionum in praecipuis earumdem collectionibus hactenus praetermissarum, collectore Ludovico Antonio Muratorio*, 4 vols., Milan.

NGSL = E. Lupu, *Greek Sacred Law: A Collection of New Documents*, Leiden 2005.

Nilsson II² = M. P. Nilsson, *Geschichte der griechischen Religion 2: Die hellenistische und römische Zeit*, 2nd ed., Munich 1961–1967.

NSER = A. Maiuri, *Nuova silloge epigrafica di Rodi e Cos*, Florence 1925.

OGIS = W. Dittenberger, *Orientis graeci inscriptiones selectae*, Leipzig 1903–1905.

Ohlemutz, E. 1940. *Die Kulte und Heiligtümer der Götter in Pergamon*, Giessen.

Oliver, J. H. 1939. "Latin Inscription from Samothrace," *AJA* 43, pp. 464–466.

———. 1966. "A Roman Governor Visits Samothrace," *AJP* 87, pp. 75–80.

OMS = L. Robert, *Opera minora selecta: Epigraphie et antiquités grecques*, 7 vols., Amsterdam 1969–1990.

Palmer, L. 1961. *The Latin Language*, London.

Parisinou, E. 2000. *The Light of the Gods*, London.

Parker, R. 2000. "Theophoric Names and the History of Greek Religion," in *Greek Personal Names: Their Value as Evidence*, ed. S. Hornblower and E. Matthews, Oxford, pp. 53–79.

Perlman, P. 2000. *City and Sanctuary in Ancient Greece: The Theorodokia in the Peloponnese*, Göttingen.

Picard, C. 1922. *Éphèse et Claros: Recherches sur les sanctuaires et les cultes de l'Ionie du nord*, Paris.

Pickard-Cambridge, A. 1988. *The Dramatic Festivals of Athens*, 3rd ed., rev. J. Gould and D. M. Lewis, Oxford.

PIR = P. de Rohden and H. Dessau, eds. part III, *Prosopographia imperii romani saec. I, II, III*, Berlin 1898.

PIR² = E. Groag, A. Stein, and L. Petersen, eds., *Prosopographia imperii romani saec. I, II, III*, 2nd ed., Berlin 1933–.

Portes du désert = A. Bernand, *Les portes du désert: Recueil des inscriptions grecques d'Antinooupolis, Tentyris, Koptos, Apollonopolis Parva, et Apollonopolis Magna*, Paris 1984.

Pouilloux, J. 1954. *Recherches sur l'histoire et les cultes de Thasos* (Études thasiennes 3), Paris.

———. 1955. "Actes d'affranchissement thessaliens," *BCH* 79, pp. 442–463.

Pounder, R., and N. Dimitrova. 2003. "Dedication by the Thessalian League to the Great Gods in Samothrace," *Hesperia* 72, pp. 31–39.

Reinach, T. 1892. "Inscriptions de Samothrace," *RÉG* 5, pp. 197–205.

Rigsby, K. 2004. "*Theoroi* for the Koan Asklepieia," in *The Hellenistic Polis of Kos: State, Economy, and Culture* (Boreas: Uppsala Studies in Ancient Mediterranean and Near Eastern Civilizations 28), ed. K. Höghammar, Uppsala, pp. 9–14.

Ritschl, F. 1852. *Monumenta epigraphica tria ad archetyporum fidem exemplis lithographis expressa commentariisque grammaticis illustrata,* Berlin.

———. 1866–1879. *Friderici Ritschelii opuscula philologica,* 5 vols., Leipzig.

Robert, L. 1935a. "Inscriptions de Lesbos et de Samos," *BCH* 59, pp. 471–488.

———. 1935b. "Notes d'épigraphie hellénistique XLII: Décret de Samothrace," *BCH* 59, pp. 425–427.

———. 1936. *Collection Froehner* I: *Inscriptions grecques,* Paris.

———. 1963. Rev. of *Samothrace* 2.1, in *Gnomon* 35, pp. 50–79.

———. 1966. *Monnaies antiques en Troade,* Geneva.

Rohde, E. 1987. *Psyche: The Cult of Souls and Belief in Immortality among the Greeks,* trans. W. B. Hillis from the 8th ed., Chicago.

Rose, B. 2003. "The Temple of Athena at Ilion," *Studia Troica* 13, pp. 27–88.

Rubensohn, O. 1892. *Die Mysterienheiligtümer in Eleusis und Samothrake,* Berlin.

Rutherford, I. 1998. "The Amphikleidai of Sicilian Naxos: Pilgrimage and Genos in the Temple Inventories of Delos," *ZPE* 122, pp. 81–90.

———. 2000. "*Theoria* and *Darśan:* Pilgrimage and Vision in Greece and India," *CQ,* n.s., 50, pp. 131–146.

Salač, A. 1925. "Z Malé Asie, Samothray a Thrakie," in *Niederlův Sborník* (Obzor praehistorický 4), ed. J. Schránil, Prague, pp. 156–160.

———. 1928. "Le grand dieu d'Odessa-Varna et les Mystères de Samothrace," *BCH* 52, pp. 395–398.

Salač, A., and J. Frel. 1968. "Inscriptions de Samothrace," *Listy filologické* 91, pp. 105–106.

Salomies, O. 1996. "Contacts between Italy, Macedonia, and Asia Minor during the Principate," in *Roman Onomastics in the Greek East: Social and Political Aspects,* ed. A. D. Rizakis, Athens, pp. 111–126.

Salviat, F. 1962. "Addenda Samothraciens," *BCH* 86, pp. 268–304.

Salviat, F., F. Chapouthier, and A. Salač. 1956. "Le théâtre de Samothrace," *BCH* 80, pp. 118–146.

Samothrace = Samothrace: Excavations Conducted by the Institute of Fine Arts of New York University

   1 = N. Lewis, *The Ancient Literary Sources,* New York 1958.

   2.1 = P. M. Fraser, *The Inscriptions on Stone,* New York 1960.

   2.2 = K. Lehmann, *The Inscriptions on Ceramics and Minor Objects,* New York 1960.

   3 = P. W. Lehmann, *The Hieron,* Princeton 1969.

   7 = J. McCredie, G. Roux, S. M. Shaw, and J. Kurtich, *The Rotunda of Arsinoe,* Princeton 1992.

   11.2 = E. B. Dusenbery, *The Nekropoleis: Catalogues of Objects by Categories,* Princeton 1998.

Samuel, A. 1972. *Greek and Roman Chronology: Calendars and Years in Classical Antiquity,* Munich.

Sanchez, P. 2001. *L'Amphictionie des Pyles et de Delphes,* Stuttgart.

SB = Sammelbuch griechischer Urkunden aus Ägypten, Strasburg (later Wiesbaden), 1915–.

Schwabacher, W. 1952. "Cabiri on Archaic Coins of Samothrake," *ANSMN* 5, pp. 49–51.

Seure, G. 1911. "Archéologie Thrace: Documents inédites ou peu connus II," *RA* 18, pp. 423–449.

SGDI = H. Collitz, Sammlung der griechischen Dialekt-Inschriften, 4 vols., Göttingen 1884–1915.

Sherk, R. K. 1984. *Translated Documents of Greece and Rome* 4: *Rome and the Greek East to the Death of Augustus,* Cambridge.

Skarlatidou, E. K. 1993. "Κατάλογος μυστῶν και εποπτῶν από τη Σαμοθράκη," *Horos* 8–9 (1990–1991), pp. 153–172.

Smith, D. R. 1972. "*Hieropoioi* and *Hierothytai* on Rhodes," *AntCl* 41, pp. 532–539.

Stephanis, I. 1988. *Διονυσιακοὶ τεχνῖται,* Iraklion.

Stoian, I. 1962. *Tomitana: Contributii epigrafice la istoria cetÍatii Tomis,* Bucharest.

Syll.[3] = W. Dittenberger, *Sylloge inscriptionum Graecarum,* 3rd ed., Leipzig, 1915–1924.

Tacheva [Tatschewa], M. 1995. "The Last Thracian Independent Dynasty of the Rhascouporids," in *Studia in honorem Georgii Mihailov,* ed. A. Fol, B. Bogdanov, P. Dimitrov, and D. Boyadziev, Sofia, pp. 459–467.

———. 2000. *Sevt III, Sevtopolis i Kabile (341–252 g.pr. Khr.) spored epigrafskite i numizmatichnite danni /Seuthes III, Seuthopolis und Kabyle (341–252 v. Chr.) nach den epigraphischen und numismatischen Angaben,* Sofia.

TAM = E. Kalinka, R. Heberdey, F. C. Dörner, P. Herrmann, Tituli Asiae Minoris, 5 vols., Vienna 1901–1989.

Thomasson, B. 1991. *Legatus: Beiträge zur römischen Verwaltungsgeschichte,* Stockholm.

Tit.Cal. = M. Segre, Tituli Calymnii, in *ASAtene* 22–23, n.s., 6–7 (1944–1945 [1952]), pp. 1–248.

Tit.Cam. = M. Segre and G. Pugliese Carratelli, Tituli Camirenses, in *ASAtene* 11–13 (1949–1950), pp. 141–318; 15–17 (1952–1954), pp. 211–246.

Točilescu, G. 1883. "Inschriften aus der Dobrudscha," *AEM* 6, pp. 1–52.

Touchais, G. 1986. "Chronique des fouilles et decouvertes archéologiques en Grèce en 1985," *BCH* 110, pp. 672–761.

Traill = J. Traill, Persons of Ancient Athens, Toronto 1994–.

Triantaphyllos, D. 1985. Αρχαιότητες και μνημεία Θράκης, *ArchDelt* 33, B´ (1978), pp. 302–314.

Trümpy, C. 1997. *Untersuchungen zu den altgriechischen Monatsnamen und Monatsfolgen,* Heidelberg.

Velkov, V. 1991. *Kabile* 2, Sofia.

Vidman, L. 1965. "Inscriptionis Samothraciae fragmentum Pragae asservatum," *Zprávy Jednoty klasických filologů* 7, pp. 5–6.

Walbank, F. W. 1979. *A Historical Commentary on Polybius* 3, Oxford.

Walton, F. R. 1963. Rev. of *Samothrace* 2, in *AJP* 84, pp. 98–101.

Weaver, P. R. C. 1966. "A New Latin Word," *AJP* 87, pp. 457–458.

Ziebarth, E. 1896. *Das griechische Vereinswesen,* Leipzig.

———. 1906. "Cyriacus von Ancona in Samothrake," *AM* 31, pp. 405–414.

CONCORDANCE OF PREVIOUSLY PUBLISHED INSCRIPTIONS

Cat. No.	IG XII.8	Samothrace 2.1	CIL
1		23	
2	164		
3	165		
4	168		
5	170		
6	171		
7		24	
8	161		
9	162		
10	163		
12	169		
13	160		
14	173		I 581, I² 667, III 716
15	174		I 580, I² 671, III 715
16	176		
18	175		
19	177		
20	166		
21	167		
22		22	
24	172		
25		app. III A	
28		13	
30	216		
32	196		
33		46	
34		47	
35	178		
36		58	
37	195 and IG XII Suppl., p. 149		

Cat. No.	IG XII.8	Samothrace 2.1	CIL
38	209		I² 666, III 12319
40	215		III 7368
41	220		
42		42	
43	217		
44	218		
45	221		
47	190		III 12323
48		59	
50	186		
51	184		
52	183		
53	206		
54	223		
56	188	app. IV	
57	189		III 12322
58	191, 192, 211, 212, 259	29	III 718, 719, 721
59	194		
60	222		
64		25	
65			I² 662a–b, III 7367
67		28	
68		30	
69		31	I² 2505
70			I 578, I² 663, III 713
71	205		
72		32	
73			I² 665, III 12318
76		17	
77	208		I² 669, III 12320
78	207		I² 668, III 7369
79		33	
80		34	
82	210		III 7370
87	214		III 717
88			III 7372
89		36	
90			III 12321
91		41	
92		40	
93		39	
97	219		
98		51	
99		52	
100		53, 53bis	III 7371

Cat. No.	IG XII.8	Samothrace 2.1	CIL
101		50	
102		54	
103			I² 664, III 720
106			I 579, I² 664, III 714
107			III 7373
108			III 7374
112			III 722
113	213		III 7375
117	180		
118	181		
119	182		
121	185		
122	IG XII Suppl. 344		
129	204		
130		26	
132	197		
134		27	
135	201		
137		37	
139	179		
141	199		
142	224		
143	225		
144		19	
145	203		
149	IG XII.8 Suppl. 346	60	
150		35	
152		48	
153	193		
154		49	
155		55	
156		56	
157	200		
159	202		
161		43	
162		57	
163		61	
164	187		
165	198		
168		62	
169		63	
170	156	app. I	
171		6	

CONCORDANCE OF INSCRIPTIONS IN MUSEUMS

Archaeological Museum of Samothrace

Inv. No.	Cat. No.	Inv. No.	Cat. No.
01.1	63, *a*	50.632	76
38.355	100	51.98	80
38.376	22	51.501	168
38.380	99	52.779	1
38.393	102	53.2	64
38.401	169	53.560	67
39.12	150	53.616	155
39.16	58, *a*	53.7	137
39.23	58, *b*	53.73	156
39.79	98	53.74	152
39.83	33	53.84	42
39.332	34	56.2	91
39.338	154	56.5	163
39.348	101	57.856	72
39.545	161	60.559	167
39.547	48	61.502	4, *a*
39.548	79	62.1	128
39.549	107	62.1464	74
39.914	28	62.2	127
39.1071	92	62.885	104
39.1072	89	65.981	123
39.1131	7	68.354	126
49.4	68	68.55	47
49.418	97	68.56	133
49.437	93	68.673	115, *a*
49.438	36	68.700	151
49.440	134	68.856	124
49.441	144	68.857	114
49.442	69	68.858	95
49.444	130	69.556	96
49.445	149	70.456	27
49.447	171	70.771	158
49.995	162	70.939	147

Inv. No.	Cat. No.	Inv. No.	Cat. No.
71.950	166	93.576	115, *b*
71.953	109	C 81.2	49
71.954	86	C 81.3	55
71.956	see 93	–	11
71.957	140	–	12
71.958	136	–	21
71.960	see 93	–	31
71.961	46	–	35
71.962	61	–	50
71.963A, B	166	–	66
71.967	125	–	82
74.83	116	–	84
76.16	75	–	85
76.18	105	–	90
88.510	146	–	110
89.2	160	–	117
93.47	63, *c*	–	129
93.48	63, *b*	–	148
93.49	63, *d*	–	170

MUSÉE DU LOUVRE, DEPARTMENT OF GREEK, ROMAN, AND ETRUSCAN ANTIQUITIES

Inv. No.	Cat. No.	Inv. No.	Cat. No.
Ma. 4182	20	Ma. 4189	53
Ma. 4183	6	Ma. 4190	38
Ma. 4184	15	Ma. 4191	30
Ma. 4185	18	Ma. 4192	41
Ma. 4186	16	Ma. 4193	45
Ma. 4187	19	Ma. 4196	83
Ma. 4188	118		

EPHOREIA OF PREHISTORIC AND CLASSICAL ANTIQUITIES

Inv. No.	Cat. No.	Inv. No.	Cat. No.
02.50	81	C 80.106	17
25	138	–	9
68	39	–	14
69	131	–	121
C 80.105	62		

ARCHAEOLOGICAL MUSEUM OF KAVALA

Inv. No.	Cat. No.
Λ 70 (old 465)	29

INDEX OF NAMES

Theoroi

[Γ]λαυκί[ας] . ὁλωνος, 67
Γλαφυρ[ί]δ[η]ς, 41.v
Γοργίας, 49.i
Δαλεῖνος, 122
Δαλι[άδας Ἀντιπά]τρο[υ], 50
Δαμαγόρας Φιλίσκου, 57.B.ii
Δαμασα[- - - - - - - - -], 50
Δαμάτριος Ἀμφοτεροῦ, 50
Δᾶος, 19
Δάφνος, 142
Δημέας, 49.i
Δημήτριος, 49.i (two people)
[Δ]η[μήτ]ριος, 49.ii
Δημήτριος Ἀπολλωνίου, 53
Δημήτριος Ἀρτεμιδώρου, 119
Δημήτριος Δημητρίου, 58
[- - - - - - Δ]ημητρίο[υ], 42
[- - - - - -]ος Δημητρίου, 159
Δημοκράτ[η]ς Οὐλιάδου, 119
[- - - - - - - - - -]λης Ἀκ[- - καθ᾽
    υἱοθεσία]ν δὲ Δημον[ίκου], 113.i
Δημῶναξ, 49.i
Δημοχάρης Λάμπωνος, 138
Δίδυμος Διδύμου, 53
Διαγόρα[ς], 141
Διζάσσκος, 79.i
Δίναρχος Ἀγαθ[- - - - -], 79.i
Διογένης, 53
[Δι]ογένης Διονυσίου, 118
Διογέ[ν-, 124
[- - - -]ς Διογένους, 51
Διοκλῆς Εὐάνδρου, 57.B.ii
Διονυσίας Ἐπικράτου, 138
Διονύσιος, 49.i
Διονύσιος, 49.i (two people), 141, 143
Διονύσι[ος], 49.ii
Διονύσιος Ἀρχεπόλεως, 37
Διονύσιος Διογένου, 131.i
Διονύσιος Διοδότου, 79.i
Διονύσιος Διοδώρου, 14
[Δ]ιον[ύσιος] [Δ]ιονυσ[ίου], 67
Διον[ύσι]ος, 50
Διονύσιος Μαντας, 37
Διονύσιος Σκοπίου, 15
Διονύσιος Τιμο[κλ]είους, 119
[- - - - -]νδρος Διονυσί[ου?- -], 128
[- - -] Διονυσίου, 117
[- -Δ]ιονυσίου, 117
[- - - - - -]ION Διονυσίου, 44
Διονυσόδωρος, 49.i
Διονυσοκλῆς Μητροδώρου, 79.i
Διοσκουρίδης, 49.i, ii (three people)
Διότιμος Διοτίμου, 120
Διοφάνης, 130
Δωσίθεος, 19
Εἰρήνη, 35.ii
ΔΙ . ᶜᵃ·⁵ . β τοῦ Εἰσιδ[ώρου/-ότου], 144
Εἰσίδωρος, 41.v

Ἕλενος, 79.i
Ἐλπιδηφόρ[ος vel -υ - - -], 146
[Ἔ]νδημος?, 47.ii
[Ἐ]ξήκεστος, 49.ii
Ἐπαμινώνδας, 19
Ἐπαφρᾶς, 121
Ἐπαφρόδε[ιτος], 41.v
Ἐπιγένης, 79.i
Ἐπίγονος Μενεστράτου, 119
Ἐπίγονος, 49.ii
Ἐπίλογος, 63
Ἐπιτυγχάνω[ν], 63
Πό(πλιος) Ἐρέννιος Λεοντεὺς Ἀζηνιεύς,
    30
[Ἑρ]μίας, 122
[Ἕ]ρμων Δημητρίου, 52
Εὐβούλα Διονυσίου, 41.iv
Εὔβουλο[ς] Ἀρχιπόλιος, 61.i
Εὐήμερος, 19
Εὐήμερος Λεόν[τ]ιδος, 52
Εὔηνος, 142
Ε[ὐ]μέν[ης], 79.i
[Ε]ὔνομος [- - - - - -], 118
Εὔνου[ς], 144
Εὐπόριστος, 63
Εὐπορίων, 121
[Εὐπ]ορίων Κυαίου, 31
Εὐριπίδης, 49.i
Εὐσύης, 50
Εὐσχήμων Χρυσέρωτος Πειραιεύς, 30
Εὐφρόσυνος, 125
Ζηνοδώρα[- -], 141
Ζήνων Ζήνωνος, 58
[Ζ]ωΐλος, 122
Ζώπυρος, 127
Ζώπυρος Μενίππου, 62.i
[Ἡ]λιόδωρ[ος], 67
Ἡραῖος Ἀλεξάνδρου, 120
[- - -]Ἡρακλείδα, 117
Ἡρακ[λ . . .], 49.ii
Ἡρακ[λῆς?], 49.ii
Ἡράκλειτος, 49.ii
[.] . ολλᾶ[ς] [Ἡρ]ακλέο[υς], 67
Ἡρακλέων, 49.i, ii (two people)
Ἡρακλέω[ν], 49.ii
[Ἡ]ρακλέων, 49.ii
Ἡρακλεώτης, 49.ii
[Ἡ]ρακλῆ[ς] [Ἡ]ρακλέ[ους], 67
[. . . .]Ἡράστρατο[ς?], 63
Ἥρων Ὑγιαίν[ο]ν[τος], 149
Ἥρως, 125
Θασίων, 49.ii
Θεμισταγόρας Ἀπολλοδώρου, 31
Θεογείτων Σατύρ[ου], 118
[Θεο]δόσιος [[Μενοικέως, 46.i
Θεόδοτος, 49.i
Θεόδωρος, 118
Θεόκριτος, 49.i

[Θ]εόμνης Θεοδώρου, 118
Θεόξενος, 55
Θεόξενος Μητροδώρου, 79.i
Θεότιμος Ἀριστοδάμου, 120
Θεοφάνης, 49.i, ii (two people)
Θεοφάνη[ς], 49.i
Θεοφάνης, 49.ii
[. . .] . ος Θεοχάρου, 59
Θερσίων Ἡρογείτ-<ονο>ς vel -<ου>, 58
[Θ]ευδᾶς, 49.ii
Θεύδ[οτ]ος vel Θεύδ[ωρ]ος, 130
Θεύδωρος Θεοδώρου, 120
Θεύδωρος Ἡραγόρ[α], 50
Θέων, 49.i
Θέων Δημητρίου, 52
Θηβαΐς, 34
Θήρων, 50
Θήρων β τοῦ Μ[ενάνδ?]ρου, 144
Θόας, 49.i
Θρασύμαχος Πολυδ . [- -], 118
Θρέπτος, 63
Ἱεροκλῆς Δημητρίου τοῦ Μοσχ[- -], 13.ii
Ἱεροκλῆς Δ . . . ΟΥ, 31
[Ἱ]ερομαχο[ς vel -υ] Ἀτ[τ]άλου, 67
[- - - -]ς Ἱέρωνος, 51
Ἱκ[έ]σιος Ἀντιόχου, 41.iv
[Ἱ]ουλία Γηπαιπυρον, 44
Γ. Ἰούλιος Αὐφιδιανός · Τι(βερίου) ἀδε(λφός), 97
Ἰούλιος Ἕρμιππος, 30
Τιβέ]ριος Ἰούλιος [Εὐφ]ρόσυνος, 53
Γ. · Ἰούλιος Νίγερ, 45
Γαῖος Ἰούλιος Ρασ[κος], 46.i
Γάϊος Ἰούνιος Λυσίμαχος, 53
Ἱππίας Αἰσχυλίνου, 120
Ἱππόδαμος Ἀναξάνδριδ[ος], 61.i
Ἱππομέδων] Ἀγησιλάου, 170
Ἰσίδοτος [- - - - - - - - - -], 50
Ἰσίδωρος Νικοστράτου, 29
Ἰσίδωρος, 143
[. .]νος Ἰσίω[νος], 122
Γα · Ἰτύριος Πούδης, 34
Κάδμος, 53
Καιρέλλιος Γάλλος, 46.i
[Κ]αλλικλῆς, 49.ii
Καλ[λ?- - - - - - - - - - -Ἡ]ρακλέ[- - - - - - - - - -, 167
Καλλικράτης Δαματρίου, 50
[- - - -]ΙΑ Καλλικράτου, 44
Κάρπος Παπᾶ, 39
Πο. Καστρίκιος Ἀπφοῦς, 39
Κάστω[ρ] Ἐπικράτ[ους], 156
Κέρδων [Ἀ]ν[τ]ιμάχου, 52
Κλᾶρος Κλάρου Αἰξωνεύς, 30
Τι · Κλαύδιος Εὔλαιος, 34
Κλαύδιος Σύμφορος, 36
Κλεοπάτρα Θεοδότου, 37

ΚΛΕΥ[- - - - - -] Νικασιβούλου, 61.i
Κόλλις Κόλλιδος ὁ καὶ Μάρεις, 53
Κομμέν[ι]ος, 143
Κόνων, 130
Κορινθία, 125
Κορνηλία Ἀλεξάνδρα Κορ(νηλίου) Ἀδειμάντου θυ(γάτηρ), 30
Κορνηλία Φιλότροφον ἐξ Ἀζηνιέων, 30
Κορνήλιος Ἀδείμαντος Ἀναφλύστιος, 30
Κορνήλ(ιος) Πολύδωρ[ος], 63
[- -Κορ]νήλιο[ς?], 91
Κοτυς Γλαυκίου, 37
Κρατίδαμος Ἀπολλοδώρου, 31
Κράτων, 49.i
[Κ]ροῖσος [Λ]υκόφρον[ος], 67
Κρόν[ι]ος Ἡλιοδώρου, 53
Κυβερνήτης Μηνοφίλου, 58
[.]άνθος Κυδί[μου], 118
Κυϊντία Μίλωνος, 44
Κῦρος, 142
Τίτος Λέπιδος Νύ[μ]φιος, 53
Λεύκιος Ἄκαι[ο]ς Διοφάνους, 79.i
[Λ]ούκιος [- - - - - -] (Ἀθηνίων), 91
Λούκιος Μάρκου, 131.i
Λοῦππος, 125
Λυσιμένης Ἀπολλωνίδου, 14
Λυσίων Ε[- - -], 32
Μαγιανός, 48
Μάμιος[- -], 115
ΜΑΝ[. . .], 49.ii
Μάρκιος Μυρισμός, 36
Μειλάσιος, 55
Μελάνιππος, 57.B.ii
Μέμνων, 63
Μεν[. . .]ος, 49.ii
Μένανδρος, 35.i
[Μέ?]νανδρος, 118
[Μέ]νανδρος Μεν[- -], 136
[- - -Μ]ενάνδρου, 117
[- - - - - - - - - - - - -Βε vel Με]νδιδώρο[υ], 134
Μενέδημος Μενεδήμου, 52
Μενεκράτης, 49.i
Μενέμαχος Μητροδώρου, 53
Μένυλλα Ἱπποστράτου, 35.ii
Μένων, 49.i
Μηνόδωρος Τέχνωνος, 119
Μηνοφαν[- -], 47.ii
Μηνόφαντος Φιλοκράτους, 14
Μηνόφιλος, 49.ii
Μηνόφιλος Φιλίππου, 79.i
Μητρόδωρος, 49.i
Μητρόδωρ[ος], 122
Μητρόδωρος Βιθυος, 37
Μητρῶναξ, 118
Μητροφάν[ης vel -οφαντος], 118
[- - - -]ίων Μίκα, 51

Μίκα Θάσιος, 51
[Μοι?]ραγένης, 57.B.ii
Μόσχος Μενεκράτου, 58
Μύρμηξ, 49.ii
Μύρων Πρόκλου τρόφιμος, 39
Νεικήτης, 63
Νεικόλαος ΟΛΙ . ΟΥ, 45
Νεικόστ[ρ]ατο[ς], 41.v
Νέων, 49.i
Νικήρατος, 49.i
Νικησίλεως Σωτέλους, 135.ii
Νικηφόρος, 19
Νικηφόρος Μητροδώρου, 62.ii
Νικίας, 49.i
Ν[ι]κίας, 49.ii
[Ν]ῖκις Μνησισ[τρ]άτου, φύσει δ[ὲ] Ἀσκληπιάδης Ἀττάλου, 56
[Νικ?]ογένης Ἀττάλου, 59
Ν[ικό?]λαος, 143
[- - - - -]ΩΝ Νικομήδ[ου- - -?], 128
Νικόστρατο[ς] . . Ν, 142
[- - - - - -]ΠΗ Νίκωνος, 44
Νουμήνιος, 49.ii
[Ν]υμφικός, 48
[Ν]υμφόδωρος, 118
Νυμφόδωρος Νυμφοδ[ώρου], 38.iv
Ξένων, 49.i
[- - - -Ὀ]βρίμου, 57.B.i
Γάϊος Ὀκταούιος Βᾶσος, 53
[Κοίν]τος Ὀκτάβιος Ἀπε . [- - -], 46.i
[- - -]ος Ὀλυμπιοδώρου, 117
Ὅμιλος, 15
[Ὀ]πτάτα PAN[- - - - - -], 46.i
Ὄπ[τ]ης? Μενίσκου, 52
Μ. Ὀρφίδιος Ἀγησίλαος, 36
[Ὀ]τρύας Στησικλέους, 118
Οὐλπία · Ἀλεξάνδρα, 34
Οὔλ Ἀλκιβιάδης, 63
Οὔλ Ἀρείων, 63
Οὔλ Εἰρκεῖνος, 63
Οὐλ · Εὐτυχιανό[ς], 63
Οὐλ · ΧειρΙ [- - - - -], 63
Οὔριος, 49.i
Παλαίστρικος Διοκλεῦς, 120
Πάνταυχος, 49.ii
Παντε[- -], 135.iii
[Παπεί]ρ(ιος) Ἐλπίν[ικος], 63
[.]Παπείριος Ἰοῦστο[ς, 63
Παπείρ(ιος) Ὑάκινθ[ος], 63
Παράμονος, 34
Παράμονος Ζωίλου, 33
[- - - -]τειμία Παραμόνου [ἡ] καὶ Ζωσίμη, 41.ii
Παρμενίσκος, 49.ii
Παρμενίσκος Ἀριστέω[ς], 58
Παρμενίσσκος, 35.i
ΠΑΤ . . . ΟΣ Ἀλεξιμάχου, 14
Παυσανίας Διφίλου, 15

Latin (including Thracian names written in Latin)

GEOGRAPHIC INDEX